# Libraries and Learning
# Resource Centres

## Second Edition

# Libraries and Learning Resource Centres

## Second Edition

## Brian Edwards

AMSTERDAM • BOSTON • HEIDELBERG • LONDON • NEW YORK
• OXFORD • PARIS • SAN DIEGO • SAN FRANCISCO • SINGAPORE
• SYDNEY • TOKYO
Architectural Press is an imprint of Elsevier

Architectural Press is an imprint of Elsevier
Linacre House, Jordan Hill, Oxford OX2 8DP, UK
30 Corporate Drive, Suite 400, Burlington, MA 01803, USA

First edition 2002
Second edition 2009
Copyright © 2009 Elsevier Ltd. All rights reserved

**British Library Cataloguing in Publication Data**
A catalogue record for this book is available from the British Library

**Library of Congress Cataloguing in Publication Data**
A catalogue record for this book is available from the Library of Congress

ISBN: 978-1-85617-619-4

For information on all Architectural Press publications visit
our web site at http://elsevierdirect.com

Typeset by TnQ Books and Journals Pvt Ltd
(www.tnq.co.in)

Printed and bound in Italy

09 10 11 12 13 10 9 8 7 6 5 4 3 2 1

# Contents

# Acknowledgements

The author wishes to acknowledge the support of the Royal Danish Academy of Fine Arts, School of Architecture. Thanks also go to Edinburgh College of Art for financial support to allow the author to interview clients and their architects, and to visit and research the case studies which form an important element of the second edition. Thanks also to Wilson Smith, Head Librarian at Edinburgh College of Art, for directing the author to relevant articles and for his ceaseless enthusiasm for libraries generally. Thanks also go to the research students and former colleagues attached to ACE at Edinburgh University for subjecting the author to rigorous examination of some of the ideas in this book through the Research Seminar series.

There are too many organisations, architectural practices, academic colleagues and users of libraries to single out any for special thanks. All of them provided in their different ways the intellectual material, support, plans, photographs and documentation contained in subsequent pages. However, the author is particularly indebted to the *Architectural Review*, *the Architects' Journal* and *Architecture Today* for allowing plans produced in those journals to be incorporated in this book.

The author is also greatly indebted to Ayub Khan, Head of Libraries (Strategy) at Warwickshire County Council who provided valuable advice in connection with the author's chapter on libraries in the Metric Handbook, some of which is incorporated here. Thanks also go to Andrea Kerr of Hampshire County Council for assistance with the Discovery Centres.

Many librarians provided help in various ways, making their collections, buildings and facilities available often at short notice. Without their support, this book would not have been written.

Many architects, engineers and designers provided material upon which the argument and case studies are based. Their help and constructive criticism have been invaluable, as have the drawings and photographs provided to illustrate the book.

Finally, there is a considerable debt to Godfrey Thompson whose *The Planning and Design of Library Buildings* (1989) for the same publishers provided some of the tables and whose arguments are updated in this book. In similar spirit Anthony Thompson's *Library Buildings of Britain and Europe* (1963) proved a useful source of case studies and plans. Thanks also go to Biddy Fisher, my collaborator on the first edition, for her support, guidance and in directing me to important new material.

Brian Edwards

# Preface

Like any other tourist, he made his way east ... until he reached the Public Library. He had already heard about this curious place ... it was a circular building ... with seven or eight cubicles along the circumference. In the cubicles were shelves of books along two sides and a window in the third. In the centre of the circle was a small wooden enclosure where a ... librarian sat.

Tom Wolfe describing the public library in Nassau, Bahamas in *A Man in Full*, Picador, 1998, p. 537.

Even the most misfitting child
Who's chanced upon the library's worth
Sits with the genius of the Earth
And turns the key to the whole world

Ted Hughes (an introductory verse to New Library) quoted in *Quarto*, the newsletter of the National Library of Scotland, Number 4, Autumn 1998, p. 2.

# Introduction

## Knowledge and the library

When fire destroyed the library at Alexandria in 4000 BC, over half of all mankind's recorded knowledge was lost, or as Ted Hughes put it in his poem, *Hear it again*, the burning of the library 'brain-damaged the human race' (Oxford Dictionary of Quotations, 1999). It was not until the development of monastic libraries in Europe around 1200 that humanity again amassed in a single place what approached the collective wisdom and knowledge of the age. Libraries may be exchanges of information and market places for ideas but they are also the buildings which contain the bulk of human knowledge. Or at least they were until the electronic digitally stored information revolution of the 1980s. Now knowledge is virtually everywhere; it has broken free of the constraint of buildings. Today if you were today to destroy all the world's libraries, it is unlikely that more than 20% of human knowledge would be lost. Certainly, a large amount of archival material would disappear forever, but a substantial volume of knowledge would survive. If a library is a repository of knowledge, this is now just one of its functions. The library's prime function is now making that knowledge available and encouraging exchange and reflection upon it.

Electronic knowledge is nowadays available to everybody – in the home, workplace, airport terminal, school, etc. The Internet has liberated the library but it has not removed the justification for library buildings. It has though changed the balance of functionality – there is still the agenda of storage with all the difficult balances of provision and service this entails – but other functions now demand greater attention. Libraries today need to facilitate multi-modal access to information and, at the same time, encourage the creative use of knowledge. This was not considered essential when libraries had a primary storage function, but when information is everywhere the challenge is one of knowledge use and dissemination.

The importance of the library to knowledge and hence power is considerable. Knowledge, both in a practical and cultural context, is a commodity which libraries contain and make available. The public accesses knowledge and wisdom via the book shelves and archives of the public library, and the researcher via the technical reports and journals of the academic library. Increasingly, both use the library's Internet facilities to keep up to date with the unfolding world of digital information.

Historically, the library was a private building dedicated to an individual, monastery or college. Today, the library is electronic and virtual – a building which loosely and casually contains the diverse tentacles of knowledge. Yet the more the library diffuses under the influence of the computer, the more important become the architectural anchors of the building type. These reside in space, not rooms, in the shared theatre of knowledge. Important as the electronic screens of the library have become, there is no denying the social function of the library to a sense of identity, community and nationhood. The growth in 'national' libraries is an expression of the cultural function of the library in a world increasingly dominated by global values.

Modern libraries began their life as adjuncts to monasteries – secret and sacred worlds within an enclosed, sheltered environment. They developed into private book collections associated with colleges and, more rarely, wealthy landowners. Via the college quad, they evolved into places where scholars could gather for private study. With the printing press, the library became larger but less exclusive. The mass production of books changed the library in important ways. The printing of books reduced their cost but expanded their social value. By 1500, the printed book became relatively common and the library was born. Early examples chained books to walls and operated the stall system whereby readers perched on high seats using books anchored to heavy masonry walls. Later the books were placed in locked bookcases and eventually on open shelves, arranged in the fashion of a picture gallery. The long top-lit library with bookcases between the busts of benefactors was eventually replaced by the circular library with a reading room at the centre and bookcases around the circumference. The rotunda form (e.g. the Radcliffe Camera, Oxford, and the library of the University of Virginia) became the pattern of the eighteenth century.

The growth in books and readers in the nineteenth century changed the library into a rational container of reading rooms, control points and book stacks. For the first time, book stacks and reading areas became zoned into separate functional areas, and with the emergence of journals and newspapers, the dominance of the book began to be challenged. By the turn of the twentieth century the form of the modern library had begun to appear – thanks partly to the liberal influence of great benefactors such as Andrew Carnegie and to the expansion in higher education. For it was the universities which generated and tested new approaches to library building design, not the countless smaller civic libraries of Europe and America.

If libraries express one of society's clearest embodiment of the politics of knowledge and the historic dissolution of closed sources of power, how have they responded to the world of electronically stored information. Just as the printing press changed access to knowledge, information technology (IT) has revolutionized the library. The supremacy of the book is now challenged and the journal is as likely to be electronic as real. Does the library have any justification to survive as a building type when the media it holds have undergone such profound transformation? The answer is, of course, yes for the library is not a functional container but a cultural icon. It is the library as social symbol that matters – as a centre of community interaction and as a place to celebrate learning. Just as the stadium, airport and museum symbolize their respective functions and transcend limited utilitarian need, the modern library celebrates a deep social ideal. The library would be needed even if we abandoned the book merely because it brings people together in the pursuit of knowledge. So essentially, the library is a place for people not books. The computer, Internet and electronic media are not 'ends' in libraries, but the means of establishing social contact in what would otherwise be a private world of scholars and books.

Changes in how we store and disseminate knowledge alter the form and content of libraries but they do not make the library redundant. The evolution from the scroll to the hand-written book, printed book, mass-produced scientific journal and Internet has had the effect of increasing the importance of the library. A society dedicated to knowledge creates a thirst for new information: that the library can provide it efficiently and democratically is confirmed by every change libraries make to accommodate the unfolding technology of media. When Caxton developed his printing press at Westminster in 1477, he opened up a demand not only for books but for libraries in which to store them. The broader knowledge of a few became the public knowledge of the many. This fundamental change – the bedrock of the Renaissance and the industrial revolution – depended upon the essential symbiosis of book and library.

But the shift from a book-based library collection to an electronic one has profound implications for library design. What is the role of the reading room in an IT library? What purpose does silence serve in a library of team-based electronic learning? What is the right balance of provision between social space and study space? In the electronic library, do we need rooms at all or just a large open marketplace of digital interaction? Ultimately is open space more important than rooms or, given the library's social or cultural role, is the provision of snack bars and cafes as important as the study collection?

## The nineteenth century awakening

Although libraries had long existed up to the nineteenth century, it was only after the Public Libraries Act (1842) that working class people in Britain could experience the building type. The public library was not alone as the physical expression of civic duty towards education. Mechanics institutes for the education of adult working people became established between 1830 and 1860, the Municipal Corporation Act (1835) led to modern local governance, the Museum Act (1845) spurred construction in that sector, and the Elementary Education Act (1887) gave rise to compulsory formal schooling. The Public Libraries Act was one of several initiatives aimed at creating a modern, knowledgeable, literate society.

Although some civic libraries initially charged for book loan, they became free institutions. The library was an essential expression of a caring public authority, and where resources were scarce, Andrew Carnegie came to the rescue. Constructional ironwork was essential for carrying the loads of books and sometimes for the fabrication of the bookcases themselves. In the early years (1840–70), ironwork was hidden in the walls and roofs, but towards the end of the century it was freely expressed as a structural material. Sometimes cast into free Gothic or Renaissance forms, the iron members gave both modernity and enlightenment to the library interior.

The civic library learnt from the academic library to be symbolic of learning. Sometimes linked to the municipal art gallery, sometimes to a new technical college, it invariably carried an inscription about the value of reading or education. Unlike the university library, there was space for newspapers and popular journals, and many of the dispossessed used the library as shelter from the elements as well as for daily news-gathering. In this regard, the civic library became truly a community anchor in a period of social and technological change. Some more enlightened libraries (as in East London and Liverpool) provided space for local literary and philosophical societies. Here people would gather to listen to lectures or watch displays of the latest scientific experiments. Luminaries of the nineteenth century such as John Ruskin and William Morris often addressed their audiences in the lecture rooms of larger public libraries. Just as today the library is a high-tech gateway to learning, a century ago it provided the opportunity through book, newspaper and lecture to keep abreast of a rapidly changing world.

## The library of the future

There are three perspectives which will fashion the library of the future:

- the library as high-tech access to learning
- the library as community focus
- the library as an adjunct to 'cultural' tourism.

These views, essentially post-industrial (and hence post-modern in spirit) give a role for the library beyond that of its functional origins. Just as the modern art gallery has become an object of cultural value irrespective of the collection it contains (the Guggenheim Gallery in Bilbao is one of many examples which could be cited), the library is a building which increasingly exists independently of the printed word.

The agent that will make the future library relevant is electronic media and all the access it provides for non-mobile tourism, education and social discourse. The problem is not so much what the library should contain, but what form it will take. Is the electronic library a large flexible interactive space or should there be rooms in the sense of enclosure of subject territory? Also, since our global infrastructure of libraries is already a largely constructed one, the question is increasingly that of how to adapt old libraries to new ways.

These are the challenges libraries face and the reason why this book was written. If society loses sight of the library as an essential building type, it faces the prospect of devaluing the book, learning and ultimately of one of its greatest cultural anchors. Libraries have seen more change in the past twenty years than at any time in the past hundred. The library as a building type and as a public institution has been put under great strain by the introduction of non paper-based information systems. The supremacy of the book has been challenged by the digital revolution. Computer screens now stand side by side with books and journals. IT suites eat into the space once reserved for special collections, newspaper reading rooms, children's libraries or bookstack areas. As computerized data and retrieval systems encroach upon book territories, the library takes on a different character. It becomes more open and interactive, it becomes a digital market place and readers become navigators of electronic systems. Books are not replaced by the changes but take on a different role. They tend not to be the first point of contact, but are used after the reader has scanned electronic databases. Visitors to libraries are now confronted by computer screens, which act as traffic lights directing the flow of inquiries into different directions.

Librarians have had to adapt to these changes as much as library buildings. Library staff have had to learn to navigate the new electronic data systems, to accept that CD-ROMs have an equal place to that of books, and that

their role is to guide the reader through the systems available, both electronic and traditional. If librarians and their buildings are stressed by these changes, so too is the very word 'library'. The library has become the 'learning resource centre'. This new title helps signal the new emphasis upon all resources – electronic and book, upon learning (not just reading) and upon the concept of 'centre' as against building. Academic libraries led the change in name in the 1990s, but public libraries are now commonly called 'resource centres'.

There have been inevitable stresses in so profound a change of use and identity. This book seeks to draw together recent experience, looking via a series of case studies from the UK and elsewhere, at best practice in different types of libraries. From these it has been possible to draw some conclusions and offer the following insights: libraries are essential buildings in cementing together communities of all types (city, village, academic, professional); libraries remain meeting places but need to be designed to be more welcoming and accommodating to non readers; IT does not destroy the library but liberates it into providing new kinds of public services, attracting a potential new audience; the library is a knowledge channel which complements schools and college, and supports directly 'life-long learning'; for many the library is the vehicle of IT skills transfer – it is the gateway for technology migration to society at large; as an institution the library is an essential element in a trilogy of investment in public services aimed at intellectual enrichment. Its partners include the art gallery and museum. All three are undergoing cultural transformation.

These perspectives point to a different type of library in the twenty-first century. Many of the case studies illustrate this argument and offer a model for others to follow, either in terms of the refurbishment of an existing library or the design of a new one. Typical of the new generation of libraries is that at Peckham, winner of the Stirling Prize in 2000 as the UK's Building of the Year. Designed by Alsop and Störmer in the inner city suburb of Peckham in South London, the new library is a people's building bedecked in strong coloured glass, filled with Afro – Caribbean collections, surrounded by new public space and divided on the inside into meeting areas of various kinds. This large new public library combines traditional carrels around the perimeter with ship-like structures towards the centre which, in Noah's ark fashion, house the library's special collections. The building pushes at the frontiers of library design, taking the challenge of IT, the needs of young people and multi-culturalism as the agenda for a fresh approach to library architecture. Peckham Library serves as a symbol of economic and intellectual regeneration amongst the broken streets of South London. Equally importantly, it ushers in a new dawn for library architecture – one where people come before books and colour before drabness.

**Part 1**

# History of the library

# 1

# History, form and evolution of the library

## How libraries evolved

The emergence of the library, as distinct from the museum or picture gallery, did not occur directly as a result of the invention of the printing press but as a consequence of the growth in rational thought. Most commentators note that the library as we know it first occurred in the Renaissance with the Biblioteca Malatestiana in Casena and Michelangelo's Biblioteca Laurenziana in Florence. The first from around 1450 and the second a century or so later were libraries rather than bookstores. Earlier notable libraries such as the one at Wells Cathedral and the Ptolemy Library in Alexandria (which contained perhaps half a million scrolls) were depositories of written material with only a casual distribution of reading space for scholars.

To be a library in the modern sense, there needs to be a collection of books, clear access to the study material and a well-designed arrangement of seats and tables for readers. This last requirement implies a satisfactory level of light, a functional plan with a logical structure of bookstore, bookshelves, study space and corridors, and a level of control over the use and management of the space. A library, therefore, is a controlled environment designed for the benefit of both book and reader. Against this criterion, the modern library emerged not in antiquity but on the back of the growth of European rationalist thought from the sixteenth century onwards.

The great flowering of the library as a recognizable building type occurred in the eighteenth century. It was then that the library emerged with its own taxonomy of forms, functions and details. An early example is the Wolfenbüttel Library in Berlin (1710), with its elliptical reading room set symmetrically within a 'golden section' plan. This library also was one of the first free-standing libraries (as opposed to a library as a wing in a larger composition as in the Bodleian Library, Oxford, 1610). It had the authority of formal composition which marked the presence of the library in countless cities for two centuries. Dome and cube – the former as reading room, the latter as bookshelf accommodation – became the elemental architecture language for the library. The dome, usually surrounded by high-level windows formed in the circumference of the cylinder as it pierced the cube, allowed even light to filter down upon the reader. Those in the reading room could also (as in the former Reading Room at the British Museum in London) ponder upon their material within a volume designed for intellectual reflection.

The eighteenth century plan had a large area for book storage within a semi-basement. The position allowed books and journals to be delivered easily at road level, temperature and humidity could be controlled more readily than at high level and, by elevating the public to a first floor approach, the entrance could be grandly marked architecturally.

The plan, evolved and perfected through the eighteenth century, remained largely unaltered until the early twentieth century. A few changes occurred such as the introduction of cast-iron construction (notably at the Bibliothèque Nationale in Paris, 1868), greater sophistication in the control of temperature and humidity (with early air-conditioning in some pioneering American libraries at the turn of the century) and improved security of the stock; but fundamental change had to wait until the 1930s. Then the old dependencies of plan and section were rejected – the modern library introduced fluid space for more fluid functions. The formal repertoire of recognizable forms, inside and out, gave way to new unfamiliar arrangements. The dominance of the reading room became eroded, the division between book storage on shelves and in store became less certain, and the library became more open and egalitarian in spirit. More recently, even the primary role of the book has been questioned. New technologies in the form of computer-based data and electronic images have changed the old assumptions again. As the library material becomes more freely available via information technology (IT), the library itself has begun to adapt to fresh arrangements of space and new inventions of form. Whereas it was once an exclusive and often private

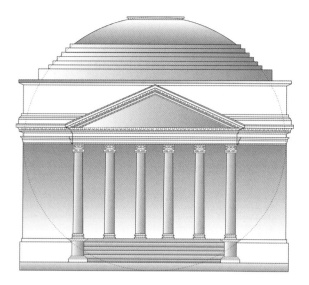

Example of a dome and cube library at the University of Virginia by Thomas Jefferson, 1819. (Brian Edwards)

building type, over some 500 years the library has become a truly public building with genuine social space and community purpose.

In some ways, the library's fortune has followed closely that of the museum. Both building types share a common root and there was not much difference in the architectural arrangement between the Renaissance art gallery and that of the library. Both were long, evenly lit buildings with wall niches for books, sculpture or paintings. Often the library sat above the museum in a wing of a larger building. In both cases, the user stood or perched on a high seat as a spectator of the collection. Construction technology did not then allow for wide span buildings, so the column and wall bay became the unit of display. Sitting down did not occur in libraries until the sixteenth century and in museums until the nineteenth century.

The common root of library, art gallery and museum owes something to the nature of patronage. Art collecting and book collecting depended upon a sense of history; both were revised and made systematic by the Renaissance. Paintings, bronze statues and leather-bound hand-written books were trophies to be displayed. Collecting is the common basis of both library and museum buildings; use of the collection for study purposes tended to occur later. In some ways it was the growth in education in the seventeenth and eighteenth centuries which split apart the library and museum as building types. Education certainly was behind the development of the library as an essential aid to higher learning. The book became less an object of treasure and more an object of use. It was this change in the status of the book, coupled with the expanding use of the printing press, which led to the removal of chains from many civic and university libraries.

Education too played a large part in forging the separation of the library from the cultural precinct of the museum and gallery. The formal repertoire of the library was developed in the colleges of Oxford and Cambridge and in the universities of Paris, Milan and Glasgow. The library, initially built as a wing in a college, matured in the seventeenth and early eighteenth century into a self-contained building. With physical separateness went architectural ambition; the library became a building to be viewed in the round. The Radcliffe Camera in Oxford by James Gibbs (1740) is a notable example. The museum, however, did not reach such heights of architectural distinctiveness for another century. Without the impetus of higher education to propel the building type forward, the museum stagnated architecturally. It remained a gallery-type building – a sequence of rooms leading to further rooms on a rather dull circuit. Where the circle interrupted the order of the rectangle, it was to form small sculpture courts (e.g. the National Gallery of Scotland, 1845). Without the impetus of the universities, and then of the civic authorities, the museum was not able to develop architecturally as fully as the library at least until

Reading Room, New York University, 1895, designed by McKim, Mead and White. (New York University)

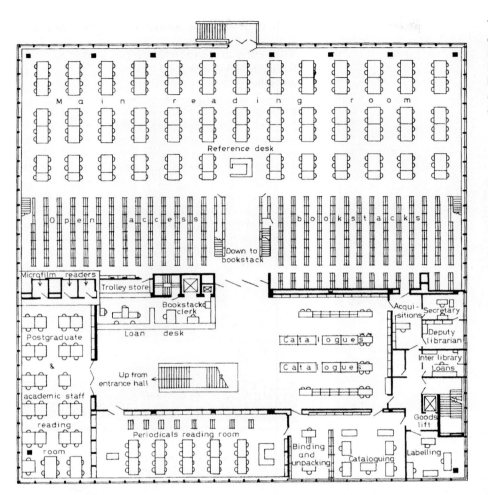

Typical twentieth century library plan. Sheffield University Library, 1958, designed by Gollins, Melvin, Ward and Partners. (D. Insall and Partners)

the nineteenth century. When the museum did evolve architecturally, it was the correspondence between space and light which, like the library, led to innovation.

In the library, the introduction of the central dome allowed daylight to penetrate to the interior. With the museum, the need to display works or walls without the glare of sunlight led to the introduction of large roof lights. This was an innovation which revolutionized the museum in the early nineteenth century, just as it had done to the library a century or more earlier. How differently libraries and galleries organize the relationship between space, study material and light is one key way in which the two building types can be distinguished. Even today with their different demands, it is the environmental servicing of space, as well as the collection, which fashions plan and section.

## Libraries and the history of space

Libraries are essentially collections of study material based upon the written, and increasingly electronic, word. Being collections, they are not unlike other depositories of human artefacts such as the museum and, in the need to display the material, they are not unlike art galleries. They are also similar to museums in their compact between the formal language of the container (in the shape of the building) and the nature of their contents. The integration of material and container allows the library to reflect higher ideals: the status of learning, the importance of the written word and the symbolic celebration of free access to society's knowledge.

The correspondence between the book and the building flowed from the rational nature of thought in the Enlightenment. The library became a 'safe, well-lit warehouse' (Markus, 1993, p. 171) where the readers' needs became as important as that of the collection. In the nineteenth century, and increasingly since, the text of the building and the text of the books within shared a common ideal. The formal organization of architectural space and the space in the mind liberated by the power of the written word became symbolically united. It is this symbiosis which led to the domed

5

Library at Toddington Manor, Gloucester, designed by Sir Charles Barry in 1829. (Country Life)

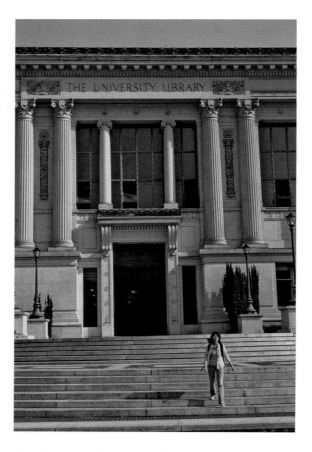

The University Library in California supports Berkeley's intellectual vitality and innovative thinking in all departments, for both faculty and students.

reading room – itself a metaphor for the human brain. The books, inventories, journals, maps and catalogues of the modern library are in this sense merely an enlarged version of the human intellect. Inevitably, the building sought simultaneously to both control the sum of human knowledge within its walls and to celebrate its presence.

It is not sufficient to see the library as a storehouse of knowledge, especially in the age of information technology. It is the delicate relationship between the books and architectural space which defines the library and helps us classify libraries into various categories – national, civic and academic. Reading and accessing knowledge via the computer screen requires a bond of dedicated effort between the book, reader, screen and space. The nature of the space varies according to the type of collection, the nature of the library and the ambition of the reader. Space is therefore essential, but the character of the space is not uniform. The social, cultural, political and educational aspirations of the library and its collection alter the type and the use of space.

In the library, a distinction needs to be drawn between private and semi-private reading. It is sometimes argued

that private reading is an inappropriate activity in a public library (Roche, 1979). The library is a place of semi-private reading at best and it follows that total silence is an ideal that cuts across the nature of discourse which the modern library seeks to promote. The library is like a bank: there are the catalogues with details of customer accounts and secured areas with ready currency, but the main activity is at the interface between the customer, bank teller and bank note. The library too exists to encourage production at a similar interface and often the necessary human exchange is via the spoken word.

The nature of space reflects the type of library, the activity in different functional zones and the needs of the reader working from book, journal or screen. Book and computer screen have quite different environmental needs. Reflected light on the screen impairs the ability to work effectively over a long period: sunlight on the book also creates eye strain (and can fade the printed page). Lighting levels for reading are not the same as for computer-

| Changing arrangement of library book storage and use | | | | | |
|---|---|---|---|---|---|
| Type | Material | Date | Reading position | Type of space | Typical example |
| 'Combined' library and museum | Scrolls | Antiquity | Standing | Open with vaults | Alexandria, Egypt |
| 'Cloister' system with book cupboards | Illustrated religious books | 6th–13th century | Sitting | Open cloister | Tintern Abbey, Monmouthshire |
| 'Lectern' system with open shelves for chained books | Hand-written books, then printed | 13th–16th century | Standing with foot rests | Linear and narrow | University of Leyden, The Netherlands |
| 'Stall' system with integrated shelved partitions and seat | Printed books | 16th–17th century | Sitting | Linear | Bibliotica Laurenziana, Florence |
| 'Wall' system with perimeter bookcases | Printed books | 17th–18th century | Sitting | Circular and rectangular | Bodleian Library, Oxford |
| 'Reading room' system with attached book galleries | Printed books, maps, journals | 18th–20th century | Sitting | Open plan centre with enclosed perimeter rooms | Bibliothèque Nationale, Paris |
| 'Open plan' system with integrated open shelves and PCs | Printed books, etc. plus CD-ROMs and other digital information systems | Late 20th century | Sitting | Large, open plan | Law Library, Cambridge University |

accessed material, while ventilation standards vary according to the type of retrieval activity. So space in the library is both a question of politics and working environment. The abstractions of function and the dictates of health via eye strain and gaseous emissions are increasingly expected to fuse.

Over the past two centuries, the balance of power has shifted from the book to the reader and more recently from the book to digital data systems. This is reflected in the emergence of the 'reading room'. When first introduced in the eighteenth century, the reading room was a domed space surrounded by books on a wall system (bookcases first, open shelves around the perimeter later). After about a century, the space in the reading room was colonized by bookcases arranged as spokes in a huge wheel of learning. Early in the twentieth century, the reading room became a foyer space for the library, signifying the importance of entrance and exchange with library staff. Books were now in rectangular galleries disassociated from the public area, which had been transformed from the form of the old reading room. Even more recently the library has itself become little more than one large reading room – a kind of trading floor of electronic learning. Light is carefully controlled so that the screen is dominant and ventilation is achieved by the use of lofty volumes with roof lights, or via air-conditioning.

The shifting politics of power in the library has been to the advantage of architectural space. As the importance of the reader has grown under the influences of falling book prices, and the ever-lowering cost of information technology, so there has been a growing recognition of the value of space as the medium of interchange. Space allows staff and readers to exchange, readers to interface with books and digital systems, the public to experience the democratic ideals of the public library and students to engage in the pedagogy value of the university library. Space, and how it is variously treated, is as important as the book.

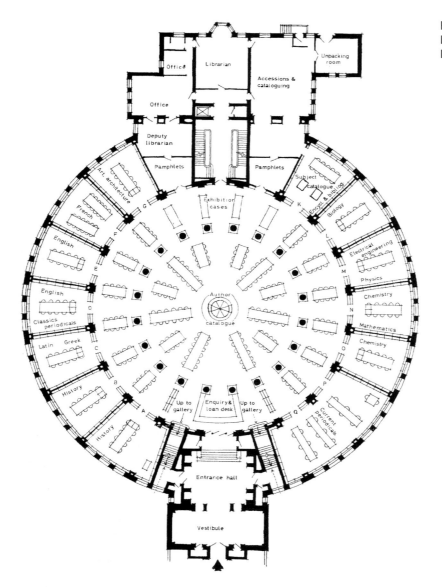

Brotherton Library, University of Leeds, 1935, by Lanchester and Lodge. (D Insall and Partners)

## Resolving the demands of space and time

There has always been a correspondence between the type of communication medium, the method of distributing it, the nature of the space in which communication occurs and society. Over 2,000 years of written communication (or 3,000 if you include China) the politics of media and space have inevitably been closely related. The building in which the dialogue between word, book and society has taken place is, of course, the library.

But before the public library, there was the private library with its archives of contracts, laws, plans and written cultural artefacts. Much more recently, the emergence of electronic data utilizing websites accessed freely from home

computers has again led to a questioning of the role of the traditional library. Print, post and electronic media provide everyday contact with words and the ideas behind them. If the library's role is to remain a centre of word culture and democratic freedom in the digital age, then there needs to be a smooth interface between books, computer screens and people. This requires the integration of two types of space: book space with the traditional arrangement of shelves, tables and chairs, and computer space with its special demands for non-reflective light, keyboard elbow room, and places for electronic gossip. For unlike the almost universal spread of literacy, not everybody at present is at home with the media of electronic data.

| Technology and the library | | | | | |
|---|---|---|---|---|---|
| **Type of communication** | **Method of communication** | **Type of storage** | **Method of reading** | **Type of library** | **Date** |
| Hieroglyphic | Stone, clay or papyrus | Vault | Standing | Private | 500–1000 BC |
| Alphabet | Papyrus (rolls) | Vault | Standing or reclining | Private or state | 500–1300 AD |
| Alphabet | Animal parchment (decorated books) | Room | Standing or sitting | Monastic | 500–1200 |
| Cursive handwriting and numeracy | Paper (books) | Chapel above cloister | Standing | Monastic | 1200–1500 |
| Printing press | Paper (books) | Library | Standing with stall system | University and civic | 1500–1800 |
| Mass production printing | Paper (books, journals, newspapers) | Library | Sitting with tables | Civic and local public | 1800–2000 |
| Electronic digital | Electronic | Computer disk | Screen | All types and personal | 1990– |

Adapted from Hall, P. (1998). *Cities in Civilization*. Weidenfeld and Nicolson, pp. 509–510.

Historically, the pattern of communication has moved from durable media (carved stone, parchment) to non-durable media (electronic messages). The word power and memory of a modern computer equals that of many older libraries. With computing you can access whole books and reach data sources across the world. Cultural barriers are eroded in such a process: 'place', whether of countries or of libraries, is undermined by the breaking down of traditional media structures. The decentralization of the medium of knowledge has led to lighter, flexible, portable societies and transparent, open libraries. It is not the library which has changed society, but society and its technologies which have altered the library.

In the process society has shifted from one tied to space to one related to time – a distinction between 'place' and 'time' was developed by Harold Innis and quoted by Hall (1998). Late twentieth century humanity is time-structured with spatial perceptions eroded by mass communication whether physical or electronic. The library is caught in a dilemma – the medium of the library is space expressed in rooms and corridors, yet the media of communication is increasingly unrelated to space. The library historically consisted of rooms for books classified neatly into subject areas. Today the book exists alongside the computer screen – the first is space-tied, the second could be located anywhere. How the tension between space and time cultures is resolved is the essence of modern library design.

## The library as a cultural symbol

It is evident that in the evolution of the library as a distinctive building type, the library has spawned certain spaces which have both a symbolic and functional purpose. By reserving a special place in society for books and reading, the library signals the importance of learning. In this sense the library is, like the art gallery, a cultural signifier. But not all of the library spaces need to gesture towards this social or cultural role. Whilst the book stacks and offices are not worthy of celebration, the reading room certainly is, and so are the routes and staircases which provide promenades through the building. So if the library is a special type of building redolent with cultural meaning, the focus of celebration is primarily an internal affair. How the balance of symbolism and function is resolved gives character and meaning to library design.

Like a theatre, railway station or stadium, people gather inside libraries: the building is a container which looks inwards not outwards. The library is not a building from which to view the city but one where the intellectual realm of urban society is captured within its walls. The library was always so: private libraries of the Renaissance were splendid, comfortable rooms with tall windows set between built-in bookcases which lined the walls (e.g. Escorial Library, 1570). These early libraries were lofty well-proportioned galleries which contained the book collection, seats and writing space within a single room. They are

Sunken reading room,
Viipuri Public Library,
1933, by Alvar Aalto.
(Alvar Aalto Foundation)

more obvious precursors to the modern library than the rooms set aside in monasteries for storing and producing books. In the latter, books were held in locked chests or vaults, removing their sense of presence from within the space. Books were not normally read in the library but in alcoves set in nearby cloisters.

It is the ambience created by the books which makes a library. The library of the Renaissance was both a celebration of the book and of reading. The book was set within its framed enclosure just like a painting. Bookcases were built-in fittings, which ordered the space and determined the layout of furniture, windows and lighting. The book was prominent and its symbolic presence displayed. In these libraries the reader entered the world of books (and hence wisdom) rather than as in some modern libraries where the book enters the realm of the reader. The reader had a special place too, often a bay window or a special seat and table set by a window.

The identity of the library as a building type emerged as the importance of the book grew. When universities became

established as a by-product of the widening of the teaching duties bestowed upon monasteries, the book assumed a new status. Without access to books there was limited spread of education and a new university, once in receipt of its Papal Seal, quickly gathered books and built libraries. Influential early examples, such as those at the Sorbonne (1485) and at Leyden University (1562), placed the library up high to avoid damp attacking the paper and chained the books in long open lecterns. Reading was conducted in a standing position since the chains did not allow the book to travel far. But the space was not ordered by the books but by security.

It was the Renaissance that changed the relationship in favour of books. Books were beautiful objects (now cheaper with Caxton's invention of the printing press) and their leather bindings became an art form. The spines of books framed in their ornate bookcases became the wallpaper of the library. As a consequence the library emerged as a room to be seen in: a place in its own right in the palaces of Europe. This was essentially the model adopted by the UK universities with the lecterns converted first to

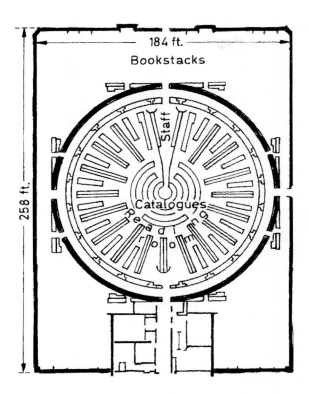

Plan of the Reading Room at the British Museum, 1852, by Sydney Smirke. (Brian Edwards)

Interior of the Reading Room at the British Museum by Sydney Smirke, as restored by Foster and Partners. (Nigel Young/Foster and Partners)

stalls, complete with fold-down seats, and then in the seventeenth century abandoned in favour of bookcases. The adoption of bookcases revolutionized the concept of space in libraries. With bookcases lining the walls, the reading area in the centre became the focus of attention. The Bodleian Library (1610) adopted the form, though it was a century before centralized libraries based upon circular forms were evolved. Wren's unbuilt centred plan of 1675 for Trinity College Cambridge Library was an early anticipation of a form which became common from the eighteenth century to the 1950s.

The wall system with locked bookcases and then open shelves lent itself to non-rectilinear planning. Centric layouts gave the benefit of perceiving the library as a whole, with every book visible at a sweep of the head. It allowed for a grasp of the totality of learning since all wisdom (at least in the early days) was contained within the books on display. Late Renaissance man (not women, who were usually banned from libraries until the nineteenth century) could stand in the centre and comprehend the world. Such libraries were like the globes which often stood within them – a gesture towards control and measure.

The circular library (or oval as it was often built) allowed for ease of supervision and, by setting a circular

reading space in a square building, the peripheral areas could be developed for staircases and offices. The circular library, often lit by a central roof light, contained an inner ring of reading desks and an outer ring of bookcases beyond which was placed a circular corridor. This essentially was the form of the Radcliffe Camera in Oxford by James Gibbs (1740) and the Reading Room at the British Museum Library (1852) by Sydney Smirke. In these examples, the cultural value of reading and scholarship was expressed in a grand and often domed space. The intellect had in a sense won over the book. The library was not just a place for storing and reading books, but also a public space for the expression of collective scholarship.

The Reading Room at the British Museum had a major influence on library design for nearly a century. The plan form with staff at the centre of a radiating system of bookcases, reading spaces and controls had the logic of marrying space, function and administration. Although the British Museum's stock at the time exceeded a million volumes, only the most important works were on display with the remainder kept in iron-framed book stacks behind the scenes. It was a library essentially of public parade and many, such as Karl Marx, benefited from its uplifting ambience. Such was its reputation that Smirke's circular design was repeated at the Library of Congress in

Washington (1897), the Prussian State Library (1914) and the Stockholm City Library (1928) (Graham, 1998, p. 74; Markus, 1993, pp. 172–178).

In an ideal library, readers, books and staff coexist in the same space. The circular library allowed this to happen because the book collection was not that large, the arrangement of books on the shelves corresponded directly to the catalogue and the reader could browse unimpeded by subject walls. Space in this sense ordered knowledge. But as libraries grew and subject boundaries became more rigid, a single centric library became untenable. The eighteenth century ideal of the 'universitality and perfectibility of knowledge' (Graham, 1998, p. 74), which the circular library expressed so vividly, failed to meet the demands of growth in stock and specialization of knowledge. Lateral thinking, which the circular form encouraged, was replaced by the idea of subject libraries each with their own rooms and disciplines of storage and use.

This change in emphasis grew directly from the growth in the number of books and the diversification of fields of knowledge. Before the concept of the self-renewing library where new stock is balanced by the withdrawal of old material, the library simply expanded to house the growth in publications. Rigid walls and equally rigid management can, however, impede the effectiveness of a library. The system of a central reading room with peripheral subject libraries and separate book stacks evolved as a means of accommodating the uncertainties of future change. The latter could expand without undermining the quality of the library's most important inheritance as a building type – namely, the reading room.

By the nineteenth century, the idealized circular library of interdisciplinary scholars sharing a common cultural space was replaced by the introduction of specific rooms for elements of the collection (science, humanities, etc.). The development of classification systems (such as that evolved by Melville Dewey) encouraged the division between open-shelf and book-stack storage. The sequential arrangement of books led to subject partitioning which effectively undermined the symbolic value of the library as social signifier whilst, admittedly, improving its usefulness. It was a victory of functionalism over meaning. The present day library has necessarily to grapple with the demands of both.

If the central circular reading room suggests the ordering of knowledge, how is the modern library to evolve given the unprecedented growth in the scale, complexity and format of knowledge? How is the library to communicate its high cultural duty whilst also satisfying the demanding strictures of almost instant access to book and electronic-based information? The answer lies in the balance between single monumental spaces and functionally specific ones. The new national libraries in London, Paris and Frankfurt all distinguish between the two although in quite different ways. In each case a large foyer space, rotunda or central

garden signal the presence of an intellectual realm – or space for reflection. The functional parts – specific reading or research rooms – are accessed via these bigger uplifting spaces. Each feeds upon the other as knowledge and theory interact. The science reading room at the new British Library is enclosed and studious, and hints at the indisputability of facts. The foyer spaces are lofty interpenetrative volumes where the mind is encouraged to wander – seeking perhaps to join together knowledge gathered elsewhere but in new ways. Monumental spaces have a role in libraries but their role is not primarily functional.

Until the mid-twentieth century, the library was generally classical in plan with a central reading room about which were placed, normally on sub-axes, various subject libraries. This was the form most commonly adopted after the public library movement of the 1860s. In fact, of the 600 new public libraries built in the UK between 1885 and 1920, the main element of interior design was provided by a central, often circular, space (Whittick, 1953). A fine example from Sweden is Gunnar Asplund's design for the city library in Stockholm (1928), which sits within a rectangular embrace of subject libraries, study rooms and offices. Books are placed in three tiers of radiating shelves around the perimeter of the reading room with a large bookstore in the basement immediately below. A slightly different form is Manchester City Library, designed by Vincent Harris a year later. It is modelled closely on Smirke's design for the British Museum but here there is a further band of libraries and exhibition space forming an outer ring to the building. In each case the reading room is not just pivotal in plan, it is also lofty, ordering the section as well.

Such spaces are monuments to the mind and its imagination, but difficult to justify in practical terms. By the 1930s more strictly functional solutions became commonplace. They tended to give equal weight to the parts of the library, arguing that use legibility was more important than hierarchy or symbolism. Typical of the modern functional approach to library design is Alvar Aalto's library at Viipuri (originally in Finland but now in Russia). Designed in 1933, the distribution of parts and outward architectural forms give direct expression to the internal arrangement. There is no grand shared space or reading room: instead there are wings of libraries and lecture rooms for different purposes. Only the double flight staircase of the lending library hints at finding time to reflect upon the books or journals read. Even in the hands of a master architect, the library seems bereft of symbolic calling. After all, books are not read for the purpose of gaining knowledge alone: they are the means by which both facts and wisdom are acquired. The traditional reading room was an expression of non-linear thinking.

This critique of the history of libraries helps clarify the issues designers and libraries face today. If a library is to celebrate the triumph of scholarship over the acquisition of

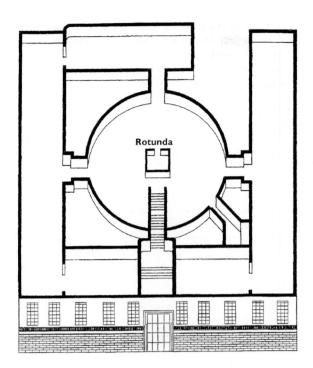

Plan of Stockholm Public Library, 1928, designed by Gunnar Asplund. (Stockholm Public Library)

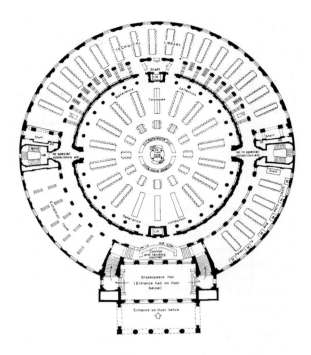

Manchester Central Public Library, 1935, by Vincent Harris. (D Insall and Partners)

mere knowledge, then its form should perhaps transcend strict functionalism as the basis for building design. What is more, when the vehicle for gaining knowledge and hence wisdom is the computer and its systems of e-mail, Internet, web pages and CD-ROMs, then is not the computer suite the contemporary version of the reading room? Or taking the argument further, is not the space to be given meaning not physical space but electronic space? Is not the modern library really a virtual world which we access if not from our homes at least from a special kind of building? If that is so, should not the library be a kind of cybercafe – a place where minds meet rather than a building where the reader joins the book? Ultimately, new technology makes space redundant: it leads to the death of distance as a factor in building design. When the reader can access every text from a single screen the assumptions upon which library design are based erode. With the loss of functional space goes the need to reappraise the purpose of the library as a building type and the spaces within it.

Some new lightweight, flexible, interactive libraries have begun to address the new agenda. Built mostly for expanding universities, these libraries for a digital age are fundamentally different from their predecessors. They resemble call centres or the trading floors of stock exchanges. Readers face electronic screens, scanning various sources of information in parallel. The screen on the desk provides

access to more information than was available in Smirke's library – a single scholar can virtually dip into all the world's information with a click of the mouse. But do new media make all of the old ideas obsolete? What is evident from new electronic libraries is the presence of generous communal space – a kind of modern computer-centred reading room. These spaces perform much the same symbolic role as the traditional centric library. It is space for the collective intellect: a volume in which to gaze hazily at the impossible, to share in the experience of inquiry with like minds. In this important sense the library has not really changed: it remains a special kind of building which signals the value we place upon learning and culture irrespective of the media we employ (Graham, 1998, p. 72).

## From hybrid to specialization: the emergence of the modern library

The cultural quarter in Alexandria contained a typically Hellenistic collection of public buildings and civic spaces. Here in the second and third centuries there existed a library, a museum and a debating chamber arranged in a typically Greek composition of loosely flowing parts. The grouping set the pattern through the Renaissance and beyond of library, museum and art gallery in planned relationship. For economy, library and museum were often in the same building, either directly above each other (as in the Royal Museum in Munich, 1570) or as separate wings

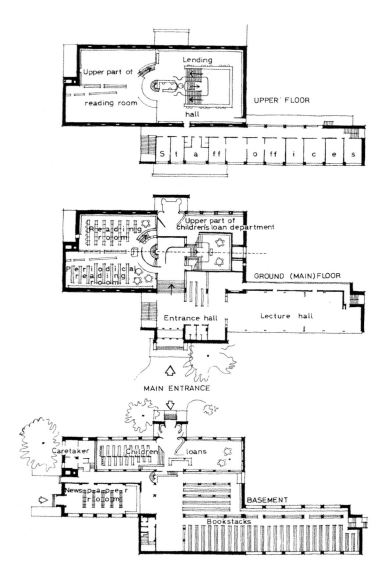

Plans of Viipuri Public Library, 1933, designed by Alvar Aalto. (Alvar Aalto Foundation)

in a larger public building. It was largely the need for roof lighting of museum exhibits which, from the early nineteenth century onwards, formerly split the two buildings apart. The public library (normally positioned above the museum because books were more easily moved than statutry) emerged as a distinctive building type when the display and lighting problems of the museum and art gallery were resolved around 1800. Although academic libraries had gelled into a recognizable taxonomy of arrangement by about 1600, the public library did not mature as a building type for a further two centuries.

Many examples of joint museums and libraries existed, however, in the nineteenth century (e.g. the British Museum, 1855, and Grenoble, France, from 1862) and into the twentieth (e.g. Huddersfield, UK, in 1930). The technical problems of lighting galleries and libraries were so different that the impetus for functional separation was more practical than cultural. But the division was reinforced by the nature of finance available. The Peabody Trust from around 1860 and the Carnegie Trust from 1896 accelerated the development of library buildings in the USA and UK largely on philanthropic grounds. The library (rather than the museum or art gallery) was seen as essential for the education of ordinary people. Often in partnership with civic authorities or local benefactors, both trusts spawned countless new library buildings, mainly in the new industrial cities of the late nineteenth century. Most acknowledge that the first public library was built at Peterboro in New Hampshire in 1833 (Pevsner, 1976). Boston Public Library, which opened in 1854 and was

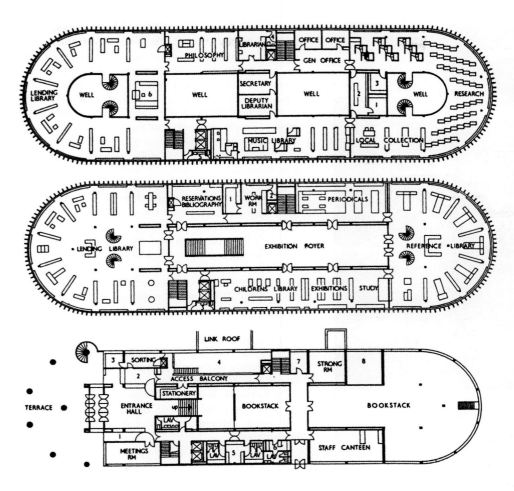

Plans of Swiss Cottage Library, Hampstead, London, 1966, designed by Sir Basil Spence. The building captures the spirit of the modern democratic public library. (*Architectural Review*)

significantly extended in 1890 by McKim, Mead and White, is an important early example in the USA. The first public library in Britain was the Warrington Public Library (1848), followed by Manchester Public Library (1852) (Pevsner, 1976).

The public libraries of the nineteenth and early twentieth centuries differ from university libraries in three important respects: they were free and open to all, they had welcoming interiors with direct entrance from the street and there was less emphasis upon the 'Reading Room' and rather more upon the book stack. As a consequence, the plan of dome and cube which had marked development hitherto became replaced by the use of separate departments. The modern library contained a reference section, a journals and newspaper area, a children's library and so forth. The library desk too became important, both in terms of security and providing information for users, many of whom were ill-educated. As the social function of the public library grew, so too did the volume of the entrance space. In some libraries the circular reading room migrated in the plan to become the reception foyer. These

changes necessitated alteration to the arrangement of windows. By the 1920s, long low bands of windows had replaced the tall lights of earlier libraries. Horizontal not vertical light was needed for the low tables and book-shelves of the modern public library. Rooms were not high and deep, but shallow and friendly. Democracy had altered the plan and the details of construction just as the advent of higher learning at the universities had altered the form of the library three centuries earlier. This change is most evident in the smaller public libraries, such as those built in the new suburbs by the London County Council and the many small town libraries of East Coast America designed by Henry Richardson.

The pursuit of openness and horizontality was made possible by innovations in construction technology. The development of iron-framed construction and then structural concrete liberated the walls from providing anything other than symbolic enclosure. The library structure became increasingly high-tech, allowing bookshelves to be placed almost anywhere. Walls and partitions could be freely disposed, altered over time to suit change in

15

Children's Library at Mission Bay Public Library, San Francisco. (Brian Edwards)

management philosophy, and kept low to encourage the sense of fluidity of space. The introduction of new construction technology liberated the library from old constraints (such as structured span lengths, vertical movement via stairs and opening windows for ventilation). By 1900 the library had a steel or concrete frame divorced from the brick or stone external envelope, a lift to move people and books, and primitive air-conditioning. These innovations occurred not in academic libraries but in the major public libraries of France, Germany, England and America.

The public library has been described as a building where the 'curious and impatient enquirer and the bewildered ignorant might freely repair' (Fletcher, 1894). The key aspects of the modern library are free, unhindered access to the reading material, the lending of books and other material, and the provision of a physical environment which not only invites entry but encourages users to dwell upon the material. These elements, coupled with new approaches to design and construction, led inevitably to countless modern public libraries around the world. Differences in form and arrangement are slight compared to the variation in academic libraries which, with their greater focus upon computer-based study collections, remain fundamentally different. Another group of distinctive library types are the national libraries where the scale of the collection (many in excess of 15 million books), the extent of scarce or valuable material, and the fusion of traditional and digital retrieval systems makes for another key classification.

Learning Resource Centre, University of Sunderland, 1996, designed by Building Design Partnership. (BDP)

Horizontal space boldly expressed in the Hallward Library, University of Nottingham, designed in 1973 by Faulkner-Brown, Hendy, Watkinson and Stonor. (University of Nottingham)

## The twenty-first century library

After years of relative neglect as a building type, the library enjoyed a renaissance towards the end of the twentieth century and into the twenty-first. Interesting new solutions to the architecture of the public library appeared, first at Peckham and Whitechapel in London to designs by Will Alsop and David Adjaye respectively, and in Vancouver and Seattle to designs by Moshe Safdie and Rem Koolhaas. In parallel, national libraries underwent exciting transformations, as in Paris to designs by Dominique Perrault and in Alexandria by the architectural practice known as Snohetta. The libraries of colleges and universities were also transformed into dramatic enclosures for knowledge dissemination, research and learning such as at Thames Valley University designed by the Richard Rogers Partnership and more recently at the Saltire Centre at Glasgow Caledonia University to designs by BDP. These and countless other examples examined in the new edition of this book signal the re-emergence of the library as a building of architectural significance. In this it is following in the footsteps of the art gallery and museum – buildings where cultural and social engagement matter as much as the collections they house. In

| Major libraries and their collection | | | |
|---|---|---|---|
| **Library** | **Type** | **Date** | **Collection (books)** |
| British Library, London | National | 1998 | 15 million |
| Bibliothèque Nationale, Paris | National | 1992 | 12 million |
| Library of Congress, Washington | National | Various | 21 million |
| Mitchell Library, Glasgow | Civic | 1892 | 8 million |
| New York Public Library | Civic | 1849– | 5 million |
| Manchester Public Library | Civic | 1852– | 4 million |
| Harvard University | Academic | 1880– | 10 million |
| Bodleian, Oxford University | Academic | 1610– | 4 million |
| Glasgow University | Academic | 1540– | 3 million |

Seattle Public Library, designed in 2004 by OMA/Rem Koolhaas, signals a new approach to the design of the building type. (Brian Edwards)

Interior of Saltire Centre at Glasgow Caledonia University, designed in 2005 by BDP. This IT-based library creates a variety of spaces for informal learning and socializing. (Brian Edwards)

many ways the library has 'shrugged off its origins as a sternly patrolled repository of knowledge' to become a place for 'encounter, communication and research' (Bertolucci, 2004).

The reasons for the revival of interest in the library are threefold. First, new media technologies, particularly IT-based knowledge packages and universal Internet usage, led local government and universities to a reassessment of the role of libraries in a digital and multicultural age.

---

**Main factors leading to change in design of library buildings**

- New information technology especially electronic data collections

- Greater community and educational role for libraries

- Expansion in higher education and growth in life-long learning

- Impact of popular culture on libraries

---

Second, the resurgence of interest in other building types – notably shopping malls and art galleries – encouraged often conservative public clients to see libraries as buildings to visit in their own right rather than merely providing a desk on which to read a book. Third, the expansion of higher education has led to a radical reassessment of the role of the academic library in teaching and learning, and this in turn changed attitudes in the public library, especially in the area of IT provision and widened access. In fact, one trend in recent provision is the blurring of types of library, with university libraries increasingly providing facilities for the general public and public libraries incorporating seminar and study space for use by students at local schools, colleges and universities.

By the early twenty-first century, libraries with exciting public spaces, interesting exterior forms and more 'market place' interior qualities had begun to appear. Typical examples in the UK were Brighton Public Library by Bennetts Associates and in Canada the new Montreal Public Library by Patkau Architects. What these have in common is their attention to urban presence as well as building design, the creation of study areas and cafes which invite

Brighton Public Library
signals the importance
of the library as an
expression of
democratic space –
a place for people to
meet as well as read.
(Bennetts Associates,
Brian Edwards)

contemplation and reflection on the knowledge gained, floor layouts which encourage information exchange across media types, and the abandonment of the sterile silent world of the typical library. As a result different areas of the libraries took on the qualities of bookshops and cafes on the one hand, and computerized trading halls on the other. The library in effect began to assume many functions and guises reserved for other types of building in an attempt to adjust to wider changes taking place in society.

Of all modern building types few have been as stressed by the twin currents of technological and social change as the library. New digital media, ready access from home to the web and lowering costs of laptops have conspired to change the role of the library from a book to a multimedia depository. Coupled with this, wider changes in society, such as the need for language support associated with the growth of people migration and the greater emphasis on higher education and life-long learning, have added to the stresses of technological change. The two are not unrelated: technological innovation has fuelled social change whilst new patterns of work have required new skills and these in turn have generated new forms of information and entertainment media. The affects on the library have been twofold. First, there is pressure to adapt existing library buildings to meet the needs of the twenty-first century whilst, second, a fresh generation of libraries has emerged under various names such as mediateques (mainly in France), idea stores, discovery centres and the like. This book focuses upon the design challenge posed by libraries in an age of rapid change. Through various case studies under the four headings of national libraries, public libraries, academic libraries and special libraries, the book seeks to explore the architectural consequences of these social and technological shifts on one of our most familiar and cherished building types.

In a remarkably short generation libraries have changed from being repositories of books, newspapers and journals to being local knowledge centres playing their full part in the modern age of digital media. Today the typical library is an interactive network which encompasses books, journals (many of which are electronic), CDs, videos, Internet sources and sometimes special collections. Increasingly the network contains links to the home and study centres, thereby supporting independent learning and reinforcing the role of schools and colleges in the community. Many university libraries have done the same thing with links to private research centres and local businesses. This widening of the economic, cultural and social role of libraries has been accompanied by a change in design values and a broadening of the brief of a typical library. In effect the twenty-first century library is a knowledge grid and information gateway with tentacles spreading across continents, into homes and offices via laptops and ipods. Wire or wireless, these tentacles are synchronized, managed and often cultivated within libraries by librarians whose role is to guide readers through the ever-expanding world of knowledge. The role of the library building is not so much to contain that knowledge but to make it available in such a fashion that the process of discovery is stimulating, pleasurable and uplifting.

Rather than lead to the obsolescence of the library, new technology has liberated the building from increasingly unpopular stereotypical forms, and altered the fundamental assumptions behind their design. One such is the dominance of the book and the associated requirement for

19

A strong street presence is needed for today's libraries as here at San Francisco Public Library. (Brian Edwards)

silence in all but designated areas. The strategy today is to encourage the sharing of knowledge and to welcome the use of the spoken word either between individuals or in groups. Since the library is often used for teaching and learning within the community, silence is expected only in private study areas. Elsewhere the pleasure of discovery and exchange is welcomed, as is the talking computer and the tapping of keyboards. Restricting silence to special areas allows the remainder to become a place for sharing ideas and jointly pursuing knowledge. In an age where knowledge and creativity are the new forms of wealth creation, the library, whether academic or public, has a crucial role to play in equipping people with the skills needed in a changing world.

Another change is the assumption that print is paramount: although books remain vital to the library, the first point of contact is usually the computer screen. The interaction between digital knowledge and the printed word is a dynamic one which requires space characteristics different from the traditional library reading room. Many modern libraries place the computer screen at the front door allowing the reader to pass through knowledge layers as they navigate the library. The role of library staff is to aid navigation through types and modes of knowledge rather than exercise security or merely sit behind a desk stamping the books as they are borrowed. In directing readers to the material, there is a great deal of interaction, both verbal and digital, which inevitably affects the interior layout.

In charting the impact of the IT revolution on the design of libraries it is tempting to dismiss the book as an obsolete form of media. This is far from the truth. Books are essential to the justification of the existence of libraries. In fact one of the key roles of national libraries is to be a deposit of every printed work, and the public library owes its local justification and remit to the ability to make available books on loan to the community. In spite of the growth of e-books, people still like to read from hardcopy books rather than from a screen. Downloading books is becoming ubiquitous (especially for students and professional readers) yet society still enjoys books for their cache and flexibility. Digital readers are limited by both copyright law (you cannot copy an e-book to a friend) and the availability of technology. Books are physical entities which communicate to the world that their readers are culturally informed and hungry for knowledge. To borrow a book is to send a message that the screen denies. That is why readership and buying of books continues to rise in spite of the growth of anti-book technologies.

A significant shift over the past two decades has been the increasing role of libraries in life-long learning, in providing community information, and in supporting the needs of the elderly. By 2020, 50% of Europeans will be over 50 years old and for this section of the population, the library

**Contemporary role of the public library**

- Helps cement together a community
- Provides meeting places
- IT learning and support centres
- Complements art gallery and museum as cultural investment
- Life-long learning centre

| Library types and functions | |
|---|---|
| **Library type** | **Characteristic features** |
| National library | Legal deposit (all published books deposited) |
| | Comprehensive book and journal collection |
| | Attached special collections (e.g. Kings Library at British Library) |
| | Reference rather than loan |
| | Wide range of supporting activities (conservation centre, bookshops, exhibition area, cafe) |
| Public library | Loan rather than reference |
| | Supporting community or social activities |
| | Mainly book-based (as against journal or electronic) |
| | Special libraries for children, elderly, local study |
| Academic library | Emphasis upon supporting learning |
| | Extensive research material |
| | Large journal collections |
| | Extensive electronic/computer systems |
| | Networks to departmental libraries |
| Virtual library | Electronic/IT-based |
| | Can be associated with cybercafes or traditional library |
| | Exists independently of buildings |
| | Requires home or office based computer network |
| Special library | Collection based on famous individual, topic, event or place |
| | Not normally for loan |
| | Mainly research-based |
| | Provides archive and conservation function |
| | Visit often by appointment |
| Professional library | Special collection to serve professional body |
| | Material not normally for loan |
| | Often associated with exhibition area |
| | Extensive archive and journal collections |
| | Contains a wide variety of material (photographic, letters, plans) |

has particularly important services to provide. This has ramifications for the design and layout of library buildings, the level of lighting and provision of such things as toilets and disabled access. For people who do not possess English as their first language, for the poor seeking welfare support, and for individuals who are newly arrived in an area, the library is often the first point of contact with a neighbourhood. Hence, the qualities and values expressed through architectural design leave a lasting impression. For these reasons the library today is seen as a gateway to learning and a shop window of both knowledge dissemination and access to educational or community services.

The dynamic relationship in the former generation of library buildings between the lending library, reference library and reader room has been replaced by a new set of interacting functions. Today the library contains spaces for the print collection, the digital collection, and associated cafe, community and educational areas. This change has fundamentally altered the nature of the building.

Rather than face declining numbers of users, today's library is full of life and activity, and many of the new users were not visitors to the old generation of libraries. One important challenge into the twenty-first century is to accommodate these changes without destroying the library as a familiar and much loved building type. For in spite of the many examples discussed later, many library managers and their architects 'seem fixated on the classic book-dominated library and have great problems redefining libraries for the electronic age' (Latimer and Niegaard, 2007).

## 'Library' – a definition

The standard dictionary definition (derived from the *New Collins Concise English Dictionary*, 1974) of a library distinguishes between the library as space, the library as collection and the library as institution. A library is either:

- a room or set of rooms where books and other literary materials are kept
- a collection of literary materials, films, tapes, etc., or
- the building or institution that houses such a collection.

However, a more contemporary definition of a library is a building where knowledge is collected, stored and made available mainly free of charge. Such knowledge can be in book, journal or other forms of paper format, may consist of photographs, maps and graphic representations, or may be based on digital and other forms of electronic media.

As such, for the sake of this edition a library is a building designed to contain and make available for use a collection of book and other forms of published paper-based material, plus the facility to access information by electronic means. In this context the word:

- 'contain' means to secure, preserve and present the collection
- 'designed' refers to a conscious act of creating such a building with the dual purpose of meeting the needs of the collection and the library user
- 'make available for use' embraces the ability to borrow, retrieve, read and copy aspects of the collection. It also includes the ability to access electronically information held in digital formats and to interface this with paper-based material.

Consequently, a library is a building where books, e-knowledge and people meet in largely convivial surroundings without the obligation to purchase. Such definitions can be further expanded to include types of libraries. For example:

- A *national library* is one where depositions of books and other material of national importance are housed. In such a library, the emphasis is upon comprehensiveness of collection, plus the safe housing and conservation of scarce material.
- A *public library* is one where depositions of books and other material are housed primarily for loan. Such a library would normally provide study and other material for use by community groups or for local social advancement.
- An *academic library* is one where books, journals and other material, particularly electronic information systems, are housed primarily to support learning or research.
- A *virtual library* is a collection of library material housed primarily in electronic formats and accessed via networked computers. Such a library may be partly or wholly independent of physical enclosure.
- A *specialist library* is a collection within a room or building dedicated wholly to a specific subject. Normally special collections are based upon individuals, topics or places.
- A *professional library* is a collection developed specifically by a professional body to serve its members. The collection would normally contain a wide range of library material which would not normally be for loan. Such a library shares characteristics with the specialist library.

The characteristics of libraries vary according to type, but there are overlaps in provision. For example, virtual libraries often exist with traditional ones, and material of national importance may, for historical reasons, be housed in a central public library. Also, special libraries may be annexes to public or academic libraries as in, for instance, the Ruskin Library at the University of Lancaster.

## References

Bertolucci, C. (2004). Cave of knowledge. *Architectural Review* January, p. 22.

Fletcher, W. I. (1894). *Public Libraries in America*. Boston. p. 12.

Graham, C. (1998). Libraries in history. *Architectureal Review* June, pp. 72–74.

Hall, P. (1998). *Cities in Civilization*. Weidenfeld and Nicolson, pp. 506–507.

Latimer, K. and Niegaard, H. (2007). IFLA library building guidelines: developments and reflections. *KG Saur*: 31.

Markus, T. (1993). Buildings and Power: Freedom and Control in the Origin of Modern Building Types. Routledge.

Pevsner, N. (1976). *A History of Building Types*. Thames and Hudson, p. 105.

Roche, D. (1979). Urban Reading Habits during the French Enlightenment. *British Journal of 18th Century Studies,* 2, p. 141. (I am indebted to Professor Markus for drawing this to my attention.)

Whittick, A. (1953). *European Architecture in the 20th Century 1924–1933.* Vol. 2. Crosby Lockwood and Son Ltd. p. 20.

# Part 2
# Planning the library

# 2

# Location and site factors

## Urban design

The public library needs to be well connected to civic life and the academic library located at the centre of the college or university. Good access to pedestrian flows and public transport is essential, as is the ability to service libraries with their ever-evolving collections and needs. Hence, there will normally be a public front and a service rear or undercroft. However, the public entrance is not normally the library door but a gathering space immediately outside it. This should be designed with the characteristics of a public square with attention to landscape design, public comfort (i.e. seats) and community or personal safety. The library 'square' is where users will meet, escape from the confines of the library to reflect on the material, take short breaks to eat sandwiches or visit local cafes or other cultural facilities, and engage in the ambiance of the public realm. Aristotle refined the city as 'a collection of buildings where men live a common life for a noble end' and no building embodies this ideal better than the public library.

The external library space should be free of cars although public modes of transport can (and often should) pass nearby. There also needs to be provision for disabled access and facilities for the storage of bicycles. Hence, a level access is preferable and ramps essential where changes of level are inevitable. The public space alongside the library entrance provides an opportunity for the building to make a statement and this in turn can help signal the significance of the library. It also provides the chance to incorporate sculpture or other forms of public art into the city – some of which may contain text references to the library collection.

With university libraries the building needs to be centrally placed on the campus and located where 24-hour surveillance is possible. There is often a linear plaza at the centre of campus where other academic institutions are located, such as senate house, refectory, gymnasium and registry. This provides an opportunity for the formation of a student-centred academic mall which ties together the key shared facilities with links to the separate faculty buildings further afield. Hence, one role of the academic library is to define the centre of the campus both spatially and in terms of building hierarchy.

The flows from the external public space to the main building entrance are more clearly defined if attention is paid to urban design at the briefing stage. The choice of site often dictates external relationships. Proximity to public transport and existing pedestrian or cycle flows is imperative. There are parallel flows too which need to be considered such as the delivery of books, newspapers, furniture and access for staff. The service entrance needs to have good road access and a limited amount of delivery and parking space. Increasingly, information is electronically delivered using wire or wireless technology and this eases the demand upon physical service areas. However, delivery and storage of the library material is a major consideration at the site planning level.

To fulfil its duty in the widest sense the library needs to be well connected to civic life. This means good access to public as well as private modes of transport with facilities provided for library users who arrive on bicycle or are disabled in any way. Since most visiting the library will arrive on foot, the needs of pedestrians must take priority.

Not all sites provide ideal conditions for access, but too often the functional needs of book delivery or emergency vehicle access take priority. Readers' needs should take

| Principal site planning considerations | Issues to consider |
|---|---|
| Civic presence | • Relationship to other public buildings<br>• Visible presence |
| Public access | • Access to public transport<br>• Disabled access |
| Service access | • Access to road system<br>• Delivery and storage areas |
| Urban design | • External public gathering space<br>• Safe, secure and legible routes |

precedent over those of the books (except where rare or fragile material is involved) and this alters the balance of convenience between public perceptions and library management ones. A successful library is one which is conveniently accessed via attractive and safe urban spaces, and where there are areas to pause and reflect upon the material read. Few modern libraries do this though they are well serviced by road, giving the superficial impression of functional efficiency.

Libraries are part of the civic infrastructure of towns. The library has a key role to play in the realization of the 'common life' – socially, economically and culturally. Placed in this context, the library becomes part of the web of civic facilities embracing education, art, administration, justice and sport. In many ancient and modern towns, a central meeting place contains a grouping of public buildings forming an interconnecting network of civic facilities. The library is an important element in the ensemble but because it addresses access to knowledge and wisdom, its natural neighbours are the art gallery, college and town hall.

If the library is part of the civic realm, it is important to differentiate between public and market functions. Most towns have a clearly defined civic centre around which public functions are grouped, and a retail centre for trade and commerce. Although the two realms connect, the library belongs to the former. This is the pattern found in most towns up to the twentieth century, though many recent libraries have abandoned the principles of civic proximity for the convenience of vehicle access. The expression of a civic place containing the library as functional and formal anchor is best expressed in the American Plaza of the late nineteenth century. Here, under the enlightened patronage of

Andrew Carnegie, the new libraries of cities such as Boston and Buffalo were developed alongside art galleries and town halls to form cultural and administrative foci embodying the spirit of accessibility and democracy.

A good location is one, therefore, which integrates the library into the civic and cultural life of the town. A poor one is where the library is isolated physically and psychologically. The design of the library needs to promote, not hinder, linkage with space, which is the medium of connectivity expressed through both interior and exterior volumes. People movement through space is more important than vehicle movement, even if those vehicles are providing deliveries to the library. A good location is one which gives priority to the library user, not to the convenience of library staff; and to the reader rather than the book.

The library necessarily sits between two strong currents: that of the user accessing the material and that of the staff, library systems and delivery vehicles which service the collection. Since the library reader may well wish to visit other civic facilities (such as the town hall and gallery) as well as borrow a book, there are obvious connections to establish. Likewise, for the library to function effectively it needs ready access to roads for service and emergency purposes. But the library should not be located simply because of the servicing or functional argument. To do so would be to scatter indiscriminately the library and other public buildings about the town, thereby undermining any sense of centre. This is true of the city library and of the university library where the effect of a centre is equally essential.

Thus the first priority in locating a library is civic. There are two main ramifications that follow: the first is a matter of effect and grouping at the level of urban design, especially

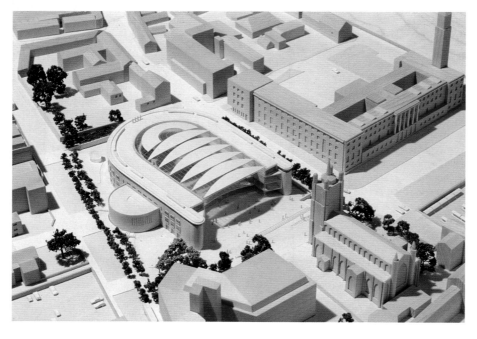

The new Norwich Public Library is served by attractive pedestrian routes and approached by an urban square. (Tom Miller)

The Idea Store in Whitechapel, London is designed to be part of local street culture. (Brian Edwards)

that of external space planning. Second, there should be ready access to railway and bus station with ramps—not stairs — to provide ease of movement for disabled users and those

with children in prams. The route to the library should be clear, safe and attractive to use. Where there is vehicle access to cross, the road user should be subservient to the pedestrian. As the library is likely to be used in the evening, the design of access paths and squares should encourage safety and security by ensuring a high level of use (by employing mixed land-use development around the library) and by employing natural and closed circuit television (CCTV) surveillance in conjunction with high levels of lighting.

The routes to the library need to offer legibility and the library itself should have a high degree of visibility. The hierarchy of function implicit in the library as a building type should be expressed in the use of distinctive architectural form. The various routes to the library, whether on foot or by vehicle, should present an imageable sequence which culminates in a memorable library. The question of access, therefore, needs to address the psychology of place as well as its functionality.

So far the emphasis has been upon the characteristics of good location – particularly from an urban design point of view. Bad locations are ones where, no matter how well the library is designed, the building cannot be stitched into the infrastructure of the civic realm. This may be because of distance from the urban centre, because of the effect of barrier buildings or roads, or because the brief gives undue priority to functional needs. The aesthetic or formal vocabulary of the library should balance the demands of utility or, put another way, the long-term value of the library in terms of achieving Aristotle's 'common good' needs to take priority at the level of civic design.

As a practical measure, it is important to plan libraries so that they do not open directly onto busy streets at their front or flanks. The reader does not want to have to rush directly

Large civic libraries, as seen here in Copenhagen, need space outside for people and bicycles. (Brian Edwards)

into a busy thoroughfare after the quiet refuge of a library. Busy streets directly abutting the library pose considerable problems of interior noise as well as adding to the disorientation of the reader. Far better to place the library in a square or have a recessed 'place' at the entrance where readers can meet friends and gather their thoughts before confronting the bustle of modern urban life. A good example of this approach is the new British Library in London with its recessed square behind the busy Euston Road. Another is the new Peckham Library in South London by architects Alsop and Störmer, which is set within the newly created Peckham Square – intended to act as a catalyst of urban regeneration and refuge from congested arterial roads.

Few librarians or architects have the option of choosing their site. Frequently the location is decided by the time the design team arrives. However, it is still possible to turn a poor location into an acceptable design by addressing some of the points above. For instance, it may be possible to link the library directly into a bus or railway station (to avoid tortuous routes later), to form a shared piazza with an adjoining building placed at right angles to a busy road, to bridge across a ring road with a high-level entrance away from traffic noise, or to give the library a leafy oasis at the centre (a kind of refuge for reflection as at the Bibliothèque Nationale in Paris).

It is also worth remembering that the effect of well-designed public buildings is lost if they are placed in ordinary streets. What they need for totality of effect is a distinctive site. Part of the architect's duty is to turn an average site into a memorable place through the process of design. However, not all locations have the potential to achieve this transformation. This is why design guidance is needed right at the beginning of a project and before the architectural team is appointed.

The totality of effect is also dependent upon neighbours. Some locations offer advantageous adjoining buildings, others a disadvantaging background. As a general rule, the library requires contrast from a domestic or mundane physical context and harmony, but stylistic differentiation from a civic background. Where the site is surrounded by poor quality and under-scaled buildings (such as warehouses, car showrooms and business premises) the library building can lift the area aesthetically and enhance its status culturally. The design here needs to have measured contrast. Where on the other hand the library is located alongside neighbours of similar civic status, there is the opportunity to enhance the group effect. Here the library should not contrast in size, material or scale, but add to the ensemble. It does, however, need to read as a library (and not an art gallery) so differentiation based upon functionality is an essential element of architectural design.

The library of a town is part of the cultural quarter not the commercial quarter. On the university campus it is an element of the central learning environment not the peripheral research park. Location is essential if the right connections are to be made. It may be more convenient or cheaper to find a site away from the centre, but to build a library there would be to reduce its value to the community (civic or academic). Since libraries are one of the longest surviving building

Peckham Public Library forms a cultural space at its entrance designed for impromptu civic events. (Brian Edwards)

St George's Library in Sheffield, designed by Building Design Partnership, is a useful symbol of regeneration. (Roy Wooding/ICS)

types, it is important that the 'big picture' is considered at the outset—the library as cultural capital as against building cost.

The library is not a static building type. More than most, the library is subject to considerable pressure for change – from innovations in information technology, the growth of knowledge with an ever-increasing volume of books and journals, and in the move from a manufacturing to service economy with its emphasis upon education. A successful library is one which is able to grow externally and adapt internally. A good location is one, therefore, which provides the space for change. However, ultimate change is destructive of civic and architectural values. A balance is needed between permanence of form with attendant cultural value attached to fabric, and flexibility of operation. It is important that the library takes its place amongst the community of public buildings and has a character which is recognizably that of a library (so that meaning can mature through association), yet is able to grow and respond to programmatic changes. A good site is one therefore which provides some space for growth – either outwardly or upwardly. If total flexibility and extendibility are required, however, this will be at the expense of urban design. It is better to allow for limited physical growth (say 20%), which can occur over one or two generations with substantial growth accommodated by new satellite buildings. This is the pattern adopted at

| Hierarchy of deliveries at a typical library | |
|---|---|
| **Timing** | **Item** |
| By second | Electronic mail<br>Telephone calls |
| By hour | Users<br>Staff |
| By day | Newspapers<br>Inter-library loans |
| By week | Books<br>Popular journals |
| By month | Reference journals<br>Government publications |
| By year | Special collections<br>Furniture and equipment |

the National Library of Scotland where a new annex nearly as large as the original building has been constructed a mile away. This too is how many university libraries expand, taking advantage of separate faculty libraries to accommodate growth.

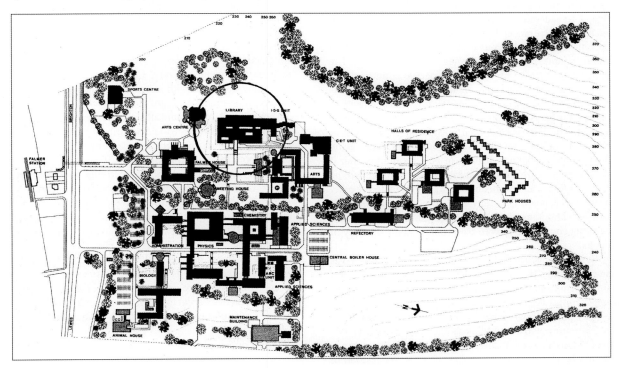

Libraries are normally free-standing buildings with space around for outward growth. Sussex University, master-planned in 1958 by Basil Spence. (Feilden and Mawson)

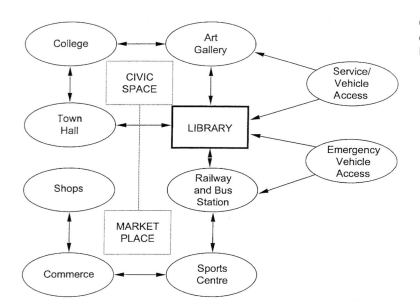

Conceptual diagram of the relationship of library to civic functions. (Brian Edwards)

## Issues of access for people and books

The visit an individual makes to a library may be the sole purpose of the journey, but people often combine their visit with other activities. How they travel to the library is thus a consideration in planning the location and ease of access to its entrance. The vicinity outside the library can become an obstacle course if attention is not paid to where people can leave bicycles or baby buggies. The popularity of travel by bicycle in specific countries such as Sweden and China and, in the UK, by users of academic libraries, means that people will expect places to leave their bikes securely. Bike parks should therefore be a feature of planning (as seen outside the new public library in Malmo, Sweden), as should dog rails. Baby buggies are a common feature in public libraries and, if the building interior is not parent-friendly, storage will be required to prevent prams becoming an obstacle for other users and a potential safety risk. However, for most library locations users will arrive at the door on foot and carrying something – often the accoutrements of study or books.

Storage is needed at the library entrance for prams, coats and shopping. It normally takes the form of lockers for small items and secure rooms for larger ones. Public storage facilities help reduce the risk of theft of library property by placing bags outside the book and journal areas.

The entrance to the building should either be central or in an obvious relation to other public buildings nearby. It should be placed to take account of traffic (pedestrian or vehicular). Most libraries will be large enough to make locating the entrance an issue for the first time user. Easily interpreted visual clues should be provided from a variety of approaches, including car or bike parks, bus and train stations and other major facilities. The entrance itself should be an attractive feature but easily negotiated. It is necessary for the entrance to be accessed via a ramp in instances where steps are featured. In common with many civic buildings, it is usual for libraries to have only one public entrance/exit. This provides for the security requirement by cutting down the number of exits where checks have to be carried out. Entrance in some libraries has to be controlled, i.e. granted to bona fide members only. Card entry systems are increasingly common, with a reception function to provide access to non-members. A growing number of libraries offer 24-hour access. All day and all night opening puts particular stress on staffing systems and security. Controlled access and CCTV within the library are a common response to protect both the collection and the staff.

Library users will normally be carrying books or other materials, making mechanically operated doors essential. Automatic doors or electric revolving doors are appreciated by users (especially those with some form of physical impairment). Doors that close after use are necessary to prevent heat loss or weather ingress. The size, design and position of doors helps signal the presence of the public entrance to the library as against the staff entrance. Out of hours 'book-drops' are a facility which needs to be located in a convenient external location, but also one which has an internal relationship with the main circulation desk.

### Internal entrances/exits

Libraries are multifunctional and sophisticated buildings which often challenge the first time user. Library users are often required to anticipate their needs in advance of entry.

Multi-modal access to Bournemouth Library. Design by Building Design Partnership. (BDP)

External seating at San Francisco Public Library. (Brian Edwards)

The library entrance is also a place to meet. Temasek Polytechnic, Singapore. (Michael Wilford and Partners)

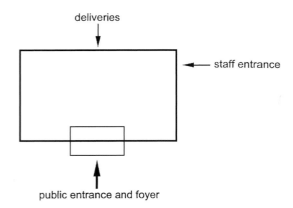

Conceptual diagram of entrances. (Brian Edwards)

It is essential that, once inside, users are allowed a place for some reflection or overview of the internal layout. From a central vantage point, the user should be able to assess the physical arrangement of facilities in consultation with an information board, electronic noticeboard, printed material or other guide. Some users will not have the confidence to approach personnel at this stage of their investigation, but a reception desk in the entrance area allows for face-to-face consultation. This is often repeated on all the floors of the library. It is necessary for some commonality of layout to be introduced alongside any variations of service provided in specific locations within the building.

### Staff access

It is important to include a separate staff entrance, especially where opening hours are not concomitant with working hours. In any library, there are a number of daily routines, including cleaning, which need to be undertaken before or after the public areas are open. Staff entrances avoid a library seemingly admitting some people (staff)

Protected entrances at Seattle Public Library provide a sheltered route for users. (Brian Edwards)

whilst others (users) are queuing. The location and design of the staff entrance should not lead to ambiguity over the status of private and public gateways into the building.

Similarly, at the end of the day, locking the public entrance/exit is made easier if the staff can then leave by a separate door. It should be remembered that most library employees are female, and libraries stay open until late evening. Exits for staff should therefore give them access into well-lit, public spaces and not into alleys, cul-de-sacs or less busy areas of the locality.

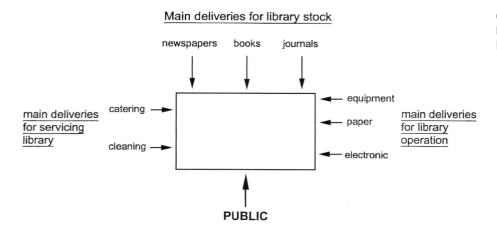

Conceptual diagram of library deliveries. (Brian Edwards)

The elevated student entrance to the Saltire Centre at Glasgow Caledonia University signals the distinction between public and private access to the library. (Brian Edwards)

Vertical and horizontal movement from the entrance or towards the exit should be allowed by placing lifts, stairways and other routes in a pattern of logical and functional relationships. There are well-defined patterns of interrelational usage for the public use of facilities (see Chapter 4). Staff communications are different and are best accommodated separately.

*Service access and deliveries*

There is a constant delivery schedule in all libraries which includes post deliveries, stationery requirements, paper for photocopiers, daily newspapers and books, journals and pre-requisites for the cloakrooms, kitchens and catering. This necessitates access to the building for vans and trucks, as well as internal delivery methods within large organizations with centrally provided services such as postal delivery.

Once inside the building, the goods need to be directed to the appropriate floor, area or level. Goods entrances must be serviced by doors that do not conflict with the users' needs, for example to avoid the need to manoeuvre trolleys or delivery carts through an area where people are queuing for book issuing or photocopying. In some libraries, postal deliveries include a large number of books and items obtained through the interlibrary loan service. Sorting areas have to be provided and, in large departments, space may need to be dedicated to service functions like the periodicals or interlibrary loan departments.

The integration of movement within a building should enable all functions to operate without conflicting demands on space, lifts or stairs. Just like finding the library within the city, getting around library buildings should be natural and self-instructing. The principles of the self-instructing library and how this is translated into design are a feature of the public library in Malmo, Sweden (see Chapter 10).

# 3

# Planning the library

## Achieving design quality in libraries

The value of design is often overlooked by those who procure library buildings and draw up the brief. Yet good design and comfortable environmental conditions can make a big difference to the perception of the building and, by extension, to the organization which commissioned it whether it be a local council (public library), a national government (national library) or a university (academic library). Excellence in design is not, however, easy to measure especially in advance of construction. According to CABE, good design is 'design that is fit for purpose, sustainable, efficient, coherent, responsive to context, good looking and a clear expression of the requirements of the brief (CABE, 2006). Moreover, it is now widely accepted that the quality of design affects the attitudes and behaviour of library users. There are some pointers which can be employed such as:

- is there a 'wow' factor in the overall design and in the interior spaces?
- does the building connect well with neighbours?
- is the library well lit and naturally ventilated?
- has acoustic quality of the different spaces been addressed?
- have potential adverse conditions such as solar glare, overshadowing and traffic noise been resolved?
- are there views out onto attractive areas?
- are there views within the building which promote use legibility and aid navigation through complex facilities?

In the competitive world of higher education, the impressions gained of university facilities are important to both students and their parents. They can affect the choice made between different colleges or universities (CABE, 2005). Similarly, the quality of design in the public realm in civic buildings such as libraries affects the choices made by people in both the facilities they use and more widely in where they choose to live.

Increasingly, there is an expectation that sunlight, fresh air and operable windows will be provided in all or part of the library. This may be just on the top floor where the cafe is provided, or in a central atrium, or in study rooms around the edge. Either way, a number of surveys of users have highlighted the importance they attach to natural conditions and there is some anecdotal evidence that this also affects their ability to concentrate.

Public buildings and those on campuses are also expected to display best practice in the area of sustainable design. This is often incorporated into the brief and where it is not, architects and engineers have a duty to seek to reduce the carbon footprint of their designs. The role of the library here is important as it stands for knowledge dissemination and intellectual discovery – and nowhere is this more pertinent today than in the arena of global warming and sustainability. It is no accident that many recent public libraries, such as the one in Brighton designed by Bennetts Associates, have innovated in the area of energy efficiency. Here the green technologies have been visibly displayed in order for the building to carry the message of sustainable design and thereby teach through the building rather than just the books. This issue of wider citizenship learning is a key characteristic of library buildings whether in towns or on university campuses.

## Establishing the brief

Much useful information can be found in the literature of library planning which will assist those beginning to draw up a design specification for the first time. This is true for architects as well as for library staff. However, nothing that is written or read can fully prepare anyone for the experience of seeing a building arise from plans. This chapter derives from direct experience of contemporary projects in addition to the wisdom of those who have created library buildings elsewhere.

Libraries have historically illustrated the highest cultural values of society. The building of a new library will not be a singular decision – it will be the result of committees and policies. All the considerations which lead to a project need to be retained as information for the architect's brief. The priorities for the building should be listed and assessed before agreement is reached to include or dismiss features which accommodate them. This is an intellectual exercise which can become influenced by personal crusades. It is important that the process of determining priorities is managed by those who embrace a vision that accommodates democratic, social and technological innovations. Teamwork is an essential characteristic of the successful brief.

Visions give a building integrity and are critical to understanding purpose and function. Without a shared vision, the concept can become vulnerable to abuse and even become disregarded. Any successful building will, therefore, be created by a team of people who have a common understanding of what is to be achieved and what is to be avoided.

The visions realized in library buildings stem from disparate sources. The commissioning body or authority will have ideas and influence the final outcome. The artistic interpretation of architectural principles and professional service requirements may lead and dominate. The practical elements of library management will appear to direct the interior layouts. All parties mentioned so far will have a particular view of the relationship of the building to its community and within the wider society in which it is to exist.

It is also important to distinguish in the brief between aspirational and functional need. For instance, the library could be seen as a gateway to knowledge rather than a collection of purposeful rooms. It could be a centre for information or technology transfer as against a warehouse for public lending books. Too few briefs address the big question, preferring instead to list accommodation as if a schedule of rooms were sufficient to guide the designer. A good brief has good ideas, bad briefs none at all.

## General considerations and assessment of needs

It is important that a vision should be created and applied to all the considerations given above. There must be room for imagination and creativity in the practical areas of layout

and servicing as well as in the design. Where harmony can be achieved between architect and librarian, the resulting building is likely to have a flow and charm which is felt by all users. If such harmony is not forthcoming, the building will retain harsh juxtapositions. Users will find conflicting messages which deny them any understanding of how the building is to work. Harmony is the result of dialogue between those who commission, design and ultimately use the library.

## First stages in planning

Assessments of current and projected user needs provide vital information to the architect. Until such information is received, the design cannot begin. Needs should be analysed by library staff in terms of current service delivery and provision of facility. The anticipated growth or atrophy of users and services must be assessed and presented within the brief. For public libraries, data are available from sources such as population statistics for the town or region. Student numbers can be obtained from the annual plans of the governing body or the educational authority. The membership services department of a professional body or specialist organization can provide data for specialist libraries.

The way in which particular users retrieve and exploit information is important to planning services. Library staff will need to understand how their users approach information and plan for provision that responds positively to the nature of the enquiry. Despite the growth in Internet or web-based information, library buildings have not diminished in importance. The vast amount of information which is publicly available has led to an increased

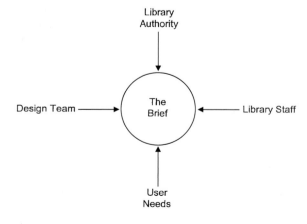

Key influences upon library brief. (Brian Edwards)

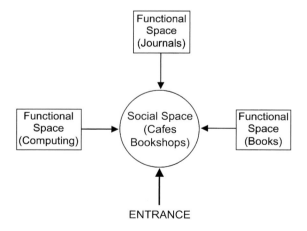

Changing relationship between reading room and book stack areas in twentieth century libraries. (Brian Edwards)

dependence on the authoritative order of the library catalogue and classification scheme. Thus, services which allow free searching in a controlled environment are proving ever popular. Space and equipment must provide for all types of information retrieval.

Internal space requirements should be formulated using the latest data and statistical information. Service descriptions of current and projected demand can be produced in terms which allow architectural interpretation. As the information which libraries contain become more virtual, the provision of services to those distant to the building also require consideration. Services to those present in the immediate community may be easier to assess. It is also important to discover what is required to make a non-user find the library an essential part of their work or leisure. Information from assessments carried out as part of a library's regular user surveys will provide valuable planning evidence.

As well as continuing what is currently done, it is just as important to do what is not done but ought to be. Librarians and architects will use their professional networks to understand the contemporary challenges to their respective professions. There is a responsibility on both to engage with new ideas. The last decade of the twentieth century was marked by a significant number of examples of innovative library building – all pointing to provision in the twenty-first century. Web-based information pages of companies, organizations and universities offer a rich

resource for anyone planning new library buildings. Virtual visits to websites, followed up by actual visits to the most promising sources, have led to the creation of some stimulating library environments.

## Technical criteria

Standards and guidelines for the particular type of library will inform the final design. Besides the regulations for public buildings that will necessarily be followed by the architect, the library and information profession offers advice on standards for library service provision for different types of library. In the UK, the Library Association's Colleges of Further and Higher Education Group produces guidelines based on actual provision for the university sector. The British and Irish Association of Law Librarians and the Law Society both contribute to standards for law libraries. These and other publications provide the useful criteria, but it is also recognized that for many projects the ideal is rarely attainable.

For the librarian, familiarity with relevant technical criteria may be all that is required. The architect's team will be far more involved with ensuring that specifications for heating, lighting, ventilation and air-conditioning are met. This will involve consultation over areas of law (health and safety), relevant local conditions (risk assessments) and meeting current environmental standards (eco-auditing).

## Accommodating change

Changes in the parent organization's environment may inform the nature as well as the location of the building provided. For example, as shopping spreads to the outer perimeter of towns, so the location of community libraries needs to reflect that move. Contemporary universities are concentrating on student learning centres rather than teaching spaces, and so libraries need to provide learning environments in the widest sense. The challenge to library management is to retain traditional strengths whilst providing new equipment and spaces that enhance the users' perception of the value of the library.

## Forming the teams

### Commissioning

The exact nature of any commissioning team will depend upon the method chosen to procure a plan. If the library is part of a wider infrastructure of buildings, such as within a university or town centre, then plans will need to include a holistic approach to the site. Some authorities choose to employ an architectural competition for a new library

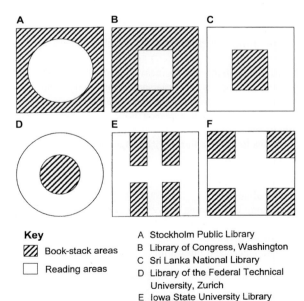

**Key**

▨ Book-stack areas

☐ Reading areas

A Stockholm Public Library
B Library of Congress, Washington
C Sri Lanka National Library
D Library of the Federal Technical University, Zurich
E Iowa State University Library
F Bibliothèque Nationale, Paris

Different patterns of reading area and book-stack areas in the twentieth century libraries.
(Brian Edwards)

design, such as in Paris for the new Bibliothèque Nationale. This grand project of the late twentieth century was finalized in an English versus French selection by President Mitterand. The architect Dominic Perrault was appointed in 1989, work commenced in 1990 and 1997 saw the first full year of operation. Design competitions can be especially useful when a prestigious library is under consideration.

In some instances, commissioning authorities have very particular ideas which they wish to see implemented. These can take decades to implement – as in the case of the British Library. Originally commissioned in 1962, the architect Colin St John Wilson waited until 8 July 1999 before the final reading room was opened. Most teams will retain a more dynamic momentum over the period between idea and inception, and will work expediently to see their visions realized. Overlong commissioning and project delay undermine team spirit and lead to an inferior design.

### Planning

The feasibility or visionary documents that represent the thinking behind a project do not always indicate the make-up of the teams who realize them. There can be no blueprint for an ideal planning or implementation team. Projects will take on an identity as they progress and wise leadership allows for timely contributions from those best placed to make them. Communication between project team members is the most critical feature which will affect eventual success. The Royal Institute of British Architects (RIBA) Plan of Work provides a useful template of the commissioning and planning stages of a typical project.

## Major players

All projects will require an architect and a librarian: their functions are interrelated. The architect to design and plan, to work within the brief, to create and inspire: the librarian to advise, analyse and specify the requirements of the building. Both are charged with the need to discuss and refine ideas and to evolve the practical requirements of the vision. The nature of building projects is such that the architect will normally emerge as the leader of the planning team. The architectural firm selected will arrange for a dedicated person to undertake liaison with the librarian.

### Other contributors

Other significant roles are required in order for projects to evolve into reality. A major one is that of financial overview; this is normally undertaken by the parent organization. The architect will appoint a quantity surveyor to liaise with the client's cost consultant and both will normally be part of the planning team. Most large organizations (e.g.

public library authorities and universities) will have estate managers. Staff from these departments will be the direct 'client' and will appoint a 'clerk of works'. During the building work, these people become invaluable as negotiators between the eventual occupants, the building firms and other contractors. The RIBA Plan of Work sets out clearly the phasing of operations, client input at different stages and the role of key players (clerk of works, quantity surveyor) for those in the UK.

Specific projects may need specialist advice at various times during the planning or building processes. These will vary from geological expertise in areas where land is volatile (earthquake or volcanic activity) to pollution experts and maybe industrial archaeologists for brownfield sites. There will also be experts in health and safety, IT systems, security advisors and many others whose expertise will need to be embraced.

### Representatives of the user community

Some planning teams allow the users of a new library to be represented. Within universities, it is common for projects to be discussed within the academic community via bodies such as the senate. Contributions may be sought at an early stage and be obtained through focus groups or other such forums. It is important that the views of those who are likely to use the library (local residents, academics, researchers, students) have a direct input into the brief preparation and planning process.

## Managing the process

Instrumental to the effectiveness of the planning team is the person acting as chairperson. Objectivity and understanding are the most essential qualities for this position. Normally, such a person is likely to be the chief librarian.

Issues to address in the early stage include:

• initial planning
• involvement of others
• consultation
• defining and refining
• 'ownership'
• staff involvement
• experiences and innovation.

Issues to address in the middle stage include:

• meeting the pressure of change
• incorporating the views of users
• technology
• staff
• organizations
• transitional states.

Issues to address at detailed implementation include:

- agreeing performance targets (including architectural quality)
- specifications and generalizations
- timetables for occupation
- managing diverse expectations
- understanding the contracting process
- knowing what will cost money and time (especially late alteration to the brief or design).

## Design criteria for libraries – a generic list

The architect of several new libraries in the UK, Harry Faulkner-Brown, listed 10 design criteria for successful libraries (Faulkner-Brown, 1987). These were that libraries should be:

- flexible
- compact
- accessible
- extendible
- varied
- organized
- comfortable
- constant internal environment
- secure
- economic.

To this list one may add:

- sustainable
- uplifting to the spirit.

The benefits of this list are rather obvious but too rarely adopted in their entirety. *Flexibility* is often compromised by poor initial design or subsequent changes to building fabric. *Compactness* is sacrificed by excessive pursuit of functional zoning where each library activity has its own space. Compact buildings require close connection and overlapping functions. *Accessibility* is not always good for all, especially the disabled or those with small children. An accessible library is also one which has readily perceived entrances and routes.

*Extendibility* can be limited by the nature of the site and the choice of building location within the site. An extendible library must have perimeter space for growth and a design strategy that recognizes and orders subsequent expansion. As noted by Faulkner-Brown (1987), *varied* libraries allow the provision of freedom of choice for readers, managers and those intent upon exploiting different information technologies. Since libraries – especially academic ones – undergo waves of management change, a variety of types of accommodation at the outset is important. *Organized* libraries offer an effective interface between readers and books, but a plan which

starts life by being well organized can be compromised by the inevitable complexity of changes over time. Since libraries are amongst the longest lived of mankind's built artefacts, the passage of time stresses the most organized of systems.

*Comfortable* libraries tend to be well-used ones, but excessive comfort can lead to their being used as lounges with readers taking periodic naps. A *constant internal environment* is important for the preservation of library material – a point noted by Faulkner-Brown – but a balance has to be struck between naturally ventilated libraries with fresh air and sunshine, and air-conditioned ones which, though they control temperature and humidity well, can lead to drowsy conditions for readers.

*Security* of libraries is essential to avoid the theft of books (a point obviously more acute in libraries with special collections) but the reader too needs to feel safe. Both staff and readers require a secure environment – their needs are as important as the study material. An *economic* library is one which is efficiently built, maintained and operated; this involves finance, staff and resource consumption. Since libraries are long-lived buildings, attention to quality of materials, staff morale, reader access and community well-being is important.

To Faulkner-Brown's comprehensive list, one should add two further criteria. First, that the library should be *sustainable* in the use of resources consumed in its construction and operation. It is no longer sufficient to just think in terms of being efficient or low cost; the sustainable library may entail slightly higher initial investment in order to reduce running costs or to create more satisfying conditions for staff and readers. The sustainable library will be of low-energy design (this means shallow not deep plan), use natural materials in construction and finishes, conserve water and avoid car-based travel (see pages xx – xx). Few modern libraries have addressed the agenda of sustainability though some have made brave attempts. A good example is the naturally ventilated low-energy Queens Library at Anglia Polytechnic University, which substantially avoids air-conditioning.

The other additional criterion is the need for the library to *uplift the spirit*. As a cultural anchor the library, like the art gallery or stadium, is a significant expression of civilized values. The library not only provides access to books; its role is also that of celebrating the written word (and increasingly the electronic one). Whether it is an academic library, a national library or a small town library, architectural design must provide meaningful form as well as functional space. The reader needs to have an 'experience' which marks the passage of reading time or which gives dignity, pleasure or stimulation to a visit to the library. Too few libraries of the past generation can be said to achieve this criterion.

Such a list begs the question whether all 12 criteria are equally important. In a university library, for instance,

Architecture library at
the Royal Danish
Academy of Fine Arts,
Copenhagen (Andreas
Trier Mørch)

flexibility may be more important than comfort; in a national library, security may be more crucial than economy; and in a town library, accessibility may be of greater concern than compactness or environmental standards. Certainly, judgement is needed and some weighting (depending upon circumstances), with the design brief itemizing the key criteria. Ultimately the choice and balance within the listed criteria are not a question of right or wrong, but what is appropriate for the library in question. Here political judgement is needed and the skill of the designer exploited to achieve a building which is ultimately valued by the community it serves, and not just by library staff.

An area of frequent conflict is that between security and accessibility. A fortress library is hardly an inviting one, yet a library designed with the openness of a supermarket runs the risk of losing a great deal of stock. Whereas a branch library with no rare books and limited stock can operate a fairly liberal entrance regime, far greater security is needed in a major civic or national library. An accessible library needs a wide entrance, without steps and preferably some seating near the threshold. The entrance should be perceived as welcoming and safe for the reader. For library staff, the ideal entrance is overlooked, narrow, controlled by electronic tagging devices and monitored by closed circuit television (CCTV). In a national library where scarce and valuable material is housed, there can be some justification for such an entrance, even with (as at the National Library of Scotland) mandatory searching of folders and briefcases. The concerns of security reach their limit at the National

Library of Iceland housed at the university in Reykjavik. Here the National Collection of Icelandic sagas, ancient maps and manuscripts is controlled by a member of staff who responds to an entry bell, conducts searches and patrols the vault and reading room above against burglary, flood or fire. The connecting staircase is protected by glass-enclosed walls, which provide visibility at all times. Such security measures are only justified in national libraries or where valuable collections occur. Elsewhere reader-friendly spaces are needed in order to maximize library use.

## Learning from shopping malls

The traditional library was not always a welcoming building. Often the needs of security of the book stock, limited opening hours, poor location and excessive steps resulted in unpopularity. One has only to compare public libraries with retail malls to see how uninviting many libraries have become. Typically a shopping mall has a level entrance from the street, there is a glazed area or atrium running through the centre of the complex around which the various shops (often on several levels) are located, floors are connected by wide escalators, and security is subtle, understated and electronic. Although there are limits to the similarities between these two building types, the popularity of the mall as a place to visit especially for young people should influence thinking by those who procure or design public libraries.

Old and new wings of the Sydney Jones Library at the University of Liverpool make a powerful composition. Notice the new Library square in the foreground. (Peter Durant)

banded new libraries such as that in Montreal look superficially like shopping malls. Another answer is to employ proximity to retail malls to ensure the library is well-connected to consumer culture. This is the approach at Brighton Public Library in the UK and Vancouver Public Library in Canada. In both cases the libraries were designed as part of larger civic developments and integrated spatially and aesthetically with the retail aspects of them. As a result the shopper can include in one journey a trip say to Marks and Spencer with the loan of a book, a pot of tea, and a scan of the Internet.

Another answer is to employ 'library streets' rather than library buildings. Here the idea is to extend from a retail mall a separate street or sub-mall devoted largely to library activities, or perhaps library and other civic functions such as a museum or council shop. The idea of a library street allows people to browse without making the formal commitment to engage in the library services (in the same way that one window-shops). By creating permeable and pervasive spaces linked to retail developments libraries may be able to attract a new clientele and expand their visitor numbers. However, one problem with the retail mall is its tendency towards environmental anonymity – what Marc Augé calls 'non-place' (Augé, 1985). Being 'lost in space', as commentators put it, is the opposite of the ideal library experience. Unlike shops and department stores, libraries need to generate a specific environment: one where the character of the building derives from the nature of the collection (Eco, 1985).

Large libraries such as national libraries or the public libraries of major cities pose a particular difficulty, not unlike major retail parks. They can be massive in scale and form a major barrier to urban movement. The answer, as with shopping malls, is to draw people inside by forming

Norwich Public Library designed by Michael Hopkins and Partners is one example where the spirit of the mall has been an influence on the building's architecture. Here a mixture of functions from local radio station to small museum have been combined with cafes and bookshops to form an attractive crescent of activity around the library. All of these activities are housed within a large glazed atrium-type space, which opens onto the stalls of Norwich's street market. To use the public library is to experience civic life in all its attractive complexity.

By engaging in more of a retail culture, architects can use the design of the library to attract users who previously were discouraged by the staid overtones of the modernist or Victorian library. Certainly the colour-

The branch library in the small town of Dunsmuir in California, built in 1964, uses materials from nearby forests in its construction, controls glare without loss of daylight levels, has its own bus stop and set down area for staff and users, and a simple library name sign. (Brian Edwards)

The library at the Jubilee campus, University of Nottingham, is a building to visit in its own right. Architect Michael Hopkins and Partners. (M Hamilton-Knight)

A large library is a small city of streets and spaces. Joule Library, UMIST, Manchester. Design by Building Design Partnership. (BDP)

social spaces and cross-routes within the centre of the building. People should be able to pass through libraries as they do retail malls, rather than have to walk around a forbidding perimeter wall. As Dominique Perrault (the designer of the Bibliothèque Nationale in Paris) notes, 'the façade of a library should be a filter not a barrier, letting light in and views out, and encouraging people to enter' (Arets, 2005).

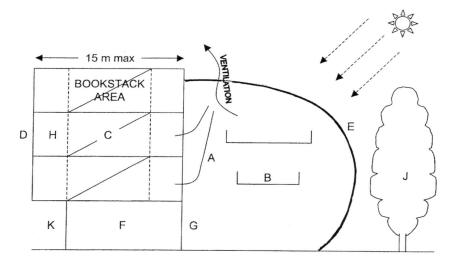

A - Open Plan Learning Resource Centre
B - Banks of computers on decks
C - Library floors, bookstacks in centre
D - Fully glazed north façade
E - Solar protected south façade, freely ventilated at top
F - Café, exhibition area
G - Entrance into library at central point
H - Reader carrels at building periphery
J - Planted shade on south side
K - Sheltered routes to library

Ideal template for design of academic library. (Brian Edwards)

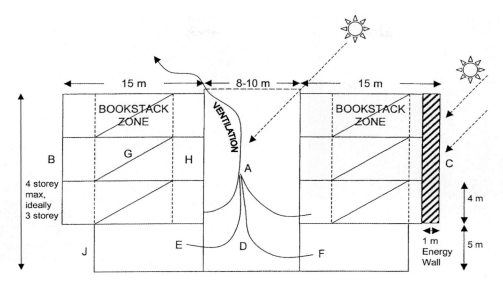

A - Atrium in centre for stairs and lifts.
Direct sunlight and natural ventilation.
Acoustic ceiling and walls.
B - Fully glazed north façade.
Reader desks against periphery
C - Solar protected south façade.
Shaded reader desks against periphery.
D - Well identified, sheltered entrance.
Disabled friendly, pram and bicycle storage.
E - Café and exhibition space.
F - IT Resource Centre.
G - Library floors, bookstack in centre for thermal capacity.
H - Computer terminals in bays around atrium.
J - Sheltered routes to library.

Ideal template for design of public library. (Brian Edwards©)

## Should library space be functional: the need for reflection as well as access to knowledge

Compared to museums and art galleries, few public libraries offer an environment that is deliberately attractive or stimulating. Whereas some people visit art galleries just for the experience of the building, not many will go out of their way to visit a library in a similar fashion. When Frank Gehry designed the Guggenheim Museum in Bilbao (1998), he did more than create a rational container for viewing the exhibits. His approach was to give visitors a memorable architectural experience and to provide Bilbao with a landmark. Too few libraries are designed in a similar spirit, with the result that not many recent buildings provide an appeal and friendliness beyond that of accessing the collection.

Such appeal is substantially the challenge of architectural design. To create a library worth visiting as a building in its own right, functional space should not dominate aspirations towards cultural meaning in the broadest sense. Space is not only the medium of function or purpose; it is also the medium of social value. In a world of rapidly expanding knowledge and growing access to it via the Internet, the 'wholeness' of intellectual endeavour should

be reflected in the design of libraries. Fragments of knowledge, each captured in a book, website or CD-ROM, should be subservient to the totality of wisdom. The public library is a place where reflection upon the whole should take place in parallel with the search for information. Architectural design should, therefore, create less a 'supermarket of knowledge shelves' and more a gallery of contemplation or stimulation. It should, if you like, allow the reader to set the fragment of information into the wholeness of wisdom.

Within such reflective volumes can exist the ingredients of appeal and friendliness. Space, natural light and comfort are essential. These are the 'lounges' of the library — distinct in character from the book stacks that are necessarily arranged according to functional rules. In addition, there may be other elements of social interaction — perhaps a cafe or bookshop. Music and conversation may be permitted, with the resulting atmosphere akin to a large city bookshop. Thus the library becomes less a homogeneous space and more a collection of volumes of slightly different function and character. These volumes are zoned not only according to the nature of the material — books, journals, newspapers, children's collection, computing, etc. — but as a response to changing social or cultural purpose. This is

Architectural design should help the users navigate the levels by providing clues to perception. (BDP)

the lesson of the public museum and art gallery, which the library service has yet to grasp.

The rebalancing of cultural space and functional space is necessary not only to provide areas where the wholeness of knowledge can be contemplated, but also to attract new client groups. If libraries were more inviting, their appeal would increase. Demographic change results not only in additional elderly people for whom the library is a valuable social magnate, but also creates a more culturally varied community. In much of the world, the drift into cities from rural areas places a particular responsibility upon the library to provide access to information in a building that is friendly and appealing. In the developed world, growing affluence shifts the emphasis to quality of life issues. Here not only is the public library an element in urban competitiveness, but its design has an important role to play in delivering a quality experience. This sense of community or public realmness revolves around a handful of building types – schools, museums, sports halls, railway stations and most importantly libraries. If the library is not designed to reinforce and express civic values, then it will fail to fulfil its mission in a holistic fashion.

This appeal to social values should avoid the 'theme parking' of the library experience. It is desirable to use design to make the library more popular and to anchor it visually in the perception of a neighbourhood as long as the cerebral nature of the library survives. Superficial branding and shallow images should not replace what are essentially 'deep' experiences.

It is in the area of depth that space comes into its own. Social values are always expressed in space and the greater

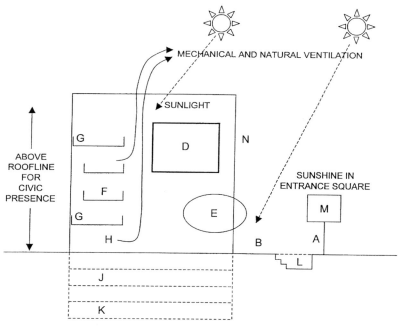

Ideal template for design of national library. (Brian Edwards)

A – Civic presence on street
B – Gathering square
C – Spacious entrance with exhibition space
D – Special collections readily identified
E – Auditorium near entrance
F – Library floors by subject
G – Reader spaces against perimeter
H – Computer catalogue access and toilets
J – Conservation
K – Storage of research collection
L – Amphitheatre for external performance
M – Conference
N – Energy conscious façade

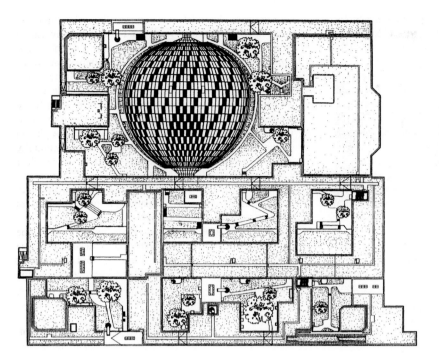

The plan of the Free University Library in Berlin, designed by Foster and Partners, creates a legible sequence of malls and squares dominated by the dome of the library; such large developments as this need to be structured at the urban and building scale. (Foster and Partners)

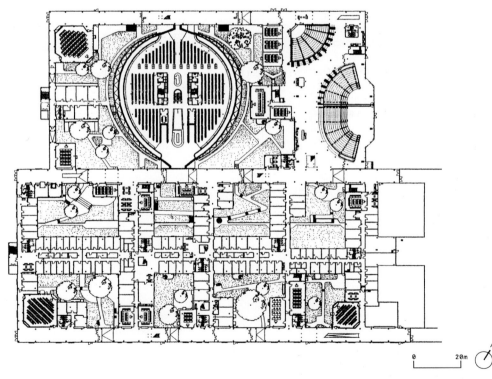

the cerebral content, the deeper that space becomes. Libraries, like art galleries, are exercises in 'deep space'. It is only architecture that can give space depth and meaning for the users of these public facilities.

Space, however deep, is perceived differently according to the type of library user. For example, the librarian sees space as an issue of function, efficiency and security. The regular library user sees the space as familiar and cherished territory – a refuge perhaps from life elsewhere, certainly a place where escape through reading is possible. The casual user sees the same space as unfamiliar volumes to be negotiated in order to gain some specific library return. The visitor with no interest in using the collection may see the space as pure architectural volumes – rooms bathed in light and clad in books. For some the library is a refuge, for others a place to gain specific information, or a building in which to meet friends or a place of work. All these users perceive the same space in different ways – this pluralism of experience highlights the need to consider the value of complexity over rigidity. Spatial order may help cement social order or reflect the intellectual order of a library collection, but in a world of rapid demographic or knowledge changes, old orders soon become obsolete. Space has instead to appeal to the diversity of users, providing legibility and orientation through the maze of knowledge. It has to achieve this efficiently and elegantly whilst ensuring that some places exist not just to support functionality in a mechanistic sense, but also spiritually.

Within the diversity of users, it is also evident that different expectations exist between the young and old. Whereas the teenager seeks a lively, stimulating and essentially contemporary library where electronic data access is to the fore, the older user seeks a tranquil, comfortable book-based experience. Young and old, the two principal groups of library users, have their own distinctive perceptions of architectural value and library character. Somehow the library not only has to present the 'pastness of the present' but the 'futureness of the present' in a space which shares two contrasting media technologies: the printed page and the electronic screen.

A large library is akin to a small city. The spaces should be designed as streets, squares and buildings as opposed to corridors, foyers and rooms. The adjustment to a city scale has advantages in terms of how areas may be managed or designed. For instance, the passage through the building with points of distraction, pause or crossing becomes similar to the negotiation of urban areas. There are places of social intercourse, elements which landmark the route, rooms where you can shop or take refreshment, seats where the world can be observed, places in the sun and others in shade. Big libraries are small cities, not just big buildings.

## References

Arets, W. (2005). *Living Library*. Prestel. p.172.

Augé, M. (1995). *Non-places: Introduction to an Anthropology of supermodernity*. London and New York: Verso Books.

CABE (2005). *Design with Distinction*. OPDM, London.

CABE (2006). *Better Public Building*. DCMS, London, p. 5.

Eco, U. (1985). *Travels in Hyperreality*. Picador, London.

Faulkner-Brown, H. (1987). 'The open plan and flexibility' in Anthony Vaughan, *International Reader in Management of Library Information and Archive Services*, UNESCO.

# 4

# Space and interior design

## Is a library a 'place' or a 'service'?

Architects view the library as a building and librarians as a service. This paradox touches upon the nature of provision within the library and the design of the building itself. Not only is the technology of the library currently undergoing rapid change, but the relationship in academic libraries between teaching and research, and between teaching and learning itself, further destabilizes old structures. In public libraries where the cutting edge of new technology is less evident, libraries too are changing as they cater for an ever-ageing population and demands for community-based information. Typically the services provided by a library are:

- access and loan of traditional book-based materials
- access to journals and newspapers
- use of workstations
- electronic access to research journals
- access to the Internet
- guidance through the information maze by staff
- community and visitor support.

These services are provided by a building with a variety of spaces tailored to specific needs. In a large library, there may be bookshops, exhibition space and a cafe/restaurant – adding to the blurring of library functions. The services provided affect the nature and dimensions of space on the one hand, and staff roles and relationships on the other. Space in this sense is not neutral but filled with operational, political and management consequences.

The library as a place may be increasingly altered by changes in information technology (IT), expectations of its roles in building a community, or as a means of reinforcing new modes of service delivery. It is also modified by new concepts of 24-hour access. The permanently open library (a frequent feature of the academic estate) changes the nature and perception of provision. Besides being a building where information is held, accessed and exchanged, the library becomes a place of refuge or encampment. It is, at least for some, an escape into a sane and quiet environment – a place to reflect and renew at any time of the day.

## Space stress in libraries

The growing popularity of libraries, the relative cheapness of books and the expansion of IT provision and related social areas have stressed many existing libraries. Rooms, corridors, stairs, reading areas, stack areas, reference and archive areas all find themselves used more intensely than in the past. In order to accommodate more space for people and their laptops, a greater area of the library is given over to casual seating and workstation provision. There are three ways in which these stresses are commonly resolved: firstly, by building new libraries and either demolishing or altering the use of existing ones. Secondly, by extending existing libraries, altering internal configurations in the process, and, thirdly, by reconfiguring existing libraries without physical extension. The latter is often employed as a short-term solution to the wider social and technological pressures on libraries described elsewhere in this book. A recent survey of American libraries found that 76% of public libraries had their ability to cater for growing IT usage limited by space provision whilst 31% reported that the existing infrastructure curtailed routes for computer cabling and electrical outlets (American Libraries Association, 2004).

Where internal modification is employed, it usually entails the creation of extra space for IT users at the expense of traditional book users. Here the answer employed, especially in college and university libraries, is to employ compact mobile stacking systems. Effectively, it cuts down on the 1 m wide space required between each parallel row of book stacks. With mobile stacking systems only one corridor of space is needed for up to eight rows of book stack – in effect saving 7 m of library provision to use for other purposes. This can result in compact shelving systems doubling the storage capacity per metre of library compared to traditional library book stacks. However, compact shelving has two main drawbacks: the weight of the compressed stacks can exceed the floor loading capacity, and only one reader can browse the stacks at a time. So with large book collections and lower usage it provides a sensible economy of space (and associated heat and light) but in smaller libraries where there is much demand, it is

Space in a library is not neutral but fashioned by functional need. Learning Resource Centre, Sunderland University, designed by Building Design Partnership. (BDP)

a false economy in spite of the claims made by manufacturers of such systems.

As a rule of thumb the book-stack area of the public library accounts for around 50% of the total area whilst for a university library, where greater IT provision is provided, it is nearer to 40%. It is a common problem to find too much space allocated to shelving and furniture resulting in restricted space for browsing and casual meeting. However, much depends upon whether the stacks are compact or on open access for use by all readers, whether there is storage elsewhere (say in a basement), and what level of workspace and IT-based provision is to be accommodated. An economy can be achieved by providing book-stack galleries within double height reading rooms – the mezzanine being employed for relatively low stacks which can be reached without ladders. This is a modification of double height book stacks of eighteenth and nineteenth century libraries, which in turn led to lofty reading rooms. The benefit of mezzanine book galleries is not just functional: the space for reading has the quality of space and light needed for reflection whilst the retrieval of books is undertaken in more utilitarian surroundings – perhaps using sensor-based artificial lighting.

Historically, the three main areas of a library have consisted of the general stack area, reference stack area and reading room. Although we have today many other functional zones (e.g. children's library, IT suite) the primary three part division remains true particularly for larger libraries. However, there is a tension between the major parts which has been exacerbated by the growth in the number of books and the invasion of CD-ROMs and Internet information systems. As a consequence, the reading room is often sacrificed or combined with other library functions. As the nature of the collection changes so too does the library that serves it.

The book is a major part of our cultural heritage: readers will continue to study them, books will be borrowed, ideas will be shared, and groups will meet in surroundings which respect this heritage (Arets, 2005, p. 311). The library somehow has to accommodate these traditional functions whilst also becoming the shared living rooms of an IT literate society. The ability of the library to encourage intellectual collaboration and knowledge exchange between people will be an important measure of the success of the building. Since knowledge is rapidly evolving into new fields and modes, space will inevitably be stressed in the process of delivering these important services. As Rem Koolhaas (the architect of Seattle Public Library) puts it 'rather than being a space to read' the library of the future will be 'transformed into a social centre for multiple responsibilities' (Arets, 2005, p. 212).

## Space standards

There are no international standards for space in relation to public libraries, as the range of groups served is deemed to be too variable (Khan, 2006). University, college and school libraries do have some recommended space allowances related to the numbers of students. For all types of library there are several guides available on the Internet to help work out the space required for a new or refurbished building. In the context of the whole space required, various resources agree on the following seven types of space to be considered in a new library building:

- *Collection space* – to take account of books (open access and closed), periodicals (display and back issues) and non-print resources. Digital resources may need some space allocation.
- *Electronic workstation space* – for staff use, public use in the main area, as well as any requirements in meeting room areas. A public access catalogue used from a seated position requires 4 sq. m.
- *User seating space* – plan for 5 seats per 1,000 users. Table seating requires 2.5 sq. m per reader, a study carrel 3, and lounge chairs 3–4 sq. m. A useful average is 3 sq. m per seated reader.
- *Staff workspace* – including areas in the public part of the library and separate workroom facilities. 15 sq. m per staff work area (e.g. issue counter, help desk) is a good planning guide.
- *Meeting space* – including conference space, a lecture theatre or a room for children's activities. When calculating seat space, the square footage for lecture-style chairs would be the total number of chairs multiplied by 10. For conference-style seating the figure would be multiplied by 25. Seating for children's activities would require 1.5 sq. m per child. Space would also need to be

allocated to other functions like cafes, with storage space for equipment.

- *Special use space* – e.g. a local history room, job centre, tourist information centre or special collection with appropriate facilities for users to access the material. Generally, suppliers of equipment should include this detail in their catalogues.
- *Non-assignable space* – including toilets, stairs, lifts, corridors and space required for heating or other systems on which the library depends. In general, non-assignable space accounts for between 20% and 25% of the gross floor area of a typical library.

## Flexibility in design

One of the most valued qualities of a library building is flexibility. This is not a finite commodity and should be realistically anticipated in designs. It is not feasible to design in total flexibility for future needs other than for those currently anticipated. Flexibility therefore needs to be built in through a sequence of options, rather than un-limited movement of all aspects of the collection. In-corporating flexibility will result in some compromise in terms of lighting and layout, which can result in an overall blandness in design.

Each library will have unique features that require specific solutions. Even the most basic library service has some element that will lend itself to a different treatment. It is these differences that allow more interesting designs to emerge. It is far more normal for libraries to accrete functions than to discard them. Changes of function are to be expected if buildings are to evolve over time. Libraries, with their quick take-up and adaptation of computer methods for records management, have had to considerably adapt desks and work areas to hold technological equip-ment. A major change over the past 30 years has been the move from card issue and catalogue systems to automated, computer-based ones. Thus, issue desks designed to hold wooden trays of one set of 'Browne' issue cards have been adapted to hold several computer terminals, bar code wands and desensitizing equipment.

### Flexibility and growth

Using shelving as an example, it is clear that any growth in collections either by annual addition or the incorporation of book stock from other libraries will need more shelves. The rate of growth can be calculated accurately and thus de-signers can determine an optimum amount of shelving for a period of years. Most librarians will also be able to project any estate changes that will have to be integrated into the new building. For example, during the building of the Adsetts Centre at Sheffield Hallam University, it was agreed to close two of the university's other libraries. The

---

**Space standards for public libraries**

30 sq. m for every 1,000 population

5 reader spaces per 1,000 population

Storage of 110 volumes per sq. m

Circulation areas around 20% of total floor space

1 staff member per 2,000 population

**Library provision for colleges**

1 sq. m for every 10 students

1 study space per 10 students

Library floor area approximately 10% of total college floor space

Library floor area approximately 20% of total teaching area

2.5 sq. m study space per student

**Library provision for universities**

1 sq. m for every six students

1 study space per six students

Library floor area approximately 12–15% of total university floor space

4 sq. m study space per student

---

new building therefore included the space needed to con-tain the collections previously housed at these two site libraries.

---

**Key factors to consider in interior design**

**Technical**

Are the floor loadings adequate for the collection?

Is the wiring layout suitable for future IT needs?

Are the environmental conditions acceptable for the planned use?

Is the collection secure from fire or theft?

**Aesthetic**

Is the building welcoming as well as functional?

Are the routes and major spaces legible to the user?

Is there space for reflection?

Do readers have good access to daylight?

---

Integration of old and new technologies within same library area at Norway's National Library. (Brian Edwards)

Open-plan designs are utilized as a solution to the need for flexibility. Open-plan designs normally incorporate shelving on floors, with sections for user spaces woven between them. Shelving is used to create flexible barriers to noise, movement and distraction. The fixed features of any design will create inflexibility. Lifts, building structure, emergency exits, purpose-designed areas for photocopiers and similar features will provide static features around which the other elements of provision have to be fitted.

## Subdividing large volumes for growth

Accommodation growth in libraries can be achieved by constructing a large initial volume, which is then colonized over time by new floors and mezzanine levels. In effect, the building is filled in to absorb the inevitable growth in the library collection. In theory, this is an economical way to proceed since the perimeter of the library remains static. However, the internal disruption caused by periodically constructing new floors can be damaging to the life of the library. But it does allow the new floors, rooms and decks to be tailored to the specific requirements of that part of the library. For instance, if growth is mainly towards IT provision then the building fabric needed for this can be designed accordingly. Likewise, if growth is to accommodate a special collection (such as historic photographs), then the specific floor loadings and environmental conditions can be met.

There are three advantages to this approach to library growth. First, it allows for phased construction, shifting the initial financial burdens to future generations. It also gives the library greater flexibility in meeting needs that cannot always be predicted at the outset. Finally, it allows the library to invest in the perimeter shell and basic structural elements knowing that such investment will be long-term. The disadvantage of the physical disruption to the interior can be offset by using prefabricated elements of construction (no wet finishes) and designing the initial shell so that roots of colonization are in place at the outset. The latter entails well thought-out service runs, good overall access to natural light and a robust circulation system.

## Flexibility in layout

### Circulation desks, movement and ergonomics

Circulation desks are complicated work areas. The commodity of books and the recording, return and reservation of materials mean complex operations at the counter area. Computer systems are now widespread; few libraries use manual issue and recording systems. Security tags need desensitizing and most of this equipment is clumsy and space-intensive. In addition, most systems require fines to be taken and thus tills have to be accommodated in the work area. Counter areas more typically resemble those

Large simple volumes provide greater flexibility than irregular shapes, University of Hertfordshire Library. Architects: Architects Co. Partnership. (Forster Ecospace)

**Typical services provided within a public or academic library**

Access to and loan of books

Access to journals and newspapers

Use of workstations

Access to the Internet

Electronic access to research journals

Guidance to sources of information

Community and visitor support

Cafe and refreshment area

found in supermarkets than the reception areas of hotels, and models based on retail practice are now commonplace. However, it is an area where staff opinions are very important. The physical variations of members of staff and users (many of whom may have degrees of disability) ensure that solutions to the counter design are usually generic. This has the advantage of providing some standardization of practice according to type of library, giving the further benefit of mass production of equipment and furniture.

*Managing the stock*

The management of book and journal stock involves elements of processing, recording, handling and storage; all these bring about movement that is usually managed by trolley. All areas in libraries must allow for the safe and easy movement of book trolleys between them. The main circulation consists of:

- movement to and from shelves of mainly book-based material
- movement to and from shelves or storage of CD-ROMs
- network issues between libraries or departments
- printing, photocopying and other paper-based material.

*Space design for staff as well as stock*

### Staff accommodation
Library support staff and maintenance functions normally occupy about 12–15% of notional floor area. There are three main types of staff accommodation, the

first being the circulation or information desk which provides guidance to library users. Normally this is inside the library entrance, facing visitors as they arrive, and needs to be welcoming and conspicuous. Here library staff can provide surveillance of the library entrance whilst dealing with the registration of new readers, the issue and return of loan books (assuming electronic systems are not in place) and general guidance on the facilities available.

The second main area is the back-up staff room where librarians can undertake their administrative duties, process and catalogue books and journals, provide copy

| Considerations for layout of book stacks | Secondary issues |
|---|---|
| Position book stacks to define routes through library | Ensure safety exits are visible |
| Use book stacks as acoustic barriers | Consider acoustic and thermal properties of book stacks together |
| Compress stacks to create reader areas at perimeter of building | Provide adequate space for safe use in dense stack areas |
| Provide light sensors in deep stack areas | In large libraries lighting is the major energy user |
| Ensure floor loadings are adequate for dense book stacks | Changing internal layout can be constrained by structural limitations |

services and hold meetings. In larger libraries there will also be a separate room for the head librarian and possible assistant, and the facilities listed earlier will be duplicated on each floor.

Each specialist or reference library will also be serviced by a team of librarians who again will have their own accommodation. This represents the third main type of library staff area. Here repair and conservation may also take place, plus digitizing of the rare book collection.

Although it is common to have staff accommodation related to the circulation desk, in larger libraries the staffing areas are more closely related to the delivery point for books, journals and newspapers. However, a trend evident particularly in academic libraries is for the staff accommodation to be related directly to the collection with librarians being accessible at all times. This enables the librarian to act as subject navigator for the student with the added benefit of proximity to the books and journals, as well as providing a point of contact regarding electronic sources. This arrangement works well with either open desk library staff provision or the use of glazed library offices within the study collection. The change in role of the librarian from that of security of the collection to subject guide has altered the interior layout of many library buildings. The librarian also provides guidance on the IT equipment available, both hardware and software elements. Again visibility of staff is crucial if this role is to be effectively delivered and this militates against the provision of anything other than a desk.

The unique features of library management require the application of various planning and design strategies to meet staff accommodation needs. Many library staff work in office-based areas, but their tasks are not regular office tasks. Space norms for offices have to be extended to accommodate the additional features of library-based routines. The obvious additional feature in the working space for those library staff engaged in processing or cataloguing is the physical presence of books and other printed matter. Materials have to be brought into the working area and stored for short periods. Every item in a library is subject to some particular treatment. Books and media items require processing to increase durability and to be individually catalogued and security tagged. Journals and newspapers also have to be logged in and recorded. Working spaces thus have to be larger than those in regular offices and desks have to reflect this feature of working practices.

Depending on the type of library, all functions have to be defined with space standards developed with the staff responsible. These are the basic functions associated with the collection: acquisitions, cataloguing and classification, journal accessioning, binding, security systems, preservation and repair. In a public system, it is usual for these functions to be carried out in a central library. Branch libraries do not normally undertake these activities unless they have specific functions (e.g. a local studies area or business service) which are unique in the overall system and are managed locally. Specialist libraries, national libraries and academic libraries normally have collections with unique processing requirements. Practice here is less standardized than in public libraries, with the result that microsystems exist within areas of more generic practice.

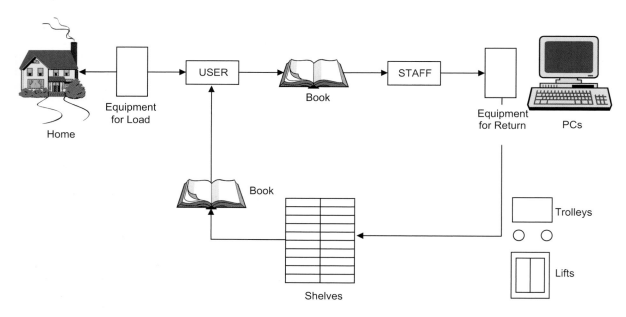

Pattern of flow in lending library. (Biddy Fisher)

Reader space against window at University of Lancaster Library. (Brian Edwards)

## Personal and working space in the library

Whereas the nature of the space needs to reflect the organization and character of the collection, space in the library is also a personal matter. Library space for the reader consists of:

- table space
- book-stack access space
- circulation space

plus also:

- ambience and reflective space.

Personal space is real and a question of perception. It is both measurable and atmospheric, fixed and elastic. While it is possible to have precise dimensions for workbays, table width and space between book stacks, personal space is a matter of taste and preference. The library designer needs to ensure that the mechanistic function of space is well planned, but also that the personal, spiritual and atmospheric nature of space is considered equally.

Well-designed working space at the Scottish Poetry Library, designed by Malcolm Fraser Architects. (Malcolm Fraser Architects)

A reader's personal space is deepest at the front, and narrowing to the sides and rear. The 'bubble' of reading or working space extends for about a metre forwards and downwards from the face. Some people's personal space is larger than others and, as a general rule, the longer you occupy the space, the bigger the bubble. We tolerate small spaces for short periods but if the library is of an academic or specialist nature, where readers study for long periods, additional working space is required.

### Carrels

It is normal to create carrels for personal study in libraries, but the percentage of provision to readers varies according to library type. As a general rule, allow 10–20% of carrel space per user in a public library, 25–50% in an academic library, 50–70% in a national library, and 70–90% in a specialist or research library. Carrel size may vary as well: from 3 ft (0.9 m) wide in a public library to 4 ft wide (1.2 m) in an academic library, and 5 ft wide (1.5 m) in a specialist library. The width and depth of a carrel are based upon the likely number of books or periodicals jointly referred to and also whether maps, drawings or photographs form part of the expected study material.

Carrels defined by task lighting at Phoenix Public Library, designed by Will Bruder. (Andrew North)

Carrel depth too varies from 2 ft (0.6 m) to 3 ft (0.9 m) and partition height from 4 ft (1.2 m) to 5 ft (1.5 m).

Carrels are simple work positions with low dividing screens affording some privacy and, in larger carrels, the presence also of a single shelf. Larger carrels may have space for a computer, thus allowing the reader to move between paper and electronic sources without leaving the chair. Carrels are best positioned in quiet enclaves or bays away from through traffic. Ideally, readers should face readers (though screened by a dividing partition), with backs facing backs. This affords privacy and allows for the 'bubble' of personal space to be contained without violation of cross-movement to the front. Circulation behind the reader can also be disturbing and should not consist of frequent through movement – only access by readers to other carrels.

The area of carrels in a library should form a 'study territory' – perhaps within a cleared area of book stacks or, more commonly, as a bay near the perimeter of the building. The latter allows the readers to enjoy access to views and sunlight, which can offer temporary relief from the rigour of intensive study.

*Tables*

Tables are commonly employed in libraries both as a working space and an area to lay out larger material such as newspapers, maps, prints and photographs. Tables and chairs are cheaper to provide than carrels and offer greater flexibility of layout. Normally, a group of readers shares a table – normally rectangular – with up to 10 chairs positioned on either side. The larger the table, the easier it is to avoid the domination of the space by a single individual. With a table shared by two to four readers, the personality of a single reader can disrupt the whole. Small tables are consequently less useful than large ones and small tables for two tend to be occupied by a single reader. In tables for six, those sitting in the centre tend to spread out, making those at the end of the table feel uncomfortable. So, in spite of their flexibility and relative low cost, carrels are preferred to tables in all but school or branch libraries.

Tables, however, are useful for group working and discussion is permitted at them. The trend towards group

Chairs and tables arranged to encourage social exchange at Sunderland City Library. (LFC)

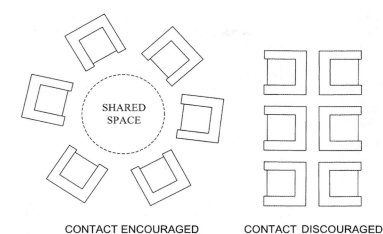

How furniture layout influences social contact. (Brian Edwards)

CONTACT ENCOURAGED        CONTACT DISCOURAGED

project work in universities has encouraged certain academic libraries to designate areas for 'quiet discussion'. Tables are obviously more useful here than carrels and round ones are preferable to rectangular ones. It is well known that circular tables are best for conversation and the round form helps to avoid territorial demarcation. As a general rule, conversation should take place within groups of individuals seated no more than 6 ft apart (1.8 m). Above this distance voices are raised and the sense of a small, collaborating study community eroded.

The layout of tables and chairs can encourage conversation or promote privacy. When the chairs face towards each other, eye contact and verbal exchange occur; when they are placed back to back, no such intercourse takes place. In parts of the library where silent working and privacy are expected, furniture layout should reinforce the lack of contact between readers (or staff and readers). On the other hand, where exchange is encouraged – perhaps in an entrance foyer or larger concourse – chairs may face each other.

The position of the counter should provide surveillance over the library collection. (LFC)

If furniture layout is the product of working needs in different types of library and their constituent parts, tables, chairs, carrels and book stacks can also be employed to articulate the architectural order of the library (SCONUL, 1996, p. 38). Furniture can help to reinforce the spatial or structural pattern of the library with the position of tables and chairs creating territories that help zone functions or express routes. In this regard, furniture layout is a matter of reader need and that of the building where functional order should be expressed or highlighted for the sake of legibility or convenience. Poor furniture layout can disrupt the flow of architectural space.

## Security planning and design

Before libraries as distinctive buildings or rooms became commonplace, a learned person's books were kept in locked chests. This arrangement provided security from theft and protection from water penetration or animals. When a scholar needed to resort to a book or manuscript, all that was needed was a key and table on which to spread the material. As books were mainly in manuscript form until about 1600 and hence rare, the chest afforded balance between security and accessibility. For example, before the widespread use of printed books, the library of Oxford University (as against the separate college libraries) was held in chests in a nondescript room adjoining St Mary's Church. It was only after Duke Humphrey's Library of 1445 was incorporated into the Bodleian Library (1610) that purpose-built accommodation for medieval manuscripts was provided. Here books and manuscripts were arranged according to subject in locked cabinets and read standing using the stall system. The key holder was personally responsible for security of the material.

The main threats today to the library collection are the theft of books, the removal of pages (particularly valuable plates) from books, fire and water damage. The main threats to library staff are personal attack and to readers of

| Considerations for layout and design of library furniture | Secondary issues |
|---|---|
| Provide visible staff desks on each floor to guide readers | Library staff should be visible to aid readers |
| Provide reader tables in areas well served by natural light | Place tables at edge of library or in internal atria spaces |
| Divide large reader tables into personal study areas | Provide separate power points along length of table |
| Ensure mix of table sizes and layouts to suit nature of collection | Atlases and newspapers require different table designs |
| Ensure tables are connected to IT systems | Encourage mixture of media usage at study tables |

theft of personal belongings (wallets, briefcases, laptops). Security and safety are questions addressed at the design stage and kept under review when the library is in operation. Different strategies are needed according to:

- the type of library and consequent degree of risk
- the type of risk
- the location of the library.

*Type of theft*

Four types of theft commonly occur at libraries and different strategies are needed to overcome each. Generally speaking there is:

- theft of books and journals
- theft from books and journals
- theft of equipment
- theft from the person.

The degree of threat from theft varies according to the type of library. Where the library collection has high financial

Fireproof compact shelving, provided by Forster Ecospace at the Bodleian Library, Oxford University. (Forster Ecospace)

value, books are commonly taken. When on the other hand the equipment has high value, it is electronic goods which are stolen. Where there is a high turnover of trusting young people (as at a university library), the greatest volume of theft is from handbags, briefcases and jackets. Theft is not a uniform problem across all libraries but a problem whose characteristics vary according to library type and location.

*Risks in different types of library*

National and specialist libraries face the greatest risk (at least in monetary terms) of theft. Here security has to be both real, comprehensive (covering all areas including toilets) and visible. Thieves should be aware of the extent of security: this acts as a general deterrent and, with guile, can be used to trap thieves in areas perceived to be less secure. The normal approach in libraries at high risk is to have rooms within rooms whereby the most valuable material is kept away from general readers. Such libraries, for example the King's Library at the British Library in London, are in effect vaults with far stricter security than occurs elsewhere (see pages xx – xx). Related to this approach are two further refinements: the secure library may be encased in glass on the assumption that transparency is an effective crime deterrent. In addition, only a limited amount of the valuable collection is ever on display – the remainder being in locked storage.

In academic, town or professional libraries, the security risk is not so high but even here a hierarchy of protective measures is required. The library may have to be zoned (horizontally and vertically) into highly secure, secure, semi-secure and open access areas. Each level of security will have its own management responsibility, its own level of locks and cameras, and its own evacuation policy in the event of fire or other disaster. The most secure accommodation is commonly placed furthest from the general reader. In addition readers often need to make appointments in advance to view the most valuable material, providing administrators with the chance to confirm the visitor's credentials. The determined thief will not risk

**Environmental considerations**

Restrict plan depth to 15 m for maximum daylight penetration

Create internal atria in large depth libraries

Provide solar shading and internal blinds on large south facing glazing areas

Use external light shelves to increase daylight penetration

Place reader tables in well-lit areas

Avoid air-conditioning except in 'hot spots'

Employ mixed-mode ventilation systems

Maximize natural ventilation in public areas

stealing a whole book in a secure environment, but may be tempted to extract a plate or slip a rare photograph out of a folder. Hence visual surveillance is required, backed up by security cameras in the areas most at risk.

Since the number of people using branch libraries is declining, library managers need to consider whether some theft is a price worth paying for keeping the library attractive to users. The casual removal of a dog-eared paperback or back copy of a car magazine does not justify expensive and off-putting security measures. The concept of an open library is one where some theft is inevitable, especially in inner city areas. Where security needs to be addressed in such libraries is in local study areas (which may contain old maps or photographs) and in parts of the library where computers are housed. As in national or major civic

The library environment should provide conditions which do not discriminate. Here lighting levels, table layout and counter height all encourage use by people with disabilities. University of Westminster, Marylebone Campus Library. (Forster Ecospace)

libraries, the designer and librarian need to plan for levels of risk rather than adopt a policy of blanket high security.

### Type of risk

Although theft is a major problem at some libraries, the greatest threat is fire and attendant water damage. Some 80% of fires in libraries in the USA are caused by arson and these account for more loss of material overall than theft. For example, the fire started deliberately at Los Angeles Central Library in 1986 resulted in the destruction of half a million volumes and water damage to the same number again (SCONUL, 1996, p. 38). Since libraries are public buildings and consequently attract disgruntled individuals, the threat of arson needs to be considered at the design stage.

The 'fuel' load of book stacks is extremely high and, in newspaper and periodical rooms, there is an abundant supply of paper which can be readily ignited. Fire protection is a question of planning and detailed design. In such areas, the architect should avoid quiet cul-de-sacs that are not easily patrolled by library staff. Openness and transparency are preferable. However, if a fire gains hold in an open-plan library, it is difficult to contain. A large number of books may be damaged by the attendant smoke. In addition, the water employed either by the local fire service or as part of a sprinkler system will probably have an even more damaging impact. The normal strategy in library design is to employ both open planning and compartmentation. The latter consists of concrete floors and fireproof walls that effectively contain a fire, limiting spread and hence damage throughout the library. In many early libraries, the building was open over several storeys allowing a fire, once it got hold, to devastate the collection. Today horizontal compartmentation with only single storey book stacks is the norm. In most modern libraries, the construction of the floor provides fireproof sandwiches that hold the books of a group of related subjects in close lateral proximity. To move from floor to floor, the reader passes through fireproof doors and smoke containment lobbies.

Though compartmentation is the most frequently adopted strategy for dealing with library fires, sprinkler systems are also commonly employed. These are automatically triggered and drench a small area to put out the fire. Of course, they also damage the books but it is assumed that the damage will be of limited extent. Modern automatic sprinkler systems are beginning to change the approach to fire engineering in some recent libraries. Rather than have a blanket system, the current practice is to employ localized controls related to sensitive smoke detectors placed throughout the library but at a higher density in sensitive areas. Sprinkler systems remove some of the justification for rigid structural fire compartmentation, allowing greater flexibility for the architect at the design stage and the librarian once the library is in use.

Sprinklers are not suitable for rare or valuable collections. The best solution is to protect such rooms from external fire by employing fireproof construction and having a clear strategy for the evacuation of the stock. All involved in fire security should be aware of special collections and have a readily understandable procedure for removing the collection to safety in the event of fire. Most large libraries have an emergency planning handbook that allocates clear duties for library staff and fire brigade personnel. The architect would normally be expected to contribute to the handbook at the handover of the building.

Since water is a major threat to books and electronic data systems, the design of the building should eliminate any risk of water penetration, condensation and accidental overflowing of cisterns. With the exception of those required to serve the sprinkler system, water pipes should not cross library areas (in the suspended ceiling or the floor slab). To avoid flooding in the toilet areas, taps should have automatic cut-off valves or be of a spray type. Unless the construction guarantees humidity control, book storage in basements should also be avoided. Similarly roof spaces should not be employed for storage unless entirely free of water penetration and condensation. With global warming and the resulting climate change, what may be water secure today may not prove so in a generation's time.

The avoidance of unnecessary activation of sprinkler systems means that no-smoking policies must be rigidly enforced. Sprinklers should be checked regularly for leaks and blocking of nozzles. A design that relies upon automatic sprinklers for fire safety entails a recurring commitment to maintenance of the system.

### Location of the library in relationship to security

Libraries in high-risk areas are more vulnerable to a variety of safety and security problems. Arson is more prevalent in urban than rural areas and in big cities rather than small ones. If a library is built near other high-risk buildings (such as railway stations or public houses), the problems may be greater than elsewhere. The brownfield site in the inner city poses dangers which need to be recognized at the outset. Although a library built here could do much to invigorate a neighbourhood, the crime prevention measures may need to be stricter.

A problem location poses additional risks to the collection, library staff and users. All three need to be addressed by the addition of safety lighting at the perimeter of the building, extra security cameras inside and at the entrance, a human safety policy on opening hours, and robust design. Although individuals may be at risk, the problems often extend to the building itself, to staff cars, and those using nearby streets. Hence, correspondence between the library security strategy and nearby policing is needed. As with the fire service, the local police crime prevention officer and library management staff need to develop a security strategy together.

## Getting books to readers

Libraries increasingly employ outhousing as a means of accommodating the expansion of the stock. The physical limits of the library building provide an obvious constraint upon the number of books that can be stored. With new libraries, it is possible to anticipate growth by providing room for subsequent expansion but in older buildings such space, if it exists, has already been exhausted. The usual solution for both large reference and academic libraries is to use nearby buildings for the storage of less frequently accessed material.

Outhousing has the advantage of providing ideal conditions in purpose-built warehouses for storage without compromising the library itself. Where special collections are involved (for example historic manuscripts, photographs, plans) such storage can be linked to conservation departments. For the reader, however, outhousing can cause delay in obtaining access to the material. Without almost instant access, there can be a lack of spontaneity and cross-referencing of types of material. Where a scholar is involved in interdisciplinary research, this can be a particular problem.

As a general rule, it is easier to get the reader to the books than the books to the reader. IT data systems do, of course, remove the problem of distance altogether but, until all books are converted into electronic formats, the reader is normally left with CD-ROMs and with a few key headings rather than the book itself. Providing direct access for the reader to the books has implications for the location of the library as well as library design. It means for instance that the library should be centrally placed either on the academic campus or in the town. Storage of study material can be elsewhere. To some degree, special libraries such as the Ruskin Library can be in special places. However, the reader must be able to gain ready access to the books and, where space or scale of collection prohibits, it should be easy to get the book to the reader. This places a limit on the distance storage can be from the library itself. A reader may reasonably wait an hour or two, but to be asked to come back another day is not acceptable.

The split between reader and storage is well handled at the National Library, Paris, where the four towers mark the corners of the podium that houses special collections and rarely used books. A similar split occurs at the British Library in London, where a three-storey basement holds the bulk of the material, supplemented by special collections further afield. At the National Library in Edinburgh, the library and storage are a kilometre apart, with the result that readers wait an hour or two for any material ordered.

## The importance of the reading room

Readers and books are normally connected to each other via open reading rooms where book stacks are located directly alongside tables and chairs (or reading desks). Here the reader

Study spaces overlooking atrium at Vancouver's Public Library. (Brian Edwards)

can browse, retrieve a book and sit nearby at a desk to use the material, which is then returned to the shelf. Such an arrangement typically places computer terminals in banks at the end of tables, producing a triangular relation between books,

Traditional lofty reading room at the UMIST Library, Manchester. (BDP)

Modern Reading Room, University of Lancaster Library. (Brian Edwards)

reader and screen. Alternatively, there are closed access reading rooms where the reader spends a long period of time at a desk consulting material drawn from storage elsewhere (sometimes from a warehouse outside the building). The closed reading room (used predominantly by researchers in reference libraries) is quite different from the open reading room preferred by humanities scholars and casual readers (Wilson, 1998; Davey, 1998).

The type of reading room has implications for interior design – especially lighting, furniture layout and standing space. In open reading rooms, a great deal of browsing is undertaken – often without resorting to a chair. The reader is searching for an idea or the right book without a clear sense of destination. Some readers are in a sense beach-combing, hoping to stumble upon a treasure as they scan the shelves. Standing space is as important here as seating and, where chairs are provided, they need to provide a range of positions and conditions. The closed reading room, on the other hand, is a reference library where readers know in advance what they are looking for and roughly where to find it. Specific books or journals will be employed with the reader or researcher knowing in

59

advance on which shelves to search. Here the reader will spend a long time writing at a desk – taking breaks maybe for refreshment. The ambience in the closed reading room will not be casual or cafe-like, but formal with a disciplined arrangement of desks, chairs and lighting. Since the closed reading room will contain few books on open shelves, the emphasis here is upon furniture as against bookcases.

The open access reading room is the form of almost all modern libraries. The closed access reading room remains the basis for most major reference libraries, many academic ones and for private libraries. The open reading room depends upon relatively cheap books, good security and an inquisitive readership. The closed reading room is normally in response to the presence of expensive books or scarce study material, the need for high levels of security, and the demands of a research community. The relationship in a large library between open reading rooms and closed reference collections provides the basis for architectural order and interior expression (Brophy and Craven, 1999). The former establishes the democratic ambience of the building, the latter the points of security, enclosure and focus. The library as a building for the enjoyment of all is necessarily compromised by the particular, the scarce, the rare and the fragile. It is a dialectic which the best library designers turn to their advantage.

## Interior design

Although in an ideal world paper and electronic sources are physically integrated on the reader's desk, in reality the technical demands and characteristics of different types of media result in separate zones being allocated for each. There is usually a zone or room for computer users, a separate area for those referring to journals or newspapers, the library book stacks and collections of reading desks, and perhaps special study carrels. The separate zones may be distinctive functional areas but they are generally linked by wide connecting corridors. It is an arrangement that allows one area to adopt a different policy on noise or security than another; it permits internal change without disruption to the whole; and it allows different users to employ the library resources in different ways. A varied interior culture is preferable to one where there is a corporate standardization across the whole estate. Such variety can be engineered or left to grow as the nature of users and the collection changes. At Peckham Library there are three pods within the main book areas designed specifically to house the special collections. Each is specific to the collection and tailored to the tastes of potential users.

Zoning the interior of the library into distinctive areas rather than separate rooms is the policy generally adopted in all but national libraries. Here the nature of the collection or its conservation requires much more attention to security and environmental stability. Elsewhere, integration is the norm within the constraints imposed by

noise, screen conditions and general comfort. It is important that the interior layout provides space for reflection on the library material employed rather than its use in strictly functional terms. Hence, the nature of the spaces created, how they are lit and the interior views available, all deserve attention. Even if the information sources cannot be gathered into one place, the reader should be encouraged to use imagination to join them together. This is the basis for the traditional domed reading rooms of public libraries.

The library is a building type where users often spend a great deal of time in private contemplation. For many students the bulk of their private study time is spent in libraries and for the non-academic user the library is often a place where many hours are devoted to intellectual pursuit. There is, therefore, growing demand to provide facilities of a non-library nature within the building. This normally consists of a cafe and sandwich bar, but can also include gallery space for showing local art works or displaying community projects. As libraries broaden their social role to become 'ideas stores' there is pressure to increase the extent of non-library accommodation within their walls. The problem for the architect is how to bring the library and non-library functions into a coherent whole.

### Room layout, furniture and shelving

Most libraries are subdivided by book stacks that provide the basis for zoning areas into functional parts. The stacks also provide acoustic protection, have important environmental qualities (they provide thermal mass), and help define routes through the library. The position and type of shelving is essential to the smooth operation of a library; it needs to be located carefully in relation to the fixed parts such as columns, lifts, stairs, walls and doors. The book stacks also dictate the layout of seating, tables and the position of workstations.

Growth in IT provision is sometimes at the cost of areas for book storage. As a result shelving is often closely spaced and increasingly aspects of the book collection are stored elsewhere. Growing use of libraries is sometimes at the expense of space standards, both in seating area and library shelving. Designers need to consider both the needs of readers and of staff who have the task of servicing the collection. Although books are generally decreasing in size, art books are getting larger, and whereas PCs are also shrinking with the growing use of laptops, the number of readers who arrive armed with the latest digital technology is increasing rapidly. Hence, layouts and service points need to accommodate these changes.

Academic libraries provide much more computer space than public libraries. In some university libraries the areas given over to IT-based learning resource centres can exceed that of book and journal storage. The use and loan of CDs and the development of a learning rather than teaching culture have led also to the academic library being

Furniture and finishes are crucial to the experience of a library. Cranfield University Library designed by Foster and Partners. (James Morris/Foster and Partners)

extensively employed in group teaching. Rooms are set aside for seminars within the library itself and often the Internet provides the main resources on which students draw. As a result the nature of the interior spaces change into a hybrid between the traditional library reading room and something more akin to a stock market trading floor. The use of the library for seminar-type teaching also puts pressure on the lifts, stairs and corridors at the end of timetabled teaching and this can disrupt private study areas.

Table layout is an important consideration since the distribution of reader spaces can influence the configuration of columns and interior walls. The layout of tables and shelves is largely dependent upon the type of library in question. Libraries with large book collections increasingly store less frequently used material in basement areas or in other locations. Here modern rolling book stacks can be employed, thereby saving on space and cost. Basement storage is useful because the high loadings can be more readily accommodated than on upper floors and the reader is not kept waiting too long for the material to be accessed. Reader tables, rather than individual study desks, are the norm and these are usually placed near the perimeter of the library or in special reader rooms. Tables usually have the facility to use a laptop and often there is a desk lamp and small storage area provided per reader space on a shared table of perhaps eight seating positions. Much depends upon the type of library and the proximity to specialist IT areas.

An area needs to be set aside also for special library use such as employing large atlases or maps, broadsheet newspapers and archival material. There may be security issues to consider as well as furniture needs such as large tables. Often there is the need to make copies and this can

Study desks against the curved perimeter wall of Vancouver Public Library, designed by Moshe Safdie, provide an attractive environment for reading. (Brian Edwards)

61

pose a noise and environmental problem. In public libraries there is often a sharing of tables for a variety of purposes, but in academic and professional libraries study areas are set aside for specific purposes.

Dedicated areas for the use of electronic media are increasingly provided in libraries of all types. Although the integration of digital and paper-based systems is the ideal, often the constraints of security, noise and readership needs lead to the zoning of an area for the prime us of CD-ROMs and other forms of electronic media. In many academic libraries a dedicated learning resources centre is provided catering specifically for computer use, often with associated mixed-media, printing and teaching spaces. These areas require provision not unlike that of a computerized office floor in business premises. Hence, the design breaks the mould of the traditional library in the type of lighting, wiring layout and acoustic provision. As a result there is often a library and IT learning centre side by side either as two joined buildings under the same envelope (Thames Valley University) or two separate but adjacent buildings (University of Sunderland). In public libraries where the level of IT provision is lower, the two activities are normally integrated.

## Environmental considerations

Natural light and ventilation are preferable, especially in the reader areas, but security and plan depth can make this difficult to achieve. As a result most libraries employ a mixed-mode ventilation system which incorporates a mixture of natural and mechanical systems, often employing atria spaces and sometimes wind turbines. Since libraries use a great deal of artificial lighting, solar heat gain can be a problem especially where large areas of glazing are provided on south facing elevations. It is better to avoid a southern orientation but where unavoidable solar screening

This sketch for the Liddell Hart Centre of the Military Archives Library at King's College London, by architects Shepheard Epstein Hunter, shows the integration of seating, lighting and book stacks necessary in modern research libraries. (Shepheard Epstein Hunter)

The top floor reading room at Oak Park Public Library, Chicago, invites contemplation. (Brian Edwards)

or special glass may be required. However, the use of solid façades to exclude adverse external conditions is not advisable if the library is to assume a level of social engagement.

As a matter of course low-energy light fittings and sensors should be fitted in all areas. The use of task lighting can result in lowering general light levels, but with a growing elderly population reducing overall light levels can result in accidents and poor user satisfaction. Light reflection on computer screens is also a consideration and generally results in PCs being in more central areas.

In order to maximize natural light and ventilation, the plan depth should not exceed 15 m. However, this is difficult to achieve in all but the smallest of libraries and hence artificial conditions are provided in most areas. Since most libraries are constructed in urban centres, the main

Meeting tables and soft chairs mixed to encourage discussion at the War Veterans wing of the Oak Park Public Library, Chicago. (Brian Edwards)

environmental factors are normally external air and noise pollution. Thus a great deal of attention should be directed to site choice and layout, the design of external façades and the internal zoning of the building. For example, by placing book stacks against noisy external walls a more satisfactory level of comfort is provided internally.

As general rule readers like to work in natural light. This normally results in the perimeter placing of reader tables. Some seating areas can also be provided in inner sunlit spaces, particularly where magazines and newspaper are read. The creation of relaxation areas as distinct from study areas should take into account the different environmental conditions.

## Furniture and interior character

The act of reading places library users in close proximity with furniture. Tables, chairs and bookshelves are not only used but also touched. The quality of the furniture is a significant element in the perception of the library experience (Brawne, 1997). Furniture is seen and used: its tactile characteristics of texture, smell, naturalness and warmth are directly experienced.

The small-scale environment of the library furniture is arguably more important than in other public buildings. Reading is normally undertaken sitting at a desk, while retrieving books or journals requires immediate contact with shelves. Furniture, book stacks, carpets and lighting are all closely experienced as a consequence of library use. Table surfaces, chair finishes (whether plastic or leather), bookshelf construction, the type of task lighting, the construction of floors and much else make up the readers' direct experience of the interior. In this sense, the functional and tactile are equally part of the designer's responsibility with regard to interior design.

Reading is a cerebral and sensual act. Many library users gain pleasure from the books, newspapers and periodicals: the search for knowledge is balanced by the pursuit of leisure. For some the book itself is a treasure, handled with reverence and placed carefully with companions on a table or back on the library shelf. In some ways, the bookshelves are a frame enclosing and protecting works of cultural value. The library room too is not just a storage area for reading or retrieving books; it is almost a treasure chest. Certainly with rare or valuable books, there is often a correspondence at the level of detailed design between the book, the bookshelves and the room. Each is usually subscribing to the same system of values; as a consequence, the collection and the library share a common character.

The relationship between the type of library material and the characteristics of the building itself allows the designer to moderate or style the interior to suit the qualities of the collection. For instance, a library of ancient leather-bound books will quite reasonably have an interior to match – incorporating in all probability solid oak furniture, bookshelves with cornices, and panelled doors or cupboards. Some of those qualities are to be found in the contemporary Ruskin library at Lancaster University designed by MacCormac Jamieson Prichard in 1997. Here Ruskin's collection of books, sketchbooks and letters are housed in a building which evokes the artist's interests. The materials of the interior – hardwood furniture, leather, slate and thick hand-made glass – reflect Ruskin's love of authentic construction and colour. The leather is stained red; there is gold inlay and blue slate. The resulting interior captures the high Victorian age and provides a sympathetic context for the Ruskin collection.

By way of contrast, a modern computer library will probably be housed in a high-tech building. Not only do the functional and technical demands of IT drive the building into a particular form, the characteristics of the collection require the building to take on a specific character at a psychological level. At both macro and micro level, form and meaning need to correspond to the media of the library. So in a computer-based library one may expect to find: neutral, even lighting (to avoid screen glare); soft grey interior colours (so that the screen colour dominates); and steel, aluminium, plastic and glass (to reflect the materiality of the computers themselves). There is also likely to be the soft background purr of air-conditioning to absorb the low buzzing tones of the computers and tapping of keyboards. The total environment will therefore be fundamentally different to that of a traditional library. This applies not only to the interior as a whole, but to the design of tables, chairs and furnishings. These, like the elements of construction, will be of steel, glass, aluminium and synthetic fibre to create a sympathetic working framework for the IT library.

## Material considerations

Most modern library buildings are concrete or steel frame structures. This allows light to enter the building through large areas of glass whilst also freeing the floors of structural walls, thereby providing flexibility of layout. However, concrete and steel are not attractive materials in their own right and this has encouraged designers to employ a wider palette of materials for internal finishes. This includes glass, either on its own or with textured or coloured finishes, wood of various types, cork, linoleum, wool carpets and other natural fibre fabrics. The aim is to increase the level of comfort by using materials which introduce into the library, as the architect Dominique Perrault puts it, a 'more sensual, sensitive and smooth feeling' (Arets, 2005, p. 172)

Natural materials create an ambience of warmth and reflection in the Scottish Poetry Library, designed by Malcolm Fraser Architects. (Malcolm Fraser Architects)

The dialogue between structure and finishes is a dynamic one, not unlike that between books and the Internet. Coloured or decorative glass is increasingly being employed in contemporary libraries. It has many benefits — aesthetic and environmental — whilst also creating the ambiance of a social centre where, as Rem Koolhaas puts it, 'all available technologies to collect, condense, read and manipulate information' can coexist (Arets, 2005, p. 212). In the Seattle Public Library the glazing system becomes an envelope of unfolding planes which opens up the rich interior of wood veneers and coloured walls to exterior gaze.

The tactile quality of materials extends to their touch, their visual texture, lustre and to their smell. The books themselves have similar characteristics. To read is to get close to the material of the book and to do so in surroundings which invite comfort and leisurely reading is to express the deeper nature of being inside a library. Architects can alienate users by excessive employment of hard synthetic materials. As Jacques Herzog notes, libraries are 'fantastic places to read, to study, to meet, to hang around with books and people' (Arets, 2005, p. 182). The choice of furniture and finishes made by designers should reinforce these qualities not undermine them.

## References

Arets, W. (2005). *Living Library.* Prestel.

Brawne, M. (1997). *Library Builders.* Academy Editions. p. 216.

Brophy, P. and Craven, J. (1999). The Integrated Accessible Library: a model of service development for the 21st century. BLRIC Report 168. British Library Board.

Davey, P. (1998). Book Cases. *Architectural Review*, June, p. 6.

Khan, A. (2006). Personal communication. The author is indebted to Ayub Khan of Warwickshire County Council who provided the bulk of this information in July 2006.

SCONUL (1996). In *The Development of Learning Resource Centres for the Future.* Proceedings of a conference held at the Royal Institute of British Architects, 10 October, 1995. Standing Conference of National and University Librarians (SCONUL).

Wilson, C. St J. (1998). *The Design and Construction of the British Library.* British Library. pp. 19–20.

# Part 3
# Technical issues

# 5

# Impact of new information technology

As early as 1980 people were heralding the demise of the book. Yet the earliest use of computers in libraries was not to replace text but to streamline cataloguing systems. This was an appropriate response to an emerging technology as it offered the ideal, but unreachable, aim of bringing together all the bibliographic references of recorded literature. Visions of large printed volumes containing universal catalogues of publications were replaced by visions of banks of computer terminals giving direct access to those catalogues via the most powerful communications technology – the Internet.

New technology has impacted upon the library in three major ways: issue systems, records management and accommodation. The repercussions are felt by users and staff alike. It is inevitable that these impacts are reflected in library design and building use but information technology (IT) has not led to the demise of the library as some have predicted. Observation suggests that libraries accrete functions and systems – they do not normally shed them. Libraries have moved from the chained book and manuscript to the provision of closed access shelving, to open access and to on-line information via the Internet. The printed book and library as we know it have survived through all these transitions. The mixed mode of information supply suits the mixed readership and the mixed economy of data.

Library buildings will be required to house print collections for as long as society requires the use, preservation and conservation of words and artefacts which are represented by the book. Library buildings will be needed to fulfil the essential community function and to express culture and values. That technology is integrated into our libraries, not replacing them, is a measure of the social function of libraries. The library community has embraced the appropriation of technology. The challenge of harnessing powerful tools for the manipulation of data appeals to a library profession whose philosophy requires multiple use, multiple access and multiple functionality of expensive resources.

Technological impact has been a major force in libraries from the late 1960s. For staff the immediate concern was the translation of daily tasks from manual to technological systems. The most usual projects involved moving from manual to automated issue for book/borrower records and the conversion of the records of the library collections from 5″ x 3″ catalogue cards to automated systems of records management.

Manual systems involved routine filing activity bringing together slips of paper or card 'pockets' containing book cards into date and borrower sequences. Such systems were space and labour intensive and could not cope with cross-manipulation of data, making them vulnerable to chaos if the drawers containing the records were upset. This led to the introduction of large-scale projects involving retrospective catalogue conversions. In the UK, academic libraries were encouraged to engage in this activity by the University Grants Committee. Teams of people worked upon the records of individual libraries and, after a decade or so, it was possible to buy in records from catalogue banks – thus eliminating all but the most specialized of catalogue activities. Those catalogues which required a specific record or those collections that contained items which would not be covered by the agency approach

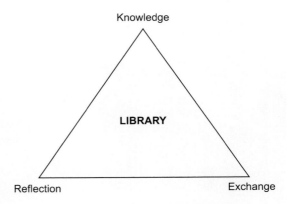

Key relationships in the library. (Brian Edwards)

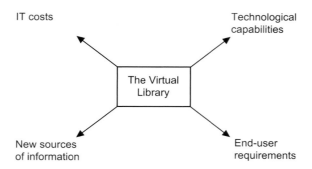

IT costs

Technological
capabilities

The Virtual
Library

New sources
of information

End-user
requirements

Main factors affecting the generation of virtual libraries.
(Brian Edwards)

continued to require a catalogue team to create records. Generally, however, standardized automated catalogues replaced card systems.

Today there is worldwide commonality in the provision of automated catalogues. This has transformed the ease by which the public have access to catalogues, particularly by the adoption of an on-line public access catalogue (OPAC) and a dedicated PC terminal. Library planning is affected in two ways: there is the need for more public space to be provided for the terminals and their associated cabling system, and less space is needed by the cataloguing team.

The accommodation required for computer hardware and software has also changed over the years. In the 1970s, computer hardware took up considerable space in specifically designed environmentally suitable areas. Basements were usually chosen as the floor loading was suitable and the climatic conditions generally stable. Air-conditioning or air-cooling systems were needed and basements made the provision of such systems and the associated ductwork easier. Modern 'server rooms' are, however, little more than flexible cupboards. The significant change is in the sophistication of the wiring and cable management systems. Buildings are required to incorporate the most flexible power distribution possible. This feature is one of the most difficult to accommodate in older buildings and, in new buildings, requires the time lapse between design and commissioning to be as close as possible.

Libraries are becoming places where on-line information is processed by users who provide the 'plug-in' technology themselves. This creates a social divide between the information-rich and the information-poor. It is a situation that does not sit well alongside a key principle of librarianship – the free access to information for all in society. In this sense, modern technology which serves society at large can, in the domain of libraries, lead to an underclass as serious as the problem of illiteracy.

## Managing IT complexity

The art of managing the various information systems in a modern library lies in reducing (or at least concealing) the complexity between systems. Users should be able to access available services without 'having to worry about switches, nodes, cables and connectors' (Whitehead, 1994, p. 17). There should be a smooth interface, especially between traditional library material and electronic sources. The characteristics of effective interface are:

- physical proximity
- language compatibility
- simplicity.

New technology expressed by huge satellite discs outside the library at California State University, Sacramento. (Brian Edwards)

It follows, therefore, that one key factor in deciding upon an IT system is its user-friendliness. Over-complex multimedia packages, for instance, appeal only to computer experts and can have the affect of alienating mainstream library users. Although the cost of moving information has fallen, low transmission costs overall have resulted in globally more complicated systems. The library has to manage interface complexity to the benefit of all users, rather than satisfy the enthusiasms of those who are IT-literate.

Part of managing information will be the linking of library and home systems. This is already happening in academic and research libraries, where faculty connections exist at some distance from the main library. In the future people will be able to access the digital material held in their local library via the Internet. The library will become more virtual than real — at least for those who have networked computers at home. Just as home shopping allows you to browse and choose goods with your personal computer, the future holds the prospect of the 'home library' (Whitehead, 1994, p. 20). Here it will be possible to read and download book and journal material, to call up CD-ROMs and to search both traditional and electronic sources via author or topic. The virtual library will be dependent upon a few real libraries around the world, but few expect it to make the local branch library invalid. In the latter, social exchange takes place and facilities are provided for those without IT skills: ultimately the library is a community resource rather than a stepping-stone on the digital superhighway.

Global digital information highways potentially offer libraries the chance to enhance their store of information and encourage users to use that knowledge more intelligently. Interaction between databases will be made easier and will interrelate book, journal, visual image and a multitude of electronic sources. If libraries harness the new electronic technologies in a user- or data-friendly fashion they can improve the level of service provided, leading to greater visitor numbers and higher regard for libraries by society at large. The IT revolution provides the means to amplify the human imagination, leading to greater creative outlook and more innovation (Whitehead, 1994, p. 20). In this sense the library is a window into another world — just as it was with the advent of the printed book and the introduction in the nineteenth century of the public lending library. What the future offers is a library which lends ideas and knowledge rather than just books. But it will take a new kind of library building to serve this function. The library in effect becomes a set of services on a network, with the storage of print on paper part of an overall information infrastructure strategy (Ford, 1994, p. 23). The technological architecture (i.e. IT systems) then drives the physical architecture — changing the nature, functionality and form of libraries at the most fundamental level.

After a decade of growing technological complexity, there are signs of global convergence in the IT field. Multimedia has become a vehicle for integrating systems, delivering new library models that bring together education, media and communications (Ford, 1994, p. 15). The distance (in virtual terms) between sources of information and users of information is shrinking. The library of the future will need to capitalize on current global convergences in order to integrate into a coherent whole the world of books, IT, telecommunications and media. This will have obvious benefits: it will enhance access, improve the

User-friendly IT equipment integrated into furniture designs by Folio. (Folio)

efficiency of data gathering and knowledge use, establish new opportunities for the delivery of training or research and, equally importantly, add to the pleasure of using a library.

## IT and space

IT has not only changed the way we use libraries, it has also led to more fluid space use (less walls) and less demarcation between librarians, support staff and information managers. To some extent, users become their own subject librarians as they search through electronic catalogues and download information. Libraries are essentially a balance of space and structure, yet both are made redundant to a greater or lesser degree by the IT revolution. As libraries stabilize after the first shock waves of universal e-information (1980–2000), one can begin to take stock. The library is still a 'repository of knowledge, a focus for reflection and a centre for exchange' (Worthington, 1994, p. ii). The medium of knowledge has changed: reflection may be via the screen as against the book, and exchange is more likely to be electronic than paper-based, but the library still exists as a distinctive type of contained architectural space. Added to this, the tools of virtual information retrieval – the PC and associated networks – are space-demanding in the same way that books consume the volume in which they are housed.

As digital technology becomes more universal, it could be argued that space should become more specific. In a placeless world of electronic data, the real world of place takes on greater meaning. This paradox allows new library buildings to take on a character which transcends the immediate needs of technology. Certainly within the lifespan of a typical library (100–150 years) many technologies come and go. Buildings as intergenerational assets should rise above the transient pressures of emerging technologies. Whilst they need to accommodate new ways of storing and accessing information, libraries are more than giant containers for the technology they house. Meaning is an essential ingredient beyond that of function, and space is fundamentally more important than technology.

## The library: space or service

Architects perceive libraries as space, librarians as service. The reader on the other hand exploits both space and service to satisfy need. The problem with space is that the virtual library makes concepts of architectural volume redundant. The IT library exists in a kind of zero space. The virtual library shifts space need from that of a large public building to a myriad of private working areas in the office or home.

Service provision in libraries is also changing under the impact of IT. The fusion of library and computer provision into a single building blurs the distinction between librarians and information technology managers (Worthington, 1994, p. 24). Librarians now manage the IT collection and IT managers enhance access to library information systems. So both the provision and use of library space is changing, and computing has altered the corresponding pattern of service delivery. There is now less emphasis on fixed elements such as the reference library and special collections and more emphasis upon improving access and support systems. The function of the library, both public and academic, has changed from that of book storage to information exchange (Worthington, 1994, p. 25).

As a consequence of changing patterns of work and education, the library is also less a place for individual study and more a place for team projects or group working (Worthington, 1994, p. 24). Librarians see their task today as 'navigators of knowledge' with architects designing the ship in which the knowledge is housed. It is a ship which has to be capable of changing direction and which has, at the same time, to be recognizable and cherishable as a library. So while the computerized library has made traditional concepts of space redundant, it has not removed the need for social and cultural space. After all, the library's worth, as the poet Ted Hughes put it, resides in being able to sit 'with the genius of the Earth' whilst being able to 'turn the key to the whole world' (Hughes, 1998).

## IT and the public library: financial and ethical considerations

Although the popular image of a library is that of a book-based service, electronic systems increasingly undermine the centrality of the book and frequently replace it. The public has a well-established belief in the free provision of books and the free reference to them in national or specialist libraries. There is the feeling, however, that other services, such as the loan of videos and software, should entail some form of charging. If a charge is not made for the borrowing of non-book media, the fear is that funds will not be available for purchasing books. In an IT age, the dilemma for the library service is how to cater for both traditional and new services: how to keep the book collection up to date whilst accommodating the expansion of computer or video-based facilities.

Whereas the UK academic network was established to facilitate electronic information transmission, no such infrastructure exists for public services. Thus the public library has generally been slower to engage in new IT than academic libraries. However, there are four areas where computer-based systems occur in a typical civic library (ASLIB, 1995, p. 76):

- electronic databases which integrate information from different sources providing a multimedia interface

New and old technologies integrated into Malmo Public Library using Gresswell-designed furniture and shelving. (Gresswell Projects)

- electronic databases of specialist reference material (historic photographs, plans)
- access for the disabled to special electronic information or reading systems
- access to the Internet.

As a result of these innovations, the public library has had to adjust its budget allocations, its space and the training of staff to provide an effective IT service. The library is no longer seen as exclusively a book repository but a building that caters for different information media. Library staff too need to manage the wealth of information rather than store it. The library, as a building, is having to reassess its role in a computer age in ways which bring in new readers without alienating old ones (Association for Information Management, 1995, p. 78; Follett, 1993). The library will in effect exist to serve two parallel technologies — paper and electronic — each with their body of users. These parallel worlds are increasingly integrated within the physical space of the building and bridged by the expertise of library staff.

The integration of physical and electronic data is important to avoid a kind of library apartheid where distinct worlds exist for those with IT skills and those without. Information technology is a major liberator and source of knowledge, but also a significant barrier for those who are not computer-literate.

Besides the general benefits of IT systems, they also allow the public library to cater more effectively for life-long learning. Independent education and training (that which occurs before or after student years) is dependent upon a well-resourced public library. This is particularly true

in the knowledge industries where many of the journal (and increasingly book) sources are published electronically. Updating skills throughout one's working life requires the support of appropriately designed and equipped libraries. Not only is interface needed between traditional and electronic systems, but between home IT and library IT ones.

Multimedia will provide the means of interaction in the future — electronic systems will erode both space and distance as limiting concepts. However, they will not invalidate the library as a building for social interaction or a place where users, library staff and stock interface. Neither will the electronic library destroy the need for tranquil internal space: in fact the computer-based library should offer a contrast from the bustle of city life or the private cloister of the home. As external distance is destroyed, there is more importance attached to the quality and dimensions of internal space. IT, whether integrated or

**Information technology trends relevant to libraries**

Increase in capacity and lowering of computer prices

Increase in network capacity and lowering of transmission costs

Fusion of various kinds of media (text, sound and pictures) on single compact discs

PCs which act simultaneously as telephone, radio, TV

Fusion of printer, fax, photocopier and scanner

accommodated as a separate suite, offers the library the means of its own liberation.

There is a further sense in which the building matters, even in an electronic age. As words and information migrate to electronic text, it also glows in extent and access. The human mind cannot absorb this in its entirety and learns to accept fragments (Heim, 1993). The big mental picture upon which notions of wisdom are based is sacrificed in a kind of information overload. The library itself can remind readers that 'facts' are no substitute for 'meaning', and that time must be set aside for reflection. The library as a space should, by its very design, engender a respect for the whole rather than isolated knowledge.

## Planning of library IT workstations

Where workstations are dispersed throughout the library (as opposed to being grouped into an IT suite), their position is critical in terms of user requirements. There are two distinct aspects to consider – social and technical. On the social front, the computer screen acts as a draw, usually bringing more than one user within its immediate orbit. Sometimes two or three people discuss the information on the screen at the same time. They may be assisting each other in navigating the highways available or evaluating the data (Drake, 1994, p. 64). Either way there is likely to be noise – both keyboard tapping and talking. Often too there is the trek to printers or to other workstations that could be engaged in similar pursuits. The sociability of computer stations is distracting to other readers and changes the whole culture of the library. Hence, workstations need to be planned to facilitate use and interaction in

a fashion which does not undermine the library as a place for quiet reading and reflection.

There are two main strategies followed: either the positioning of workstations in clusters where the noise can be controlled by the positioning of book stacks, etc. or their dispersal in the library on tables deliberately designed for single person use. Where the two are used in conjunction, there can be workstation provision which promotes the exchange of information but which can also, with a different layout, encourage private study.

The technical problems are as taxing as the social ones. VDU screens act as mirrors reflecting light sources; this is tiring to the eyes and annoying for the user. VDUs should not, therefore, face windows or be beneath sources of artificial or direct light. Where VDUs are near windows, the glare of natural light – especially sunlight – can be irritating. The answer is to place VDUs at right angles to windows and to ensure that nearby windows are protected by internal or external blinds (Drake, 1994, p. 65). Where placed on peninsulas arranged perpendicularly to the outside wall there is, however, the problem of exposing the cables and back of computers to view. The answer here is to arrange for computers to face outwards on double desks, so that users face each other divided perhaps by a low screen that can incorporate task lighting whilst also hiding the cabling.

Computers and users create more heat than readers and books. The heating load of a person studying via a VDU is generally about twice that of a person employing only books. This excess heat will require extraction by natural or mechanical means. Opening windows is the traditional answer to high internal temperatures, but this is not usually possible in a library where theft is a perennial problem. The

Computer noise leads to physical separation of IT suites as here at Putney Public Library. (Biddy Fisher)

solution is to employ fan-assisted ventilation or full air-conditioning in areas of intense computer provision. Where computers, people and artificial lighting come together the problem is not generally one of heating but cooling.

The trend towards multimedia use in libraries has the added problem of acoustic control. Here voice and vision are equally important. Noise separation becomes as important as thermal control, adding to the complexity of provision. Increasingly, audio-visual and multimedia facilities are placed in their own secure rooms where specific conditions can be most effectively met. However, the provision of rooms within libraries restricts flexibility of use and makes such space inefficient when new technologies are introduced. What is evident is that, whilst the fabric which houses the library changes at the same rate as library functions change, technology is usually the motor of library innovation.

Noise, thermal control and the social use of space are interrelated factors in planning the layout of library workstations. The environmental conditions required often result in the use of raised floors to house ventilation ducts, IT cables and orthodox electricity supply. The trend, however, towards cableless IT does bring into question the concept of universal raised floors. Suspended ceilings are also frequently employed where both lighting and acoustic control are needed. A common dilemma relates to the use

Learning Resource Centre, Sunderland University, designed by Building Design Partnership. (BDP)

of the perimeter of the library for quiet study. Carrels positioned against the building façade offer ideal conditions for book study, but poor conditions for use of VDUs. The usual solution where reading and IT facilities are integrated on the same floor is to zone the library into noisier 'streets', where issue desks, short loan, electronic catalogue, computer suites and printers are located almost as shops along a high street. This is the solution adopted in the extension to the Lancaster University Library (MacCormac Jamieson Pritchard, 1994). Beyond this central area are book stacks acting as visual and acoustic screens to the quieter non-intensive IT areas at the building perimeter. Such zoning requires not a universal architectural solution to environmental conditions but the planning of the library into parts, each with their own strategy for sound, thermal management, privacy and security.

## Computer areas

All new libraries contain large areas devoted to the space and technology needs of IT provision. This may account for 40–50% of the floor area of a typical public library and possibly as much as 60% in a college or university one. Computer areas, known as 'computer commons' in the USA and generally as 'learning resource centres' in the UK, normally contain a central well-lit (but excluding direct sunlight) space that is secure and supported by local networks which extend to other parts of the library or outreach beyond the building. Practice varies between types of library but all libraries now contain extensive IT facilities which, ideally at least, are integrated with paper-based collections.

In computer areas desktop PCs are usually provided along with printers and scanners. However, students in university libraries and readers in public libraries now tend to come equipped with their own laptop and merely log onto the system. Shared computing facilities complemented by personal laptops usually makes the computer the first port of call in many libraries. When there exist adjacent meeting rooms, each with their own computer network and data projector, plus possibly training and support areas, the IT suites of a typical library have become the focus for infrastructure investments. These are in fibre-optic and wireless systems, in new furniture needed for integrated study use (paper and digital media) and in support services from cafes to media shops. In under a generation the library has become a media centre with an information agora at its centre (Neuman, 2003).

## Learning spaces in libraries

Post-occupation studies of public and academic libraries have highlighted the extent to which users employ the library for IT-based informal and sometimes formal

The computer-based catalogue and the study collection should be placed in close proximity. Cambridge University Library. (Forster Ecospace)

learning. Where seminar rooms and lecture theatres are provided, there is an obvious overlap between library activities and educational ones. However, a great deal of casual teaching and learning takes place and this is sometimes encouraged by providing informal spaces for socialized education. The blurring of education and library services within one building has been encouraged by a number of UK local councils. At Tower Hamlets in London a new generation of libraries known as 'idea stores' have been built which provide teaching and seminar

Informal learning spaces and cafe area at the Saltire Centre, the new inter-active library at Glasgow Caledonia University, designed by BDP. Designed for wireless technology, the area encourages a range of learning methods to take place. (Brian Edwards)

space for use by local schools, colleges and universities. A similar strategy has been followed in Hampshire in the Discovery Centres which, although primarily library-type buildings, provide also a range of group learning spaces and rooms for community use.

To maximize the potential of these initiatives it is important that the providers of libraries (whether public or academic) articulate a broader learning plan which includes libraries rather than just a library strategy. The integration of learning modes and spaces in the library is not without its own difficulties or cost consequences. It requires, for instance, changes to the planned technological infrastructure and space utilization and to the management of the library in terms of personnel and policy on opening hours, noise and refreshment facilities. However, if libraries are to fulfil their full potential as hubs of knowledge storage and use, there are obvious overlaps with both the world of work and of education.

Where the twentieth century library was mainly concerned with the acquisition and sharing of knowledge and ideas (through the loan mainly of books to registered readers), the twenty-first century library has somehow to support society's needs for critical thought, creativity, skills in problem solving and the ability to articulate ideas clearly. From developing basic skills in language to using sophisticated modes of thought, the library has always supported the acquisition and application of knowledge. What makes today's library different is not just the complexity of information modes and the richness of the knowledge base, but the speed with which old knowledge and technologies become obsolete. It means libraries need to stay flexible in their provision if they are to retain a central role in facilitating social, cultural and educational change.

One key area where the library looks set to expand its influence is in e-learning. Here facilities in the library (both public and academic) have a key role to play in bridging between the home and college. The full potential of e-learning to transform the educational landscape at school, college and university level could be released if libraries provided more facilities for interfacing between IT and mobile technologies. The latter are the main vehicles of communication employed by 15–24 year olds yet many libraries prohibit the use of mobile phones. Future changes in educational technologies will undoubtedly impact upon the library but, rather than adapt to change, libraries could be at the cutting edge of evolution.

## References

ASLIB (1995). *Review of the Public Library Service in England and Wales.* Association for Information Management. pp. 76–78.

Drake, P. (1994). Eternal values and changing technologies. In *Building Libraries for the Information Age.* Institute of Advanced Architectural Studies (IAAS), York.

Follett, B. (1993). The Follett Report on libraries for the HEFCE, SHEFC, HEFCW and DENI, *Joint Funding Council's Libraries Review Group.* (This report paved the way for the changes to academic libraries which helped fashion the new generation of public libraries in the UK.)

Ford, J. (1994). The intelligent library: a supplier's viewpoint. In *Building Libraries for the Information Age* (S. Taylor, ed.). Proceedings of a symposium held in York, 11–12 April 1994, pp. 64–65. Institute of Advanced Architectural Studies (IAAS).

Heim, M. (1993). *The Metaphysics of Virtual Reality.* Oxford University Press. (The quote is a paraphrase.)

Hughes, T. (1998). An introductory verse to new library. *Quarto,* No. 4, Autumn, p. 2. (*Quarto* is the newsletter of the National Library of Scotland.)

MacCormac Jamieson Pritchard (1994). Lancaster University Library extension and the Ruskin Library. In *Building Libraries for the Information Age* (S.Taylor, ed.). Proceedings of a symposium held in York 11–12 April, 1994. Institute of Advanced Architectural Studies, (IAAS).

Neuman, D. (2003). *College and University Facilities.* John Wiley and Sons, London.

Whitehead, G. K. (1994). The library of the future: global information highways in the information age. In *Building Libraries for the Information Age* (S. Taylor, ed.). Proceedings of a symposium held York, 11–12 April 1994. Institute of Advanced Architectural Studies (IAAS).

Worthington, J. (1994). Planning the virtual library. *Architects Journal,* 18 August, pp. 24–25.

Worthington, J. (1994). Preface: planning the virtual library. In *Building Libraries for the Information Age* (S. Taylor, ed.). Proceedings of a symposium held York, 11–12 April 1994. Institute of Advanced Architectural Studies (IAAS).

IT area at Sydney Jones Library, University of Liverpool, designed by Shepheard Epstein Hunter. (Brian Edwards)

**LEARNING
RESOURCES
CENTRE**

# 6

# Technical factors and engineering design

## Environmental sustainability and the library

Like all public buildings, libraries have a major impact on the environment. This extends from the energy used for heating, lighting and ventilation to energy consumed via computers and in transport reaching the building. In addition, a large amount of water is consumed and libraries have an impact on biodiversity via the materials used in construction. The subject of sustainable design is a broad one but in the context of libraries there are a number of factors to consider at the briefing, design and operational levels, which are discussed in this chapter.

### Energy usage

To heat, light and ventilate buildings consumes around 45–50% of global energy consumption. Most of this energy is normally in the form of fossil fuels. Added to this, libraries consume additional energy in providing the power for computers and other forms of multimedia. To achieve a low carbon footprint, the architect needs to maximize daylight and opportunities for natural ventilation, exploit solar energy for winter-time heating and summer-time stack effect cooling, control excessive solar gains and internal glare, and employ construction materials which have low embodied energy. To achieve the latter, it is usually advisable to source materials and products locally since this uses less transport energy (the main component of embodied energy for heavy materials).

Energy conservation can also be achieved by ensuring the building is well insulated, air-tight in construction, and uses such things as sensors to prevent artificial lights being employed when there is nobody present. High thermal mass also helps reduce energy consumption though the effects of transparency sought elsewhere for aesthetic delight can undermine this. However, much can be achieved at little or no extra cost. By simply reducing the footprint of the building to the dimensions needed for natural light to penetrate the full depth of the interior can

achieve considerable energy savings. Similarly the employment of atria can help with energy efficiency especially in larger libraries and these sunlit spaces can provide social and way-finding benefits. Also the reduction of the surface area to internal volume ratio can deliver further energy savings (and hence carbon emissions). However, the nature of libraries can limit the opportunity for sustainable design. The book-stack area is normally deep in plan and lit by electric light, and rare book and map collections require specific conditions for their conservation. But within these constraints efficiencies can be achieved by, for instance, reducing background light levels and employing task lighting at desks.

It may be possible to zone larger libraries into: areas which can be naturally ventilated; those which need to utilize mechanical ventilation and air-conditioning; and those areas which could operate on mixed-mode cycles. The latter employing night-time cooling would be suitable in parts of the library where strict air quality requirements are not needed, such as staff rooms and in the general book-stack collections. However, in IT areas the workplace standards normally prohibit natural light and ventilation. Security of stock and equipment also poses a limit to the degree of permeability of the building's fabric.

Libraries are particularly dependent upon electrical energy. It is needed for lighting and to power computers, surveillance and security equipment, lifts and air-conditioning. As about a half of all energy consumption worldwide goes into constructing and servicing buildings, libraries have their part to play in achieving more sustainable practice. Libraries, with their high electricity consumption, pose a particular problem as electrical energy is relatively inefficient per unit of delivered energy compared with oil or gas. For every unit of electricity, about twice as much carbon dioxide pollution is generated for the same unit of energy delivered via gas or oil.

There are three important energy conservation practices to follow in the library:

- to reduce energy demand by utilizing sound environmental design practices (high insulation, passive solar ventilation, etc.)
- to exploit renewable energy sources to maximize natural light and ventilation and, where appropriate, to generate electrical power directly from the sun (using photovoltaics) and the wind (using microgenerators)
- to reduce energy use in the operation of the building by using low-energy lamps, lighting sensors, computer cut-off systems and task lighting for key tasks.

The library should be designed as a closed system whereby energy by-products from one area become the energy input for another. For instance, heat recovery technology allows waste heat to be recycled – cutting down on initial demand. Similarly, the heat emitted from computers and lights can become an important source of heating or ventilation if the section of the building allows for passive solar or assisted stack effect ventilation. Since libraries are particularly dependent upon electricity for their operation, energy can also be generated at the building exploiting emerging technologies such as photovoltaics. Effective energy consumption requires the client, designer and operator of the library to share responsibility. There may be some additional cost, perhaps 2–5% above normal budgets, but since libraries are amongst the longest surviving building types, sustainable design will give long-term benefit through lower exposure to environmental problems in the future. Since libraries are visited by people in pursuit of knowledge or leisure, they can also act as a useful demonstration of good environmental practice: the building as well as the books it contains can teach the message of sustainability.

There is considerable regional variation in the low-energy strategies that need to be employed. In the cold north, passive solar gain may be useful for seasonal heating, but in the warm south the problem will be one of preventing overheating. This is often exacerbated by the accidental heat gains which flow from lights, computers and people. So whilst solar aperture is desirable where heat gain is needed, protection from direct sunlight is imperative. Even where solar heat gains are undesirable, the sun's energy can still be exploited to drive natural ventilation systems (especially when wind towers are incorporated) and thus reduce or eliminate the need for environmentally damaging air-conditioning.

With low-energy design, it is important to consider the different needs of people and books. The temperature and humidity standards for each vary and, in hot dry climates, the tolerances for book conservation can be stricter than those for human comfort and computer use. Whereas people prefer contact with direct sunlight and can accept some variety in ambient temperature, the same is not true of books (especially rare ones). A highly glazed building may be welcoming and attractive to use, but as a library it will undoubtedly be costly to heat and ventilate and may damage the book collection and make computer operation difficult.

### Indoor air quality

Related to energy consumption is the question of air quality and internal ambiance. A healthy library environment is obviously needed by all but sometimes the interests of energy efficiency can undermine the quality of light and air within the building. People tend to like daylight and natural ventilation so every effort should be made to maximize their presence in the library. Air quality is affected also by the materials used for finishes, especially their surface treatment. Natural materials provide healthier working environments than those where a great deal of paint, lacquer and artificial fibres are employed. Man-made synthetic materials such as carpets and floor tiles should also be avoided in spite of their benefits elsewhere (e.g. noise control).

Indoor air quality is also related to external conditions. The choice of site, orientation and position of the building can greatly influence internal conditions. The relationship between the internal and external environments should be considered at the briefing stage so that the working conditions for library staff and users are considered early in design preparation.

### Green travel plan

The site chosen for the library has a significant impact upon the amount of energy consumed by those using the building. Since about 25% of global energy use is related to transport, decisions affecting the location of the library are important. First, the building should be well served by public transport and this needs to be available during the opening hours of the library. Hence libraries should be centrally located, preferably adjacent to bus, tram and railway stops. Where they are not the routes from the bus or train stop to the library should be visible and legible.

Since many people choose to walk to the library, their needs should take priority over those using wheels. Too often pedestrians have the spaces left over after everybody else has taken a slice of the urban landscape. Their routes are often obstructed by barriers, used only with the help of traffic lights or urban tunnels, sometimes poorly lit and dangerous. People will only choose to walk to libraries if the routes are designed for pedestrians, i.e. attractive and tree lined with seats every few yards. Many elderly people carrying their books and perhaps groceries are not able to sustain a lengthy journey on foot without periodic rests. Too rarely is the pedestrian put first and often the library car park has to be crossed to reach the public entrance.

The cyclist also needs to be accommodated. Again, safe cycle routes to the library are required and secure storage of bicycles is needed but rarely provided. Cyclists also need showers and changing rooms on arrival. The needs of car users, whether staff of readers, generally absorb what investment is needed in wider access provision. The ability of the library to help deliver a green travel plan is dependent upon fresh thinking by both building clients and their designers. The brief is the place to provide the framework for sustainable thinking.

## Water conservation

Libraries have the ability to capture their own rainwater for use in flushing toilets and in irrigated landscape areas. The large flat roofs of typical library buildings provide an opportunity to direct the water into roof tanks where it can then be fed by gravity to the various toilets in the building. With climate change water is becoming an issue in many regions of the world yet libraries rarely incorporate features in their design to conserve water stocks. As a result potable water is used for the relatively low grade tasks listed earlier.

Water can also be conserved by employing spray taps, self-closing taps and low-flush toilets. Here the benefits are threefold. First, the cost of utilities is reduced (thereby saving money for use on other library services). Second, water can be conserved for other more essential purposes such as drinking, cooking and agricultural irrigation. Third, the use of water conserving apparatus can help educate the public into practices they should be using in the home or workplace. However, since libraries are urban buildings, the opportunity to recycle water is limited. Water is used typically in sanitation, heating and sprinkler systems. The water arrives in a potable state and leaves polluted. On-site treatment of low-level polluted water (grey water) via reed-beds is not usually possible, nor is local catchment of water to reduce the scale of importation. However, in regions of the world where water is scarce, roof catchment may be possible and local water treatment with recycling desirable.

As with energy conservation, the approach to follow is site catchment, efficient use, recycling and recovery. Water conservation sets an example which is generally more visible than with energy conservation. It is also important to use localized valves and water metering to help educate library staff about the importance of water conservation. In many parts of the world water is a scarcer resource than energy (or more critical in terms of building performance). In hot climates, wastewater should at least be recycled for

irrigation and perhaps also (after purification) for evaporative cooling of the library itself.

## Biodiversity

The choices architects make in the selection of construction materials and finishes has a large impact upon local and international biodiversity. By bulk around 60% of global raw materials end up in the construction industry. The impacts are on rainforests (for structural timber and veneers), mountain ranges (crushed aggregates and building stones), natural riverbed deposits (sand and clay), remote regions (ores for steel, copper, lead) and farmed animals (sheep wool for carpets, etc.). Libraries are long-lived buildings where the initial impacts can serve society well over generations as long as the initial choices are intelligently made. Generally it is better to choose materials with a low ecological footprint. This can be achieved by using locally sourced products where the supply chain is easier to monitor and impacts are nearby rather than further afield. Second, by using recycled materials or construction products which lend themselves to reuse (in whole or part), the ecological damage can be reduced.

Biodiversity can also be addressed at the level of landscape design. The linking of the library into the local landscape, providing ecological richness through the choice and extent of planting, the creation of sheltered and safe areas for people and wildlife alike can all benefit biodiversity. Also the minimalization of waste both during the construction phase and once the building is in use can also reduce the environmental footprint of the library. Here facilities for waste recycling by library users and staff can be beneficial.

Since libraries consume a large amount of resources in construction (stone, steel, concrete, glass) and in operation (energy, water, carpets, paper) it is useful to consider their recycling potential as well as their wider environmental impact. Some resources are renewable (timber), others not (stone); some are recyclable (steel), others not (concrete); some resources also become contaminated by library use (air) and others require global ecosystems to assist in purification (water). Library buildings can be seen as environmental systems with inputs and outputs.

The scale and location of environmental impacts vary according to the nature of the construction material. With stone or concrete there are significant landscape and

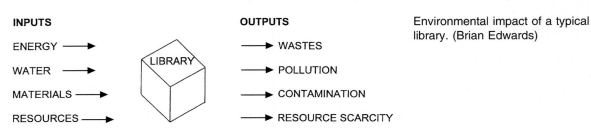

Environmental impact of a typical library. (Brian Edwards)

transport impacts; with steel or aluminium there are impacts upon air and water quality at the works, foundry or smelter; with paper, there are impacts at the mill and in the forests. In the UK, each person accounts for about six tonnes of building material use annually (DETR, 1999) – some of this ending up in the construction of libraries. Energy is needed to extract and transport this material (the embodied energy in a typical brick will, if converted to petrol, drive a family car up to 7 miles), water is used in much manufacture of building components (plasterboard, concrete tiles) and raw materials are used non-renewably. Like other public buildings, libraries have a significant impact on global ecosystems, both directly and indirectly. For example, the timber used in construction or furniture may have derived from a distant rainforest or a local wood. Paper (of which libraries are great consumers) has a chain of impacts from manufacture to use and reuse.

There are four principles to follow with regard to reducing the impact of resource use at libraries:

- source heavyweight construction materials locally to reduce transport energy costs and general environmental disturbance
- source lightweight materials globally but ensure that overseas companies follow sound environmental practices (look for local eco-labelling or eco-auditing schemes)
- design for reuse or recycling of elements of construction
- design the library so that it can readily adapt to future change.

Most libraries worldwide were planned and constructed by previous generations. We inherit libraries and add to the global stock. The libraries designed and built today become the resources for future generations – our buildings in this sense are part of society's cultural and operational capital. The way we design and construct today's libraries shapes the options available for meeting the needs of future generations. It is only in making them environmentally responsive that they will fully serve the changing social and sustainable agendas of the future.

### Recycling and waste

It is important that the library buildings, their components, systems and materials are capable of adaptation, reuse and recycling. Each element from the whole to the smallest construction part should be capable of being recycled. Reuse to serve a new function is preferable to recycling because it involves less material change. But recycling is preferable to waste – a material of no social or environmental value whose disposal will eat into the library's operational budget and add to landfill problems.

The outputs from a building vary according to the nature of the inputs and their conversion. Burning oil to provide heat or energy also produces $CO_2$ (carbon dioxide –

'Green' Library and Learning Resource Centre at Sunderland University. Designed by Building Design Partnership. (M Hamilton-Knight)

a major greenhouse gas) and other toxic emissions (e.g. $SO_2$ – the main pollutant in acid rain). Materials such as carpets, furnishing and finishes may give off gases such as volatile organic compounds (VOCs) and $NO_x$ (nitrogen oxides) and may have involved the use of ozone-depleting chlorofluorocarbons (CFCs) in manufacture. These wastes often have a damaging impact upon global or human health. Since a person in Europe typically spends 80–90% of their time indoors (some of which is spent in public buildings such as libraries), the impact upon health and the sense of physical well-being are important.

## The relationship between plan depth, book-stack position and glazing

The book stacks provide a convenient heat sink which can be used to moderate temperatures in the library. The thermal capacity of the books evens out peaks and troughs in temperature – a particular advantage with low-energy designs. Where narrow configurations in plan are employed, the relationship between orientation, glazed area, building depth and building fabric is critical. Ideally, the book stacks are centrally placed with readers around the building perimeter. This arrangement provides advantageous conditions for the reader (daylight, view) and the best conditions for books and computers (glare-free, sun-shaded). Without the employment of deep plans, there is little justification except in special areas for either air-conditioning or suspended ceilings.

Where the library has a southerly orientation, the book stacks can be placed against the south wall with clerestory lights above. This allows the stacks to act as solar shading, reducing the problems of both heat gain and glare elsewhere in the library. With a northerly aspect, the opposite strategy should be employed. Here, for maximum sun-free daylight penetration, the stacks should be placed towards the centre or back of the library. Light-shelves can also be employed to deflect daylight deep into the library. So whereas the southern library façade has only limited glazing, the northern one is fully glazed. Since readers do not like sitting in direct sunlight, it is on the northern side of the library that desks and workstations are normally located. A sustainable library is one which has distinctive elevations according to orientation and a corresponding layout of desks, stacks and computers according to aspect.

In low-energy design, it is commonplace for lighting, heating, ventilation, plan depth and sectional arrangement to be considered as a series of connected issues. The design philosophy should be robust enough to engineer solutions that are mutually compatible. The light-shelves for instance can double up as solar shades and incorporate air supply grilles, which connect in turn to ducts placed within floors or internal partitions. Artificial light is best provided by a combination of low-level overall illumination and task lighting at desks. Glazing systems can incorporate internal uplighters and have sensors that detect movement in the room (useful for security and energy conservation). Since nearly 40% of all energy use in modern libraries is associated with lighting, this is the area where economies have greatest impact. Four simple, cost-effective lighting strategies are to:

- maximize the use of daylight by avoiding plan depths greater than 15 m
- employ atria to introduce natural light and ventilation into deep-planned areas
- use task lighting generally and to avoid light flooding except in selected areas (library counter, corridors)
- use low-energy light sources.

There is a growing tendency to employ solar-assisted ventilation in libraries. Atrium spaces provide the motor to move air naturally around the building, perhaps aided by solar chimneys. Natural ventilation and natural light benefit from the atrium concept, but there are two obstacles in the library that limit the universal application of atrium-based solutions. The first is the problem of noise, especially in academic or research libraries. Group working by students can cause widespread disturbance in the open-plan, atrium-centred library. The need for interconnected spaces (necessary for air movement) provides the channel for the transmission of noise. The second problem is one of walls and the book stacks themselves. For natural ventilation to be effective, there should be the minimum of obstruction to airflow. Where walls are necessary, these should not rise to the ceiling and, for such libraries to be

Rooftop conservatory and conference suite at Chicago Public Library allows for environmental moderation of building. (Brian Edwards)

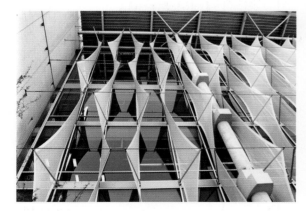

This library addresses sustainability to create a lively display of shading sails on the façade. Phoenix Public Library by Will Bruder. (Andrew North)

successful as low-energy buildings, the ceiling heights themselves should generally be fairly high (at least 3.5 m). This adds to construction costs and can offset the gains in energy efficiency. Airflow, acoustic separation, flexibility and simplicity of control are key components of the sustainable library (Long, 1995).

## Options for lighting

Lighting is important for comfort, safety, legibility and energy efficiency. Working areas need to have good conditions for reading or screen use. Circulation areas need to be well-lit with pools of light employed to guide users around the library. Lighting also needs to be carefully considered in the energy strategy because, in large libraries, energy consumption as a result of artificial lighting often exceeds that of heating. The most immediate benefit is gained by exploiting natural light to its limits as opposed to employing artificial light. However, there are both dimensional and technical constraints in doing this. As a general rule, working areas should not be further than 7 m from a window – this results in a maximum plan depth of 14 m or 15 m with a central corridor or open passageway. Where libraries require deeper plans, the daylight should

Daylight and security screens used at Hirata Public Library, Japan. Note the use of trees to provide further solar shading. (Teramoto Architects)

be introduced into the core via lightwells, atria or roof glazing. Hence, as the user moves through the depth of the building a deep library will normally have a sequence of solid and ceiling glazed sections.

Two design strategies are normally employed to maximize daylight penetration: to use high ceilings (3–4 m

Combined daylight canopy and shading screen used at the Law Library, University of Cambridge. Designed by Foster and Partners. (Dennis Gilbert/View)

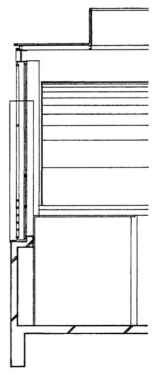

Section of interior daylight and security screen at Hirata Public Library, Japan. (Teramoto Architects)

high) and to incorporate light-shelves into the external glazing or cladding system. Light-shelves and louvres for solar control are frequently combined into a single system — the light-shelves are needed to bounce daylight back into the interior and the louvres are employed to provide glare-free working conditions at the building perimeter. There are benefits in relating lighting and ventilation design: the high ceilings also aid passive ventilation and often allow the building fabric (normally concrete columns and beams) to be exposed (which assists passive cooling). Tall ceilings also provide space for high-level windows which can be opened mechanically with building management systems. High opening lights reduce the problem of theft or vandalism and ensure that draughts do not occur at desk level.

Lighting is also substantially a question of artificial light. The 24-hour access library has major consequences for energy efficiency. The use of artificial lighting adds to heat gain and hence ventilation requirements. Night-time cooling will not occur at the same rate when lights are left on. Hence the importance of employing energy efficient light sources (such as compact fluorescent lamps) which, by using less energy for the same level of illumination, release less heat into the environment. Light sensors may also be employed (e.g. infra-red detection) which activate the lights according to occupation. This is particularly useful in cellular office areas but could be employed more widely in areas of the library subject to occasional use. Solar cells can also be employed to regulate the level of illumination according to daylight conditions.

## Options for ventilation

There are three main options in terms of library ventilation:

- natural ventilation
- mechanical ventilation
- full air-conditioning.

The first requires a shallow building depth, an open-plan design and predominantly open section. If the library is large, the building needs to be fairly high (at least three storeys) and would normally include lofty atria. The building fabric will also assist cooling and the glazing area (including orientation) needs to be carefully considered. Being open plan and of fluid section such libraries can suffer from noise transmission problems. Future adaptability can also be compromised by the need to maintain the building's essential openness.

Mechanical ventilation offers greater choice of plan depth, sectional arrangement and interior subdivision. Air is moved through the library via fans and ducts, leading

Low-energy library which maximizes daylight and natural ventilation. University of Hertfordshire Library, designed by Architects Co. Partnership. (Forster Ecospace)

The naturally ventilated atrium at The Queens Library, Anglia Polytechnic University. Designed by ECD Architects. (Anglia Polytechnic University)

inevitably to floor area being sacrificed for plant rooms and service routes. Sometimes mechanical ventilation uses the concept of 'comfort cooling' whereby the thermal mass of the structure assists with moderating temperature. Here a variety of passive and active systems are combined, depending upon the need for fresh air in different zones of the library. With mechanical ventilation it is normal practice to employ heat recovery technology in order to conserve energy.

Full air-conditioning requires a totally sealed building and thus separates internal conditions entirely from those in the external environment. It is usually employed in large libraries (national libraries and major academic ones) and in locations where outside conditions are extreme (particularly hot or cold climates). Air-conditioning allows the building to be of any shape or size, and to be practically of any form of construction. The main price paid for this convenience is the large areas lost due to duct runs and building plant, and the cost of operating and servicing such buildings. Air-conditioned libraries are not unlike four-wheel drive vehicles – they give the library high performance under difficult conditions but at an environmental and financial cost.

In many modern libraries no single system is used. Instead there are combinations of natural and mechanical ventilation, and of mechanical ventilation with full air-conditioning in special areas. The density of occupation and the type of library collection or equipment stored in a particular part of the building determines the ventilation strategy. Even the 'greenest' of libraries may have air-conditioning in photocopying or archive areas. For the architect and engineer, the choice of system depends upon five variables:

- the level of people occupancy in different parts of the library
- the vulnerability of the collection to changes in temperature or humidity
- the diversity of equipment (copiers, computers, printers) and attendant pollution levels
- the need for zoning to allow for extended opening in particular areas
- the arrangements for fire escape and smoke extraction.

The trend towards the 24-hour access library limits the options available. Natural ventilation is normally dependent upon night-time cooling. This will not occur if the library is open all night with the lights on. With all-night opening, only parts of the library are usually accessible and a different heating and ventilation will be required here. As a result, the modern library is more likely to be a hybrid of systems rather than a thoroughbred – with each area being as lean, flexible and efficient as conditions allow.

## The air-conditioned library

The air-conditioned library offers flexibility of layout but at a price. Such libraries are often stifling environments with background fan noise, which can be distracting. Although temperature and humidity may be carefully controlled to suit both the reader and the collection, the working environment may feel stuffy and lifeless. In order to avoid fluctuations in temperature, air-conditioned libraries are normally relatively windowless and often of deep plan in order to place as much of the library as possible away from external conditions. Without large windows and pools of natural light, it is not easy to identify routes, staircases or

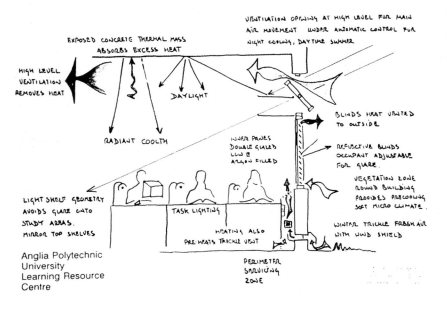

Anglia Polytechnic University Learning Resource Centre

Environmental strategy at perimeter of Learning Resources Centre, Anglia Ruskin University. (ECD Architects)

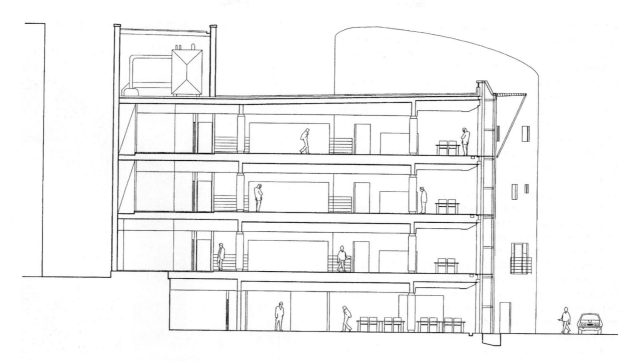

The University of Abertay Library, designed by the Parr Partnership, uses exposed concrete columns, solar screens and double façades to conserve energy. (The Parr Partnership)

use hierarchies. And without slight fluctuations in temperature, light and humidity, the reader can easily feel drowsy.

Typical of air-conditioned libraries is the one constructed at the University of Exeter in 1983. It follows closely the pattern common at the time and widely advocated by the University Grant Commission (which at the time funded academic libraries). The library is three storeys high and partly built beneath the ground. The plan is nearly square and about 40 m across. The main staircase is placed close to the centre and hence has no natural light. The entrance at first floor level leads to a deep, rather gloomy library entrance surrounded by book stacks, with seats hidden beyond in a perimeter reading area alongside the narrow slot windows. Lighting, temperature and ambience are consistent throughout the library – irrespective of the proximity in plan or section to the building periphery. Readers have, therefore, no escape from the 'ideal' conditions imposed upon every quarter. There is nowhere to work in sunlight, no space where currents of air pass naturally by and no greenery to view except through narrow windows. The banks of book stacks are bathed in fluorescent light which shines down from the remorseless grid of suspended ceilings. The reader is not conscious of natural light at all – though perimeter carrels are each lit by a tall deeply set window.

The library relies upon air-conditioning whose fans can be heard working tirelessly away from within much of the library. It is a background noise which allows

### Changing environmental strategies in the design of libraries

| Time period | Daylight | Ventilation |
| --- | --- | --- |
| 18th century | Natural light, shallow plan | Natural ventilation, perimeter windows |
| 19th century | Natural light, roof-lit deep plan | Natural ventilation, perimeter and roof cross-ventilation |
| 20th century | Artificial light, deep plan | Air-conditioning and mechanical ventilation |
| 21st century | Natural light, roof-lit, light-shelves | Natural ventilation, mixed-mode with solar chimneys |

conversation to be absorbed within its decibels. From the outside, the library is forbidding in its deep purple-brown brick box with 'ill-proportioned rows of little windows' (Cherry and Pevsner, 1989). A bridge at first floor level identifies the point of entrance, which is otherwise understated as both an external and internal spectacle. The library is cruelly described as 'extremely ugly' in the *Buildings of England: Devon* series (Cherry and Pevsner, 1989) — a description whose roots can be attributed to the decision to employ air-conditioning. Certainly, air-conditioning allowed the deep plan, shallow height, windowless configuration to come into being. The library at Exeter University is a warning against relying upon excessive engineering to temper the interior environment. The high theoretical level of flexibility provided by air-conditioning has been at the price of comfort and stimulation for readers and staff.

The problem with the air-conditioned library is not so much the energy consumption involved, the high maintenance costs or the inherent inflexibility of highly engineered structures, but the unresponsiveness of the resulting environment. Staff and readers are subject to stuffy windowless interiors and, where glazing occurs, it cannot be opened to let in external fresh air. No matter what the weather outside, the air-conditioned library is always at a fixed temperature and humidity. The regularity of such an environment may be good for books, journals, special collections and IT equipment, but it does not match human expectations so well. People require vitality and sparkle in their library, a place perhaps to read a book in full sunlight with an opening window nearby. The challenge for the library designer is how to balance the optimum conditions for the collection with those of users and staff.

In hot climates, air-conditioning is often unavoidable but libraries can incorporate external shading to reduce energy loads. Phoenix Public Library designed by Will Bruder. (Andrew North)

Façade shading at the University of Hertfordshire Library. Designed by Architects Co. Partnership. (Pippa Summers)

## Pollution from books

Books are often a source of pollution: they bring dirt, germs and mites into the library as a result of use and especially as a result of loan. Books and to a lesser extent journals require periodic cleaning. In tropical regions book contamination leads to mildew attack, especially where humid conditions occur. Mildew leads to permanent staining of the pages of the book and provides the conditions for mite attack. As a result there is greater pressure to air-condition libraries in tropical and sub-tropical countries than elsewhere. Commonly, however, library architects do not air-condition the whole space but zone the interior into air-conditioned areas and naturally lit, ventilated ones. This allows the benefit of both mechanical and natural ventilation to be combined — providing a mixed-mode building which has vitality and variety of environmental experience, e.g. the National Library of Sri Lanka designed by Michael Brawne. Here the books and journals are stored in the centre of an air-conditioned room, with the readers positioned in naturally lit and ventilated areas around the library perimeter. It is a pattern adopted too by Ken Yeang

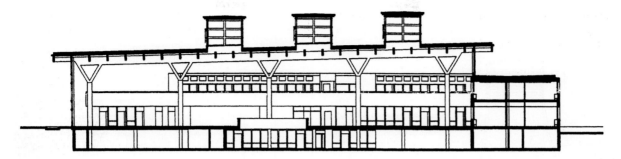

The roof lights above the reading room at Linkoping Library, Sweden, designed by Nyrens Arkitektkontor animate the space whilst proving excellent environmental conditions for library users and staff. (Nyrens Arkitektkontor/AR)

in the new national library of Singapore developed in collaboration with the building systems expert Professor Khee Poh Lam.

## Acoustic zoning of the library

Old libraries were silent places; new ones ring to the sounds of chatter, opening program melodies, mobile

Noise is an accepted part of the entrance areas of libraries.

phone tunes and keyboard tapping. Nothing signifies the changes libraries have undergone in a generation more than the attitude to noise. Some libraries make a virtue of background noise, believing that it is an inevitable expression of the life and productivity of the post-modern library. Others cling to the notion of silent areas where the spoken word is prohibited in pursuit of concentration, at least in parts of the building.

The emphasis today is to have a gradation from silent to noisier areas. The role of architectural design is to help, through the distribution of walls and layout of floors, to reinforce the mangement's policy on noise. It is better to establish through design the different noise zones than to rely upon signage or the nagging of library staff. Commonly the lower floors permit the use of the spoken word and dialogue around computers. Similarly, the centres of libraries are normally noisier than the perimeter where the study desks are located. Between these conditions a number of noise level bands normally exist in larger libraries with the position of book stacks and location of information desks providing definition of the various acoustic zones.

One problem commonly encountered is that of noise travelling vertically through the library in the atria spaces which are increasingly employed for energy efficiency. Where double and triple height reading rooms are provided the architect must employ secondary walls, screens

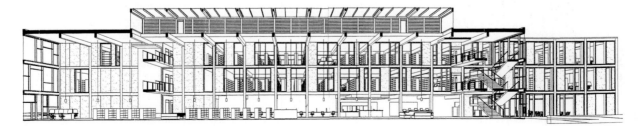

The mass of the concrete frame and high levels of glazing provide good thermal and acoustic conditions for this library at the Open University designed by Swanke Hayden Connell Architects. (Swanke Hayden Connell)

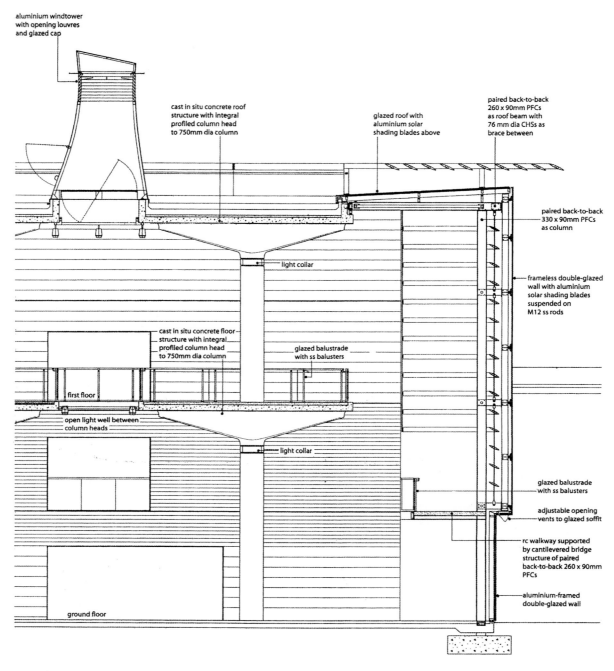

aluminium windtower
with opening louvres
and glazed cap

cast in situ concrete roof
structure with integral
profiled column head
to 750mm dia column

glazed roof with
aluminium solar
shading blades above

paired back-to-back
260 x 90mm PFCs
as roof beam with
76 mm dia CHSs as
brace between

paired back-to-back
330 x 90mm PFCs
as column

light collar

frameless double-glazed
wall with aluminium
solar shading blades
suspended on
M12 ss rods

cast in situ concrete floor
structure with integral
profiled column head
to 750mm dia column

glazed balustrade
with ss balusters

first floor

open light well between
column heads

light collar

glazed balustrade
with ss balusters

adjustable opening
vents to glazed soffit

rc walkway supported
by cantilevered bridge
structure of paired
back-to-back 260 x 90mm
PFCs

aluminium-framed
double-glazed wall

ground floor

Section of Brighton Public Library showing the key environmental features. The design successfully integrates a number of concerns from solar control to natural ventilation. (Bennetts Associates)

or acoustic baffles to prevent the working environment from becoming unusable. As a rule of thumb, university libraries are more accepting of background noise than public libraries. But here there will be designated silent areas for individual study and silence is normally expected in research and professional libraries. However, the growth of group working by students in libraries means that certain floors are allocated for this noisier type of

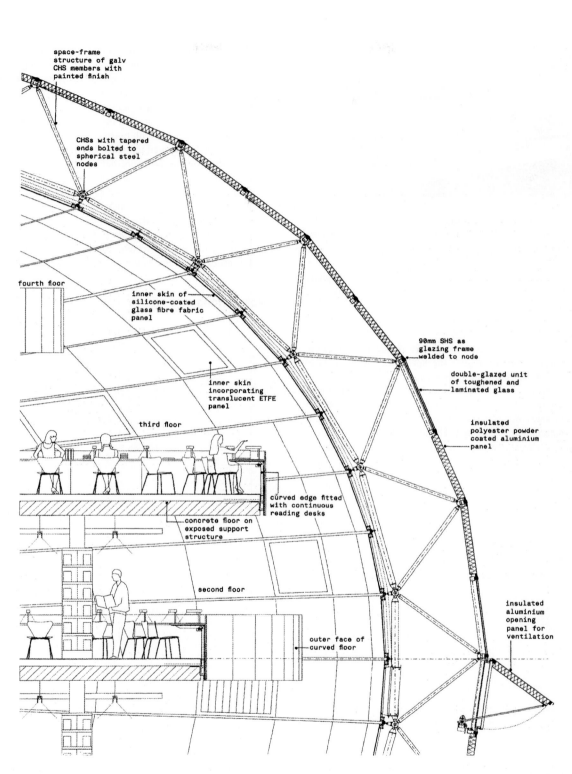

space-frame
structure of galv
CHS members with
painted finish

CHSs with tapered
ends bolted to
spherical steel
nodes

fourth floor

inner skin of
silicone-coated
glass fibre fabric
panel

90mm SHS as
glazing frame
welded to node

double-glazed unit
of toughened and
laminated glass

inner skin
incorporating
translucent ETFE
panel

third floor

insulated
polyester powder
coated aluminium
panel

curved edge fitted
with continuous
reading desks

concrete floor on
exposed support
structure

second floor

outer face of
curved floor

insulated
aluminium
opening
panel for
ventilation

Section through façade of the library at the Free University of Berlin, designed by Foster and Partners, showing the use of a double skin to deliver energy efficiency. By maximizing natural light and cross-ventilation, the library achieves good environmental standards. (Foster and Partners/AJ)

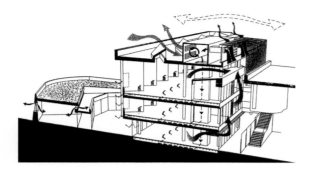

Natural ventilation strategy at Portsmouth University Library to designs by Penoye and Prasad. (Penoye and Prasad/AT)

activity, especially as it normally entails the use of study material which is frequently multimedia in nature. The integration of paper and electronic media occurs also in public libraries and here there is increasing tolerance of noise by librarians. Generally speaking the larger the library space, the more acceptable is background noise but, conversely, the bigger the space the harder it is to design out unacceptable noises.

The growing use of laptops and the expansion of mobile phones into the realm of education for many younger library users means that the architect must consider noise at the planning strategy stage. The aim is to isolate the areas which generate the most noise (staff rooms, photocopy points, control desks, group study or meeting rooms) through space planning. This is necessary in both plan and cross-section, since many disruptive noises have the habit of travelling diagonally through the building.

Acoustic disruption also occurs around lifts, escalators and stairs. Fire protection will normally require these to be enclosed and this helps with noise control. However, when open stairs are employed the noise from foot traffic can be considerable unless soft finishes are employed. Using carpeting or cork floors and book stacks which include acoustic insulation can help achieve a background noise level of 40 decibels, even in open-plan libraries. However, in many city-centre libraries the main noise source is external and here double or triple glazing may be required. Ultimately, the library which serves needs by using the minimum of resources, is the most sustainable over time.

## References

Cherry, B. and Pevsner, N. (1989). *The Buildings of England: Devon*, 2nd edn. Penguin, p. 406.

Department of the Environment, Transport and the Regions (DETR) (1999). *Sustainable Construction: Opportunities for Change*, HMSO, p. 7.

Long, M. J. (1995). University of Brighton library: the development of a building type. In *Building Libraries for the Information Age* (S. Taylor, ed.). Proceedings of a symposium held in York, 11–12 April 1994. Institute of Advanced Architectural Studies (IAAS). p. 72.

# 7

# Refurbishment

Due to their longevity as a building type, libraries are subject to much stress to keep themselves up to date. New media and organizational demands require changes to the use of space and to the building fabric. Alteration to a library is always a challenge and is resisted by two significant forces: the structure itself and the critical mass of the existing collection and the staff that service it. Managers, if they wish to implement effective change, need to address both sides of the equation with fortitude.

Planning and adroit financial forecasting are essential to smooth renovation. Plans are needed to co-ordinate space usage and physical change needed to overcome obsolescence. Unlike the design of a new facility, renovation is often compromised by some unexpected occurrence: hence flexibility of outlook, action and resources is needed.

## Overcoming obsolescence in libraries

Like all types of public buildings libraries are subject to the forces of obsolescence. However, with such a legacy of nineteenth and early to mid-twentieth century libraries, the problem is particularly acute into the twenty-first century. University libraries too are subject to the same forces of obsolescence though here the pressures are slightly different.

The five main types of obsolescence are listed below.

### Functional obsolescence

Here the building fails to perform its duties as a library. With changing expectations in both public and academic libraries, functional inadequacies are one of the main justifications for either the demolition of existing buildings or their extensive remodelling. Sometimes new functions can be accommodated, such as WiFi installation, but often new ambitions for the wider social use of libraries are hard to accommodate.

### Structural obsolescence

Here the limitations imposed by the existing structure and fabric of the building cannot be readily overcome. This may relate to the structural capacity of floors, to the distribution and quality of daylight and ventilation (a problem exacerbated by the growing use of computers in libraries), or to the position of loading-bearing walls. Structural change is both expensive and disruptive to the running of the library.

### Social obsolescence

New expectations regarding the role of public buildings generally, and libraries in particular, have stressed many existing library facilities. Libraries often do not provide the architectural qualities and character required of today's consumers who have been raised in the glitter of retail malls and the architectural glamour of buildings like Tate Modern. To many, older libraries are not buildings that they find attractive or intellectually engaging. The values carried in the design of existing libraries simply fail to connect with the cultural values of the twenty-first century.

### Locational obsolescence

Here libraries are simply in the wrong place or located where access is difficult. The library may not be well connected to the existing web of local facilities or those on campus. There may have been changes in the provision of the civic functions, transport infrastructure or commercial activities, which have resulted in the library being out on a limb. There may have been growth in traffic that has resulted in poor public access or excessive interior noise. On campus, new academic units may have pulled the centre of gravity away from the library.

### Environmental obsolescence

This is a growing problem as society comes to terms with the concept of sustainable development and particularly global warming. The carbon footprint (the amount of energy consumed) is often large in libraries especially those built in the 1960s and 70s. Such libraries are generally poorly insulated, have problems with solar gain (leading to the use of air-conditioning units), and provide poor conditions for reading or working on computer screens inside the building. With rising energy prices and

Libraries are often designed as civic or campus landmarks and are not therefore easy to extend. Oslo Public Library. (Brian Edwards)

growing environmental legislation, such libraries find themselves increasingly obsolete.

As a result of these pressures, libraries are going through a period of structural alteration to meet new functional requirements and environmental standards, and internal makeovers to improve their image; and where refurbishment is not possible there are extensive programmes for the erection of new buildings. The latter is occurring as a result of both local and central government initiatives, sometimes also triggered by an opportunity for wider urban regeneration. The latter can entail partnership with a large commercial developer such as the 'idea store' in London's Whitechapel, developed in collaboration with the building of a Sainsbury's store. New building should, however, only be employed when the options for refurbishment (perhaps entailing partial extension) have been exhausted.

The pace of change has quickened over the past decade as libraries have had to adapt to the IT revolution. But change is not that erratic in nature: each generation is faced by new technologies, organizational theory or reader preferences. If the 1990s have been subject to the currents of a digital age, this is hardly different to the expansion in leisure time and reading in the 1960s, the use of libraries as employment information and social centres in the 1930s, or to their earlier use as disseminators of mass knowledge through newspapers and journals around 1900. To argue that the modern library is witnessing unprecedented information stress is to misrepresent the path of history. Libraries have always had to adapt to survive: today's pressures are simply the latest in an unfolding pattern of information change.

Given that libraries have always had to adapt to serve changing social needs, there are three aspects to consider in parallel: two are architectural, the third is a question of management. These are:

- space distribution
- cabling and mechanical service distribution
- staff resources (skills and personnel).

Space is clearly pivotal since new functions and services require a redistribution of space. Extra rooms are sometimes required, but often the answer is to use space more effectively. There are three key aspects to consider in the detailed allocation of library space:

- equipment (electronic) and media (electronic and book-based) are getting smaller and more efficient
- people are getting larger and more numerous
- the amount of workspace equipment is growing whilst the workspace volume is declining.

The library, like much of the world, is seeing space used more extensively. There are more people doing more things over a greater period of time, and using tools and equipment that are becoming ever smaller and more efficient. As people become larger and more numerous, they become collectively noisier and more demanding. The library in this sense moves towards greater stress, space syntax pollution (the relationship between the reader's personal space and shared space) and an ever-accelerating pace of change. The task of the librarian and architect is to facilitate the necessary adjustments to allow the library to continue to operate whilst adapting to new expectations.

Change occurs above and below ground – in the rooms and in the peripheral spaces which serve the rooms (suspended ceilings, ducts, raised floors). Every time a change in library technology occurs, there are corresponding adjustments necessary behind the scenes. For every change in the use of space in the library, a myriad of alterations are required – in cable layouts, furniture upgrading, lighting provision, closed circuit television (CCTV surveillance), etc.

Cables provide the lifeblood for a modern library – electricity drives almost every service. It is needed for lighting, ventilation, lifts, hoists, telephones, computers, Internet access and much more. But cables come in different forms, have different requirements and pose different levels of risk. Traditional electronic ring mains (carrying in the UK 220–240 volts) drive much equipment and pose a risk of electromagnetic contamination. Cables and wires disseminate electrical power throughout the library: some are substantial rope-like structures threaded through plastic conduits, others are flat bands serving only computer needs. The trend is towards fibre optic cabling which serves computer, telephone and TV needs concurrently. Fibre optics offer smaller, slimmer and more efficient cabling systems than metal wires. However, as cable space becomes more efficient the gains are offset by demand.

Most modern libraries use a raised floor system that allows for almost unlimited flexibility of cable type and layout. The floor consists of panels that can be easily lifted to permit access to computing networks and traditional electrical supply without major disruption. The worst scenario for a library is to have to shut down all or part of its operations to facilitate change in the use of space (change which should have been anticipated at the design stage). With existing libraries, however, disruption is inevitable but, at each upgrading, it is necessary to build in greater long-term adaptability and not stifle it by inadequate alteration.

Raised floors, circuit ducting and suspended ceilings together provide a flexible arrangement. Lighting, furniture and equipment can all be altered without significant stress to space or building fabric. Cables can sometimes be threaded through internal partitions in order to avoid the use of relatively expensive raised floor systems, but in large libraries cable lengths are such that partition systems are inadequate. Locking cable layouts and partitions into the same system also makes the library inherently inflexible in the use of space. The answer in existing libraries, especially those with high ceilings, is to add a raised floor able to accommodate all services.

Suspended ceilings are also a useful way of maintaining operational adaptability. Air-handling equipment can be placed in the ceiling void, providing a good distribution of ventilation allied with acoustic control and an even spread of artificial lighting. However, the trend is towards more sustainable design practice where greater use of natural light and ventilation is preferred. If left exposed, the floor slab construction can act as a useful thermal buffer and aesthetic device. When articulated into bays of concrete, steel or timber construction, the soffit of the ceiling aids navigational direction to the library. The construction can therefore provide a visual grid to simultaneously accommodate

Hirata Public Library is designed to allow the various subject wings to be adapted or extended without disrupting the whole. Design by Teramoto Architects. (Teramoto Architects)

different book-stack layouts, provide orientation for the reader and moderate day and night-time temperatures. Thus the practice with existing libraries is to use the floor to distribute new cabling and other services rather than the ceiling.

Whichever method is employed, however, it is necessary to balance the requirements of space use in the long term with short-term benefits such as lower cost and tidy aesthetics. Part of the equation involves an assessment of likely technological and environmental change – the agenda of sustainability and IT together make a powerful argument for building into the renovation of libraries the flexibility that was missing at the outset. Here the guidance outlined earlier for the design of new libraries should be used as the basis for upgrading older ones. There are five principles to follow in upgrading and renovating existing libraries:

- Architectural structure is inherently inflexible and makes an important contribution to the character of the library. The basic structure should only be altered or obscured as a last resort.
- Internal space cannot be altered without adjustment to lighting, ventilation, security and fire escape provision.
- Upgrading should move towards greater operational flexibility, not limit choice later.
- Sustainability should influence renovation in the design, construction and use of space.
- It is generally cheaper to adapt than extend, and more cost-effective to adapt than demolish and rebuild. It may also be cheaper to adapt a non-library building (such as a church) into library use than build afresh.

It is sometimes argued that IT cannot be cost-effectively insinuated into existing libraries. This is not the case: new technology can be effectively integrated into library buildings of all ages. There may be a problem when the library is a listed or designated a landmark building – here internal change would be detrimental to the historic appearance or fabric of the building. There may also be a problem when ceiling heights are too low or the ventilation standards demanded by computer suites cannot be met. But these conditions are exceptions – in most nineteenth and twentieth century libraries renovation to accommodate both structural upgrading and the incorporation of new technology is relatively straightforward. Where a need cannot be met by internal adaptation, the answer is to extend to provide the specific quality of space and servicing required in the new wing.

## The problem of the listed library

Libraries which are listed as being of special architectural or historic interest pose particular difficulties. It is incumbent upon all concerned – architects, interior designers, managers – to pressure the character and

A modern wing attached to Putney Public Library to accommodate IT. (Biddy Fisher)

appearance of the building. This entails the original spatial arrangement, the internal and external finishes, and often the furniture and fittings. Listing applies to all of the building and, in libraries, the historic interest is often more extensive on the interior than the exterior.

The 'character' to be preserved is both real and atmospheric. The historic interest of a library resides, partly at least, in ambience. Although the 'feel' of a library is difficult to measure and hence take active steps to preserve, restoration of the building fabric should not destroy this aspect of character.

Historic libraries are put under pressure in various ways. Often change is required to meet new health and safety regulations, to cater for the introduction of new library technology, and to accommodate functional change in the use of parts of the library. Change rarely occurs without alteration to the building fabric and it is how these adaptations are carried out to historic libraries which is of concern here. There are three principles to follow:

- Ensure that wherever possible change is reversible (keep samples of old fittings, furniture and finishes so that reinstatement or replication is possible at a later date).
- Carry out restoration so that it is recognizably of the date of implementation – avoid pastiche of the original. The dialogue between old and new can bring the original into greater focus.
- Understand the qualities of the historic library so that its underlying character can inform the alteration. Here

The Sydney Jones Library at the University of Liverpool is now a listed building. Changing the carrels would greatly alter the historic value of this Basil Spence building designed in 1962. (Brian Edwards)

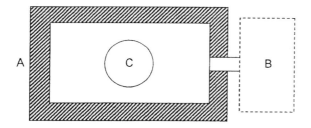

Options for renovation or extension (plan). (Brian Edwards)

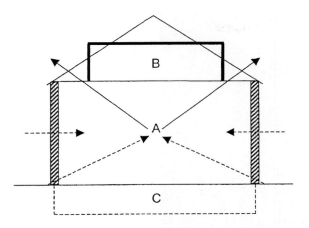

Options for renovation or extension (section). (Brian Edwards)

there may be questions of rhythm, material and effects of light on sequence of spaces which can be reinterpreted in a contemporary fashion.

Often change to historic libraries allows unsuitable alteration from an earlier phase of restoration to be reversed. At the listed Manchester Public Library (designed in 1929 by E Vincent Harris), the entrance hall has been filled with shops and display boards which disfigure or obscure the original arrangement. The flow of progression from street to reading room is impeded by well-meaning architectural additions carried out with indifference to the spatial sequence of the building.

Some would argue that the character of a library is also that of the character of the collection. The books make a historic library and to remove the leather-bound volumes

and replace them with paperbacks is as significant an erosion of character as the destruction of cornices. Unfortunately listing extends only to the fixed elements and to original furniture or fittings – in the UK at least the collection itself is not listed although it may be protected in other ways. However, any architect involved in work on a historic library must take into account the role played by books, paintings and sculpture in the totality of the environment.

Mention was made earlier of the opportunity provided by restoration for revealing the historic features of a library in new ways. Conservation is a question of preservation on the one hand and creative adaptation on the other. Few projects fail to provide a chance to establish a fruitful dialogue between past and present. Skilful restoration allows the past to be brought into clearer focus by its contrast with the materiality of the contemporary world. This debate in stone or steel mirrors the debate between books and electronic library media. A library, even if listed, is not a museum of books but a living building. Restoration provides the means to ensure that the historic building is in touch with the past and the present.

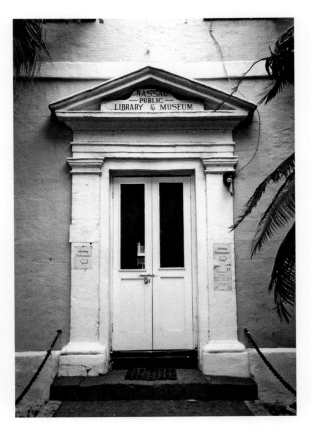

The colonial entrance to Nassau Public Library and Museum. (Biddy Fisher)

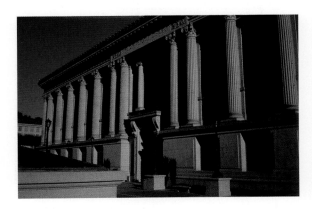

Doe Library, University of California, Berkeley, is both a campus landmark and a state monument. Designed in 1911 by John G Howard. (Brian Edwards)

View of entrance to Arts and Humanities Library, University of Melbourne. (Biddy Fisher)

The restoration of historic libraries should entail the minimum of destruction to original features. Library, Columbia University, designed in 1892 by McKim, Mead and White. (Columbia University)

## Small-scale conservation measures

Besides large-scale adaptation to historic libraries, there is also periodic restoration or repair to consider. Listed library buildings are likely to be fairly old structures and hence require specialized attention from time to time. As with major alteration, there are three principles which should guide detailed conservation works:

• minimum effective restoration is preferable to comprehensive fabric renewal
• record the work both before action is undertaken and during the contract
• ensure that the restoration or repair does not prejudice future action. Aim wherever possible for reversibility.

As with larger action, work on historic libraries should seek to convey the importance of cultural property. Restoration or use adaptation should communicate the value and meaning attached to such buildings. Restoration should not be penny-pinching, implying say in the use of plastic laminate as opposed to hardwood that old libraries do not matter. The materials of conservation, the skills of craftspeople and of specialized conservation architects or designers should all be placed ahead of consideration of cost. Historic buildings demand greater resources and effort than ordinary buildings and work on them should ensure that the key values attached to cultural property – emotional, cultural and use – are preserved (Feilden, 1982). This argument applies with particular force as libraries are one of the most public

The new wing at the National Library of Norway wraps around an atrium which now houses a cafe and reading area. The phased growth of libraries should encourage the creation of new social or exhibition spaces between the book repositories. Overcoming obsolescence often involves taking imaginative steps forward. (Brian Edwards)

forms of cultural property accessible equally inside and out.

## Putney library – an exercise in refurbishment of a listed library

The public library in Putney is an example of the extension, conversion and refurbishment of a listed library in operation. The 1999 extension retains internal features including a Victorian oak-beamed roof with centre arches and panelling, which formed part of the building's listed status. The library is situated in a residential street, adjacent to the high street of this London suburb. It stands in close proximity to railway and underground stations and bus stops. The library is a busy hub, admitting 2,000 users per day, many of whom arrive by public transport.

The entrance, placed in the modern section, is approached via a ramp and stair. The elevated entrance, which is reached via a revolving door, leads to a desk that

The Green Library, Stanford University, by Bakewell and Brown (1919), where the urban setting of this historic library has been re-established by recent campus upgrading. (Brian Edwards)

serves as a referral point for the users as well as the return and issuing counter. At this point, the ceiling is low with an expanding view beyond to other areas including the audio library and the main enquiry desk. These important visual keys allow the user to locate the main library functions easily.

The exterior is built of Portland stone and the large circular window at the front of the building is tinted blue. Internal decoration has been chosen to complement external materials. Walls are white and doors are beech or opaque glass. Door and window furniture is aluminium. The lighting has been meticulously designed in all points of the building. It is unobtrusive and uses modern fitments and features. Library staff are complimentary about the adequacy in work areas, while users find all areas of stock and work areas lit to precisely correct levels.

Linking corridor and reading area at Sydney Jones Library. (Peter Durant)

This building is successful from the point of view of both users and staff. Beyond the entrance foyer the full height of the building is unrestricted, giving a sense of space and orientation. The enquiry desk, adult fiction and non-fiction book stock, public access PCs and photo-copying facilities are found in close proximity to staff offices, which are accessed directly from this area. Also adjacent are the book and people lifts, the audio stock and the listening areas. Close proximity provides convenience but the library does not feel cramped.

The bookshelves are low and easily reached by those in wheelchairs. The attention to accessibility is apparent in the design of the building as well as the bookshelves and desks. There is an easy flow within the building from books to facilities, staff to services. It has architectural points of interest and the relationship between old and new features is handled with great effect.

The children's area at Putney Library is on the first floor with a separate children's cloakroom and washroom nearby. The round bay window overlooking the street provides a pleasant environment for the working area of the library. It is complemented by a row of individual desks, equipped with PCs.

The second floor houses a separate adult study room. Individual desks are provided, some of which are equipped with PCs, including two 'iMacs'. Printing facilities and an enquiry desk are part of this heavily used facility on the upper floor. Sunlight is controlled by external screens and temperature is moderated by a cooling system. Also on the upper floor is a high security area, with individual temperature control for the 'Aubrey Collection' of children's books. This area is purely for preservation of books and is not publicly accessible.

The older Victorian building, which was constructed in 1899, provides the staff with a rest area that echoes the layout of a home. It uses space previously occupied by the 'librarian's flat'. The architect has designed a kitchen that contains the original Victorian fireplace and incorporates a seating area within a feature bay window. The building already benefited from the presence of an undercroft, which has been employed for book storage using compact shelving. Adjacent rooms provide a workspace for processing new acquisitions and mending stock. The new library wing benefits from the storage space provided in the Victorian building as well as its architectural features. The spacious panelled corridor that was the entrance to the previous library is now used as an exhibition space. The original Victorian meeting room, adjacent to the entrance foyer, offers a public space that can be used by local organizations. Old and new accommodation complement each other, providing this unique library with a distinctive character. Skilful adaptation of a splendid Victorian building has allowed Putney Library to become the rejuvenated heart of a thriving suburb.

## Ballieu Arts and Humanities Library, University of Melbourne

The refurbishment of Ballieu Library, by architects John F D Scarborough and Partners (the practice which designed the original building in the 1950s), required the retention of the fifties style and features whilst accommodating the technology of the twenty-first century. Users approach the library entrance from the leafy aspect of the campus quadrangle. They meet a new curtain wall reflecting the eastern aspect of the building in which is positioned an entrance lobby that contains references to the building's past with memorial plaques. The lobby space has been retiled and redecorated and now contains vending machines, information boards and telephones. On entry to the building, the immediate concerns of users are dealt with by a hub of service points. Orientation points are provided throughout the building and navigation is reinforced by the choice of different colours of wood and leather furniture. Scandinavian influences are present in furniture, staircases and in the half-glazed and timber partitions – providing a link between the present and original phase of the library's development.

The Ballieu Library is the preferred choice of undergraduates studying arts and humanities at the university. It is the busiest of the campus libraries, with a collection of services points immediately upon entry. The main lending desk, a reserve collection, workstations, on-line public access catalogue (OPAC) terminals and return chutes are all in this area, providing a market place of activity. The round pillars of black marble or maroon paintwork offer islands for information points and help orientate busy students immediately upon entry. In contrast, the reading rooms are carpeted and quiet oases. Generally, with low ceilings readers have the choice of individual desks or larger work tables. There is a single, large, high reading area immediately behind the curtain wall at ground level that overlooks the trees and landscaped area, giving the space the impression of being alongside a forest.

Users access the main reading areas via a central spiral staircase. This is encased in wood and glass using a pattern echoed throughout the building. New technology has been integrated by placing terminals at desks arranged in 'buddy' clusters. Up to 10 PCs can be accommodated in angled (open hexagonal) groups. Book and journal stock surround the buddy areas. Lighting is always suited to the purpose, either above reading areas, at the end of stacks, or diffused around the computer terminals.

The refurbishment of this major university library (the sixth upgrading in 50 years) coincides with changes in the management philosophy. Grey and unexciting furniture and fittings have been replaced in order to signal the introduction of new methods of information retrieval. The changing nature of the librarian's work is exemplified in

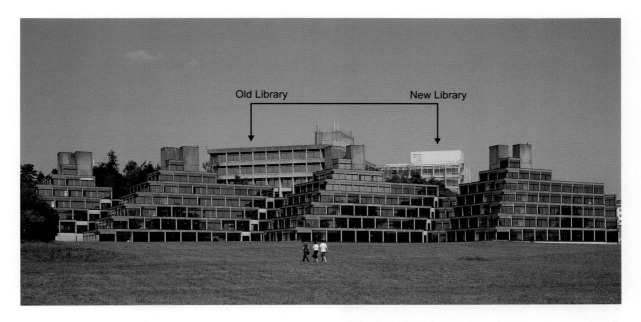

Old Library          New Library

Showing the relationship between the two phases at UEA. (Shepheard Epstein Hunter)

fresh room layouts, furniture and information systems. Users need librarians where the information sources are located, especially those using the Internet. Librarians have been relocated with their collections; this includes the on-line terminals and Internet access PCs. By placing traditional sources and electronic systems together, IT is effectively integrated in the minds of users. The restructuring of space has had to coincide with the reordering of staff timetables, offices and security systems. This, the sixth refurbishment of the Ballieu Library in less than 50 years, shows the necessity of creating adaptable libraries at the outset.

## Two examples of extended university libraries: University of East Anglia and University of Liverpool

Although this book is been mainly concerned with new academic libraries, in practice architects are more often engaged in extending or altering existing university libraries. These two examples, both designed by Shepheard Epstein Hunter, involve major extensions to university libraries designed by significant British architects of a generation earlier. The first is the extension to the library at the University of East Anglia designed by Denis Lasdun. The original library built in 1968 is now listed and the architects for the extension had the responsibility of respecting the building's architectural character. Lasdun's library sat as a promontory at the end of a 'teaching wall' and it is this promontory which has been extended.

Lasdun's six-storey library was entered from a raised walkway on the third floor. The new library follows this arrangement but turns the building through a right angle as Lasdun himself had proposed in the initial campus master plan. The new wing follows the basic proportions and scale of the original building though in lighter and more environmentally-friendly materials. Whereas Lasdun used heavy pre-cast concrete construction and a repeating rhythm of vertical concrete fins for solar control, the extensions by Shepheard Epstein Hunter employ a steel frame, gluelam fins and timber boarded finishes. The effect is to humanize the building on the outside, to establish clarity between the different phases of the construction of the library, and to address the climatic shortcomings of the 1960s building. However, this is achieved without any sense of disrespecting the proportions or ambitions of Lasdun's initial conception.

A glazed link forms the join between the extension and the original library. An earlier scheme by the architects to enclose the Lasdun library in a glass box, where it would become essentially a book deposit surrounded by 6 m deep light and airy reading rooms, was abandoned when the building was listed. Similarly, plans to extend upwards proved prohibitive both aesthetically and financially. After exploring options the relatively simple right angle extension was built. It forms part of a larger scheme for phased additions to be built as money becomes available. As such the six-bay wing as built establishes a language and footprint for subsequent expansion.

Construction of a floor at a time allowed parts of the existing library to be refurbished as books were decanted to

Extension by Shepheard Epstein Hunter to listed library by Denis Lasdun. The proportions have been respected whilst steel and timber have replaced Lasdun's concrete structure. (Shepheard Epstein Hunter)

the new wing. The double height IT centre which occupies the central two floors of the new wing is sandwiched between book-stack floors and reader carrels above and below. For obvious reasons, the IT suite is located in the new wing rather than adapt the Lasdun library for this purpose.

A similar set of problems was faced by the University of Liverpool at the Sydney Jones Library. The original library, this time designed in 1972 by Basil Spence, had proved inadequate for an expanding university and one where centralized IT was seen as inadequate. The solution again involved building an extension whilst also releasing space for internal refurbishment and alteration. Shepheard,

Epstein and Hunter were again the architects and followed a similar strategy of respecting the spirit of the earlier building whilst addressing both space and IT shortcomings in the provision of new facilities.

The new £12 m building doubles the size of the Sydney Jones Library (the university's Arts and Humanities library) and acts as link between the old library and the Senate House. Within its four storeys, the wing contains new multimedia facilities grouped around a central atrium. The atrium acts as gateway to the library both physically and in terms of the information services provided. An adjacent cafe provides a welcome counterpoint to the general scholarly atmosphere. As a member of the Russell Group of UK research-orientated universities, the quality of the library is seen as essential to winning funding and attracting students.

The new library exploits the challenge of energy efficiency in the attention paid to natural light and the use of stack effect ventilation. The atrium provides a useful environmental service by assisting with cross-ventilation in an area where intensive computer use can pose a problem. Intelligent façades also provide high levels of light at perimeter reader desks but without the fossil fuel disadvantages of the older building.

As a building, the Sydney Jones Library acts as a centre to the campus, which revolves around the Georgian Abercrombie Square. A new library piazza forms an annex to the square overlooked by the raised library cafe. Heights of the various buildings have been carefully controlled and set at four storeys to reflect the classical tradition in Liverpool (see pages xx–xx). Although the Spence library is not listed (unlike at UEA) the whole sits within a conservation area where attention to urban design was paramount. As the university librarian notes 'the whole building exudes a sense of light, spaciousness, possibility and optimism … a place (quoting Disraeli) of light, liberty and learning' (Sykes).

## Reference

Feilden, B. M. (1982). *Conservation of Historic Buildings.* Architectural Press, p. 6.

# 8

# Furniture, shelving and storage

Except in the most prestigious library, furniture is normally specified from manufacturers' catalogues rather than being designed specially for the building. Architects merely select shelving, desks and tables from what is offered by library furniture manufacturers. The choice, however, is by no means limited or the products available of inferior quality. The main problem which arises is not what is selected but who does the selecting. Often it is the chief librarian or project team which makes the choice of furniture and fittings. It is vital that the architect is involved in guiding the team in making the selection. This will ensure compatibility in terms of architectural structure and furniture layout, dimensional correspondence between book-shelving and partitions or tiling patterns, and the avoidance of conflicts of colour, style or material.

Where the architect or interior designer is responsible for both the building design and the furniture design there will be harmony in the total environment (e.g. Malmo Public Library by Henning Larson). Sometimes the designs prepared by architects are adopted by specialist library furniture manufacturers and made more widely available. This has occurred with designs prepared by Sir Norman Foster and Partners, but it is the exception. Usually, there is little professional service continuity between building and furniture design: the task is either undertaken by nominated designers or catalogues are scanned and appropriate choices made.

The principal library furniture and shelving manufacturers in the UK are British Thornton ESF Ltd and Gresswell. Folio provides a specialist shelving service adapted to many subject needs and Specialist Storage Systems provide a range of mobile or fixed shelving for abnormally sized materials (newspapers, plans). LFC provides a total package from book and journal storage to open shelving, while Ecospace specializes in compact mobile storage systems and a company called Preservation Equipment Ltd (PEL) provides equipment specially designed for conservation storage. These and other manufacturers provide a comprehensive service; library designers should be aware of their products before space is allocated to shelving or storage.

The main types of library furniture provided include:

- shelving (open and closed)
- mobile compact storage
- counter systems
- display shelving or boards
- general library furniture
- special furniture for children
- furniture for IT equipment
- map and plan chests
- photographic storage
- book trolleys
- specialist concentration furniture or storage
- security storage.

Not all manufacturers provide a comprehensive service and, for special library needs, it is better to use specialist manufacturers than adopt a standard fitting. Although storage for rare books or fragile photographs is expensive, the safe storage of the collection is paramount.

Foreg 2000 open shelving used at Wye College Library, Kent. (Forster Ecospace)

101

Open access mobile shelving at Wye College Library, Kent. (Forster Ecospace)

## Dimensional co-ordination

It is important that in their room layouts architects follow the dimensions commonly adopted by shelving manufacturers. These vary but are all based upon repeating modules in height, width and depth. Typical is the library shelving system manufactured by British Thornton ESF Ltd where the shelves are available in 700 mm, 800 mm and 900 mm lengths, there is a consistent depth of 260 mm and heights vary from 1200 mm to 2000 mm; using the same combination of elements, bookshelves can be single or double-sided and starter or extension bays. Dimensional co-ordination keeps costs down, makes erection and installation relatively simple, and provides a visually unified library environment. The basic shelving assembly is commonly available with integral lighting, a base and stabilizing top unit, and is offered in a variety of colours or laminated finishes (ash, oak, beech, etc.).

Other shelving assemblies are available for items such as CDs or cassettes and for special needs such as a children's library or display. These frequently integrate dimensionally and visually with the basic library shelving assemblies. It is better to avoid competing systems in the same library except where they can be accommodated in separate areas and where their use is justified because of a specified need (plan or newspaper storage). Normally library shelving is fixed and can only be moved by dismantling the assembly. Commonly, however, some lengths of library shelving are mobile in order to provide flexibility of layout, particularly around information points or near the library entrance. Here units of shelves are placed on concealed castors, which have a locking device for safety purposes.

Study carrels are also available in standard lengths, widths and finishes. As with shelving, they are manufactured to allow for single or double-sided assembly, and many come with optional extra such as shelves, cable access and a position for a computer or study lamp. Most are 800–900 mm wide, 1300 mm high and 750–800 mm deep, creating a double sided carrel unit 1600 mm across. Where computers are integrated, the width extends to 1000 mm and the depth should be at least 800 mm to provide space for the keyboard.

Compact mobile storage at Cambridge University Library. Note the perforations for ventilation. (Forster Ecospace)

Compact specialist storage at Thames and Hudson. Note the variety of types of storage within the shelving system. (Forster Ecospace)

## Special storage

Most larger libraries will need facilities for storing newspapers, plans, archival documents and perhaps extensive runs of journals. It is normal to provide storage floors for this material, which is brought to the reader by library staff.

Basement or sub-floor storage is common in all but smaller libraries. Specialist manufacturers provide a range of compact, mobile storage systems normally based on a fireproof construction (steel or aluminium). Such systems require heavy-duty performance and are either manually or electrically driven. Compact mobile storage is highly

Children's library furniture manufactured by LFC. (LFC)

efficient in terms of space but is expensive to install, maintain and operate. The system adopted for a particular library is usually tailored to customer needs but as with library shelving, there are common sizes of units, widths and heights. Mobile storage employs a rail system with guide wheels, gearing (to allow for manual moving of shelving units) and safety measures (to prevent trapping of users or library staff). With a system of compact mobile shelving manufactured by a company such as Ecospace, facilities exist for storing books, journals, newspapers, magnetic tapes, CD-ROMs and box files.

Deep-shelf storage systems are also available in the form of plan or map chests. Normally these use drawers 900 mm by 1250 mm and 100 mm deep fitted with telescopic runners. Although traditionally constructed of timber, modern plan chests are made of steel for security purposes. The units may be perforated to provide ventilation in situations where drawings could suffer from mildew attack. Where plan and map storage is provided, it is important that large tables are positioned nearby to avoid damage when the material is unfolded or referred to. Sharp edges or gaps between tables can lead to tears or damage to plans and drawings. Study tables should normally be large, have bull-nosed edgings and be capable of being cleaned with chemical-free products to avoid possible damage to fragile drawings. Such details are commonly overlooked by architects who frequently lack the knowledge of specialist library furniture manufacturers.

With special storage, the imposed weight on the floor can be considerable. Loading can be as high as 160 kg/m length as opposed to 75 kg/m length for a typical library shelving. For this reason, compact storage is normally placed on basement floors where other advantages such as ease of environmental control also exist.

For security reasons, compact storage is often locked using either steel cages, steel doors or sliding access panels activated by a password. Security is needed to cope with the three main threats of fire, dust and unauthorized access. Much archival material such as historic photographs, plans or drawings is vulnerable to damage from moisture, dust or natural light. Here security storage has to balance possible theft against more insidious attack from, say, dust mites. To protect against fire damage, secure storage is needed not only to preserve the contents from heat but from water staining. The most valuable books and papers are normally stored in lockable sheet steel cabinets, which can resist both fire and water damage.

With both general library storage and archival storage, it is necessary for the options agreed between library staff and the architect to be discussed with specialist library furniture manufacturers before the system is adopted. Room layouts should not be prepared without early dialogue with the companies that will ultimately be supplying the shelving, furniture or storage facilities. The impacts to consider are not only the normal concerns of room dimensions, column, window and door positions but also floor loadings and environmental control. Although specialist suppliers are normally brought in late in the procurement process, there are many advantages to be gained from earlier involvement. Pre-contract discussion can not only save money in the long term but can also lead to economies in space or equipment at the outset. This is particularly true where archive or special collections make up the library collection.

Adjustable library shelving manufactured by British Thornton. (British Thornton)

## WORKSTATIONS

combination to create four position
workstations

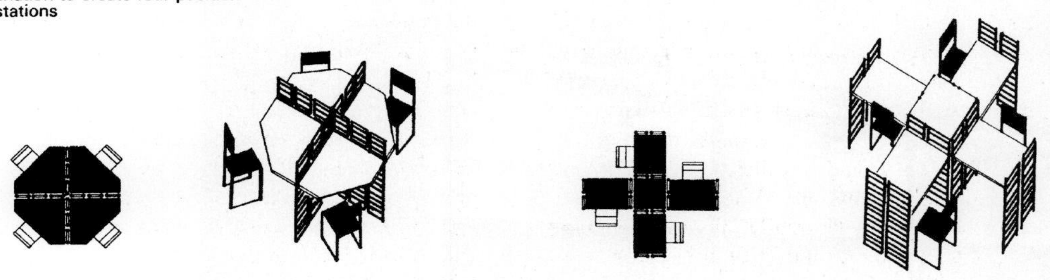

workstations or opacs with shelves,
lighting and divider boards

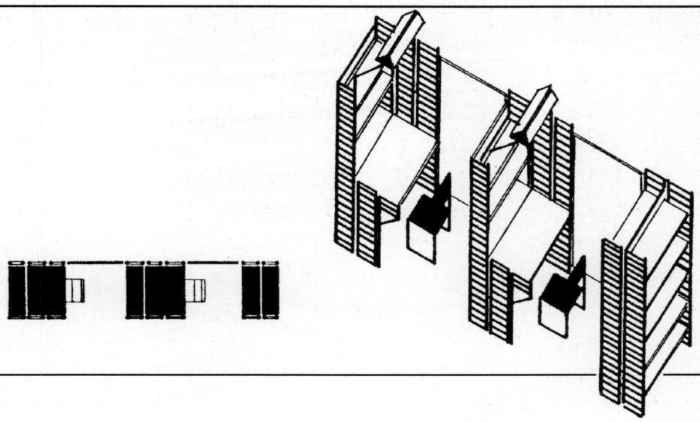

combining angled carrels

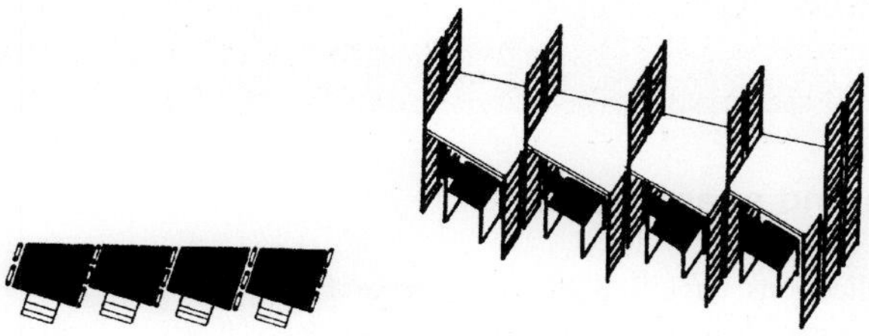

combining angled carrels

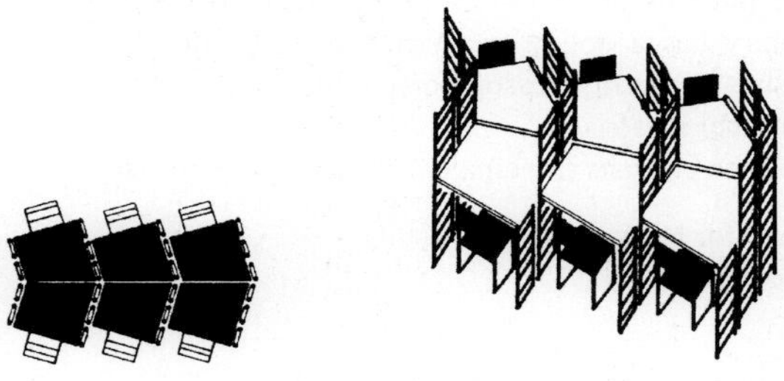

Workstations and study carrels manufactured by Borgeaud *Bibliothéques* Enem. (Borgeaud Bibliothéques Enem)

Plan, magazine and archive storage manufactured by Forster Ecospace. (Forster Ecospace)

## Shelving and space needs

Library collections have a habit of growing faster than anticipated. Growth is by no means regular or even; it is often erratic and sometimes exponential. Few collection policies allow for items to be discarded at the same rate as new books, journals and CD-ROMs are acquired. Even when a library has a policy to restrict the collection to a specific size, in reality reasons are normally found to accept additional material.

Library space consists principally of three components:

- stack space for books
- reader space
- staff space.

All three need to be planned effectively with checks and balances to avoid staff accommodation growing at the expense of bookshelving areas or reader seats. Normally, the size of the collection grows faster than the needs of staff space or reader space. Expansion in the library stock is generally the critical factor in accommodating growth. As mentioned earlier, growth in stock is often met by

outhousing rarely used material in a book warehouse at some distance from the library (e.g. the National Library of Scotland). Commonly, however, the shelves themselves are extended to meet the storage of the additional books either by cramming (e.g. the National Library, Cape Town, South Africa) or by the construction of new accommodation.

To plan effectively, it is important to understand the space needs of books, journals and IT. Most libraries have a policy of open-shelf storage for the bulk of the collection. Shelf length and density of occupation by bookshelves and of books themselves on shelves is critical. Normally, a library plans to have 80–90% of its total stock on open shelves. The collection not on shelves is either on loan, in use elsewhere in the building, or held in the reference rooms.

For calculation purposes, it is normally assumed that six volumes occupy a linear foot of shelves or 20 volumes per metre. If the bookshelves are arranged vertically spaced at between 200–300 m (8–12 inches), this means that about 80 books can be stored in every 1 $m^2$ of open shelving. If the shelving bays are 2 m high, this allows for around

Special storage for the Bodleian Library's collection of historic books. (Forster Ecospace)

150–160 books per linear metre of shelving. Hence, with a collection of 300,000 volumes, a typical library would require 2000 m of shelving. But the collection is often not that simple. A typical volume varies according to whether it is a book, atlas, bound journal, thesis or videotape. Books also vary in size according to discipline (art books are typically larger than social science books), to the time when printed (nineteenth century books tend to be larger than twentieth century ones) and the country of origin. It is thus important to decide upon typical volume sizes for the nature of the collection and also the likely rate of borrowing. Poor planning is evidenced by too many books competing for shelf space, and by additional shelves being constructed in circulation areas, across windows or directly beneath light fittings. The use of a space data record recommended by Wells and Young (Wells and Young, 1997) provides a formula for calculating the space required for specific types of libraries.

As a rule of thumb one can assume that with small, mainly paperback books that 200 volumes can be accommodated per square metre of shelving (6–8 shelves high), typical hardbacks around 150, and large reference material about 100. Allowing for room between the shelves for disabled access, this results typically in around 120–150 volumes per $m^2$ of library space (excluding staff areas and general circulation space). Thus a library with a collection of 300,000 volumes would require at least 2000 $m^2$ of floor area for the open-shelf book collection. Formulas for capacity are, however, dangerous and although general guides are useful at the initial planning or costing stage, none is entirely satisfactory (Metcalf, 1986, p. 154).

In the USA, libraries grow at around 3% per year (Metcalf, 1986, p. 155) with well-established libraries expanding generally at a slower rate than newer ones (at Harvard University the annual growth rate is 2%). In academic libraries, one assumes between 50–80 books (or equivalent) per student with a faculty or college library housing at least 40,000 volumes, and a main university one of 1,000,000 volumes. Typically, a large town library will house 500,000 volumes, a branch library maybe as few as 5,000, whilst a national library for a western country may have a total stock of 5–10 million volumes. Some specialist libraries may have a limited stock of books but an extensive collection of letters, notebooks and other archival material. These figures are an indication that space and shelf length are not uniform across types of library and that growth, though it has to be accommodated, is by no means even over time. Librarians and designers need to consider strategies for expansion shaped by the particular needs of the collection, the political or institutional framework in which they operate, and the changing technology of the printed and electronic word. In addition, librarians will have extensive data on which to base growth strategies based upon the needs of particular subject areas and budget constraints.

The spacing and design of bookshelves varies according to location, type of reader and nature of the collection. Bookshelving in reading areas tends to be of larger scale, better design and more widely spaced than in other library areas. The shelves in and forming the perimeter of reading rooms are subject to much visual scrutiny, are used casually for browsing, and house books (such as dictionaries or

King's Library encased in glazed security panels at the British Library. (Forster Ecospace)

atlases) of general use. The aesthetic impact of the book-shelves here affects the appearance of the library as a whole. In the main stack area, on the other hand, the bookshelves can be more utilitarian in character and spaced to achieve maximum efficiency.

Since reading room shelving (and furniture generally) is subject to close scrutiny, it needs to complement the architectural order of the space. Hence, the structural bays of window, column and beam should form the space discipline for bookshelves, tables, chairs and task lighting. Whereas shelving in the bookstack area of the library may

be 1 m apart, in the reading room the spacing is more likely to be 2 m, and the shelves constructed of naturally finished hardwood rather than aluminium brackets, steel and painted wood. In some high quality reading rooms (such as in national libraries and well-funded academic ones), the shelving will not be free-standing bookcases but built-in shelving around the room perimeter. This has the advantage of preventing visual clutter whilst also reinforcing the architectural language of the space, but is inherently in-flexible in terms of accommodating growth in the library collection.

Co-ordination of shelving and titling in the reference section of Chicago Public Library. (Brian Edwards)

Various types of storage by Forster Ecospace employed at the Social Studies Library, Oxford University. (Forster Ecospace)

## Special storage needs

The vast majority of storage for printed material can be met by standard shelving. Under 10% of an average library collection has exceptional dimensions and normally as little as 2–3% of books, etc. demand special storage attention. Typically, tailored shelving is required for:

- atlases and maps
- dictionaries and encyclopaedias
- journals and periodicals
- newspapers
- art folios
- manuscripts.

| Common depths and loads for types of storage | | |
|---|---|---|
| Storage type | Depth (mm) | Load (kg/m) |
| File boxes | 400 | 50 |
| File cartons | 400 | 80 |
| Books | 250 | 60 |
| Magnetic tapes | 300 | 60 |
| A4 files, upright | 300 | 40 |
| A0 drawings | 900 | 180 |
| Papers and magazines | 350 | 70 |
| Source: British Thornton ESF Ltd and LFC | | |

### Atlases, maps, aerial photographs and plans

Atlases have specific storage and display needs. They are the most frequently used type of oversized material in an academic or public library. Normally library equipment suppliers provide atlas display cases to order, but sometimes the architect is involved in their design. Atlases are frequently housed in a map room where maps, of value to historians as well as geographers, are stored. Maps are held in deep trays on rollers or hung from rigid demountable rails. Generally, it is better to avoid folding maps and, to prevent damage in use, to provide large table-top areas nearby. As a general rule, maps and atlases are stored horizontally to avoid damage to their spines.

Maps, aerial photographs and plans are normally stored in large acid-free folders or boxes. These are placed on racks or in drawer cases specially designed for the purpose. Such drawers are normally fairly flat (25–50 mm deep), but each can house up to 100 maps or plans if neatly stored. With storage of such material, it is important to consider ease of access. Drawers can be heavy to remove from a rack and maps difficult to consult without pulling out the whole shelf. Large racks full of maps or plans can also be a considerable weight for the building structure to bear.

### Dictionaries and encyclopaedias

Dictionaries and encyclopaedias are normally held in reading areas where they can be readily consulted. They are rarely stored in stack areas since their frequency of use demands a more accessible location. Large dictionaries and encyclopaedias are often consulted in the standing

Library shelving designed by Foster and Partners at the Law Library, Cambridge University. Note the co-ordination of shelving and lighting. (Dennis Gilbert/ View)

position and hence slanting topped high tables are sometimes provided. Another option is to use a consultation shelf in place of a regular shelf at an approximate height of 1 m. As with atlas storage, special dictionary shelving and stands are available from library furniture manufacturers. The same needs apply to computer manuals, which for obvious reasons need to be close to PCs or within the IT suite. Here, however, consultation is likely to be alongside the computer, using a convenient table top for spreading the material. As with dictionary storage, a place for taking notes is essential without the need to return to one's desk.

### Periodicals and journals

Periodicals and journals also have special storage, display and use needs. Current journals or periodicals are normally displayed on open racks or shelves so that the front cover is fully visible. Immediate back copies are frequently shelved nearby (perhaps behind or beneath), whilst further back copies are bound and found in open or closed journal storage elsewhere. Practice varies according to the type of

library and the frequency of use of journals vis à vis books. Since journals and periodicals are larger than books, the policy on their storage and display affects the overall space needs of the library. In addition, it is normal practice to provide some comfortable seating near to the periodicals display racks so that the reader may peruse the material in an unhurried fashion.

### Newspapers

Newspapers pose a particular problem. They are bulky and difficult to store and only infrequently used. Research libraries may justify a large newspaper archive, but the normal public or academic library will need to be selective in the extent of back copy newspaper storage. Newspapers are fragile, expensive to bind, expensive to store, and difficult to use or copy from. Large racks are needed for storage, large table tops for reference, and generally large areas for circulation (certainly trolley access to reader tables). Fortunately, microfilm and electronic formats are making newspaper access and storage more manageable,

Comfort seating at Oak Park Public Library near the magazine section. Lounge areas such as this require their own character of furniture and fittings. (Brian Edwards)

Information desk near the rare book stacks at Chicago Public Library. Notice the reflective floor finish and specially designed light fittings. (Brian Edwards)

and only national and major academic libraries in the future will store original copies of newspapers. There is good coverage of the national press through Internet services, although local papers are not usually available in these formats.

Where back copies of newspapers do form part of the library collection, they are normally stored flat in large boxes if unbound, vertically in tall racks if bound as tabloid editions, and horizontally on shelves if bound as broadsheet newspapers. Bound newspapers are heavy and should be stored where they can be accessed without risk. Over-high or too low storage will lead to problems for staff and users. Ideally, large bound newspapers (as with large atlases or art folios) should be slid horizontally onto a trolley or table for reference.

### Art folios

Art folios are normally stored flat on special shelves to avoid damage to the drawings or prints, and to the folios themselves. Since art folios rarely have spine space for lettering, the shelves should be deep enough to identify the material held at that location. Folios should be stored between 0.5 m and 1.5 m above the floor so that the reader can withdraw the material comfortably. There should be large tables nearby for displaying the material and good task lighting. Where the drawings or prints are fragile or light sensitive, special care should be paid to light levels, sources and supervision of the material. Effective surveillance is also important to reduce theft or damage.

### Manuscripts and archival material

Manuscripts and archival material are normally stored in acid-free boxes. The size of the boxes is determined by the dimensions of the archives to be housed. The storage of archival material is less easy to plan for than books and journals; their size and conservation requirements are often more specific than books and the collection grows more erratically. Also there may be security risks and, with valuable material, locked metal boxes in a specially designed chest may be required as well as wire mesh caging for large material. Valuable material may normally only be handled by persons wearing protective gloves. Storage for new gloves and disposal bins for used ones must be provided adjacent to the collection.

## References

Wells, M. and Young, R. (1997). *Moving and Reorganising a Library*. Gower, pp. 51–59.

Metcalf, K.D. (1986). *Planning Academic and Research Library Buildings,* 2nd edn. American Library Association, pp. 154–155.

**Part 4**

# Library types

# 9

# The national library

Of the four main types of library — national, public, academic and specialist — it is the national library which at present is changing the least. The relatively predictable demands of storage and conservation, plus the special nature of the readership, results in comparatively little typological stress for the national library. In their spatial characteristics, the examples described later differ not greatly from those national libraries built in the early decades of the twentieth century. There are, of course, stylistic changes, a growth in scale of provision and the tendency to separate storage from book usage, but the fundamental qualities of national libraries have remained relatively static over time and geographical space.

Like many central institutions of government, provision here is well funded and the briefs have a conservative air. Hence, from Japan to the UK, the national library remains predominantly a book deposit; it is a place for scholars rather than casual readers and the architectural gestures tend towards the monumental. National libraries inevitably carry overtones of national image; they are as much signifiers of cultural aspiration as warehouses for rare books.

In this sense the national library, as the later case studies demonstrate, is typologically distinct and formally secure in its design orthodoxy. However, as this chapter investigates, subtle evolution is taking place, particularly in the area of storage, display and exhibition on the one hand and nature or ecology on the other.

The national library is almost entirely a reference library. Being deposit libraries where every book published in the country is housed, there are necessarily extensive book stacks. As they need to accommodate all new books published, national libraries pose particular problems of physical growth. Although acquisition policy varies between countries, national libraries are a distinct type characterized by scale, readership and, frequently, grandeur of building.

The national library is essentially a reference and research library. Books are not borrowed but referred to. Although scholars may make notes from books, journals and historic documents, most resort to having copies made of relevant sections. The reader therefore requires general reading space, access to photocopying and service rooms,

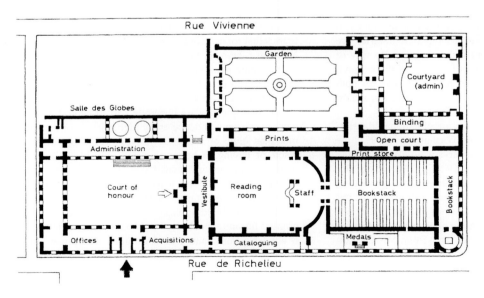

Bibliothèque Nationale, Paris, by Henri Labrouste, 1862. (D Insall and Partners)

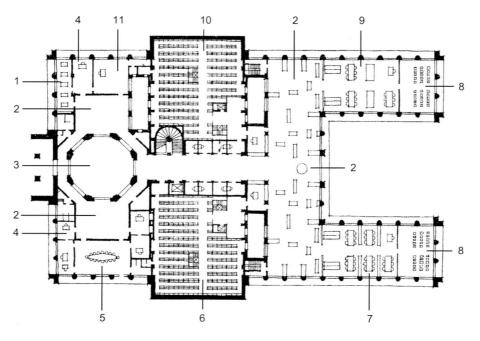

National Library of Cuba, Havana. (D Insall and Partners)

1. Accounting
2. Exhibition room
3. Upper part of grand vestibule
4. Office
5. Committee room
6. Periodic storage
7. Maps & Manuscripts
8. Seminar
9. Prints & Photographs
10. Book storage
11. Director

and areas dedicated to research. The distinction between open reading rooms and closed research rooms is a particular feature of national libraries. At the British Library in London, for instance, the various research libraries are arranged around a central open library space. By way of contrast, the National Library in Paris places the research libraries below a floor of open reading rooms. In both cases, the research libraries are secure rooms dedicated to specific subjects.

A central reading room is a feature of national libraries. The Congressional Library in Washington (1897), the National Library of Wales in Aberystwyth (1932) and the National Library in Stockholm (1928) all feature circular or octagonal central spaces. The large circular reading room has a democratic air, which suits national ideals but can cause a problem with acoustics. Noise distraction occurs as a result of readers turning book pages and leaving their seats to view book stacks, and from conversation between staff and readers. The circular form – especially if translated into a dome in section – can amplify sound. Where book stacks are arranged around the central space as

spokes in a wheel, the noise can be channelled to the reading area. It is a problem overcome in many recent national libraries by greater use of subject reference libraries that rotate about a central rotunda (e.g. the German National Library in Frankfurt am Main). In this form, the open reading room becomes rather more a symbolic space at the centre of the building as opposed to, as in the past, a working reading room.

National libraries are generally part of central government provision and hence enjoy higher levels of expenditure than civic or academic libraries. This is partly the result of having to house rare and valuable collections under specific environmental conditions. At the British Library, the new building had to store (and make available) George III's own library (known as the King's Library). It is placed in the building as a period room complete with the original furniture, bookcases and books. The whole library is almost a transplant, placed carefully in a much larger modern building. Although it is a room, the walls are constructed of glass so that the leather bindings of the books can be seen from the outside.

National and University Library of Slovenia built in Ljubljana in 1936 to designs by Joze Plecnik. (Anon)

National libraries, as all libraries do, make a distinction between rooms and space. Reference libraries are normally 'rooms' with secure walls, entrances, ceilings and specific lighting. Open reading rooms are 'spaces', often double or triple height, overlooked by walkways or galleries, edged perhaps by open books stacks and sometimes naturally lit. The dialogue between rooms and spaces is a particular feature of the national libraries. Symbolically, the open reading room is the shared intellectual space of a nation; the old reading room at the British Museum was such a space.

The general reading areas and book-stack rooms are normally separated physically in national libraries. Although some books and journals may be held on open shelves surrounding the reading room, more generally the books are held in secure stack rooms. These may be placed in a basement (British Library), in towers (National Library, Paris) or in separate buildings (National Library, Edinburgh). Basement storage of books is preferred since deliveries, security and storage can be integrated; at the new German National Library, three levels of basement storage are provided as well as a nuclear fall-out shelter. The book-stack rooms and the library areas generally have equal volumes of accommodation. For storage, conservation of the collection and space for growth, accommodation accounts for between 50–60% of the total volume of the building at national libraries in England, France and Germany.

Security from theft, fire, insect, mould and rodent attack is a key concern in book-stack areas. Humidity levels need to be adjusted to protect paper, bindings and ink. Leather-bound volumes have quite different storage needs to modern journals. Specific environmental conditions also need to be met with maps, scrolls and photographs. As national libraries expand with new deposits, it is not just a case of providing space but moderating that space to suit the particular needs of the collection.

Increasingly, storage is placed away from the main building. This allows the needs of storage and conservation to be met without compromising the quality of space and the ambience of the library itself. The main disadvantage of separation is one of delay in getting the book to the reader. However, since most readers using national libraries are specialist scholars; they can plan the retrieval of material in advance of their visit using on-line catalogues. Physical segregation has one further advantage: with urban

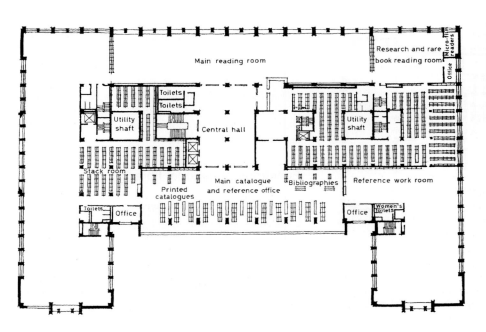

The distinction between 'rooms' and 'spaces' is particularly clear at the National Library of Canada designed by Mathers and Haldenby. (D Insall and Partners)

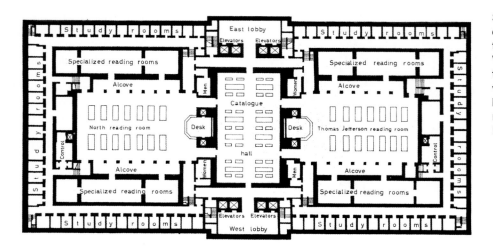

Security is an evident concern in the layout of the Library of Congress, Washington. Note how the central desks provide uninterrupted visibility over the reading rooms. (D Insall and Partners)

pollution, the environmental conditions in central locations are often not ideal for the storage of national collections. Semi-rural locations provide better conditions for both the storage and conservation of the material. As a result, some

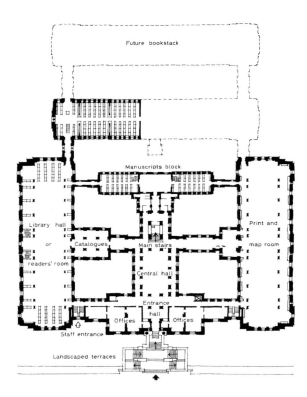

The design for the National Library of Wales, Aberystwyth, anticipated future growth. (D Insall and Partners)

national libraries have three systems of storage – one near to the reader, one in stack rooms within the building, and one in separate book storage warehouses some distance away. It is an arrangement which provides benefits for the reader (access to books), for the library (good architectural quality) and for the book (secure storage and specialist space for conservation, cataloguing, etc.).

The current expansion in the output of books and journals results in the British Library growing at around 12.5 km of shelf space per year (Jeffries, 2007). The Bodleian Library in Oxford, which is also entitled to receive a free copy of every item published under an act of parliament of 1911, received planning permission in 2007 to build a $29 million depository on the outskirts of the city. In spite of electronic publishing, books continue to be published at an unprecedented rate (about 75,000 new books a year in the UK) and those libraries that have legal deposit status have a particular problem with storage. However, it is better not to stress the architectural character of existing libraries by cramming in too many volumes especially since many, such as the Bodleian Library, are listed buildings. After all, it is the quality of their design (space, furniture and fittings) which often separates national libraries from their public and academic counterparts.

## Functions of national libraries

National libraries have four functions to fulfil:

- the collection of printed and manuscript heritage
- the preservation of past and present literary output through legal deposit
- bibliographic record production for the country
- a forum for exhibitions.

In many western countries, the national library also acts as the hub for interlibrary lending. Some national libraries are also the leading university library, as in Reykjavik, Iceland, and Helsinki in Finland. China recently established a new National Museum of Modern Chinese Literature in Beijing. Although termed 'museum' the collection is mainly literature, manuscripts and related artefacts. All projects expect the architecture to echo the cultural importance of the collections within. Thus, planning and designing within a national library context is a most complex task where function and cultural meaning connect.

Collection growth in national libraries is a dynamic feature. National libraries have responsibility for the collection and preservation of the national literary heritage. Unlike regional libraries, they will often have responsibility under a legal deposit scheme. This requires them to house one copy of every monograph and printed publication available. Publishers are required to offer their national libraries a copy of all titles published, although some national libraries are selective. The National Library of Wales in Aberystwyth has a comprehensive collection policy which states that the library will collect every title published or printed in Wales, every title in the Celtic languages, every item relating to the history of the Celtic regions and peoples as well as Arthurian legend, but excluding popular interest (National Library of Wales, 1998). The Library selects from those items published in English about Welsh subjects, but is comprehensive about the collection of titles from Welsh authors who publish in the English language.

The growth in acquisitions as a result of the practice of legal deposit means that national libraries are subject to periodic expansion. In spite of the focus in this chapter on new national libraries, enlarging existing facilities tends to be more common than the design of new. Such enlargement usually consists of new wings being added to the

Extensions to the National Library of Italy showing the recent book deposit and administration/research tower. (Brian Edwards)

existing core of library provision, sometimes resulting in a grouping of structures from different periods around the original library. Two examples can be cited; the first is the National Library of Italy in Rome: the second, the National Library of Norway in Oslo. Both bear examination as exemplars of how to undertake expansion without loss of comprehension of the building and its collection.

The National Library of Italy was founded in 1876 in order to provide a comprehensive book archive which would be an expression of national heritage to stand alongside Italy's considerable art treasures. The library was originally housed in the Collegio Romano where the Jesuit Bibliotheca Maior formed the core of the collection. This collection of manuscripts and early printed books was expanded with the acquisition of the libraries of various religious orders after the creation of the Kingdom of Italy. As a result, the National Library with its collection of 6 million books, including over 25,000 from the sixteenth century and 8,000 manuscripts, is a major research source and cultural asset.

In 1975 the library moved to the Castro Pretorio area of Rome where a new purpose-built national library was built. In 2001 it was substantially enlarged and refurbished. New reception and exhibition areas where created, plus a conference centre, lecture theatres, bookshop, bank and archive facility. In addition, a new tall administration and research block was constructed to the east of the original library. Today the National Library of Italy consists of three elements: a brick-built book deposition in the centre, a new entrance block to the north with external amphitheatre and small park, and an office and research tower to the east. The grouping into separate linked blocks allows natural light and cross-ventilation into the different parts whilst also providing space for further expansion.

The National Library of Norway is housed in Oslo's former university library built in 1913. The collection is both ancient and modern with many hand-drawn maps and early Viking manuscripts. The library interprets 'text' to include writing, sound and images and hence the building is seen as the container for the nation's cultural memory. In 1933 the original building was enlarged by the construction of a new west wing to house administration and research departments. In 1939 another wing housing a new reading room was built to the east with a service courtyard separating the two new wings and the original library.

In 1998 the University of Oslo sold the whole assembly of buildings to the Norwegian government in order to form the National Library. At this point it was decided to build a further block linking the east and west wings with an atrium where the courtyard once stood. The result is a library that rotates around a lofty glazed central space (with its history written largely in the four wings) one of which includes the original 1913 building that forms the library entrance. As this is now a listed building the architectural contrast between the new and old accommodation mirrors the historic mixture of the collection itself. Inside the atrium there is a cafe, study desks and meeting areas as well as lifts and stairs which rise through the 10 floors. The latest part of the jigsaw, built in 2002, houses seven floors of IT-based research areas constructed on top of underground book stacks. The dialogue between the architecture and its contents, and the broad definition of 'text', makes this national library notable.

## Design and planning needs analysis

For those designing new national libraries, current collection development policies will determine the calculations to establish in-built growth for shelves and stack areas. Librarians will have details of average growth and these statistics should form the basis of calculations. Open access is not a regular feature for the majority of national collections. Librarians will be able to decide what percentage of a collection needs to be available either as reference or on open access. This will form the collection that should be available in reading rooms, including printed catalogues of collections housed elsewhere, bibliographic publications

Newspaper reading room at the National Library of Norway with retained historic furniture and bookshelves. (Brian Edwards)

and reference items that assist users to access other materials. The feature of the reading area will be access to computers which provide the catalogue's library, often within a web-based system. The environmental features of areas to be used for PC use therefore apply here.

The area to be dedicated to the preservation of national library material has to be analysed in three discrete ways. The area for storage will have specific environmental considerations, which vary according to the type of material involved (books, photographs, drawings, etc.). Second, the area to be used for exhibition needs planning within parameters (including lighting and humidity) that do not pose threats to the collection. Lastly, there will be a particular area for activities related to the practical aspects of preservation, including equipment for professional lamination used in page restoration, rebinding, photographic recording of scarce documents and other specialist conservation tasks.

## The British Library

Compared to the (Bibliothèque Nationale in Paris or the German National Library in Frankfurt, the British Library lacks a sense of conceptual clarity. This is partly the result of an over-long gestation period (nearly 20 years between design, construction and opening), and the crisis in English architecture that followed the intellectual rejection of the Modern movement in the 1970s. The British Library came into being when there was little central purpose in terms of government perception of the role of public commissions. It was also designed when certain post-modern tendencies were eroding central modernist values. Implicit in the building's post-modernity is the exploitation of a certain architectural ambiguity to provide spatial richness.

If the British Library suffers as a consequence of its formal uncertainty, there is no denying the success of large parts of the building. The main problem is the lack of a coherent whole: the sense that a national building of this scale requires a corresponding public architectural statement. In many ways, the British Library is the antithesis of its French equivalent. The Bibliothèque Nationale is a clear, almost posturing proclamation of national pride, whilst the British Library almost hides itself behind the gothic skyline of St Pancras Station and is approached via a series of understated pavilions and screen walls facing Euston Road. Although the British Library was described in *The Times* as 'spectacularly beautiful on the inside, an uplifting vista of sleek white lines and exhilarating perspectives' (British Library, 1999), it remains a modest building from the outside.

The British Library is one of the world's largest libraries. It contains over 150 million separate items – substantially larger than the French and German national

Refurbished reading room from the 1930s at the National Library of Norway with contemporary study tables. (Brian Edwards)

libraries and equalled only by the Library of Congress in the USA. In addition, nearly 10,000 items are added each day resulting in a library that grows by about 3 million items a year. Put another way, the British Library will expand to twice its size every 50 years. The problem for the architects Colin St John Wilson and Partners was how to reconcile the scale of the collection with that of the individual scholar (Brawne, 1997, p. 207). Part of the conflict in the resulting building results from the ambiguity needed to conserve and make available the collection whilst providing personal study space for readers. The first requires large volumes with ideal environmental conditions; the second requires private study space centred on the book or manuscript (preferably with a view), lighting which the reader can adjust and perhaps a breeze to help maintain personal attention. In seeking to satisfy both conditions (book and reader), the building makes many adjustments in scale and character of space.

Besides the collection, the British Library has three exhibition galleries, lecture theatres, a conference centre, bookshop, restaurant and cafes. It is a building that many visit for the exhibitions on temporary or permanent display, for the bookshop (which also sells gifts) and in order to meet friends in the restaurant or cafe areas. Taken together the building is rather more than a library – it is a blending of library, museum and civic activities which takes us back to the library in classical times (e.g. Alexandria). The historic precedent is reinforced by the generous provision of outdoor gardens and a public piazza for events. These provide space for the reader to contemplate on the material between bouts of intense study.

The British Library is not a public library; its reading rooms and collection are available to those who need access to the unique nature of the material. The emphasis is upon research and scholarship, not casual or recreational reading. Readers need to register upon arrival before being given access to the three main floors of reading rooms. The entrance handles the large number of visitors by dividing them into separate groups within a large lofty foyer area. Visitors who wish to use the bookshop, lecture theatres, exhibition galleries or cafes are directed to one side while readers are taken to the other. This immediate segregation orders the plan and allows for security at the same time.

The entrance foyer is the culmination of a pedestrian sequence from Euston Road via symbolic gates, terraces, a portico building and finally across a large piazza to the

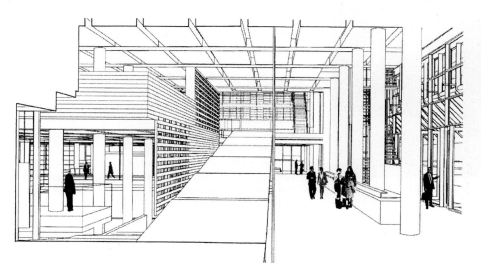

The design for the National Library of Quebec, Montreal, provides large foyer spaces for housing exhibitions. The design is by Patkau Architects with Croft-Pelletier Architects and Gilles Guite. (Patkau Architects)

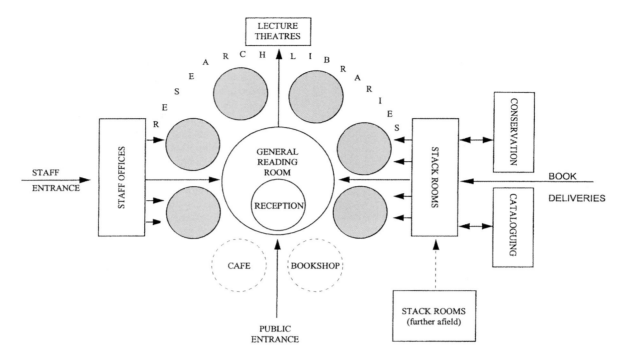

Diagrammatic layout of a national library. (Brian Edwards)

library steps. The relaxed handling of urban design prepares visitors for the building by providing a promenade that gives ample opportunity to view the various parts. The piazza is not rectangular but a parallelogram formed by the angled alignment of Midland Road to the east. Within it sits

The National Library of Denmark, known as the Black Diamond, is an amalgam of old and new structures facing the water. The black angled section is the new entrance lobby, cafe, bookshop and exhibition area for the whole library. (Brian Edwards)

an amphitheatre that helps deflect movement towards the library entrance. Compared to the ruthless orthographic geometry of the entrance spaces to the French national library, the piazza has a welcoming blend of formal and informal elements. The area is used for gathering parties of tourists and schoolchildren, and for displaying public sculpture in a pleasant sun-filled outdoor room.

The entrance foyer is a handsome space flanked by grand flights of steps – making it a fine setting for the major works of art on show. The largest is a 7 m square tapestry to a design by the painter R B Kitaj, which hangs high on the west wall. Being roof-lit, the space is bathed in natural light with tall slender columns defining the cross axis which leads to the bookshop and galleries. Readers seeking admission to the reading rooms turn to the right, those wanting to use the restaurant and view the building pass straight on. The play of light, processional staircases and structural columns signal the route with graceful understatement, making the need for aggressive signing unnecessary.

Many visitors to the British Library do not wish to consult books but to see the many valuable items on exhibition. The Lindisfarne Gospels (c.700), the Magna Carta (1215), the Gutenberg Bible (1455) and Shakespeare's First Folio (1623) are displayed in the John Ritblat Gallery, one of the three permanent galleries. These items are major public draws and the John Ritblat Gallery is sensibly placed near the library entrance.

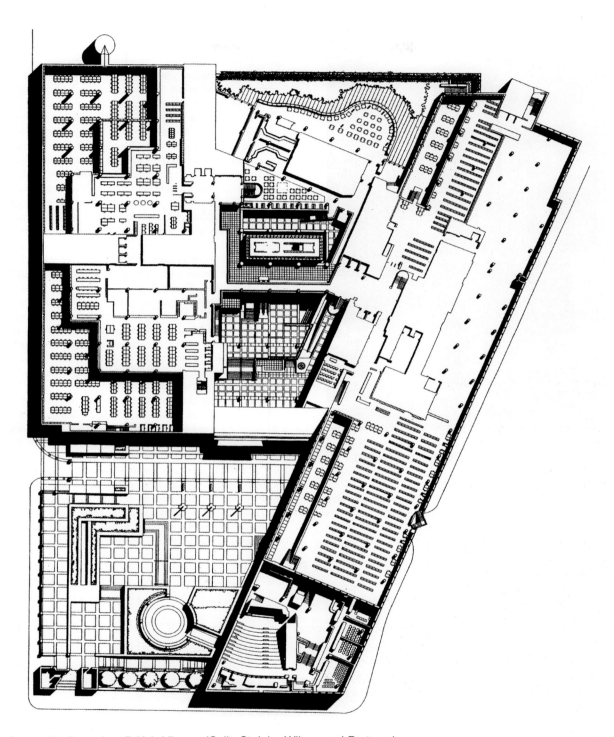

Composite floor plan, British Library. (Colin St John Wilson and Partners)

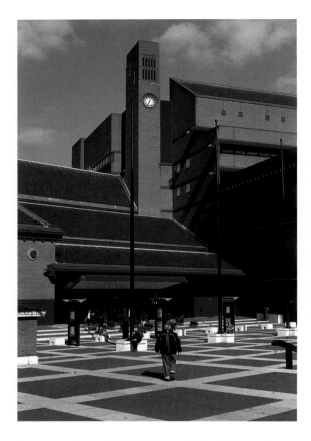

Entrance plaza, British Library. (Brian Edwards)

Another attraction is the King's Library – the personal library of 60,000 books belonging to George III. It is a collection of great beauty and is housed in a six-storey high, 17 m long glass-walled tower in the centre of the building. It acts as a point of navigation in the library and is overlooked by lifts taking readers to different reading rooms as well as the main restaurant. The artificial lighting is designed to allow the rich colours of the books to contrast with the white paintwork and subdued natural materials employed elsewhere.

The disposition of the main library responds directly to conservation need. The bulk of the library collection is housed in a massive four-storey basement where conditions are ideal for storage. Staff retrieve the books, manuscripts, journals or maps which are then transported to the readers, who are positioned on the upper floors. Readers are given a desk whose number is illuminated when the requested material is available. A limited amount of stock is housed on open shelves at the sides of the reading rooms. Study desks have their own power, IT connection and reader lamp. The tables and chairs in matching American white oak and green leather form large study areas beneath high, coffered ceilings. Personal space is provided in large reading rooms by differentiating the long tables into separate study desks and by providing smaller, more intimate study bays at the library periphery. The reading rooms are rarely rectangular spaces; they are often stepped in plan to provide a variety of table and bookshelf layouts. Choice of study ambience is deliberately provided to give a choice of conditions for readers.

Views through the library are cleverly engineered to exploit the scale and complexity of the building. Light is introduced by various means (portholes, roof lights, walls of clear and coloured glazing) to remind readers of the rhythms of the day and as a stimulus to thought (Brawne, 1997, p. 207). In general, clerestory and lantern lights light the larger circulation and study spaces, with domestic-sized windows lighting offices and smaller study areas. The result is a building which has more the properties of a small city than a large public building. In this, it is different from other recent national libraries which have greater grandeur

| British Library, London | | |
|---|---|---|
| **Architect** | **Special features** | **Cost** |
| Colin St John Wilson and Partners | Houses the world's largest research collection. | Approx. £3,000/m$^2$ in 1998 |
| | Deliberately breaks down scale to mediate between the collection and the scholar. | |
| | Has extensive range of supporting gallery, exhibition, conference, restaurant and shopping facilities. | |
| | Places bulk of collection in three-storey basement (300 km of shelving). | |
| | Contains the 'Kings Library' as a glazed internal tower. | |
| | Forms a generous external piazza for meeting, performance, contemplation and a venue for sculpture. | |

Interior planted court-
yard, Bibliothèque
Nationale de France,
Paris. (Brian Edwards)

and geometric clarity. However, the design shows that
a building housing the world's most important research
collection can have a human touch. As the library's architect Colin St John Wilson put it 'to every scholar the
(British) Library is a personal realm of secret topography'
(Brawne, 1997, p, 207). The building is as much a statement of the importance of scholars as a grand proclamation
of the scale of the collection.

## Bibliothèque Nationale de France, Paris

In architectural terms, the Bibliothèque Nationale de
France in Paris is at the opposite pole to the new British
Library in London. Whereas the British Library evokes
a Northern European picturesqueness, the Bibliothèque
Nationale is abstract, rational and coolly indifferent to
place or context. In marked contrast to the urban enclosure
of Colin St John Wilson's design, that by Dominique
Perrault is open and transparent – except for the enclosed
fragment of forest in the centre.

The concept for the Bibliothèque Nationale is simple:
four towers of offices and book stacks mark each corner of
a low podium of public reading rooms. The public areas
look into a central forest, which forms a point of orientation
in the building. Two reception points at either end of
a rectangular circuit anchor the building between a suc-
cession of thematic reading rooms arranged on the long
sides of the courtyard. The main subject reading rooms
(philosophy, law, science, literature, art and history) are on
the upper level with research areas and special collections
on the lower level. Since the library contains over 8 million

Bibliothèque Nationale de France, Paris, designed by
Dominique Perrault. (Brian Edwards)

printed volumes and a similar number of images, maps, contracts, etc., which make up the various special collections, a clear distinction is made between reading (and research space) and the storage of material to which the readers refer. The latter is housed in the four towers, which mark the perimeter of the library and anchor the building in the urban scene.

The library is noticeable for its transparency, simplicity of form and fluidity of internal space. Except for the sweeping steps and ramparts, which form the external experience at pavement level, the building is highly glazed both in terms of the exterior façades and many of the internal partitions. According to the architect, this was to evoke the democratic nature of the library and to give the experience of reading and research a clear public expression. Access to the study material, though controlled, is highly visible from various circulation areas, cafes and exhibition galleries in the building.

The main reading rooms are of double height, some with mezzanine galleries and small internal stairs. The book stacks do not rise to the ceilings but stop some way below to accentuate the sense of internal space. Simple geometry pervades the arrangement throughout. There is a square grid, which plans everything (tables, book stacks, lighting, service runs, structural columns, suspended ceilings and partitions) rationally. It is an order which derives from the central philosophy of articulating space on the basis of constructional logic, coupled with the need for flexibility. Since the collection is by no means static, the decision was made to establish hierarchies of structural and spatial order in which operational changes could occur relatively smoothly.

For the visitor the approach is, however, by no means clear. By avoiding the deliberate expression of entrance, the new library feels as if it can be entered at any point. In reality, there are only two entrances – both at high level and at the narrow ends of the rectangular building. The approach, marked by excessively grand flights of timber steps and equally posturing ramps, eventually takes the library user to the edge of the internal courtyard. Here security checks are conducted outdoors on a windy deck overlooking the planted central garden.

Inside the experience is smooth and spacious – a wide carpeted promenade circuits the outer edge of the garden with reading rooms arranged to one side. The walls to the garden (or forest) are totally glazed, while to the reading rooms there are long cliffs of timber boarding, interrupted periodically by views into the study areas. The contrast between solid and void, between transparency and enclosure, inside and out, towers and podium, establishes a stimulating sense of opposites at every point in the building.

This drama is acted out, however, in marked indifference to the presence of the River Seine, which runs alongside the north of the building. The main sense of

| Bibliothèque Nationale de France, Paris | | |
|---|---|---|
| **Architect** | **Special features** | **Date** |
| Dominique Perrault | Clear statement of new library typology | 1995 |
| | Reading and research on separate floors | |
| | Storage and conservation in four corner towers | |
| | Central tranquil woodland garden | |
| | Rigid geometric and structural order | |

outside is that of the idealized forest in the centre of the building. Even on the podium deck, which acts as the external terrace linking the two entrances, the river is barely brought into play.

The use of mainly glazed façades gives the library a healthy sense of openness and fills the interior volumes with welcome daylight. Sunlight is controlled by the use of blinds and storey-height timber shutters which track the path of the sun. The system of environmental control gives

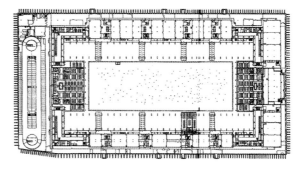

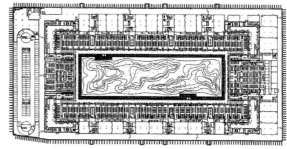

Floor plans, Bibliothèque Nationale de France, Paris. (Dominique Perrault)

126

| Breakdown of South African National Library | |
|---|---|
| **Staff** | 80 |
| Readers/researchers | 29,000/year |
| Telephone queries | 7,500/year |
| **The collection** | |
| Monographs | 750,000 |
| Bound periodical journals | 200,000 |
| Bound newspapers | 50,000 |
| Manuscript items | 35,000 |
| Maps | 20,000 |
| Photographs | 50,000 |
| **Growth in collection** | |
| Annual increase in titles | 90,000 |
| Source: Guide to the South African Library, 1997 | |

animation to the façades whilst never fully obscuring views into the library.

The division between reading space and bookstore in the Bibliothèque Nationale de France takes the trend in library design in the twentieth century to a logical conclusion. The gradual separation between study material and the scholar began in the 1850s, accelerated after 1920 and now finds expression in Perrault's four landmarking towers in Paris. There are operational and security advantages of the arrangement; by splitting storage from use, each can change or grow without impeding the other. Of course, it means that the serious scholar or researcher has to wait some time

| South African National Library | | |
|---|---|---|
| **Architect** | **Special features** | **Date** |
| W. H. Kohler | Conversion of domed reading room to exhibition gallery W. H. Kohler | 1873 and refurbishment in 1996 |
| | Growth accommodated by new double height book stacks. | |
| | Warehousing for stock elsewhere. | |
| | Café and bookshop to generate extra use. | |
| | Conservation of scarce anti-apartheid documents. | |

for the book or papers to be delivered to their desk but, with some material available in each reading or research room, the reader can be making progress in the meantime.

## The South African National Library

The South African National Library in Cape Town is typical of national collections in relatively young countries. From its beginning as a legal deposit library in 1873 to the present day, it has undergone periodic expansion in the form of new wings and independent structures some distance away. The latter are employed for the storage of infrequently used material such as early journal runs, newspapers and special collections. In the library itself, the lofty interior volumes have been colonized by ever more bookcases, some of considerable height. The new bookcases are constructed as an open steel framework with their own staircases — the whole structure being set as a central spine within older reading rooms.

Whereas the departmental wings have been used more intensively as the demands imposed by a legal deposit and copyright library have expanded, the former circular reading room has been stripped of books altogether and is used today as an exhibition space. The exhibition gallery serves to present the library's collection of maps, drawings and prints, as well as staging touring exhibitions. It attracts visitors to the library who are not intent on using the book collection and has a cafe to reinforce casual visiting.

The management of the library has had to adapt to considerable change. As a national reference library devoted to research, it remains central to South Africa's sense of its own history, geography and future. During the apartheid years, the library continued to collect banned publications and to make them available to authorized researchers, who themselves helped bring about the liberalization of the country in the early 1990s. Like many national libraries, its fortunes as a building and collection reflect the changing ideals of the society it serves.

The main difference between civic and national libraries is the extent of unpublished material. National libraries necessarily hold national collections both of published and unpublished material. Implicit in this role is that of collection, preservation and presentation of the material. Unlike a typical city library, national libraries devote a great deal of space and expenditure to conservation measures of various kinds — binding, photographic preservation, cleaning of drawings, etc. As such, just as space is needed for the legal deposit function, even more room and resources are required to preserve what is often a delicate and fragile collection of ancient books, political leaflets, maps and images. This is particularly true in South Africa where many of the most valuable publications were printed unofficially by underground political organizations based in townships or rural areas.

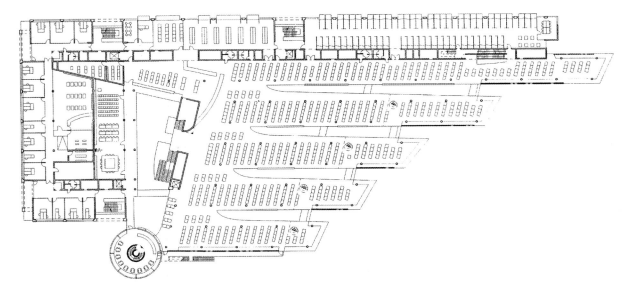

Plan, National Library, Göttingen, Germany. (Gerber and Partners)

The South African National Library (unlike the State Library in Pretoria) has the main duty to maintain a microfilm collection of newspapers, journals and political pamphlets. These are relevant to the whole African continent and aid staff in bibliographic research and publication. The dissemination of the collection is supported by a policy of direct funding of facsimile editions of rare African items. The library acts as its own publisher, using some of the equipment employed in rebinding and other preservation tasks for new publications.

It is clear that national libraries have quite distinct functions. The emphasis on size, scope and rarity of the collection has ramifications for storage and presentation; the need to publicize and disseminate the material adds further to the outreach function; and the political sensitivity of what is collected requires a commitment to balance irrespective of party pressure. Added to this, national libraries perform a vital conservation role, ensuring that books and journals remain accessible to future generations of scholars.

## National Library, Göttingen, Germany

In Germany and the Netherlands, the national library is not a single institution but a number of national collections dispersed amongst other publicly accessible libraries. This largely federal system has two advantages: it offers a fairer distribution of national treasures than the system in London or Paris which disadvantages large numbers of people by geography. Second, it allows for the integration of national, academic or public collections around subjects, thereby providing regional centres in the sciences, arts or literature.

The German National Library is dispersed into five main centres, each attached to a major academic library. Typical is that at Göttingen where the national collection in the humanities, amounting to nearly 4 million volumes, was built alongside one of the major academic libraries in the country. The library at Göttingen has thus become the national focus for scholars wishing to access books or journals in the humanities. Since the university on whose

| National Library, Göttingen, Germany | | |
|---|---|---|
| **Architect** | **Special features** | **Cost** |
| Gerber and Partners | National library absorbed into university campus | Not available |
| | Arts and humanities library with emphasis upon traditional reader spaces | |
| | Articulation of design into separate functional parts aids legibility | |
| | Brings external landscape into view by using glazed 'fingers'. | |

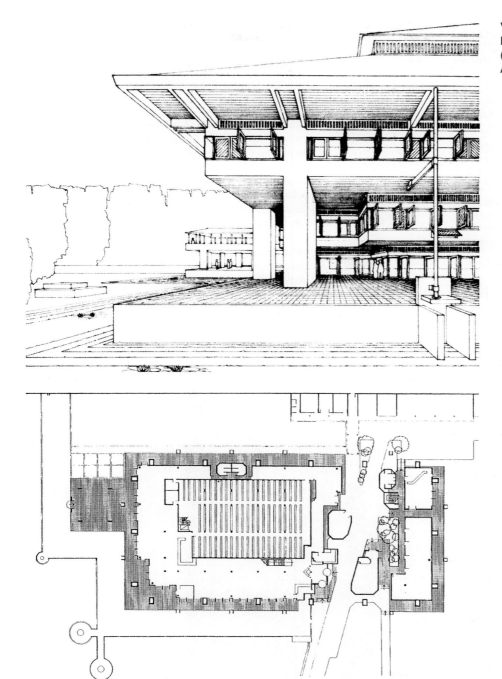

View and plan, Sri
Lanka National Library.
(Michael Brawne and
Associates)

campus the national library is built is a centre for study in
the arts and literature, the integration of facilities also
benefits the 20,000 students and 1,000 academic staff.

The new national library is constructed in a large
courtyard formed by existing faculty and library buildings.

It stands alongside a deep-planned humanities library and
shares with it a new tree-planted entrance square. Visitors
therefore approach both buildings from a single space – an
effect which helps to unify the two types of library provision. Typical of German campus architecture, there is an

129

| The National Library of Sri Lanka | | |
| --- | --- | --- |
| **Architect** | **Special features** | **Cost** |
| Michael Brawne & Associates | Employs traditional architecture as a symbol of national collection. | £560/m² in 1992 |
| | Exploits passive ventilation and solar shading in a hot climate. | |
| | Places collection in air-conditioned core surrounded by open reading areas. | |

orthogonal layout of large square buildings which the new national library cleverly deconstructs. The architects Gerber and Partners have arranged the building as a hand with five fingers stretching out towards trees. It is a plan which immediately identifies the central shared functions from the collection whilst at the same time maximizing the penetration of daylight. The new library breaks the grip of deep planning whilst retaining the benefit of compaction.

The main functional zones are distributed vertically and horizontally. The public and reader rooms occupy three floors and extend along five parallel fingers of mainly glazed accommodation. Here circulation space is arranged against the perimeter, providing views out for those retrieving books. Study desks occupy the centre of the wings in a zone defined by tall concrete columns. The control desk, information point and administrative offices are housed in a four-storey compact tower which sits upon a basement floor of storage, services and parking. Circulation between floors is provided in a glazed rotunda, which sits prominently on the west side of the composition.

There is a calm rationality in Gerber's design. The reading areas are arranged as peninsulas spreading into greenery on the south side of the building. The administration, library information and control areas are in a squat tower to the north, with circulation via a beacon-like stair on the west side. The three elements break down a large building into constituent parts, aiding legibility and allowing the national library to be absorbed into the campus landscape.

Causewayside extension of the National Library of Scotland. Designed by Andrew Merrylees and Associates. (Brian Edwards)

130

## Sri Lanka National Library, Colombo

The National Library in Colombo, Sri Lanka, is a model for other smaller nations in hot regions of the world. Rather than employ expensive air-conditioning, the building acts as a moderator of climate by the means of construction employed, the nature of the cross-section and in the positioning of book stacks. The environmental and library strategies are effectively combined in this design by the UK architects, Michael Brawne & Associates.

The library contains about a million volumes, some of which are of great historic and cultural importance. Like all national libraries, this one in Sri Lanka is simultaneously a national monument and great warehouse of information (Brawne, 1997, p. 47). The design signals its cultural eminence by employing traditional forms of building, yet elevating them in scale to create a building of clear public importance. The civic element is achieved by expressing the library as a series of large horizontal and vertical structural elements. These give scale and provide effective environmental protection from the tropical sun and monsoon rains. They also allow the library to respond to local patterns of building, providing an appropriate correspondence between a national building and the national culture which its collection promotes.

The use of a modern Sri Lankan style helps make the library accessible in a cultural sense. There is an openness and ease of approach which derives from simple site planning. A large projecting canopy extends to the pavement edge, providing an obvious point of entry to pedestrians. The entrance canopy, as much a protection from the sun as the rain, takes visitors into an internal garden where a variety of routes open up. The main one to the library takes readers into a perimeter reading area and a control desk. This surrounds a central book stack which, placed in the centre of the building, provides the best environmental conditions for the storage of books and rare manuscripts.

The library has an air-conditioned core of book stacks on two floors surrounded by wide naturally ventilated reading areas. Offices, archive and meeting rooms occupy the third floor. As with many modern libraries, books are taken from a darkened and secure library core to the edge where they are read in carrels bathed in natural light. The library edge is broken down into bays of seats in pairs sharing a table, each one modelled on the dimensions of façade elements. The constructional grid of window mullions, solar shading and clerestory panels provides the framework for the carrels, which in turn help configure the layout of structural columns. It is a grid that organizes all elements, whether functional, environmental or spiritual.

By placing readers at the edge, they have the opportunity to enjoy views over the surrounding garden and to feel the fresh breezes of natural ventilation. Although windows open, theft is not a problem since readers are identified when they borrow books (no material is on open shelves). In addition, scholarship is highly valued in Sri Lanka and books are seen as a national treasure held in trust by all readers.

The powerful rhythms of construction and the use of traditional methods of cooling ensure that this national library is held within a building which mirrors national customs. This is a national library, a building which is culturally accessible whilst preserving at its centre the treasures of a nation in an air-conditioned casket.

## National Library of Scotland, Edinburgh

The original National Library of Scotland, built in Edinburgh's city centre in 1935, had filled to capacity by the 1980s. The decision was then made to construct a substantial annex a mile to the south at Causewayside. This annex was to be both a large book and journal store, and a specialist map library augmenting the original facility on George IV Bridge.

The new building, which was built in two phases, has a deep plan and is fully air-conditioned. The site is surrounded by a compact blend of four-storey Victorian tenements and warehouses arranged in Edinburgh fashion around a grid of handsome streets. The new library is five storeys high and has a regular layout of concrete columns on a 7.2 m by 8.1 m grid. This allows the building to offer a high level of flexibility whilst providing subdivisions for book stacks and partitions on 900 mm planning modules.

As a national library, there are a large number of specialist collections to house – map storage, the Scottish Science Library and geological archives. These are placed mainly in the centre of the building interspersed with reading and consultation areas. The perimeter of the library contains special areas given over to study, meeting or conference rooms in the second phase and mainly plant rooms in the first. Interestingly the perimeter of the library is planned on a grid placed at 45° to the rest of the building. The effect is to create unusual diagonal routes into the library and rooms of trapezoid shape at the library edge. This has the result of forming distinct spaces around the perimeter of the main reading areas, which relieve the rationality of the evenly spaced columns with their nearly square subdivisions of book-stack and study areas. It also creates diagonal views over the surrounding rooftops and into adjoining streets.

The use of square and diagonal grids was a rather fashionable architectural device in the 1980s. It has the benefit of exploiting the collision of the two to form spaces that are distinctive and provide space hierarchy in a building of structural regularity. At the new National Library of

131

| National Library of Scotland, Causewayside, Edinburgh | | |
|---|---|---|
| **Architect** | **Special features** | **Cost** |
| Andrew Merrylees and Associates | Deep plan air-conditioned library on dense urban site | Not available |
| | Collision of square and diagonal grids to create interesting perimeter spaces | |
| | A building of modern 'national' style to reflect a national collection | |

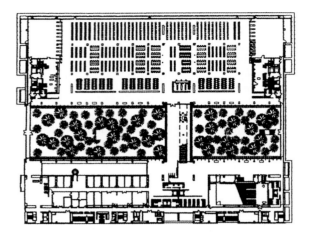

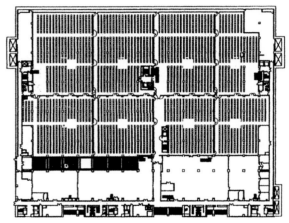

Plan, National Library of Japan designed by Fumio Toki (Fumio Toki/AR)

Scotland, this effect is used to guide readers from the street into the main exhibition and information point. A projecting glass entrance porch placed at 45° to the main building takes visitors through a sequence of roof-glazed and enclosed spaces, each of varying size and angularity. The effect has been likened to that of the approach to Scottish castles where guarded entrances are often set at an angle to the main accommodation (Edwards, 1987). The baronial overtones are further expressed in double height, prismatic entrance spaces and highly glazed, square-framed staircases; the latter project through the roofline to give picturesque massing to the skyline.

The entrance is further defined by a pair of lift shafts placed again at an angle to the orthogonal remainder. The closely spaced, angled lifts establish a distinctive reception volume on each floor. From the outside, the lifts signal entrance; from the inside, they identify the area where library staff are located.

In its stone detailing, general massing and in the measured collision of square and diagonal grids, the National Library of Scotland is an urbane building. This is no neutral container for the storing of national book treasures but

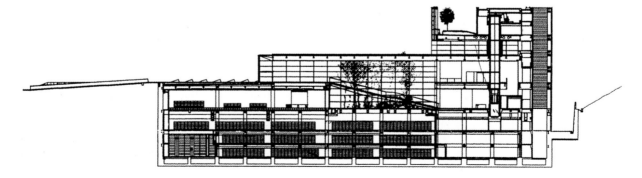

Section, National Library of Japan designed by Fumio Toki (Fumio Toki/AR)

**National Library of Japan**

| Architect | Special features |
|---|---|
| Fumio Toki | • Forms part of Kansai Science Park |
| | • Houses Imperial Library and Japanese parliamentary papers |
| | • Has tree-planted internal courtyard |
| | • Top floor cafe and roof garden |

a building which uses the contemporary Scottish style to give identity to the collection. In this sense, the cultural and spatial are drawn together – the complexity of built form perhaps signalling the evolution of a nation and its archive of written records.

## National Library of Japan at Kansai

Designed by Fumio Toki, the National Library of Japan is located on a wooded site close to the Kansai Science City, not far from Kyoto. The library houses the Japanese collection of parliamentary papers as well as the Imperial Library, and is also the nation's deposit library. Unlike the urban national libraries of London and Paris, this one near Kansai has the luxury of a spacious sylvan setting. According to the architect, the traditional elements of light, wind, greenery and transparency are the formal cues which find expression in the design (Chow, 2003).

The main reading room and three floors of book stacks housing 6 million volumes (with a capacity for 20 million) are placed in a subterranean basement. Partly roof lit, the arrangement helps with the protection and conservation of the collection whilst also reducing the visual impact on the landscape (Chow, 2003). The building is square in plan and being highly glazed has an almost Miesian quality not unlike the campus architecture at Illinois Institute of Technology with its articulation of structural frame and glazing subdivisions. In section the library steps up from its substantial basement with sunken courtyard to form a block of seminar rooms and lecture theatre with an office tower above. The main reading room faces directly onto the courtyard, which forms a leafy division between the entrance lobby and the main study areas. The reading room has a formal arrangement of tables and study desks beneath rooflights which provide diffused light by day and artificial light by night.

The use of base and tower combined with internal tree-planted courtyard suggests the influence of the National Library of France (Chow, 2003). However, the organization in plan also shares affinity with the Library of Congress in Washington with its planning discipline of axes, cross-axes and light courts. The cafe and roof garden are located on the top floor to take advantage of the views.

National libraries contain a country's treasure house of knowledge both ancient and modern. Unlike public libraries where a certain social and cultural engagement is encouraged through the medium of architecture, at national libraries the disciplines imposed by the scale of collections, their protection and preservation results in buildings that are highly rational in design. This national library is a building that also engages in the values of the country served. The combination of high-tech and tradition results in a building that is specific to place and, in an understated way, to Japan.

## Royal Library of Denmark

The Royal Library was founded in 1653 when King Frederik III established what was to become Denmark's national archive and deposit library. With links to the University of Copenhagen, the collection grew in importance to become the most complete deposit of books published in Denmark. The collection today consists of nearly 5 million books but also significant archives of musical scores, manuscripts and early maps. The original building on Christians Brygge overlooking the harbour in Copenhagen opened to the public in 1906 to nationalist Nordic designs by the architect Hans Holm. It was extended in 1968 and again in 1999 to form the present building for the Royal Library known affectionately as the Black Diamond. The latest extensions designed by Schmidt, Hammer and Lassen sought to massage the image of the collection of earlier buildings into a single entity worthy of a national cultural institution. By doubling the size of the library the Black Diamond was able to offer a range of complementary facilities such as lecture theatres, exhibition space and a restaurant whilst focusing upon its core task of recording and preserving the textural cultural heritage of Denmark.

The emphasis is upon design-led spaces rather than a collection-led national library. The aim is to draw people into the building by creating an eye-catching external image and then, upon entry, providing a dramatic sequence of entrance volumes which open up the facilities inside. The library consists of several elements: a large gallery where rare manuscripts, musical scores and pictures are permanently displayed; a temporary exhibition area near the library entrance; a concert hall for chamber music recitals of printed works in the national collection; a national museum of photography; and a large bookshop. These provide a vehicle for opening up the Royal Library to new generations of users.

The Royal Library consists of three connected structures. The original building on the site known as the Holm (after its architect) contains the bulk of the book collection arranged in wings built around a courtyard garden. In this regard it is a precursor to the courtyard layout of the National Library in Paris. From the Holm readers pass to the Hansen building which contains staff offices, conservation services and other specialist facilities. In turn the Hansen leads to the Black Diamond which is effectively the main reading room for the library. As is common practice, books and maps are brought to the readers' desks by staff from archives collections elsewhere in the building.

The Black Diamond acts as an entry portal of grand proportions to the remainder of the Royal Library. The reading rooms are placed on either side of a large atrium which rises through the six-storey building. Within the atrium a travelator leads visitors up to the main entrance floor to the library and here an escalator takes readers to the collections above. As a result the atrium provides the means to grasp the scale of the building and its collections, and gain a sense of orientation.

Unlike the earlier phases of construction, the Black Diamond has walls and floor plates which are angled to the perpendicular thereby giving the building a sculptural quality both inside and out. Since the main public facilities are located here, the loss of functional fidelity does not impede the working of the library as a national collection. In fact, the effect is to encourage intellectual discourse through the ambiguity of the faceted spaces created. The openness of the reading rooms provides many diagonal views within the building and through to the Hansen and Holm wings further afield. This sense of spatial flow helps break down the barriers between subject material and reader, and between that which is paper and image based.

As with all national libraries the main task is that of securing and preserving collections for posterity. The emphasis at the Royal Library is upon making the cultural heritage of Denmark available and accessible not just

Atrium in the new wing of the Royal Library of Denmark, designed by Schmidt, Hammer and Lassen. (Fotografisk Atelier, Det Kongelise Bibliotek)

through the archive collections but through the exhibitions and outreach facilities that are organized by the staff. The new building is the shop window for displaying the collection and the point of contact with the archive and research staff at the library. The large reading rooms of the Black Diamond signal the importance of using the collections in a space that captures the design values of contemporary Denmark.

## Parliamentary Library, New Delhi, India

Won in a competition by the architect Raj Rewal, the Parliamentary Library in New Delhi sits on a site of great symbolic importance to the Indian nation. Sandwiched between buildings by Herbert Baker and Edwin Lutyens, the building is the first major construction in the imperial centre of New Delhi for a generation. The library houses the government archives which used to be stored in the drum of Baker's Parliament Building until their volume

| Royal Library of Denmark | |
|---|---|
| **Architect** | **Special features** |
| Hans Holm (1906) and Schmidt, Hammer and Lassen (2001) | • National Archive and Deposit Library linked to University of Copenhagen |
| | • Large collection of musical scores and early maps |
| | • Design-led rather than collection-led spaces |
| | • Extensive exhibition and performance areas |

Exterior view of the
Royal Library of
Denmark (Black
Diamond). (Fotografisk
Atelier, Det Kongelise
Bibliotek)

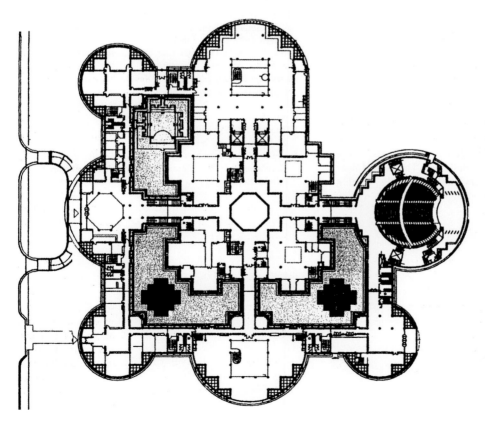

Plan of the Parliament
Library, New Delhi,
designed by Raj Rewal.
(Raj Rewal/AR)

| Parliamentary Library: New Delhi | |
|---|---|
| **Architect** | **Special features** |
| Raj Rewal | • Sits at the heart of the Imperial Centre of New Delhi |
| | • Uses linked courtyards inspired by Hindu architecture |
| | • Employs traditional shading and ventilation systems |
| | • Extensive basement storage for security |

and conservation required a separate building (Davey, 2002, p. 38). It is in effect the national library for India in terms of government archive provision and the scale of the collection.

The new library is deferential to the classical architecture of Lutyens and Baker yet more Indian in spirit, drawing directly upon historic Hindu temple precedent (Davey, 2002, p. 40). As such the plan consists of linked courtyards which draw together the various separate buildings to form a composition enclosed by a perimeter wall. The library houses a number of elements of various degrees of security. A two-storey basement houses the book-stack collection and principal parliamentary archive. This forms a safe and environmentally stable base upon which the remainder of the library sits.

On the ground floor are the main reception desks for the general public with separate entrances for parliamentarians, scholars and VIPs. The different entrances are placed axially at points of contact with perimeter functions such as the Parliament and Secretariat buildings. The ground floor houses the auditorium, scholars' library and MPs' reading room linked by corridors that face on one side into one of the courtyards and lead on the other to various offices. The first floor repeats many of the functions below with the accommodation housed in circular rooms that have their own internal staircases. The effect is like a Hindu Temple with an almost labyrinthine quality of self-contained volumes grouped around courtyards. The vertical sun overhead is skilfully used to light the interior rooms without overheating, by the use of traditional shading devices and glazed panels set into floors. A central pool of sunlight is drawn down into the lower floors from a large glazed dome which illuminates the study collection physically and metaphorically (Davey, 2002, p. 40).

Architecturally, this large library of disparate functions is united by a simple and sober palette of building materials. The main construction elements are pink sandstone and concrete whilst the interior volumes are enlivened with decorative tilework and timber screens. The effect is to remind visitors that India has its own architectural culture in spite of the legacy of European classicism left by earlier generations of builders. There is perhaps no better place to demonstrate this than in the Parliamentary Library in the state capitol.

## References

Brawne, M. (1997). *Library Builders*. Academy Editions.

British Library (1999). Quote taken from *What's on: January – March 1999*. British Library.

Chow, P. (2003). Glass Cloister, *Architectural Review*, August, p. 64.

Davey, P. (2002). Learning from New Delhi, *Architectural Review*, October, pp. 38–40.

Edwards, B. (1987). National grid. *Building Design*, 30 October, pp. 25.

Jeffries, S. (2007) Inside the Tomb of Tomes, *Guardian Weekly*, 24 November, pp. 51–55.

National Library of Wales (1998). *Statement of Collection Development Policy*. National Library of Wales, Department of Printed Books.

# 10

# The public library

The twenty-first century has witnessed considerable change in the design of public libraries. The growth of IT has led to an unprecedented level of evolution in this type of library, with a fresh relationship between books, readers and computers. The dynamic triggered by new information technologies has been paralleled by considerable social change in the nature of library users. Knowledge needs have changed and so has the means of imparting it. The examples discussed later in the chapter suggest the emergence of exciting new forms of delivering library services at both city and branch library level.

Each year in England around 60% of the population use public libraries. The majority of library users borrow books, both fiction and non-fiction, mainly for pleasure. A large number of users, however, visit the library in order to read newspapers or magazines, or to gain access to the Internet. A significant number of younger library users do so in connection with school or college projects. People looking for a job or local training opportunities use the public library as a source of information both about careers in general and jobs in particular whilst many others use public libraries to find out about community initiatives. In many urban areas one of the most frequent users of libraries are those who work from home or run small businesses. The diversity of uses of libraries by different members of the community suggests that their role beyond books is enormous.

Today the public library caters for different people in different ways. It is evident too that the various types of libraries available, from mega-city facilities to local branch libraries, fulfil quite distinct services to the community. As a general rule the 'larger the library the more often people will go to it, the further they will travel, and the better its image' (ASLIB, 1995, p. 7). This means that not only are larger libraries better and more valued, they offer a higher quality and more diversified services to the community than branch libraries. Increased scale not only provides the means to provide an enhanced architectural experience, it offers superior benefit to users. As a result the trend, in the USA in particular, is towards the creation of larger libraries as opposed to the proliferation of smaller ones. Where small ones are provided, they tend to be within other buildings (such as community centres or shopping malls)

with the result that the branch library is often an extension of something else.

Access is the key to successful library provision: access for people of all levels of mobility, and access for books. Convenient location is crucial both to serve regular users and those who visit the library on impulse. In the UK, the government set a target in 1999 of providing a library service for each person within a travel distance of 20 minutes. The relationship between libraries locally also influences patterns of use. Where a university library is available, it will be seen as serving both student and non-student needs. It is also likely to duplicate the material held in larger public libraries. As a consequence, the interaction between civic and academic libraries is one which should be planned to maximize benefit for all.

Few public library visits are made without combining the trip with other tasks such as shopping or visiting the bank. Most journeys made to main libraries are by car or public transport; most to branch libraries on foot or by bicycle. Hence, library users may visit the library carrying shopping or accompanied by small children or, having arrived by car or bicycle, will need somewhere safe to park. The brief for the design of new libraries or the upgrading of older ones should consider carefully the pattern of use and incorporate those functions which are an indirect consequence of the visit (bicycle or pram storage, etc.).

## Purposes and functions

According to a review of public libraries in the UK, there are four main purposes and 13 core functions of a public library service (ASLIB, 1995, pp. 11–12). The main purposes are:

- to meet the library demands of future generations
- to create libraries which are community assets
- to create libraries of direct benefit to people who live, work or study in the area
- to provide services that have a contingency value.

These four general purposes lead to 13 functions grouped in three broad sets:

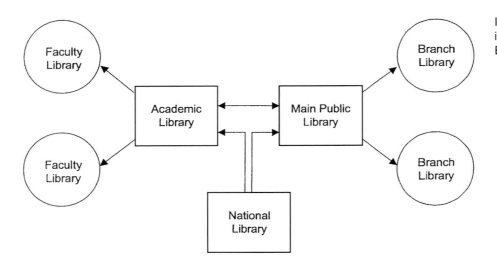

Ideal pattern of library interrelationships. (Brian Edwards)

1. Perpetual benefits:

   - enlighten children
   - provide popular reading material
   - create libraries which are landmarks in their communities
   - provide study space
   - provide 'new media' for loan or study.

2. Occasional benefits:

   - provide reference services
   - provide access to global knowledge and culture
   - provide local study sources
   - provide access to information on vital issues
   - provide local information
   - provide information for business, training or employment.

3. Social benefits:

   - create a library building of value as a familiar, relaxing place
   - create a library building which is a pleasant place and offers a stimulating environment.

It is clear that not all these purposes or functions are spatially dependent or even book dependent. These are aspirations that all public libraries should meet to a greater or lesser extent. Priorities are needed based upon local circumstance and the missions of different scales of library. However, one benefit of the list is that it encourages local context to generate the type and character of the library rather than the inherited collection or the whim of the chief librarian. The list also highlights the social value of the library and the architect should ensure that the building acts as an intellectual and social beacon by the very nature of its design. Architectural image will help the public library become an important feature of social, cultural and economic life.

## The 'street corner university' concept

In 2000, the UK Secretary of State for Culture, Media and Sport described public libraries as 'our street corner universities' (quoted by Glancey, 2000). This bold claim is dependent upon Britain's 4,160 public libraries being connected not only to the Internet but to schools, colleges and even the home. Whether the library can compete with the video shop and burger bar depends upon the presence of a welcoming and stimulating environment. It also depends on reading and study material which is fun to use. If people are to be active readers and researchers in the twenty-first century, the library needs to learn from the successes on the high street such as McDonalds, Starbucks and Virgin. There is such a mismatch between the environment of the library and the retail world that it is surprising that over 350 million visits are made each year to UK libraries (Glancey, 2000). Although each person in Britain borrows on average eight books a year, numbers are not growing adequately to meet the Secretary of State's 'street corner university' concept.

The problem is not only that of design – especially the uninviting libraries we have inherited from the past – but of presentation. Normally your entry into a public library is met by barriers (steps, doors, control points) and the first materials you encounter are books. Videos, CD-ROMs and the Internet are tucked away in their own special area. Although public libraries in the UK hold 127 million books, it is not the printed word which holds the key to the future. The 'street corner university' is an IT library first and a book library second. Public libraries need to learn the language of marketing, to exploit the techniques so deftly displayed in the retail world, and to engage more with popular culture. Peckham Library (see later) breaks the mould of the public library, opening up avenues for others to follow. Here the building is more meeting place than traditional library – the three arks floating inside are metaphors for the journey into the future. However, it is hardly a 'street corner university', being four storeys high and set back behind a new public piazza placed at right angles to Peckham High Street.

## Social role of public libraries

According to CABE (the UK's Commission on Architecture and the Built Environment):

- well-designed public libraries help revitalize neighbourhoods and cities, both physically and socially
- libraries increasingly provide support for public services in areas like welfare and life-long learning
- good library design increases the level of usage and attracts new users
- good design helps to retain staff and helps with recruitment
- well-designed libraries reduce crime and vandalism.

Hence, public libraries have an important role to play in supporting the British government's priorities for investment in the public sector. These are seen as education, skills training, health and related awareness of issues such as obesity, social inclusion, community, and neighbourhood renewal. The role of libraries is to provide the knowledge and access to information necessary to raise awareness and hence reinforce wider public debate in these areas. Similar initiatives exist in France and Sweden where the library is often the first point of contact between government social policy and the community. In the USA, libraries are normally the only place where free access to computers and the Internet are locally provided, thereby allowing communities to benefit from on-line educational facilities, job seeking opportunities and IT skills training (*American Libraries Association Journal*, 2007, p. 73). Empowering communities through the services in a library is a challenge for design as well as management. Increasingly, a library is 'a place where immigrants learn English and bridge the distance between their old country and their new adopted land' (*American Libraries Association Journal*, 2007, p. 48). The level of space provided for IT and language training as against traditional resources such as books and newspapers is a measure of a library's commitment to wider social cohesion.

However, to be effective in their social role, libraries need to be attractive and welcoming buildings. According to the CABE report *Better Public Libraries*, published in 2003 (CABE, 2003), outmoded design and poor location were responsible for the decline of 17% in the use of public

libraries in the UK over the previous decade. CABE recommended that libraries should be communication centres catering not just for residents but for the needs of businesses and tourists. There should be cafes and lounge areas to make long-stay visits to libraries more comfortable. The report also called for buildings that engendered a sense of fun in the discovery of new knowledge and the use of new technologies – not the drab world of silence and over-borrowed books which characterized many existing public libraries. The switch from books to free Internet access would result in the twenty-first century library, according to the CABE (2003) report, becoming a 'living room in the city' rather than a 'temple of knowledge'.

In being attractive to consumers, the architectural design of libraries should aspire to engage in the values of the communities where they are located rather than appeal to readers of architectural magazines. This may involve the use of colour, of cultural symbols, or of a design language accessible to ordinary people. Architectural design, which is appropriate for the context and the users of the library in question, may ultimately be more successful than one which is challenging.

Attracting more young people to libraries is important for the future of the building type and in achieving the wider social goals mentioned earlier. Surveys suggest that people in the 14–35 age group are not well catered for in public libraries. The problem is partly to do with image and design. Too few facilities cater specifically for young people or do so in an environment which is either chic or uses 'street' language (Library and Information Update, 2006). Putting the 'buzz' into libraries is a challenge for designers but lessons can be learnt by looking at other buildings. Media stores such as HMV, bookshops such as Waterston's and cafes such as Starbucks all offer a vision of a friendly ordered world which young people enjoy. Many libraries have a youth strategy but rarely an interior design message that fits the rhetoric.

Action that could be taken to put the 'buzz' into libraries includes:

- modernizing the style of existing libraries to avoid institutional connotations
- providing 'teenage' space away from the rest of library where the emphasis is upon comfort rather than noise control
- increasing multimedia and interactive collections
- extending electronic access
- widening opening hours to mirror retail practices.

It is often too easy to identify the functional and cultural shortcomings of public libraries. Changing social priorities inevitably demand new layouts as well as new collections and new modes of knowledge. The bigger challenge is to go beyond superficial functional efficiency and the limitations of service delivery. Librarians and their architects need to ask what the meaning of a library is and how social or cultural nuances are communicated through design. Libraries are repositories of knowledge: they are places where knowledge is stored and made available for use, thereby enhancing the understanding of individuals and, by extension, the empowering of communities. This is a highly elevated role for any building yet few modern libraries express this in their design image. The challenge for architects today is to go beyond function into the difficult but more fertile territory of expressing the deeper meaning of libraries through design.

Part of the cultural shift concerns the role of books. There has been a decline in the significance of the physical collection and a corresponding increase in information services of various kinds. New modes of knowledge storage and transfer have challenged the supremacy of the book. Boundaries have been eroded, costs have fallen and knowledge modes have been revolutionized, with the result that many people have libraries at home as powerful or comprehensive as public libraries of a generation before. For the first time in history, the library faces competition. Survival will depend upon meeting a new audience, providing new services, and making libraries into buildings worth visiting in their own right. The future lies in books, in the provision of quiet places to read, in areas for meeting and socializing, in IT access, and in managing the public realm of libraries so that security and control do not destroy the architectural experience of what makes a library.

## The public library as social capital

The library, as with other public institutions, highlights the fact that, with centuries of economic and social development, attention shifts from private consumption to more collective fulfilment. The book and its container – the library – ceases to be an indulgence or luxury of the wealthy and becomes a measure of quality of life for all. In this sense, the presence of books in the home and libraries in cities acts as a barometer of social or cultural maturity. The collective satisfaction of the public library assumes significance as a form of social capital as distinct from the economic capital of traditional wealth. In periods of social change, such capital can help cement communities. The point is well illustrated by, at the time of writing, threats to the future of Manchester Central Library, a distinguished circular building designed by E Vincent Harris in 1930. Located in an area of Manchester subject to change – from that of an industrial to a post-industrial economy – the library is seen by many in the community as a cultural asset in the widest sense. Campaigners argue that the collection (over a million books) and the building are points of reference in both social and physical space. Even by those who do not use it regularly, the public library is, in an important sense, perceived as a long-established community resource. Being designed as a landmark in free space,

Manchester Central Library signals the separation of public from private values – of institutions that feed knowledge as against enhanced capital wealth.

The public library service has begun to enter into partnership with other community-based agencies to provide information of various kinds. Leaflets on drug and alcohol counselling, on welfare rights, employment law, etc. are increasingly dispersed or displayed in public libraries. No longer is the book the main or sole target of the library visit: many visit the library to obtain advice or knowledge of the community and its social services. This trend has encouraged libraries to enter into agreements with other agencies and to make library space available for seminars, workshops and exhibitions.

The concept of civic participation, training and education now balance the traditional role of the public library as a source of books. Increasingly, the library is seen as the hub of a community network involving statutory and voluntary agencies. For disadvantaged communities, the library can help rebuild social life and in time economic vitality as well. To be effective here, the library needs to see itself in a different light from the spirit of the Library Act of 1850. It needs to be open when most in demand (evenings and weekends), to balance the book with electronic information systems, to encourage citizen participation by providing cafes, shops and exhibition space for use by local schools and community groups and, finally, to become a publisher of databases and other small-scale ventures (ASLIB, 1995, p. 68). Electronic publishing could transform the public library from a dull and staid asset for a few to a lively and essential resource for all. Increasingly too, the library is seen as a shop or kiosk in a large public building, for example a shopping mall, railway station, or airport. Here it can interface with the community more effectively.

Traditionally the public library is based largely upon the principle of leisure reading, mainly for those who possess the essentials of literacy and spare time. As society changes, however, new forms of library use emerge and expanding demands are made upon its resources. The agenda of social or community capital, aligned with the falling costs of electronic publishing, change the very nature of the library both as an institution and as a building.

Typical of the new generation of public libraries is that at Dewsbury in West Yorkshire, UK. The library has been constructed in a former supermarket and is combined with a careers centre funded jointly by the local authority and the Kirklees and Calderdale Training and Enterprise Council using resources available under the national government's Single Regeneration Budget (SRB). In addition, there is an Open Learning Library with an electronic database and a digital archive of 120,000 historic photographs funded by the UK National Lottery. The new library also contains a special collection for people with learning disabilities and is electronically linked to local businesses, fast food outlets and sports venues, thus ensuring that it is seen as wedded to the needs of the community. In addition, the library provides research support via IT networks to three local schools in each of which is placed a 'community study centre' used by children during the day and adults in the evening.

Although the initiative in Dewsbury was partly the result of pressure to close branch libraries in the town, the resulting rationalization has allowed the library service to have greater penetration within the community, local businesses and schools. Crucial to the success at Dewsbury was the cross-sector funding involving a partnership of local government, central government, charities and business. Equally important was the exploitation of electronic systems which eroded barriers between institutions. As a result of the changes, library use in the town increased by 36% in the first year (Taylor, 1999).

## Crisis in the public library

The dual role of the library of containing knowledge collections and making them available to inquiring minds has come under a variety of threats during the recent past. The culture of the public library has changed as people develop their own personal collection of books, have access to travel to national or specialist libraries, use university libraries on their doorstep, and find that their personal computer gives them greater access to global information than that contained in the local town library.

As society becomes more urban in character, the library becomes more accessible but perversely less used (according to the preamble to the *European Union Fifth Framework Programme 1998–2002*, 80% of Europeans and 50% of people worldwide currently live in major towns or cities). The concept of self-advancement which the public library has promoted since the 1850s has undoubtedly helped 'popularize books, reading and study thereby enhancing the lives of ordinary people' (ASLIB, 1995, p. 41), but has of late lost some momentum as society has found advancement through formal education and home-based computing access. Whereas books helped abolish time, distance and ignorance, the same is overwhelmingly true of the digital revolution. The switch from the public service element of the town library to support for private computer-assisted study at home has severe ramifications for the future of the public library.

It has been argued that the maintenance of a sound public library is as important to the community at large as to its individual members (ASLIB, 1995, p. 43). In this sense, the library is a cultural anchor in times of change – a point of reference for those seeking work, planning a career change, adjusting to a new neighbourhood, or discovering the texture of local political or social life. In theory demographic change focuses the community upon the library, but changing lives and lifestyles have cultivated

an environment of independence where the computer reigns. Without knowledge, the means of access to enhanced happiness and prosperity is denied. The traditional primacy of the library in this regard is increasingly under threat with the public library, more than any other public institution, having to develop a 'coherent response to incoherent changes' (ASLIB, 1995, p. 43) in society at large.

Besides the changes in information technology (IT), in the balance between home life and civic life, and in the expectation of life-long learning, there is a major problem in the developed world of an ageing population. An increasing number of library users will be elderly and they have special requirements as well as general ones. There are ramifications for access, type of collection (talking books, large print, Braille) and means of exchange (mobile libraries, home collections). The increase in the level of provision will benefit all users – not just the elderly – but will add to cost in an age of expanding pressure on the public purse. As the level of library use falls (due to IT and other changes in home-computing technology), the costs per reader rise. Politically the judgement rests upon value – the concept of the library as a true cultural beacon shedding light upon both the past and the future. A public library that fails to change to the pace of the contemporary agenda will become obsolete. That means that, whilst the library will become a building without walls for some, for others it will remain a special place with its own distinctive type of environment.

## The library as 'environment'

Just as museums, art galleries and stadiums have their own distinctive sense of environment, the same is true of libraries. This special ambience helps define a library as a place rather than just providing space in a functional sense. Designers and library managers are vested with creating or maintaining this distinctive quality. The library environment, essentially a stimulating and restorative place, is dependent upon the presence of four factors:

- it is an 'away' experience, different from everyday environments
- it is an experience of entry, occupation and exploration of large architectural volumes
- it is a coherent experience which is interesting and engaging
- it is a compatible experience where the spaces support one's purpose.

This list is adapted from Kaplan *et al.* (1993) (as quoted in ASLIB, 1995, p. 50).

These four factors are experiential rather than functional, and collectively give means to the library experience. They are a useful basis for evaluating the performance of existing libraries, and of establishing key principles in design briefs for new buildings.

The environmental quality of a library is dependent upon the design of both architectural and shelving elements. Fuji City Library designed by Yamato Associated Architects. (Yamato Associated Architects)

It is this distinctive quality that makes libraries worth visiting irrespective of the need to refer to books. The perception of the library being an 'away' place separate from home and work is true of the public library in particular. The university library on the other hand is rather more a place of work for the student and is, as a consequence, less symbolic. The relative neutrality of the academic library derives from its functional dimension as a place in support of learning and, to a degree, from the pervasive presence of electronic data, cataloguing and retrieval systems. The national library is even more symbolic and imbued with meaning than the public library. Here all four factors, combined with the nature and scale of the collection, create a special ambience more akin to visiting a major museum. But complexity can overwhelm the visitor if the library is a kind of information maze without spatial order. The answer to large libraries is to ensure that the architecture of the interior volumes directly reflects the architecture of the collection. Signs should reinforce cognitive mapping, not add to the confusion of navigation.

The same principles of special place should apply to libraries constructed in large buildings such as schools, colleges, research centres or hospitals. Here the library needs to be distinctive – a place which is restorative and encourages reflective inquiry. Though the library may be only a single building within a bigger complex, its distinctive ambience should be evident to all. The key physical elements which help create 'library environment' are space, light, flow, materials and collection. The first four are architectural, while the last is concerned with the collection and its

interaction via book stacks with the building itself. How the factors relate is the very essence of library design.

If there are distinctive features that make libraries into special places, one should not overlook the importance of people. A library rich in meaning and character is one which is peopled. Libraries need people as much as people need libraries – the sense of sharing with other readers is that special library experience which is at the core of 'library-ness'. The human dimension – the social interaction – is usually silent but knowing. To share in the same realm of intellectual inquiry establishes a bond not unlike that of two strangers enjoying a painting in a gallery. Part of the duty of the library designer is to create a place where such bonds are recognized as helping to nourish the intellectual strength of a community. The library in this sense is a gymnasium of the mind.

## Funding of public libraries and the effect on innovation

The public library service accounts for about 2% of a local council's expenditure (as against 8% of a typical university's in support of academic libraries). In the UK, this amounts to nearly £15 per year for every person. National libraries account for under 1% of national expenditure whereas a typical research-based company, such as GlaxoSmithKline, may invest 4–5% in its library provision. Compared to other national services such as health, defence or education, libraries are relatively poorly funded. Lack of investment is more likely to slow the pace of innovation in public libraries than elsewhere. University libraries, for instance, with four times the level of investment per capita can respond quickly to changes in technology or pattern of usage. IT libraries are better equipped and more comprehensively integrated with book-based stock in university libraries than civic ones – both public and national. Joint networking of IT systems across public libraries remains a rarity.

Innovation and diversity are often thwarted by the rigidity of management and building fabric. Lack of funds for the development of electronic libraries or microlibraries in shopping malls is sometimes used to justify lack of imagination or enthusiasm for change. This is rarely a problem with academic libraries but frequently occurs with public libraries. Building fabric can also be a real obstacle to change since new technologies require different standards of internal environment. The type and standard of lighting and the provision of new forms of ventilation and cabling can stress existing space. Equipment cost is itself an element, but the price of fabric upgrading to accommodate innovation can exceed the price of the computers themselves.

Access to the Internet is full of hidden costs; once the library becomes significantly electronic it is exposed to new legislative standards. The new information milieu and old patterns of space usage in existing libraries are not readily reconciled without significant investment. However, the problems with electronic information systems are that: they become obsolete quickly; they subject built fabric to considerable strain; they stress management regimes; and, given their all-pervasive nature, they can make the library redundant in a physical sense. The key to change may not be funding but the attitude of users and library staff to new digital technologies. Visionaries imagine a public library without walls, and mini-Internet libraries in every school and shopping centre and ultimately in every home. When this happens what will become of the traditional library building? Will it simply be converted into a cafe with a laptop by every napkin – a kind of library cybercafe with an associated 'granny web'?

Evidence suggests a polarization of library usage with a backlash by older readers who insist upon books whilst younger users avidly surf the Internet. The two worlds are increasingly becoming separate systems: they may be integrated in library space but they are not always integrated in library perception. Physical space can be used as the vehicle for system interface or can simply reinforce the division between the literate and computer literate sectors of society. In this sense, the library acts as a bridge between worlds – a place which breaks down the walls of knowledge compartmentation. It has the potential to be truly a high-tech gateway. The 'publicness' of the public library allows this to occur, or at least it would if funds and management policies permitted a fresh approach to the design of such buildings.

The architecture of library space is as important as the architecture of the collection – whether traditional or electronic. It can reinforce division and harden space into an exercise in social or information apartheid.

The welcoming entrance to Oak Park Public Library, Chicago. (Brian Edwards)

Alternatively, the architecture of internal space can facilitate freedom and access to information cyber-culture.

## Design strategies for the public library

The external square or set back public space which leads the library visitor immediately to the entrance doors needs to be inviting, wide and transparent, and arranged so that the interior can be viewed immediately upon arrival. It should also be possible to view the major library spaces from the outside, thereby providing links to the life of the city. Too frequently the demands for security interrupt the physical and visible flows between the inside and outside worlds.

Once inside the library the user should be able to comprehend the key spaces and principal routes. Hence the library control desk should not form an impervious wall but provide an inviting permeable barrier through which visitors navigate. The control desk where books are checked in and out should remain part of the entrance experience, not the sole or dominant element for the visitor. In large libraries it is often possible to form an inner foyer before the user reaches the library desk. Here there may be lockers, information boards relating to community

Public square adjacent to Alexandria Public Library overlooked by library cafe beyond. (Brian Edwards)

activities, a cafe and sandwich bar, and meeting rooms. This transition space between the inner and outer worlds requires particular attention in order to avoid disruption to the library. However, it is often the point where non-traditional users engage in the community facilities which libraries are increasingly providing.

The library desk and control barrier provide an essential element in the working of the library, as they are the main point of contact between users and library staff. The spoken word is essential to aid navigation through the collection, augmented by the catalogue and help desk. Increasingly, the next point of contact is with the computerized catalogue or the IT support area, which is usually nearby. To counter the dominance of digital information systems in some libraries (which can deter the elderly) there is often a magazine or newspaper area nearby.

There are four main strategies for arranging the book collection. The first is to stack the books near the centre of the library, arranging reading tables around the edge where there is good access to natural light and external views. The second is to place the books around the perimeter with a large central reading room often lit from above containing IT provision. Although there can be noise problems, this provides the opportunity to create an interior volume where readers can move readily between paper and electronic media. The third is to use a combination of the two: allowing the library to have a central reading room/IT space, a ring of shelving beyond which are located quiet study desks adjacent to perimeter windows. However, the integration of modes of knowledge and types of media is often difficult in practice because of the specific requirements of computers and the nature of some paper-based collections such as old newspapers or photographs. So in spite of the ideal of integration, there are often special study areas dedicated to types of media or study material. The fourth is to employ compact storage of books on shelving systems which concertina together. Here readers can access the books or journals by manually rotating the control wheel to open up the shelves in question. Compact storage releases space to meet expanding demand for computer space and community meeting areas.

Since the storage and use of knowledge is changing rapidly, libraries need to retain a high level of flexibility. The ability of the building to change over time without compromising the key attributes of what constitutes architecturally a 'library' is an important consideration at the design stage. Libraries are recognizable buildings where spaces like the reading room help to define the type. To provide flexibility at the price of character is to remove the civic dimension which increasingly is required of clients and users. However, libraries need to be able to adapt to changing information technologies and their evolving cultural or social role if they are to achieve their full relevance in the twenty-first century.

## Types of public library

The civic library consists of various scales of provision and contains a variety of library facilities. At a minimum there is a lending library with integral reading room, a reference library, children's library, a dedicated area for newspapers and periodicals, and sometimes a music room, exhibition space and local history collection. Civic libraries consist essentially of central libraries and branch libraries.

### The central library

A central library is normally the focus of a library system within a municipal area (county, city, state) which also entails branch libraries and perhaps mobile libraries for outlying areas. The central library is the headquarters of a system which services the branch libraries and undertakes any conservation or educational work necessary. In large cities, the central library is primarily a reference library (e.g. Mitchell Library, Glasgow, and New York Public Library) although some have small lending libraries attached. Central libraries also accommodate special collections of various types containing material of local interest. Normally, there is also a lecture theatre and exhibition space. Some central libraries are physically attached to municipal art galleries (e.g. Huddersfield) but generally, though detached, they form part of the civic quarter of a city (e.g. Norwich and Leeds).

The central library is both a major reference library and the hub of a system of branch libraries. As such, the main stack rooms serving the system are normally part of the central library. As libraries expand, however, the integration of storage and reader facilities is put under strain. As a consequence, book and journal storage is increasingly separated from the central library with a separate warehouse being used to house all or part of the collection.

The decision to integrate or separate book storage is based partly upon convenience and partly on cost. Even with electronic or microfiche systems, the growth in books and journals puts pressure on space. As the use of libraries increases, the increasing administration load puts strain on office space. It is often cheaper to outhouse books and journals in warehouses than to pay high city centre rent for what is essentially merely storage. By employing book warehouses just outside the city centre, the authority may be able to reduce costs whilst retrieving space for more productive library purposes.

Books are mainly distributed to the public via branch or mobile libraries. Just as the reader at a national library is not intent upon borrowing but upon gaining access to higher level provision, the same is true of the main central library of a city, country or state. Within a reference library, the integration of traditional and electronic retrieval systems is particularly important. The user is likely

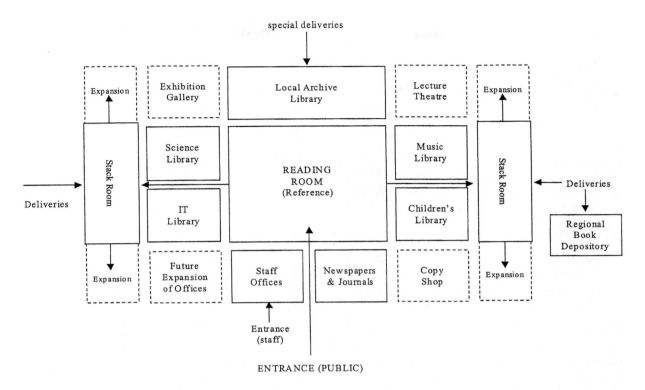

Diagrammatic layout of a central library. (Brian Edwards)

to be IT-competent – perhaps coming armed with a laptop computer. The central library needs to be able to offer high-level facilities, plus certain amenities such as exhibition space, cafe and lecture theatre. Background noise, which can be tolerated in the branch library, is less acceptable in the central library, except in designated areas.

The reference or reading room is the focus of the central library. It is sometimes used partly for book storage, giving readers instant access to commonly employed texts. The reading room is generally of large dimension in plan and section with specialist reference collections arranged around the edge. Where open shelves are used, these are arranged around the perimeter or project into the reading room forming smaller study spaces close to the material. Valuable books and journals cannot be placed on open shelves but, for the typical reader, the alcove system provides the right scale of space for private study.

As the reference library is a place primarily for study, it is important that tables, chairs and computer-based systems are integrated. Although there may be a separate IT library for viewing CD-ROMs, the reader needs to be able to refer to traditional and electronic data sources simultaneously.

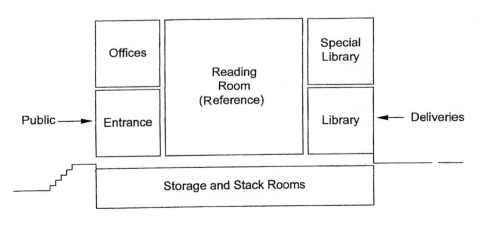

Diagrammatic section of a central library. (Brian Edwards)

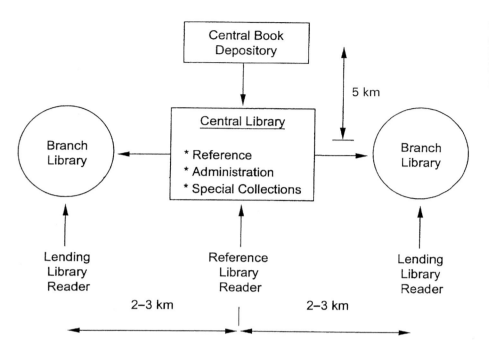

Diagrammatic relationship between central library and branch libraries. (Brian Edwards)

Separate rooms are normally provided on a subject basis, especially when the security of the collection is an issue. These can form a ring around the main reading room or overlook it as galleries. Occasionally they are grouped together into distinct wings dedicated to branches of learning. The stack rooms form a separate element of accommodation either in the form of a basement, as storage wings, or as storage floors sandwiched between public levels.

Since a member of staff using a book trolley retrieves most books or other study material in central libraries, the reading room and stack areas need to be in close proximity. Ease of access for staff reduces time and stress but, beyond a certain level of provision (about one million books), proximity is no longer possible. Here mechanical means of retrieval and movement are necessary, employing lifts, hoists and perhaps vehicles.

The layout of the reading room is determined by the spacing and position of open bookshelves, the policy of table sharing (2–12 people), whether to use armchairs (these define spaces better and are more comfortable for extensive occupation), and whether to provide low screens between reading spaces. Normally 0.6 m² (6 sq. ft) per person of table space is provided but if maps or large books are commonly referred to this may increase to 0.8 m². Gangway space between chairs of 2 m is necessary in main spaces and of 1 m in the study alcoves. Lighting is normally controlled to prevent glare from direct sunlight, to protect books and bindings from ultraviolet light, and to ensure a restful working environment. Sunlight is occasionally employed in newspaper reading rooms and in foyer spaces where it can enliven the atmosphere of the building.

The organization of a central library, which also serves in part as a lending library, is reflected well in the plan of the New York Public Library. Designed in 1932 by Carrère and Hastings, it has two entrances (public and lending) which converge upon a central exhibition space. To one side there is a domed lending library and to the other an undomed reading room. Both share a common stack room which runs almost along the whole of the rear of the building. On either side of the main entrance are the periodicals room and children's library. These flank the space, directing readers inward or upward to further reading rooms. The main public entrance faces Fifth Avenue whilst

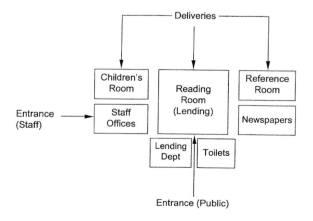

Diagrammatic layout of a branch library. (Brian Edwards)

the lesser lending library entrance faces 42nd Street, thereby reflecting the external street hierarchy in the plan.

### The branch library

The branch library normally consists of:

- lending department
- main reading room
- children's reading room
- periodicals and newspaper room
- reference room
- community meeting room
- staff offices.

In addition, there are toilets, entrance and control points, and copying facilities. As with the central library, it is important that traditional and electronic sources are integrated near or at the point of use by the reader.

Branch libraries vary in size and complexity. Some are simple affairs with a main reading room containing most of the functions listed above. Here the various sub-libraries are annexes or alcoves of the main library. In the larger branch library, there may be separate library rooms – perhaps on different levels or constructed as wings about the centre. In all cases, it is important to distinguish architecturally between the essential library spaces and the secondary accommodation.

As a general rule, the main library or reading room should be directly visible from the entrance and at the same level. Stairs and lifts should be in close proximity to the entrance but easily controlled for security purposes. The hierarchy of routes (vertically and horizontally) should be readily perceived, thus removing the need for excessive signing. Changes in level should generally be avoided and, where necessary, negotiated via ramps and lifts. The need for disabled access is paramount – doors, corridors and space between furniture should all accommodate wheelchair users.

Visual supervision of the reading areas is vital if theft or abuse of material is to be avoided. Where a main library leads to secondary libraries, it is important that a single member of staff can supervise both areas. The position of staff desks should be considered at the building planning stage. To avoid noise and visual disturbance, library rooms should not act as corridors for gaining access to other areas. Since books and periodicals are generally stored on open shelves there is little need for stack rooms, but ease of delivery from the central library and its book depository is essential.

The lending department is the hub of a branch library. Since open access is almost universally provided, security of the stock (and sometimes of the staff) is paramount. The layout of the bookcases should provide ease of supervision by staff from their regular working areas. Although closed circuit television (CCTV) can be employed, there is no substitute for staff surveillance. It is not only the books that are under constant threat, but the potential removal of sections of books or journals.

Normally the reader passes a non-electronic control point to enter the lending department and exits past an electronic scanner placed immediately after the book checkout point. Some libraries dispense with control at entry altogether, believing the public libraries should be perceived as places without barriers. Control at the library exit is obviously essential and besides electronic scanners related to security bands on books and journals, there is often a CCTV camera overlooking the point of departure from the lending library. Normally, only one reader can exit at a time. Where theft is suspected, a discrete area should be provided for searching bags or clothing.

As with all libraries, good lighting is essential if readers are to scan the books in comfort. Direct sunlight can fade bindings and cause discomfort, but natural light should not be dispensed with altogether. There are areas such as the entrance foyer or exhibition gallery where sunlight is desirable, and even in the main reading room sunlight entering via a central rotunda can produce a pleasant space in which to read. Sunlight should normally be avoided in close proximity to the bookcases – here shadows, glare and fading are all problems. Blinds, louvres and curtains can all be used to ensure that daylight enters the main reading rooms without the problems of direct sunlight. In some modern libraries, electronically controlled blinds are employed in both windows and roof lights to moderate the internal environment.

## Major public libraries

### Alexandria Public Library, Egypt

Known as the Bibliotheca Alexandria, the new and important public library in Egypt's second city of Alexandria has many of the characteristics of a national library. It

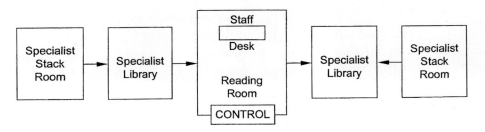

Relationship between reading room, specialist libraries and stack rooms in a central library. (Brian Edwards)

Alexandria Public Library with elevated pedestrian bridge. (Brian Edwards)

| Alexandria Public Library | |
|---|---|
| **Architect** | **Special features** |
| Snohetta | • Hybrid of national and public library<br>• Waterside site to help with urban regeneration<br>• Inspired by Egyptian iconography<br>• Large reading room over 4 floors<br>• Linked conference facilities |

contains rare and culturally valuable collections near the site of the world's first library founded by Alexander the Great in the second century. Yet it functions also as the public library for Alexandria and, having the campus of the University of Alexandria on its doorstep, also serves a large student population. As a consequence, the library is

something of a hybrid and arguably benefits architecturally from the scale, complexity and ambiguity of its functions.

Large public libraries have the habit of projecting the cultural values of the peoples they serve. They not only contain nationally important collections of printed matter, they also signify the centrality of the printed word through their approach to architectural design. This is no more evident than in the Bibliotheca Alexandria. Built in 2000, following an international architectural competition won by the relatively unknown Norwegian practice of Snohetta (named after the country's highest mountain), the library opened in 2002 to considerable acclaim.

Detail of alphabet inscribed wall of Alexandria Public Library. (Brian Edwards)

Reading room at Alexandria Public Library. (Brian Edwards)

The design of the Alexandria Public Library makes many references to both the classical and oriental worlds, yet it is decidedly modern in spirit. What makes the building significant is the way the contemporary cultural aspirations of Egypt are expressed without any hint of the building failing to serve its purpose as a major depository of printed treasures. A huge tilted disc which represents the sun and moon (images drawn from Egyptian funerary monuments) rises from the site boundary on Corniche Drive, on the edge of the Mediterranean, to become the roof of a massive seven-storey high reading room. The space inside is dramatic and fluid with seven main galleries housing seats for 2,500 scholars overlooking a central information, exhibition and control point placed half way up the building. The disc of the reading room is 160 m in diameter and lit by a number of triangular slivers of roof glazing which deflect sunlight through diamond-shaped apertures to the reading room below. At night they provide the framework for artificial lighting which complements the desk lamps at every study desk. The use of green and blue strips of coloured glass coupled with distant views of the Mediterranean provides a colourful volume in which to contemplate the study collections.

The reading room roof is supported by a number of slender concrete columns which in turn hold up the seven main gallery floors. The columns are shaped to reduce their impact upon the views out to the sea and provide the library with essential structural articulation. Widely spaced, the columns end in pseudo capitals which evoke something of a classical precedent. The columns not only define the lines of beam roof lights above, they also help structure the space below for desks, stairs and bookcases. The resulting articulation of ceiling and floor helps give meaning to the

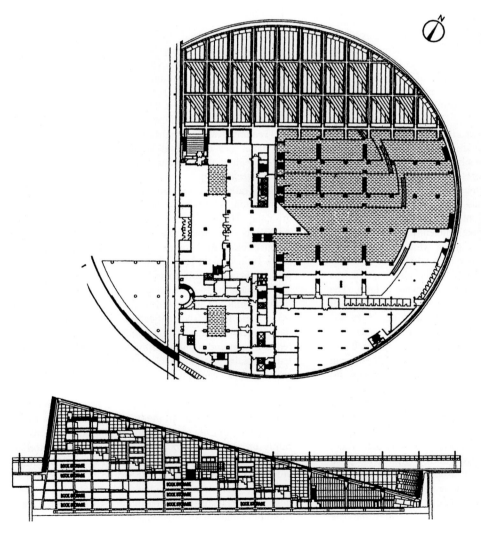

Plan and section of Alexandria Public Library. (Snohetta Architects)

space in terms of the collection and the routes through the library from the different levels.

The single big volume of the reading room with its many IT terminals represents the integration and interconnectedness of knowledge. Although separate study areas are available for specialist readership, the geometric grandeur of the reading room suggests that all of human knowledge is available in this wonderful space. Problems of noise are overcome by the extensive use of acoustic panelling on walls and ceilings, and sound absorbent floor finishes. The use of the curved shape reduces deflected noise across the reading room. The effect is to provide the library with a background hum of activity but no peaks of disturbing noise even in the reprographic areas.

The bulk of the collection of rare manuscripts and books is contained in a four-storey basement where conditions for protection and conservation are most favourable (Spring, 2000). Books are delivered to the reader (as with most national libraries) rather than the reader retrieving study material directly from book stacks. However, a limited amount of more commonly used study material is available on each of the reading room galleries, where the stacks form an acoustic barrier between the access points, stairs and lifts and the centrally placed area of reader desks. The offices of librarians occupy a segment of the disc on each floor thereby allowing staff to readily oversee readers and help with their inquiries.

From the outside the Alexandria Public Library has the eye-catching appeal of a pyramid with its allusions to the sun god Hathor. The sloping silver disc of the reading room breaks with the pattern of repetitive solid blocks of offices, hotels and apartment buildings which line the Mediterranean waterfront. The disc sits upon a circular granite wall with the alphabet in different languages carved into the stone in a fashion which evokes ancient Egyptian practice. The entrance is via a public plaza which is reached by crossing a circular lake onto a high-level walkway. This leads to a generous urban space which also contains the 120-seat planetarium, cafe and conference centre. The geometry of the entrance sequences enhances the drama of using the library and the adjoining structures. Like the British Library, attention to urban design and pedestrian routes adds to the pleasure of studying at the building. It also ensures that the spectacular views across the Mediterranean are exploited for those who wish to take a break from intensive study.

The materials of the library and the external surfaces of paving and seats are the same. The use of locally quarried granite in grey and black unifies the interior and exterior surfaces. This is most marked at the public entrance where a triple height reception area surfaced in granite leads via a glazed security screen to an information deck similarly surfaced. The use of black granite is reserved for stairs and wall panels around lifts where it contrasts with the blond wood of furniture. The theme of black, grey and pale

yellows of wood veneers establishes the language of furniture design from book stacks to study desks. One clever attention to detail is the employment of the same finishes for the top of book stacks which, because of the cross-section, are often viewed from above.

The decision to locate the library of Alexandria at the waterfront afforded the opportunity to regenerate the seaport area of a city noted for problems of decay and rapid urbanization. The library acts as a symbol of national pride and projects an image of a forward-looking nation where the past coexists with a high-tech future, for, in spite of the 8 million books (intended to rise to 15 million), every reader desk is equipped with wireless access to IT thereby providing the opportunity to work across media types. The combination of a progressive design coupled with a sense of history and environmental sensitivity led to the building receiving a coveted Aga Khan Award in 2004.

### Chicago Public Library

Known as the Harold Washington Library, the Chicago Public Library is reputed to be the largest lending library in the world. Occupying the whole of a city block in downtown Chicago, the building is densely planned over 10 storeys and finishes at the top in an attractive winter garden cum reading room. The layout is relatively simple: each floor is a self-contained subject library with associated reading desks, computer suites and quiet study areas. The latter are distributed around the perimeter of the building where they gain access to daylight and can enjoy views over the city.

This rather quirky post-modern library — won in competition in 1992 by the Professor of Architecture at Yale, Thomas Beeby, of Hammond Beeby Babka Architects — is rationally planned around a cruciform layout of circulation routes. Centrally placed escalators and stairs connect with large movement zones, which in turn provide access to information desks and banks of lifts. The axes and cross-axes open up interior views, making the library legible to users and displaying in one sweep the main aspects of the collection. The space between the circulation areas is filled with grids of book stacks, reading areas and support facilities such as copy machines. Escape stairs are sandwiched into the perimeter walls creating thick façades which, in their monumentality, recall the work of Louis Khan.

The major and minor grids of the library provide an order which extends from the building master plan to the finest detail. In Chicago fashion, the lines and patterns are firmly etched into the building establishing a metaorder, which in turn organizes the collection of over 6 million volumes into a comprehendible whole. It is a pattern of repeating geometric parts which help establish the positions of primary elements (book stacks) and minor ones (lighting, tables, floor finishes and cabling). Beeby sought

| Chicago Public Library | |
|---|---|
| **Architect** | **Special features** |
| Hammond Beeby Babka | • Inspired by Chicago-style <br> • Quasi-department store layout with escalator-based circulation <br> • Traditional book-centred library <br> • Integration of book-stacks, lighting and furniture layouts |

Detail of façade sculpture at Chicago Public Library. (Brian Edwards)

an 'adaptable yet understandable building' and, although there are similarities, each floor has a separate spatial subdivision which reflects the nature of the subject housed.

The library is rather like a department store with a number of entrances from the different streets that edge the urban block. These lead to a central information point and exhibition space, which in turn directs readers to the library on the nine floors above. Although there are lifts, users are encouraged to circulate through the library on the central bank of escalators, which in retail fashion, provide unfolding panoramas of the collection on the different levels.

The Chicago Public Library is essentially a book-based library with IT provision taking a secondary role. The book stacks are designed specifically for the building and are permanent parts of the architecture of the library. The same is true of the reader tables and the information desks. Hence, there is monumentality to the building with Beeby designing what he calls a 'library of memories' rather than an anonymous flexible shell (*Atlantic Monthly*, 1992).

From the outside, the library makes a number of references to the Beaux Arts architecture of Chicago. The building draws upon compositional ideas from the city's great architects from Adler and Sullivan to Daniel Burnham and Frank Lloyd Wright. Rich in quotation and metaphor, the library is the epitome of post-modern neoclassicism. Complete with sculpture on the roof, a rusticated granite base and arched windows which establish an immediate rhythm and scale to the elevations, the Chicago Public Library is a building which belongs to its Midwestern place. This is a building which continues the lengthy tradition in American cities of providing libraries to assert pride in books, reading and the civic realm.

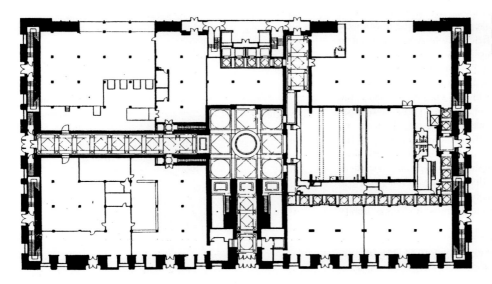

Plan of Chicago Public Library. (Hammond Beeby Babka)

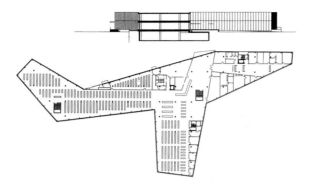

Plan and section of Des Moines Public Library. (David Chipperfield/AR)

| Des Moines Public Library | |
| --- | --- |
| **Architect** | **Special features** |
| David Chipperfield | • Part of wider scheme of urban regeneration<br>• Has landscaped roofs<br>• Irregular angular layout<br>• Part drive-in library |

## Des Moines Public Library, Iowa

Des Moines, the state capital of Iowa, is the location of another large civic library built as part of wider downtown regeneration in American cities. The library is arguably the major cultural anchor in many North American cities and caters for a wider social clientele than art galleries of sports centres. As such their location in the very heart of cities allows the public library to achieve more social gain than many other buildings. This is particularly true in Midwest Iowa where David Chipperfield Architects has designed an unorthodox yet eye-catching library.

At two storeys high the building spreads irregularly across the large rectangular urban block of central Des Moines. Overlooked by high-rise corporate offices and standing alongside parking lots, the new public library has an inauspicious location. However, the zigzag footprint and turf-covered flat roof allow the building to compete. The non-orthogonal design puts emphasis on the ground floor where a number of non-library facilities are located as angled wings contrasting with the rigidity of the urban grid pattern. Here there is a cafe, bookshop, meeting room and gallery set as an introduction to the more traditional library

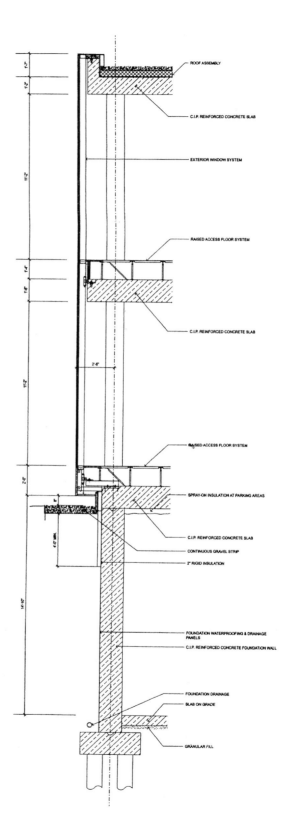

Façade detail showing window system at Des Moines Public Library. (David Chipperfield/AR)

spaces beyond. Like Seattle Public Library, this is a building for community use rather than simply for those intent upon borrowing a book. The angularity of the building creates interesting external spaces which are used for seating, external chess, servicing the building and provide that American speciality – the drive-in library. The paved area adjoining the cafe also links into a city park to the west with the new library forming a termination amongst the trees.

The books are held in open stacks on the ground and first floor with a back-up storage in the basement. Reader tables are placed mainly around the perimeter of the building and take advantage of the voids created by the colliding geometries of the wings and the stacks. An area for the special collection is tucked into an angle facing the street in one direction, and staff offices in another. In creating complex interior volumes Chipperfield has followed Koolhaas in Seattle, though here the complexity is horizontal rather than vertical. In contrast to the building's geometry the services and structure are highly rational. A 400 mm deep raised floor provides access to services whilst the exposed surfaces of concrete beams and columns exploit thermal mass to moderate temperatures. Further energy efficiency is achieved by the sedum-planted flat roof (LeCuyer, 2006).

The design of the library was chosen by the community when four options were offered by the architect. Chipperfield has produced a civic building which is sophisticated, understated and strangely appropriate. It sends a message of environmental and cultural responsibility without excessive posturing. Whilst the layout is unconventional, the emphasis placed on attracting people into the building, by careful focusing of pedestrian routes, ensures that the new library is stitched into the urban scene. In this it departs from normal urban practice in the Midwest.

### Vancouver Public Library, Canada

Vancouver Public Library which opened in 1995 is part of a large redevelopment in the heart of the city. Besides the library, there is a federal government headquarters office, retail and tourist facilities, and extensive underground parking. The whole scheme was designed by Moshe Safdie and Associates as a unified statement of both architecture and civic design.

The design is based on an oval and crescent and curved tower, producing a distinctive landmark for both library

View of Vancouver Public Library (on right) from new shopping mall. (Brian Edwards)

The central atrium at Vancouver Public Library divides the main book stacks from perimeter reading areas. (Brian Edwards)

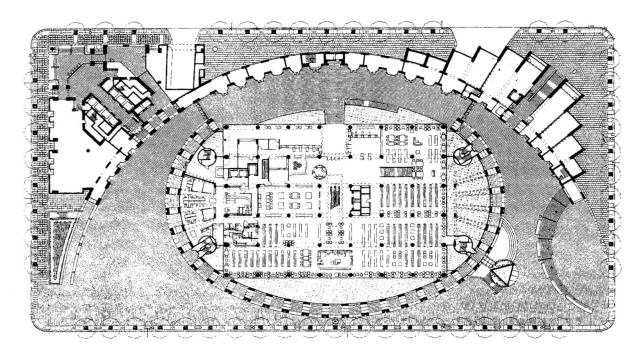

Plan, Vancouver Public Library, Canada. (Moshe Safdie and Associates)

and government administration. The public library is the central element and is designed as an ellipse separated from the other buildings by a roof-glazed crescent. This crescent is lined with shops and restaurants on the ground floor and defines the route to both library and offices. It is a wide promenade colonized by cafe tables and overlooked by the clear glazed wall of the library.

The entrance into the library is via a delicate bridge which spans the moat surrounding the library's outer walls. As visitors cross the bridge, they have the chance to look into the six-storey library. Since readers occupy the edge, with book stacks in the centre, the perimeter of the library is always animated with human life. The entrance leads to a large glazed cube which handles the control functions on

one side and the exit ones on the other. This entrance cube, defined by structural columns, has the necessary transparency to encourage the visitor to explore the library's many facilities.

The Vancouver Public Library is one of many recently built libraries which reverses the traditional pattern of placing a reading room in the centre with book stacks at the periphery. Here the stacks and computers are in the air-conditioned rectangular core, with the reader spaces arranged against the glazed curved perimeter. The library is in effect a rectangle placed in an ellipse, where readers select their book from the shelves in the centre and walk to the edge where seats are placed against the sun-filled walls. It is a pattern of movement from dark to light and from

| Vancouver Public Library, Canada | | |
|---|---|---|
| **Architect** | **Special features** | **Cost** |
| Moshe Safdie & Associates (with Downs Archambault & Partners) | Integrated library, retail, auditorium and government offices | $2,000/m$^2$ (approx) |
| | Places reader spaces at edge reached by internal bridges. | |
| | Elliptical design with rectangular book stack core | |
| | Employs daylight and sunlight to express route and volumes. | |

enclosed volumes to open ones, which Louis Kahn popularized a generation earlier in his design for the library at Exeter Academy, New Hampshire, USA. Safdie, conscious of Vancouver's dramatic setting, placed a curved perimeter reading gallery where books could be studied whilst simultaneously enjoying views of the street and distant mountains (Brawne, 1997). The bridges to the edge are both a means of expressing the movement and explaining the rationale behind the design. They also allow the edge to be separated from the core, permitting the reading galleries to be double height with lofty, fully glazed windows recalling a medieval precedent.

The clarity of the plan is not compromised by energy conservation. Everywhere is air-conditioned with raised floors for ducts and IT cables throughout. This allows for a high level of flexibility of layout, but at additional cost in terms of energy consumption, maintenance and construction. It does, however, provide the means to create a memorable library and one whose handling of daylight and space is exemplary. The separating of the core from the perimeter reading gallery allows light to penetrate deep into the library, and the curved glazed street between the library and the office tower deflects afternoon sunlight into the building. Although this is a large library (over a million books), the clarity of organization and the guidance provided through the building by light (especially sunlight) sets a useful pattern for public libraries of the future.

This library, shopping crescent and adjoining piazzas are further evidence of the maturing of libraries as public meeting places beyond that of buildings merely to read or borrow a book. Just as art galleries (such as the Guggenheim in Bilbao, Spain) have become buildings to visit in their own

| Montreal Public Library | |
|---|---|
| **Architect** | **Special features** |
| Patkau Architects | • Part of wider investment in civic realm<br>• Layout inspired by the 'mall'<br>• Adjacent to bus station for social inclusion<br>• Nature used as design metaphor |

right, the same is true of larger public libraries. The Vancouver Public Library is rather more a cultural and civic facility than a library as such. By the skilful design of the various public elements, Safdie has fashioned a building that serves as a library in the traditional sense but also caters for broader social need.

*Montreal Public Library*

The Grande Bibliotheque du Quebec is one of a number of libraries recently constructed in Canada over the past decade. Similar in scale and ambition to Vancouver Public Library and the refurbished and extended Toronto Public Library, this large library in Montreal continues with the theme of enriching the civic realm through the building of public libraries. Canada has an enviable reputation for municipal investment in the physical and cultural infrastructure of its cities. Montreal is no exception and the new library designed by Patkau Architects complements the slightly earlier provision of modern art galleries, the

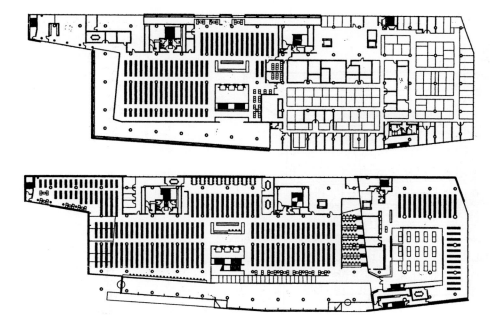

Ground (below) and upper floor plan of Montreal Public Library. (Patkau Architects/AR)

extended and upgraded Metro, and improvements to various urban spaces.

The new library has a less than distinguished location. Near to the Montreal Bus Station and several anonymous office blocks of 1970s construction, only the gothic spires of Victorian churches and French chateau-style apartments relieve the tedium of the immediate urban landscape. The design draws upon the idea of the mall, which is a triple height space along the southern frontage. It has the main entrance at one end and meeting rooms and lecture theatre at the other. With banners hanging through the three floors of the side-glazed mall and with shops, cafes and kiosks along its length, the impression suggests one of Montreal's shopping streets. However, its main purpose is to orientate users through a large and complex building, and to provide glimpses at different levels into the main library.

The book stacks are arranged on four floors in conventional fashion with study spaces around the edges. These follow a pattern not unlike that at Vancouver Public Library of forming bridges which project from the stack areas and overlook public spaces. As such, to read or study here is also to participate in the wider ambiance of the library. A more private and quiet reading room is provided at the east end of the building. This is architecturally a dramatic three-storey high space with roof lights above and timber louvred walls on all sides. Study tables are arranged in neat rows giving the impression that this is a space for serious scholars.

Like Will Bruder's Phoenix Public Library built in 1996, there is both a celebration of the book and of the reader in the Montreal Public Library. Unlike some recent libraries in the UK, there is less emphasis on youth culture, IT provision and wider social engagement. Although these

exist, the book is the dominant determinant of character and architectural order. The rational planning of the library leads to rectangular volumes and well ordered spatial sequences. In this respect, the Montreal Public Library differs from that of the similar sized Seattle Library built at substantially greater cost (Boddy, 2006).

The library is highly glazed on the south side in order to light the mall, draw daylight into the book-stack and reader areas, and provide views in from the busy pavement edge. However, the extent of clear glazing on the south side posed problems of solar gain and glare, which Patkau overcame by employing green glass louvres and tinted glass. The effect is to bathe the library in a verdant hue which, when added to the extensive use of timber inside and tall slender concrete columns, hints at the forests of Quebec. As a result, both the collection with its emphasis on French Canadian literary culture and the building seem specific to place.

### Seattle Public Library

Designed by OMA under the direction of Rem Koolhaas, the Seattle Public Library seeks almost to reinvent the library as a civic institution. It does so in the USA where the public library is one of the few anchors of civilization left in downtown areas. The building breaks certain rules of library orthodoxy such as the supremacy of the reading room, the dominance at least in terms of perception of the book, and the need for use legibility – that is the ability to recognize the building for what it is, e.g. a public library. Whereas other reinterpretations of the type (as in the public libraries at Brighton and Bournemouth in the UK, or Vancouver in Canada) still remain recognizable in function, the public

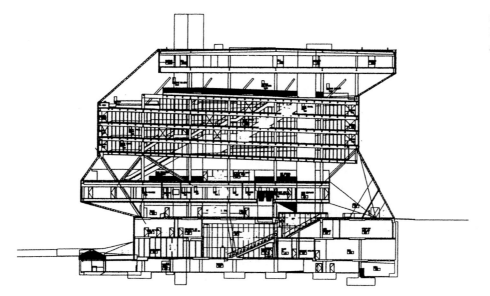

Section through Seattle Public Library. (OMA/ AR)

**Seattle Public Library**

| Architect | Special features |
|---|---|
| OMA/Rem Koolhaas | • Signature building to contrast with adjoining cityscape<br>• Spiral arrangement of collection<br>• Large vertical reading room<br>• Extensive non-library accommodation |

library in Seattle creates considerable ambiguity. OMA has created an eye-catching civic monument but its use as a library is only evident on close examination.

Commentators will argue that as the public library changes its use to better serve the needs of the twenty-first century, the form and image of the building need to change as well. Koolhaas and his team have designed a structure of facetted, cranked and inter-connected glazed walls which stand in contrast to the rectangular regularity of neoclassical Chicago Library and modernist Seattle. As such, the architectural relief upon seeing the building for the first time is enormous. However, enjoying the building as an external spectacle is only one part of the architect's challenge in designing a major public library. The others concern defining the entrance, establishing a clear boundary between inside and out, providing a hint of internal activities to external viewers, establishing a hierarchy of internal volumes and ensuring the building performs well functionally and environmentally.

The landscape of the triangulated modules of the glazed envelop encloses a huge entrance foyer where many non-library activities take place. The foyer is a public space for the community rather than a lobby to a library. Here there are exhibition spaces, an auditorium, bookshop, coffee shop, play areas for children, dens for young people and an information point for the main library. The soaring and spatially complex entrance hall, which varies in height from two to five storeys, leads to a spirally organized switchback ramp of book stacks angled at 2 degrees. The ramp is like a street imperceptibly rising to the next block although, instead of rows of houses, here there are parallel stacks of books. The ramp has the effect of removing the perception of floors, which can divide libraries into separate subject zones thereby undermining the connectivity of knowledge. There are two main entrances to the building on opposite sides of the sloping city block adding to the justification for the generous entrance volume which rises in part through all 11 storeys of the library.

Once through the spiral of book stacks the user reaches a reading room which contains a large panoramic window overlooking the city. The reading room provides glimpses down into the stack areas and up to the sky. To one side stands a tier of offices for library staff perched at the top of the building.

The Seattle Public Library has few enclosed spaces and not many walls or floors which are in normal architectural alignments. As a result, the experience is memorable if sometimes disconcerting. The disconnection between the exterior glazed envelop and the internal concrete structure,

Successful modern libraries should be dynamic buildings. Peckham Public Library designed by Alsop and Störmer. (Brian Edwards)

| Peckham Public Library, London, UK | | |
| --- | --- | --- |
| **Architect** | **Special features** | **Cost** |
| Alsop and Störmer | Seeks a popular new image for public libraries. | £1,900/m² (approx.) |
| | Raises library above ground to exploit light, view and silence. | |
| | Places special activities in sculptural pods. | |
| | Bold and radical structural form. | |

justified partly on seismic grounds (Rattenbury, 2004), allows the building to perform well socially and environmentally. This is a library which breaks with convention on many fronts. The brief was developed in close collaboration with the local community and the library staff in Seattle. As a result the building contains much art, colour and refreshing west coast innovation. OMA has exploited the current flux in library typology to create a building that promises to be a measure of municipal ambition in future library design (Lamprecht, 2004). According to Koolhaas, the continuous circulation ramp through the library allows the user to engage with the lyrical context of the surroundings whilst providing a clear statement of the programmatic diagram.

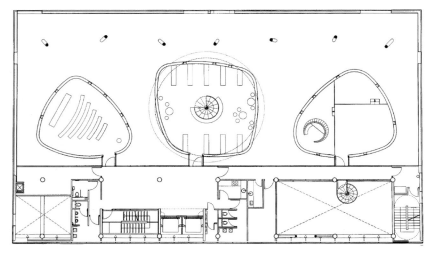

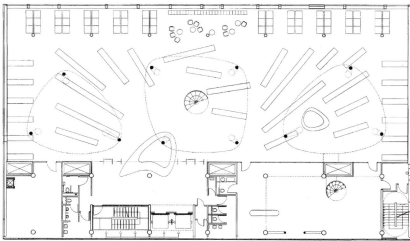

Plans, Peckham Public Library.
(Alsop and Störmer)

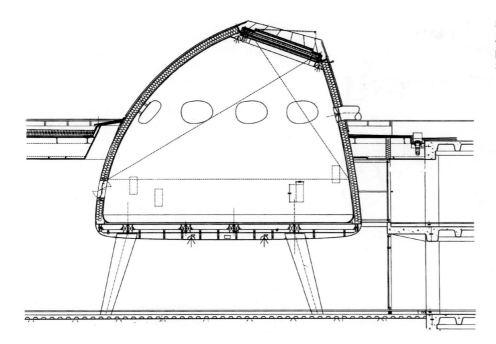

Section through
Afro-Caribbean study
pod. (Alsop and
Störmer)

## Medium-sized Public Libraries

*Peckham Public Library, London, UK*

Peckham Public Library designed by Alsop and Störmer also breaks the mould of public library design. It does so by dissolving the difference between inside and outside, creating a building of different parts united by a ground plane of crisp paving and a universal envelope of glass and bright blue panelling. Although it is a library, 'libraryness' is not evident; instead the building looks rather more like a theatre or the stage for a pop concert.

Such references are deliberate: the architect and client sought a library which would appeal across age, ethnic and cultural barriers. They also wanted a building which gave fun back to borrowing a book and which would act as a symbol of social regeneration in a deprived area of South London.

The library is built off the ground, giving the area in which it sits back to community. The library entrance is relatively understated – a timber ramp and a glazed cube viewed through a wire mesh. The main areas of the library are up high, viewed through a mainly glazed wall set back behind a thrusting cantilevered balcony. The balcony, which is set up high upon slender angled legs, affords protection to the entrance to both the library and the adjoining council information centre. The library entrance itself is minimal – a mere glazed lobby with a pair of lifts and a staircase taking visitors directly to the library above.

The library is placed up high to give maximum access to daylight on a congested urban site. Being up high also reduces the impact of local traffic noise whilst providing readers with distant panoramas over London (including a view of the Tate Modern at Bankside four miles to the north). Visitors arrive in the library proper after passing through an intermediate floor of staff rooms. The arrival is dramatic and unexpectedly airy. Where the ground level is busy with the noise and bustle of London life, the library on the second floor seems to float at roof level. The effect is enhanced by the high ceiling and the presence of three copper-clad pods positioned like giant coconuts within the main reader room. Sitting on angled concrete legs, they break through the roof to animate the skyline. Each pod holds an activity of special interest – the largest is the Afro-Caribbean literature collection while the two smaller pods house a children's library and a meeting room. They are metaphors for buildings within streets – creating in this high-level space ambiguity about inside and outside, and between collection and reading areas.

The act of reading a book benefits from the silence, view and sunlight created by placing the reading room 12 m in the air. Light is carefully orchestrated to pick out the functional high points in the building. It spills down the sides of the pods, generating tranquil reading areas at the library edge and, by forming a glazing band between wall and ceiling, gives the impression of a floating roof. By way of contrast, the north facing façade is clear glazed to bring neutral light deep into the book-stack areas.

This library breaks many conventions. It abandons the pavement level in favour of an idealized world for books in the sky. It celebrates special collections and activities by placing them in distinctive curved containers, which stand

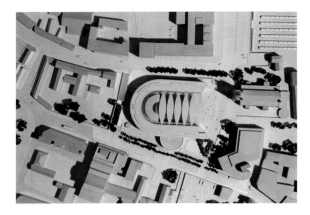

Model, Norwich Public Library. St Peter Mancroft Church is to the right. (Michael Hopkins and Partners)

free like market stalls apart from the bustle. The reading room is of double height to lift the spirit and provide a volume which gives dignity to reading and borrowing a book. As a design, the library gives more importance to the cross-section than the plan. Order in plan appears to be sublimated by spatial drama acted out in section.

The details of the library also depart from orthodoxy. Book stacks placed almost at random sit within rectangular floor plans. Although some radiate towards the library desk, others make reference to the irregular axiality of the three pods. Windows too are not evenly spaced, but patterned to create a large abstract composition of parallelograms of varying size. With tinted glass and blue cladding, the effect recalls the joyfulness of cinema or theme park design.

These various design effects are part of a deliberate strategy to appeal across social and cultural divides (Melvin, 2000). This is meant to be a popular building, cherished by the inner city community that it serves. Modern public libraries are no longer simply places to borrow books – they are buildings in which to meet friends, to hold meetings and to introduce children to the pleasure of reading. This building breaks with convention and charts a path of a more inclusive, lively and appealing public library for the future.

In spite of winning the Stirling Prize in 2000 as the UK's Building of the Year, reservations have been expressed over the library's fidelity to function. Some see the design as too influenced by pop art, claiming in the words of the Scottish architect Richard Murphy that the building is 'just a big gesture' (Sudjic, 2000). Certainly the library has the kind of impact needed in a multicultural area of South London – it uses colour and cantilevered structure to signal public presence across the rooftops. But as Murphy points out, the relationship between the parts, especially the shelving, appears haphazard and one wonders why the readers are discouraged from working at the perimeter of the building.

### Norwich Public Library, Norfolk, UK

The rebuilding of Norwich Public Library after a fire in 1994 provided the opportunity to create an architectural and civic landmark to celebrate the new millennium in England's second largest historic city. Designed by Michael Hopkins and Partners, the new building is a horseshoe-shaped building containing an atrium and library. The accommodation of the library – including a multimedia auditorium, learning and business centres – is arranged in a continuous curved wing to the rear of an atrium which provides a generous entrance space set back behind a new public square. This new public space for Norwich focuses upon the medieval church of St Peter Mancroft. A large glazed wall facing the church brings both into play as an urban spectacle and invites entry into the library atrium as part of a continuous pedestrianized network of spaces in central Norwich (M. Taylor and C. Endicott, Michael Hopkins and Partners, personal communication, 2000).

The footprint of the library responds to the scale of the surrounding urban pattern and its three-storey height shares that of the City Hall immediately to the north. The atrium has roughly the dimensions of the ground

| Norwich Public Library, Norfolk, UK | | |
| --- | --- | --- |
| **Architect** | **Special features** | **Cost** |
| Michael Hopkins and Partners | Stitched into historic core of Norwich | £1,250/m$^2$ |
| | Creates a square and public atrium on an axis with church. | |
| | Atrium-based library on horseshoe plan | |
| | Maximizes daylight to reduce energy use. | |
| | Moderates environmental conditions via a naturally ventilated atrium. | |
| | Lottery-funded. | |

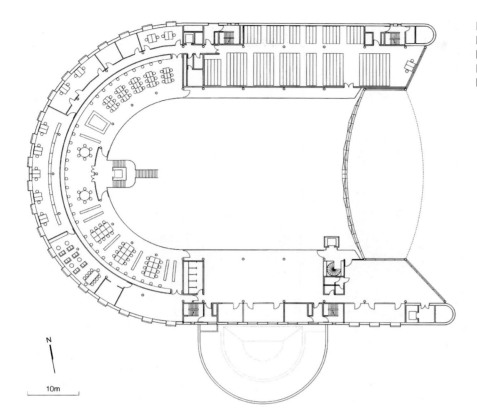

Plan, Norwich Public Library. Designed by Michael Hopkins and Partners. (Michael Hopkins and Partners)

N

10m

plan of St Peter Mancroft Church, allowing it to slide into the space conceptually. The height of the library (three storeys plus a concealed attic of offices) allows the tower and spire of the church to dominate the scene and provide a point of orientation from within the library. As with the new library in Münster, a nearby church tower is used to landmark and identify the presence of a public building.

The library is approached via a square which is at the crossing of two axes – one along the colonnaded face of the City Hall, the other on the axis of the church. These pre-existing pedestrian routes extend into the new library. This not only allows the entrance square and internal atrium space to be read as a continuation of familiar spaces, but also provides clarity of layout for the library. Upon arrival through the glass wall, all is visible and the accommodation of the library feels like an extension of the urban scene. The advantage of this strategy is to give the library a certain ambiguity as to what is inside and out, and what is front and back. It is an ambiguity which removes pomposity and invites use for a variety of purposes.

The accommodation of the library is housed in a continuous, narrow, curved wall which wraps around the atrium. The wall is 12 m deep to allow for the maximum

penetration of daylight and controlled sunlight. As a Millennium Project, the Norwich Public Library seeks to address the environmental challenge of low-energy design, whilst creating a distinctive city landmark. Since artificial lighting is the largest element of energy use in a typical library (followed closely by air-conditioning), the challenge is one of maximizing the use of natural light without incurring the penalty of unwanted solar gain. Here the solution is to employ load-bearing brick construction and exposed reinforced concrete floor slabs – taking advantage of their high thermal capacity to moderate temperatures whilst exploiting the support provided for façade shading. Hence, daylight is allowed to penetrate the library spaces but in a controlled fashion relative to potential solar gain.

The atrium within the centre of the library is designed to be used as a new covered mall in central Norwich. Arcades and covered market spaces already exist nearby, giving the atrium a sense of urban continuity. However, it serves an important environmental function as a source of solar heated air, which can be distributed to other parts of the library in the winter and readily ejected through the roof in the summer. The floor of the atrium is paved in tiles to provide a link with the external square

161

Sketch of atrium, Norwich Public Library. (Michael Hopkins and Partners)

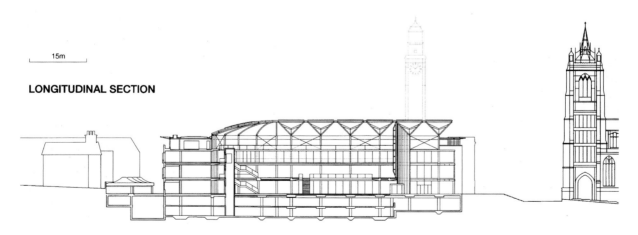

Section, Norwich Public Library. St Peter Mancroft Church is to the right. (Michael Hopkins and Partners)

| Brighton Public Library | |
|---|---|
| **Architect** | **Special features** |
| Bennetts Associates | • Part of comprehensive urban regeneration<br>• Establishes new square at front linked to ground floor reading room<br>• Innovative environmental features<br>• Mainly book-based library<br>• Won Prime Minister's Better Public Building Award, 2005<br>• Short-listed for Stirling Prize, 2005 |

and has underfloor heating to provide conditions that allow the atrium to be used for exhibitions or recitals.

Atrium-based libraries can suffer from noise disturbance. The solution employed here is to restrict the penetration of sound from the atrium by placing a corridor on the inside face of the various library areas. This double wall, together with acoustic insulation in the shelving, walls and ceiling, ensures that study conditions are acceptable in the library.

The library provides a complex range of accommodation on three floors. There are various specialist libraries (the USAF Second Air Division Memorial Library on the ground floor and the Norfolk Studies Library

on the second floor) plus a heritage visitor centre, tourist information, restaurant, auditorium, learning centre and multimedia facilities. Only the latter accommodation is differentiated in plan; the remainder of the library provides for flexibility of library and office layout. A large area of mobile storage stacks in fire-resistant accommodation exists on the second floor (built to BS 5454). The high specification here is a legacy of the fire in 1994, which destroyed much of the library collection. The main library is located on the first floor in a large semi-circular space, which fills most of the D-shaped accommodation.

The Norwich Public Library, partly funded through the UK National Lottery, provides much innovative thinking. Although primarily a library, this is a public building in the full sense of the term. It provides a range of facilities to support the community and does so in a building which is conspicuously accessible. The plan is figured as much by external conditions as by the demands of accommodation. The main atrium space, which was created as a gateway to the building, acts also as a public forum and environmental moderator. In this sense, the blurring of functionality and the blending of civic and environmental concerns are a precursor for future library design.

### Brighton Public Library

Known as the Jubilee Library, Brighton Public Library was created as part of a larger scheme of urban regeneration in the centre of Brighton (see pages xx–xx). Its immediate neighbours are large retail units, and the pattern of external spaces is one of malls and pedestrian squares. Designed by

Social space at Brighton Public Library with abstract mural. (Bennetts Associates)

Night-time view of Brighton Public Library. The building glows at night like the adjoining retail development. (Bennetts Associates)

Bennetts Associates (in collaboration with local architects Lomax Cassidy and Edwards) Brighton Public Library was shortlisted for the Stirling Prize and won the Prime Minister's Award for public architecture in 2005. The library is significant in three ways:

• in the approach to urban design and the role of cross-subsidizing the library with revenue from commercial development
• in the type of spaces created in order to broaden the appeal of the library, particularly for young people
• in the attention paid to sustainable design practices.

The master plan reinstates elements of the old street pattern lost in earlier development. A new urban cross-street (known as Jubilee Street) links together two city blocks and provides the public access to the library via a new square. The street and adjoining malls have a retail character which spreads to the entrance of the Jubilee Library. A new urban square acts as a buffer zone between the two worlds and allows the library to extend its presence outwards. Here seats and public sculpture establish the square as a civic place interacting with the commercial world.

The library has a fully glazed façade to the square thereby allowing the internal world of books, magazines and computer terminals to challenge the assertiveness of the retail environment. The dialogue across the new square between public and private interests heightens the tension of arrival at the library. The plan of the library places a large reading room in the centre with study spaces, meeting rooms, shops and offices around the perimeter. Bennetts Associates was keen that the building was a place of repose and presence where the character was civic rather than IT-based (*Architecture Today*, 2005). The repose comes from the double height reading room lit by daylight spilling from above through large apertures around the edge of the floor plate.

The library entrance faces south across the square. Inside there is a grid on two levels of four pairs of concrete columns which fan out to support the floors. The effect is to define the functional territories inside thereby ensuring that the book stacks and reading areas have an orderly relationship to the architecture. As a consequence, the layout of columns and linking bridges dictates the use of space socially and the effect is to give the book primacy over the computer screen. The relationship between space, structure and light is carefully considered and this establishes the primary order for the working of the library. Unlike other recent examples, the demands of IT provision do not override the interests of the library as a building engaging with its literary purpose and with the outside world.

Immediately inside the entrance, the library has a large magazine and newspaper area with soft seats. To one side there is an exhibition area and to the other there is a cafe which extends into the square. The effect is to provide a welcoming introduction to the library with the minimum of fortress connotations. The library is centrally planned around its columned reading room. Specialist spaces such as the rare books collection and audiovisual library are located around the edge where specific environmental conditions can be provided.

The central library space is naturally lit and largely naturally ventilated. The south facing glazed wall coupled with the thermal mass of the concrete frame, the wooden acoustic panelling on the walls and the apertures in the floors (both centrally and around the periphery) provide a high level of environmental sustainability. The ventilating chimneys and Termodeck floors reduce the summer energy load whilst giving the library the benefits of recirculated warmed air for winter heating (Evans, 2005).

### Bournemouth Public Library

Opened in 2002, Bournemouth Public Library won the Prime Minister's Award for Better Public Building in 2003, two years before a similar award was made to Brighton Public Library. Both libraries have in common their attention to both library design and to the wider challenge of reinstating former street patterns in order to enhance the civic realm. At Bournemouth the historic line of the town high street was re-established with a triangular square created opposite the library entrance, which is positioned at the corner of the site. As a result of respecting the archaeology of the place, the new library is organic in shape.

Like many new UK libraries, there is a combination of retail and library facilities within the development. A cluster of shops runs along the street frontage at ground floor level with the library above. The arrangement gives the library attractive views over the town whilst maintaining continuity in the high street activities. A triple height foyer set behind the glazed elevation to the street provides space for a generous curving staircase and open lift, and a cafe to one side. The routes into the library are legible and accessible with high levels of natural light and visibility. The stair leads not just to the library at first floor level but to a double height exhibition area and adjacent children's library, gallery space, local archives collection, music library and performance space, and a business centre.

Compared to the amoeba-like plan, the section is relatively straightforward. The three-storey building has a curved roof which over-sails slightly to achieve a measure of solar gain. Four ventilating cowls project from the roof and allow the library to be naturally cooled without the intrusion of street noise. Large areas of glass provide good visibility into the building whilst also delivering to the deep plan areas a relatively high level of natural light. The attention to sustainable construction allows the library

Elevations of Bourne-mouth Public Library. (BDP)

(as also at Brighton) to establish a benchmark for commercial development in the town.

The library is a civic building in the full sense of the term. It engages in the life of Bournemouth directly through proximity to the web of retail and commercial facilities. However, the mix of uses at the library and its elevated position ensure that the building is both inclusive in character yet set aside sufficiently from the bustle of street life to be seen as a public institution. Funded under the UK's Public Private Finance Initiative, the new library sets a useful benchmark for twenty-first century information buildings.

### Idea Stores, Tower Hamlets, London

The 'idea store' concept was coined by the Learning Spaces Consortium as a means of regenerating the concept and content of public libraries. The consortium consisted of the architectural practice Regeneration Partnership, planning consultants Urban Practitioners, the Chartered Institute of Library Professionals and branding consultants Bisset Adams (Blackman, 2003). Two libraries have been completed to date for the London Borough of Tower Hamlets based on the idea store principle – one in Whitechapel Road, the other in Crisp Street. Both are based upon the ambition of attracting more users to public libraries by diversifying the services on offer, changing the image of a library as a building type, and by refiguring the pattern of spaces both internal and external. In many ways the idea store concept is a direct response to the Cabe report titled *Better Public Libraries* which blamed outmoded design and poor location for a 17% decline in visits to public libraries over the previous decade (Blackman,

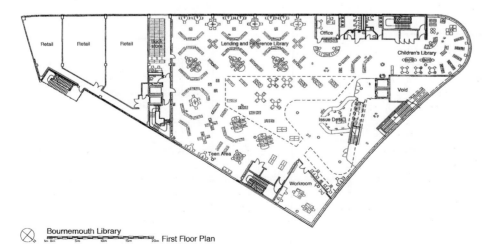

Plan of Bournemouth Public Library. (BDP)

Bournemouth Library
First Floor Plan

View of Whitechapel Idea Store from local street market. (Brian Edwards)

| Idea Stores: Tower Hamlets | |
|---|---|
| **Architect** | **Special features** |
| Adjaye Associates | • Emphasis on social inclusion<br>• Large community and educational areas<br>• Top floor cafe for meetings<br>• Coloured facades inspired by local street markets<br>• Short-listed for Stirling Prize, 2006 |

a modern dance studio, a specialist space for teaching complementary therapies, new multimedia area, life-long learning rooms connected directly to local schools and colleges, and a cafe. A feature of both libraries is the attention paid to inclusive design and the direct connection between local retail areas and the library.

The idea store name suggests openness, customer focus and an intriguing hint of something new and different (Evans, 2004). Both libraries are designed by Adjaye Associates and achieve these ambitions by focusing upon transparency, large public display areas, generous circulation spaces and interesting book-stack layouts. The entrances to both libraries link directly to the network of streets and lanes used by locals to reach shops and street markets. At the Whitechapel idea store a cross-street leads directly to a Sainsbury's store whilst the main frontage is onto the popular street market which extends from Whitechapel underground station to the new library. As a result the idea store is seen as part of the rich social mix of the community and shares architecturally in some of its imagery, such as the green and blue striped market stall awnings which Adjaye Associates translates into the curtain wall. A similar effect is seen at the Crisp Street Library where the colours of the glazing pick up those of nearby trees and the sky whilst also alluding to those of its sponsor, Lloyds bank.

2003). What was proposed in this influential report was a change of image for the library >from that of a 'temple of knowledge' to a 'living room in the city'.

The idea stores in Tower Hamlets seek to make the library a vital part of the local community by combining traditional library facilities with a wide range of social, leisure and educational facilities. The latter include

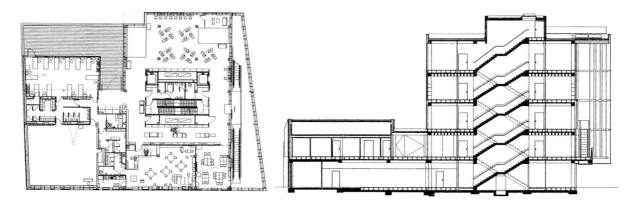

Plan and section of Idea Store, Whitechapel. (Adjaye Associates)

Both libraries use escalators as the main means of taking readers to the upper floors. The use of both escalators and stairs (and lifts for the elderly and disabled) is user-friendly, opens up the interior to ambiguous diagonal views and hints at a retail experience. The entrance doors in both libraries expose users to a variety of options. There are book return points (mostly electronic and self-operated), information desks, open learning zones, exhibition spaces and, on upper floors, there is a combination of adult, teen and children's libraries with cafes and meeting rooms above.

Both idea stores include a large number of classrooms that are networked to local colleges and universities. The aim is to erode the distinction between different types of public provision in the field of knowledge dissemination and use – blending in this case education, community well-being, social networking and library facilities. The library areas break with tradition and use curving book stacks which are kept relatively low to allow the sense of interior space to flow. Desks and light fittings were designed by the architect and when combined with red and green rubber stud flooring create a memorable and inviting interior aimed primarily at new library users. The Whitechapel idea store was shortlisted for the Stirling Prize in 2006.

*Public Library, Münster, Germany*

This library is a model of fitting a large public building into a dense urban area. Lying in the eastern quarter of the old city of Münster, the new public library is split to frame a view of the fifteenth century tower of Lamberti Church. The division of the library into segments allows the building to be less monolithic and hence more easily absorbed into historic Münster. It also facilitates the identification of separate parts of the library to serve different needs. The acknowledgement of the church tower in the articulation of plan is fitting since Münster means Minster — a clear reference in built form to the city's religious origins. Keeping the church tower in view also

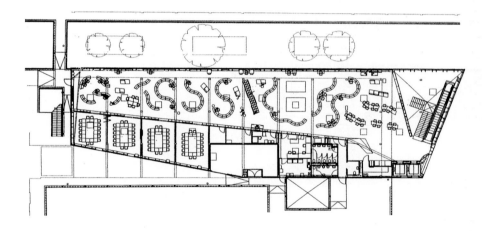

Plan of Idea Store, Crisp Street, London. Notice the retail units on the ground floor (below) and the community meeting rooms on the first floor (above). (Adjaye Associates)

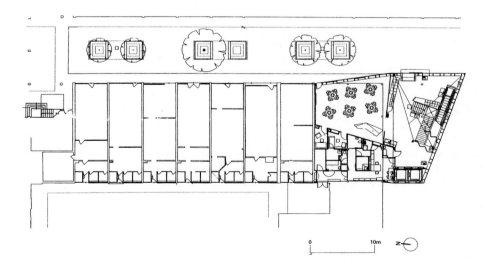

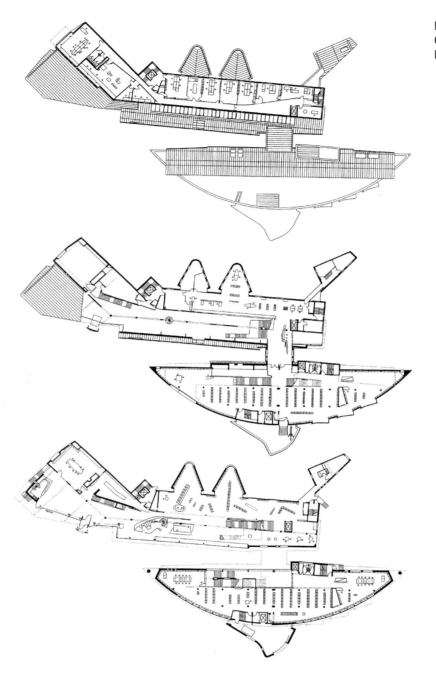

Plan, Münster Public Library, Germany. (Bolles-Wilson and Partners)

allows the new library to be located by its proximity to the older neighbour (Blundell Jones, 1994).

The split of the library accommodation into two main parts creates a central, narrow, new street in the dense urban fabric, which itself has become part of the network of pedestrian routes and alleyways. A library bridge joining the two parts terminates one end of this street and allows the other to focus on the church. Whilst new public

libraries generally derive their plan from functional needs alone, this one gives prominence to external conditions. It was the recognition of this balance which allowed its young Anglo–German architects Bolles-Wilson and Partners to win the design competition for the commission in 1993.

Initially the building was to be divided into a library and museum, but as the project developed it was decided to

168

| Münster Public Library, Germany | | |
|---|---|---|
| **Architect** | **Special features** | **Cost** |
| Bolles-Wilson and Partners | Design opens up new views of historic city. | Not available |
| | Building dramatically split between lending and reference wings. | |
| | New street formed on important church axis. | |
| | Informal, relaxed interior library environment. | |

build a library only. The division into two parts suited the split between public library and public museum use, but the architects found that as a library alone the division into two elements allowed the public lending and reference libraries to be expressed separately (Blundell Jones, 1994). Such an arrangement also gave prominence to the bridge joining the two zones together, allowing its symbolic importance to justify its urban role as a counterpoint to the axial termination of Lamberti Church.

Bifurcation expresses functionality, with the connecting bridge at first floor level being the main point of arrival and control into the library. All visitors enter via a raised terrace edged by cafes and the newspaper reading room. The entrance route is informal recalling the pattern elsewhere in historic Münster — a series of terraces, steps and curved walls. Since both wings of the library (lending and reference) are roughly of equal volume, the visitor is guided towards the information point by a slot of light drawn in by opening up the sky immediately above. The splitting of roof and wall to allow for the penetration of light at key points in the library allows hierarchy to be established without resorting to excessive signage.

This is a library of complex, subtle spaces. Although there are rooms, this public library is a series of interconnecting spaces. The circulation is given directionality by the play of light and view. Internal activities such as reading areas, book stacks and control desks are located according to external features. They almost occupy volumes left over from the wider urban scene. The building

flows and projects externally to exploit views over rooftops or to provide quiet study spaces overlooking gardens. In this sense, it is difficult to detect an internal rationale in the disposition of plan and section, but it is a delight to engage so directly in the world of historic Münster from within the new library.

This is a library of routes, views and ambiguous function. The same general shape of room serves as offices, public reading areas or lecture room. The specific demands of different activities do not alter the spaces much — this is both a weakness and strength. It denies space much functional identity, but it provides the opportunity to alter the use of different library areas over time. Only the reference library, placed in a curved wing on the south side of the building, has the scale and presence to recall 'libraryness' in a traditional sense. Elsewhere there is informality and, alongside the cafe, a conviviality which seems deliberately to break down functional barriers.

This is a public library whose measured asymmetry and fragmentation of form makes it a piece of urban sculpture worthy of a visit irrespective of the need to search out and borrow a book. It is the sort of building in which to meet friends, to have a cup of coffee and to watch the world go by. 'Libraryness' may be less evident inside and out than in other more modern public libraries — certainly the building lacks a sense of seriousness of purpose — but the informal and relaxed nature of the interior makes it an appropriate response to library design in the culturally aware city of Münster.

| Malmo Public Library, Sweden | | |
|---|---|---|
| **Architect** | **Special features** | **Cost** |
| Henning Larsen Tegnestue A/s | Major extension to existing public library | £1,400/m$^2$ for building (approx.) |
| | Uses transparency to signal democratic ideals. | £300/m$^2$ for fittings (approx.) |
| | Has unusual environmental strategy. | |
| | Places readers in tall glazed slots around building perimeter. | |

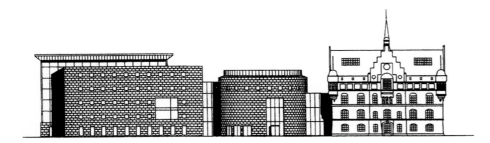

South Elevation, Malmo Public Library. (Henning Larsen Tegnestue A/s)

*Malmo Public Library, Sweden*

Malmo Public Library, which was constructed in 1901 by the national romantic architect John Smedberg, was extensively refurbished and extended by Henning Larsen in 1995. It is a large public library with a book collection of over half a million, journal subscriptions to nearly 1,500 periodicals and 1.5 million loans of books, videos and CDs every year. Larsen's extension, which more than doubled the size of the library, consists of a new shared entrance rotunda placed midway between old and new and a large three-storey non-fiction and IT library. All visitors now enter via the rotunda either from a road or an opposite entrance linked to a walk through a nearby park. Within the rotunda are placed the information desk, returns counter and an orientation display on each floor. Glazed bridges then take the visitor into the old library (fiction) or the new (reference and IT).

The simplicity is essential to steer visitors around a complex collection of study and loan material. Architecturally, the routes are clearly defined with long views through the building and out into the nearby park. The collection is generally stored within the core of the building, with study and circulation spaces around

the outside. The exception to this arrangement is on the south side of the library where the collection is placed against the walls to provide solar protection. Here, in contrast to the highly glazed north, east and west elevations, the windows are small and the walls thick in construction.

A central triple height space exists as a dramatic celebration of reading near the centre of the Larsen extension. Galleries are taken around the perimeter of this space, providing the opportunity to look into the volume from the three floor levels. Stairs rise up through the space giving further animation to the volume.

Study spaces are positioned next to the glazed library perimeter. Some of these volumes are double and triple in height, while others are reached by delicate bridges from the book-stack area. The effect is to create a unique environment for readers, not quite inside or outside the building: a transparent zone between the bookshelves and the trees outside — a place to reflect upon the material read. In other aspects too the library is a play upon opposites — of solid and open areas, long vistas and closely terminated ones, of old and new technologies, sunlit and shaded areas. The building achieves 'libraryness' without resorting to classical overtones and without disguising the open and

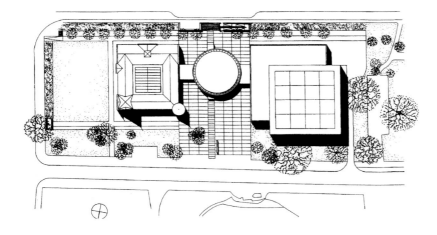

Site plan, Malmo Public Library. The original library is to the left. (Henning Larsen Tegnestue A/s)

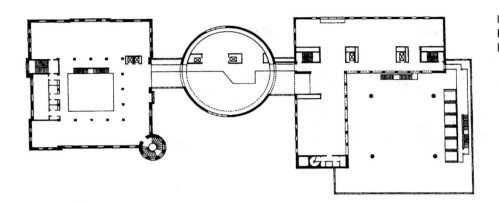

Upper floor plan, Malmo Public Library. (Henning Larsen Tegnestue A/s)

self-navigating nature of library provision. Transparency is both an architectural feature and Larsen's way of signalling the democratic traditions upon which public libraries in Sweden are based.

### Champaign Public Library, Illinois

Situated in the small university town of Champaign in America's Midwest, the new public library is an interesting example of a community-based facility. Besides a lending library there is a conference centre, meeting rooms, cafe, children's library and teens area. The library aims to be a gathering place for the local community and presents an inviting face to this nondescript town. To encourage social interaction, there is a small planted square to the west side of the library and the building itself is raised on a plinth to signal its civic status.

Although the library is only two storeys high (with a third floor mezzanine for library administration), it has a verticality in the rhythms of the façade and internally places a double height glazed spine through the building. This acts as a point of orientation whilst also providing a valuable environmental function. The library is largely naturally ventilated and lit by daylight (it has sun-tubes and ventilating cowls in the deep plan area), with solar gains controlled by external fins whose angle varies according to orientation. As a result of this and the wide use of natural materials, many of which were locally sourced, the building received a LEED Silver award.

According to Carol Ross Barney, the building's Chicago-based architect, the library seeks to create a new identity for the small town public library. Its architectural character is rather more that of 'a super-community centre than a traditional library' (Ross Barney, 2007) with 'an ambiance which appeals to the young but without alienating the older users'. The aim was to fashion a distinctive design based in part on new environmental sensibilities, and to create a 'sense of place in what is largely a placeless urban context'.

In order to stitch together the various elements into a coherent whole, the architect employed a small but consistent architectural palette. External walls are mainly of limestone and brick (this being the tradition in the town as well as on campus) with limestone used as a veneer internally where it is combined with bamboo laminated flooring. In the reading room and around the main staircase the bamboo is taken onto walls and ceilings. The seamless

Champaign Public Library, Illinois, designed by Ross Barney Architects. (Ross Barney Architects)

| Champaign Public Library, Illinois | |
|---|---|
| **Architect** | **Special features** |
| Ross Barney Architects | • Community-based library<br>• Landmark in nondescript town<br>• Received LEED silver award for environmental features<br>• Emphasis upon natural materials |

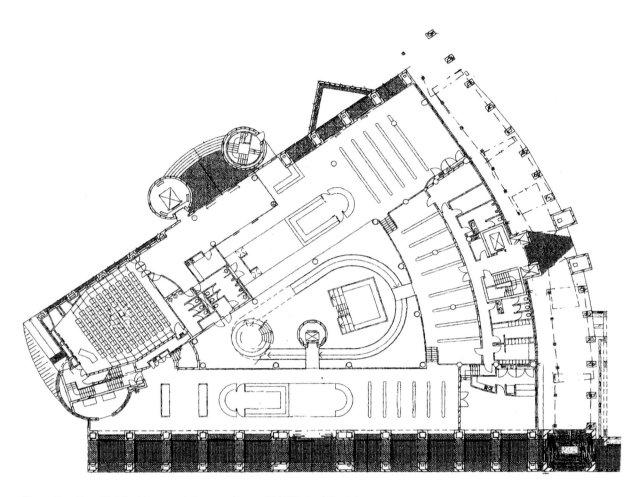

Plan, Sandton Public Library, Johannesburg. (GAPP Architects)

interior of well-lit planes of stone and bamboo veneer introduces into the building a welcome hint of glamour whilst signalling that this is a high-tech library for the twenty-first century. Built at a cost of $22 million in 2007, the library provides 121,000 square feet of accommodation for this expanding university.

*Sandton Public Library, Johannesburg, South Africa*

Sandton Public Library is part of a larger civic development in an affluent suburb of Johannesburg. Besides the library, there is an integral council chamber and office for local government administration. Adjoining the new

| Sandton Public Library, Johannesburg, South Africa | | |
| --- | --- | --- |
| **Architect** | **Special features** | **Cost** |
| GAPP Architects | Combined library and civic administration | Not available |
| | Integrated into retail and office area using public squares and colonnades. | |
| | Has triangular form and central atrium. | |
| | Moderates climate by thick brick construction and solar blinds. | |

library and civic office, there is a sculpture garden and public square which help to stitch the new development into the existing pattern of retail and office uses. The building is remarkable for the close integration of public library and civic administration, creating a hybrid of uses which break down barriers between public services and political administration. On entering you can choose between sitting in on a council debate, borrowing a book or consulting a council official.

The new library is a triangular building with a similarly shaped central atrium. It is entered via a colonnade set deeply into the building to provide a shaded route between various other parts of the civic centre. The colonnade widens in its centre to signal the library entrance. Viewed from the new public square, the changing rhythm of the brick Kahn-like façade with its giant triangular window above the library entrance expresses a clear civic purpose. In its general articulation and detailed treatment of façade, circulation and staircases, Sandton Public Library owes much to Exeter Academy, Library, USA, designed by Louis Kahn (Slessor, 1995, p. 53). Both libraries exist in hot climates where the external wall is critical to environmental control, but at Sandton the library revolves around a central atrium which pulls light deep into the core of the five-storey building – creating in the process a valuable social space and a point of navigation in a complex building.

The complexity of accommodation results in the library having to assert itself architecturally. Although the council chamber is boldly expressed as a semi-circular protrusion into the volume of the atrium, the spiral ramp (which rises from a reading area through the four floors of the library) unifies the interior experience. The ramp is used by both readers and staff, who employ its gentle incline to trolley books from floor to floor. The closely spaced horizontal rails of the spiralling ramp, bathed in South Africa's eternal sunshine, create a light and elegant interior which contrasts with the solidity of the external façades (Slessor, 1995, p. 54).

The use of an atrium allows the floor plates of the library to be fairly shallow. There are in effect three wings of library accommodation on each of the three library floors (the top floor is reference), wrapped around the atrium. Each floor is about 10 m deep with book stacks occupying the central zone. Reader spaces are at the outer edge (giving the advantage of light and views), with circulation around the inside. Structural columns and beams articulate the interior volumes forming bays for book stacks or reading areas. Although the library is fairly consistent throughout its four floors, its order is disrupted by the presence of various civic elements. On the ground floor there is a large auditorium (seating about 150) and facilities serving the council offices on the top floor. These add to the sense that the library is not a self-contained and separate building, but part of the community resources of Sandton.

It is a character reinforced by the proximity of gardens, squares and retail facilities.

This building sets an admirable example of library design for hot, dry climates. Mention has already been made of the contract between the thick perimeter walls and the open, transparent centre. This configuration is successful because of the compact plan and height of the building. Sun is never allowed to penetrate, but is deflected, screened and shaded in order to maximize daylight penetration without the disadvantage (glare and heat gain) of direct sunlight. Windows, for instance, are set deep into the thick brick façades and are further screened by projecting fabric blinds which are controlled by solar cells (Slessor, 1995, p. 53). Where library floors require a great deal of light, there are large glazed areas; on the upper floors, where staff offices are located, the windows on the other hand are small and round. Routes to the library are mostly within colonnaded walkways that follow the building perimeter. To provide further shade, the stair towers and lifts are taken to the outside where they screen the façade from low, angled sunlight. The high thermal capacity of the library – the result of concrete and brick construction – reduces temperature peaks and lessens the air-conditioning load.

Entrance court to Oak Park Public Library, Chicago. (Brian Edwards)

Top floor reading room at Oak Park Public Library, Chicago. (Brian Edwards)

## *Oak Park Public Library, Chicago*

Oak Park Library serves the relatively wealthy suburb of Chicago made famous by the presence of many buildings by Frank Lloyd Wright. Built in 2003 to designs by Nagle, Hartray, Danker, Kagan, McKay, Penny the library houses a collection of nearly a million items, many of local interest. The library faces a city park and the busy Lake Street which forms the main commercial and civic boulevard through Oak Park. It is only one block away from Wright's Unity Temple and pays mild homage to the building, particularly in its entrance sequence. As with Wright's building, the library is entered from a small paved square offset from the road, which takes visitors through a 90-degree turn into the library foyer. From here a long axis leads to the information desk with cross-axes leading to the main stair and lifts on one side and to meeting rooms and exhibition areas on the other.

From the outside the library reads as a highly glazed building with faceted walls and an irregular skyline. At the entrance (which is marked by a portal with the name of the library carved into its stone walls) an outer colonnade provides a sheltered area overlooking the park. This gathering space addresses pedestrian and cycle movements from north and south, as well as those entering the library directly across the park. It is an area where books can be retrieved from backpacks and, on sunny days, where casual reading takes place and chance encounters occur. In this sense, the space acts as civilizing transition between private and public worlds.

The library faces east across the park where mature trees provide a measure of solar protection in the summer whilst allowing high levels of daylight to penetrate deep into the building in the winter. The large upper floor windows on the second floor reading room-come-IT area enjoy good views as a consequence. The library is arranged with an exhibition area, children's library, cafe and bookshop on the ground floor, the fiction collection and magazines on the first floor, and the reference library and reading room on the top floor.

The plan at each floor level is simple: a central spine of computer and on-line facilities divides two areas of book stacks with reading tables, soft furniture and meeting rooms, a veteran's study area and a classroom for developing computer skills around the perimeter. On each level there are staff areas to the rear forming a service zone with toilets and lifts. The plan is orthogonal except facing the park where the faceted perimeter wall introduces an organic response.

Architecturally there are three features that give this public library its particular character, the first being that from outside the copper skin of the upper floors contrasts pleasantly with the sandstone base, providing a blend of earth colours which sit well in the park. The faceted façade and natural materials give the building a quality which is mildly reminiscent of Frank Lloyd Wright's domestic architecture in Oak Park, thereby helping to connect the library with the heritage of the district.

The second feature concerns the lofty reading room on the upper floor. Here the columns recall trees with branches leading to folded timber-clad ceiling panels. Readers can sit at their desks overlooking the park whilst also enjoying an internal prospect of space, light and natural materials. The third element is the main staircase, which is not an understated utilitarian structure but an open tread glazed

| Oak Park Public Library, Chicago | |
|---|---|
| **Architect** | **Special features** |
| Nagle, Hartray, Danker, Kagan, McKay, Penny | • Lofty top floor reading room overlooking park<br>• External sheltered meeting area with cycle storage<br>• Interesting stair with modern art glass<br>• Special veterans library |

stair which rises through the library bathed in coloured light and decorated with abstract art.

In many ways Oak Park Public Library is a traditional book-based loan library. IT and the world of digital metadata are relatively understated in terms of space provision. The emphasis is upon community use and particularly the needs of senior citizens and war veterans, with the library policy emphasizing the importance of respecting reading and quiet socializing. The library is zoned so that noise is permitted on the lower floors and gradually discouraged as one moves upwards. Mobile phones are not permitted in the reading areas and only texting is allowed elsewhere. Conversation is, however, encouraged with casual seating and recital areas on the ground floor. The spatial and functional demarcations at Oak Park Library reinforce the importance of reading through the building's architectural response. This is not a hybrid library but one where certain traditions are upheld. In an age of rapid change in the ethos of public libraries, Oak Park reminds us of the importance of the library to cultural continuity in the American suburb.

The new library at Espoo Public Library, Finland, outside Helsinki, is the major part of a large cultural centre which also includes a concert hall and music conservatory. Designed by Helin and Co. Architects, the group of civic buildings is part of a larger commercial development in this fast expanding new town. The juxtaposition of library and concert hall makes the project of particular interest, as does its location within a large retail development. The marriage is achieved through the use of a common palette of materials, a consistent architectural language, and the use of generous public promenade space which helps unify disparate functions.

Finland, like most of Scandinavia, sees the library as an 'essential investment in the community, providing information and entertainment... and offering solace through the frigid gloom of winter' (Webb, 2004). The building has an exterior which appears architecturally more serious than many modern libraries. This is a building with little applied colour or complex geometries; instead there is a planar discipline of horizontal and vertical lines acted out in different shades of grey. The sober exterior acts as a foil to the interior which has much applied colour in red, dark blue and white. The contrast alludes to the difference between the cold grey winter months and the gaiety of human life inside the typical Finnish dwelling. As a result, upon entering the library the visitor is faced by welcoming warmth and bright light flooding from above like a clearing in the forest.

The library forms the major element on a cruciform-shaped shopping arcade which terminates in a piazza. From the piazza the library, music school and concert hall are reached. As a result, the commercial and cultural worlds are combined in an environment which places the pedestrian first. Users of the library can combine a visit to their supermarket with the return of library books, surfing on the Internet, and enjoying a coffee and sandwich. The fusion of retail and reading makes this development particularly noteworthy, especially when one adds the evening entertainment of chamber music performed perhaps by students at the conservatoire. The cultural investment was underpinned by commerce yet the two worlds seem to exist quite happily.

The library entrance is a roof-lit triple height volume crossed by bridges and overlooked by galleries. Here the library reception is located with a childrens' library and storytelling centre to one side and shops and a cafe on the other. The fiction and music library is straight ahead and extends on a cross-axis through the length of the building. The non-fiction and reference library is on the first floor with IT and youth facilities on the top floor. The axial planning of the different facilities and the logical disposition of elements ensures that the patterns of use are reinforced by the architectural hierarchies. Added to this, large glazed panels form many of the interior

Mission Bay Public Library, San Francisco. Notice the small square and seats provided at the library entrance. (Brian Edwards)

| Mission Bay Public Library, San Francisco | |
|---|---|
| **Architect** | **Special features** |
| Santos Prescott & Associates | • Part of large community development incorporating social housing and health centre<br>• Linked to riverside walkway<br>• Special Mandarin language collection<br>• Multi-agency funding |

subdivisions thereby aiding navigation through the large library.

### Mission Bay Public Library, San Francisco

Mission Bay Public Library is the first new branch library built in the San Francisco Bay area for 40 years. Constructed in 2004, the library occupies a double height ground floor section of a larger community building which also contains a health centre, 140 units of housing for senior citizens and retail space. The library, situated at a prominent corner of the development, houses nearly

Children's Library at Mission Bay Public Library, San Francisco. (Brian Edwards)

40,000 books for loan, an archive of local interest, a children's library and a large IT area with rooms for learning support.

### Espoo Public Library, Finland

Designed by Santos Prescott and Associates, the 7,500 sq. ft library was built for $4 million. It forms part of a larger plan of urban regeneration containing a new tram station, pedestrian walkway along the sea front, new civic park, commercial office and retail space, and social housing. The new library provides the social focus to complement the commercial activities. The library was funded through a $106 million bond voted for by the citizens of San Francisco in 2000 to upgrade 17 of its branch libraries and construct three new ones in areas of multiple deprivation. Mission Bay was the first constructed and trialled the idea of mixing health, social housing and library facilities within a single building.

The library is entered from a set back lobby beneath a canopy that supports the building's name. The sheltered entrance is lined on either side with information boards displaying a variety of library, health, educational and welfare notices. Inside the entrance the library opens into a double height volume containing the main library with a central circular information desk. From here users are directed to the various facilities available, both book, IT and community-based. The latter includes a special collection devoted to Internet, language, personal health and reading support, plus information on the timetabling of classes. In addition, there is a teens area, children's storytelling centre and music rooms.

The ethos of this branch library resides in the community that it serves. Many of the books for loan are not in English and the library staff are bilingual in Spanish, Cantonese or Mandarin. The blending of library, health, drugs rehabilitation and social programmes within a single development suggests this small branch library is a useful model for similar community initiatives. By bringing in non-library activities Mission Bay Public Library was able to draw upon funding from a variety of channels, which is reflected in the size and quality of the resulting building.

| Espoo Public Library, Finland | |
|---|---|
| **Architect** | **Special features** |
| Helin and Co. | • Incorporates concert hall and music academy<br>• Part of larger retail development<br>• Triple height entrance hall<br>• Top floor IT and youth library |

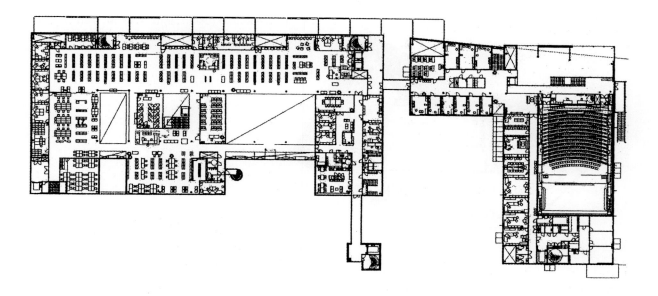

Plan, Espoo Public Library, Finland. (Pekka Helin/AR)

Sitting at the corner of the development and overlooking the waterfront, the new library provides a welcoming front to a larger parcel of urban regeneration. Outside seating and elegant stone paving allows the library to act as a meeting place and focus for local community action. In many ways, the interagency funding of the building helps bring about a shared responsibility for the needs of often disadvantaged people. The library is a small symbol of community empowerment and the importance of knowledge transfer to the local economy.

### Jaume Fuster Public Library, Barcelona

The medium-sized Jaume Fuster Public Library exploits a range of secondary functions around the core of library provision to create an irregular prism of a building which contrasts with the geometry of its neighbours. Designed by

| Jaume Fuster Public Library, Barcelona | |
|---|---|
| **Architect** | **Special features** |
| Josep Llinas | • Organic shape inspired by Catalan traditions<br>• Linked media centre, internet café and bar<br>• External square created at library entrance |

Josep Llinas, the library is close to Gaudi's Park Guell and seems to echo the Catalan traditions of spatial and material complexity. This is partly derived from the site with its organic shape, partly from the functional diversity of the brief, and partly from the architect's striving for greater expression than that afforded by International Modernism (Gregory, 2006).

The entrance is marked by an over-sailing, wave-like canopy which shades the building on its south and west sides. Its shaded edge invites people to the building from the adjacent square and provides protection for the library's cafe. Once inside the building the visitor is faced with a number of choices – to the left a media centre, to the right a cafe bar, and in front the library information desk. There is no hint of barriers; instead there is fluid space with an elegant stair connecting the library's four storeys. The spatial ambiguity is multiplied by carefully arranged roof lighting over the foyer.

Like a piece of a medieval city, this library is a place to explore. There are unexpected routes leading to intriguing rooms and study spaces. The lines of walls, roofs and windows take on forms which break down formality producing a public library which is 'eccentrically planned yet compositionally balanced' (Gregory, 2006). The building appears to be responding to the social focus of the brief on the lower floors and to the disciplines of library provision higher up. Similarly, there is a core of orthogonal planning where the main collections are housed and a periphery of study spaces, reading galleries and bridges around the edge. The arrangement allows the reader to escape into more intimate spaces for quiet study

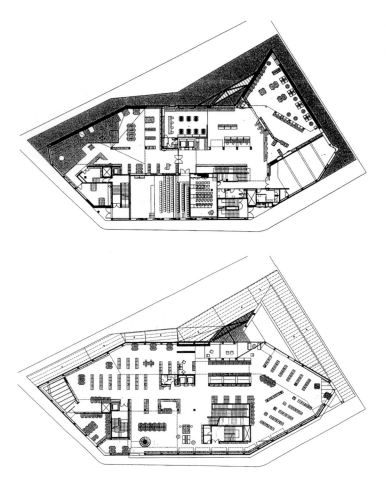

Ground (below) and first floor plan, Jaume Fuster Public Library, Barcelona. (Josep Llinas/AR)

whilst returning to the order of the book stacks to replenish reading supplies.

*Ringwood Public Library, Melbourne, Australia*

This library is situated in a small unassuming suburb to the east of Melbourne. The town developed into a sizeable suburb in the 1950s, with the adjacent Maroondah Highway and the railway providing easy access to Melbourne.

The town has a high proportion of one-parent families and illustrates the social changes which took place in Australian society in the second half of the twentieth century. The construction of the Ringwood Library was partly funded by the development of an adjacent shopping mall by an enterprising local council.

The library is located in the nearest shopping centre to the town's railway station and close to the hub of activity associated with transport, car parking, buses and trains.

| Ringwood Library, Melbourne, Australia | | |
|---|---|---|
| **Architect** | **Special features** | **Date** |
| Edmond and Corrigan | Built-in shopping mall. | 1996 |
| | Part-funded by revenue from retail development. | |
| | Landmark and civic focus in drab suburb | |
| | Design award winner. | |

Ringwood Public Library, Melbourne. (Biddy Fisher)

The library had to be distinguishable from retail neighbours and act as a local landmark. The approach to the library entrance gives a feeling of a rise in ground level, lifting the building above the surroundings. One's sight is drawn upwards to a high window of coloured glass, and the corrugated steel roofscape of sage green and grey. There is a covered walkway to the main shopping mall ensuring connectivity between library and retail activities. The façade of the building makes a bold statement among the shops in the plaza. It has a glazed brick and tiled wall of strong colour above which there is a multicoloured window. The use of colour and the varied roof heights are features that the architects Edmond and Corrigan have exploited to create a suburban landmark which contrasts with the surrounding town.

The interior design is along more simple lines; a level, open-plan interior with an entrance lobby dominated by steel sliding (automatic) doors. The approach to the library brings instant contact with the business area of the circulation desk. Once past this, the building rises into double height and the impression is one of light, space and bold construction.

An oversized signpost visible from every point of the floor indicates the location of the collections and facilities.

Human-scale shelving containing the books and media collections radiates out logically from the information desk. All are accessible and surrounded by easy chairs or desks according to purpose. The shelving provides spatial division between the discrete areas for children's books, large print and computing facilities. The only public room separated by a fixed partition from the main collection is the family history section where valuable archives are kept.

Staff work areas are located in offices around the perimeter of the building. They are found principally adjacent to the loading bay where provision is made for storage as well as distribution. (A rest room with kitchen equipment is also provided.) Their position here helps with the surveillance of deliveries and avoids competition with the public elements of the library.

The strong Australian sun is diffused by the coloured glass curtain of the main window. All other windows are low level and have large overhangs for solar protection. To the side, a small garden provides a more tranquil view and shade. Only one small clerestory window allows direct access for the sun, which is generally controlled carefully to provide a cool, glare-free working environment.

The library collections and facilities are all in a single manageable area. They are arranged to enable browsing and study to take place with ease and interaction. However, the super-human scale of certain features, for example the height of the ceiling and the oversized signpost, ensure that the users lift their eyes from the books. Perhaps this creates an analogy with the purpose of the building: to contain and disseminate knowledge through reading whilst raising the level of understanding of the world at large.

## Eltham Public Library, Victoria, Australia

The challenge for the architect Gregory Burgess, commissioned to design a library at Eltham in Australia, was to design a building to meet the aspirations of an artistically aware and environmentally active community. The library project needed to provide a cultural focus in the widest sense. The site is of historical interest, with a scheduled

| Eltham Public Library, Victoria, Australia | | |
|---|---|---|
| **Architect** | **Special features** | **Date** |
| Gregory Burgess | Provides range of cultural facilities beyond traditional library. | 1994 |
| | Irregular design as a metaphor for the fragmentation of the mind | |
| | Artistic references to Australian life | |
| | Uses local and recycled materials in construction. | |

179

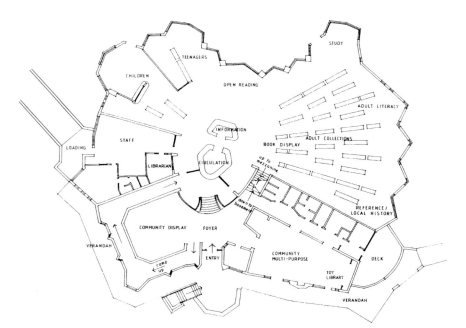

Plan, Eltham Public Library, Victoria, Australia. (Biddy Fisher)

timber-trestle railway bridge in close proximity. The resulting building offers a sympathetic translation of the surrounding landscape without any obvious compromise in the choice of structure, materials or architectural features. The building contains the additional facilities of community meeting space, toy library, coffee shop and exhibition area – all supplementing the core provision of the library.

The library, which opened in 1994, serves a population of 56,000. The book stock currently totals 59,000, with loans averaging 500,000 per annum since opening. This popularity is an indication of the success of the building and the nature of the local population. The building has become an accepted feature of local cultural life. Before entering the library, the user discovers reminders of Australian history: the approach to the building is via a veranda (a most Australian feature) with individually designed wooden seats provided under the overhanging roof. Moving into the library through blue steel automatic doors, the user encounters an entrance space which is used for public meetings or cultural events. A gentle incline around the perimeter serves a double purpose: it can be a seating area for author readings, or a ramp and steps for those who require it.

The overall shape of the building is irregular. This heightens interest and creates surprise. The building is easily understood as a cultural symbol; it can be read as a metaphor for knowledge and understanding, as it contains many corners, unique spaces and hidden features. The central circulation desk acts as a hub from which the main shelving areas radiate to the perimeter of the building. Intimate reader spaces are placed around the floor in logical closeness to the collections. A lofty gallery area has been provided allowing scholars to look down upon the more general circulation of users. Overhead a wood-clad ceiling sweeps up and down in an inspiring series of vaults unifying the various spaces below.

Low maintenance, natural materials have been chosen – clay brick, timber external cladding and recycled hardwood veranda, door and window frames. Details such as the carpet design include references to local motifs (in this case the local eucalyptus tree). Fossil fuel consumption is minimized through the use of natural light and ventilation. Brick walls, verandas and the over-sailing roof optimize passive energy. Working environments are enhanced by the use of artistic and visual reference to the locality, with materials sourced locally wherever possible.

Despite this sensitivity to nature, technological aspects of modern information provision sit comfortably within the library. The integration of PCs within reference areas is achieved simply, although modification to the lighting was necessary to prevent screen glare. Vertical blinds were also installed across some ceiling lights, contrasting with the microvenetian blinds used in the staff work areas. The changing nature of light according to the season is a positive feature and gives the library depth as a working environment.

### Dursley Public Library

This small public library built in rural Gloucestershire is a model for others seeking an appealing building which

| Dursley Public Library | |
| --- | --- |
| **Architect** | **Special features** |
| Ridge Multidisciplinary Practice | • Small community library<br>• Incorporates internet café and Citizens Advice Bureau<br>• Island site gives landmark status to library |

| Discovery Centres, Hampshire | |
| --- | --- |
| **Architect** | **Special features** |
| Hampshire County Council | • Large cultural and social spaces<br>• Colourful library interiors<br>• Links to local schools and colleges<br>• Based upon imaginative adaptation of existing buildings |

provides a range of services to the local community. Besides a traditional lending library there is an Internet cafe and Citizens Advice Bureau. The aim was to attract new users, especially 12–18 year olds, by providing services aimed at younger people and to use architecture to signal their presence.

Built at a cost of under a million pounds, the new library at Dursley is (as the brief stipulated) an 'integrated information, advice and cultural centre for local people' (*Building Design*, 2006). Designed by the Ridge Multidisciplinary practice, the library has largely transparent façades angled outwards on three sides to form an eye-catching civic building. The use of glass in slender frames and blue sheet aluminium gives the building a sleek appearance and opens up views of internal activities to the outside world. These consist of cafe and meeting rooms as well as the county library whose presence is marked by an inset entrance beneath a canopy.

Although only two storeys high, the library is a small local landmark by day and a glowing beacon at night. The island site surrounded by roads gives the library great visibility and provides an opportunity to incorporate art into the design, which includes glass stepping stones and illuminated signage onto the façade. Since the building opened in 2006, visitor numbers have doubled over the 1930s library it replaced.

## Discovery Centres, Hampshire

The Discovery Centres being pioneered by Hampshire County Council in southern England are a new form of public library based on the idea of broadening the services provided to include exhibition and dance space and community support such as Citizens Advice Bureaux and youth services. The aim is to widen the appeal of the library by creating an attractive and progressive image with state-of-the-art ICT facilities and an emphasis upon community use rather than purely library use. By expanding the services provided, the library has forged partnerships with cultural, leisure, educational and business organizations. Each Discovery Centre is tailored to the local demographics of the different communities served, with the brief developed following local consultation (Harper, 2006).

Typical of the approach is the Gosport Discovery Centre which combines innovative design with the provision of flexible library and learning spaces in a neighbourhood noted for social deprivation. The building, with its welcoming and spacious entrance, retail-type slimline borrowing desk, coloured art glass foyer and geostationary plasma screen, is far removed from the orthodox public library. In addition, there is a performance and recital area, a special zone for children and young people with coffee shop-type comfortable seating, and an extensive area for on-line learning with links to local schools and colleges. For those who want to engage in quiet study, there are silent zones around the periphery at upper levels where the bulk of the book collection is housed.

The Gosport Discovery Centre, like that at Winchester which opened early in 2008 and those planned for Basingstoke and Andover, has forged a new model for the public library. With courses offered in the Centre aimed at promoting life-long learning and retraining, the use of the building by youth theatre and contemporary dance groups, and the employment of the foyer space for touring art exhibitions, the first impression is rather more that of a community hall than a library.

However, there remains much that is library-like in the books, journals and newspapers that are available. These are positioned beyond the gallery and cafe-culture inspired public front and placed in the more silent areas within the depth of the building. Here the book stacks are fairly low and informally arranged, thereby allowing the sense of space to flow. Tables, chairs and sofas interspersed with IT facilities form relaxing clusters for reading and study within the relatively lofty general library areas. The round concrete columns, coffered ceiling and suspended lighting strips provide a robust, environmentally stable and cost-effective interior which suggests an ability to change its functional use without drastic structural modification. A reflective linoleum floor ensures that light from the vertical floor to ceiling windows penetrates deep into the building. From the outside the windows give welcoming glimpses into the Discovery Centre. Their rhythmic spacing and coloured panels, coupled with the dramatic entrance, project an image

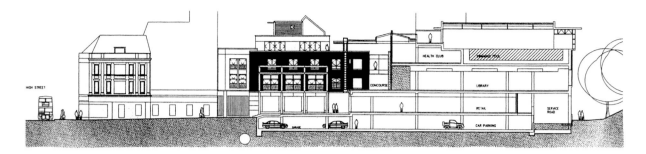

Section through Ebbisham Centre, Epsom, Surrey. The library is on the first floor (RMJM/AT)

within the town centre of an innovative and welcoming public building.

At the £7 million Winchester Discovery Centre the character is rather more traditional. Here a listed building (formerly the Corn Exchange) has been converted to contain a mixture of library and community facilities such as performance and learning spaces. The library is the hub of the 'people's network' of free IT provision, helping to erode the exclusivity of the building. The Discover Centres mark a distinct cultural change in nature of the public library. The character and design of the resulting buildings is not unlike that pioneered by the idea stores movement with the emphasis upon colour, openness and social interaction.

## Ebbisham Centre Library, Epsom, Surrey

The integration of the public library with other types of social provision is well illustrated by that at the Ebbisham Centre in Epsom. Here the redevelopment of a large part of the town centre provided the opportunity to realize an ambitious fusion of public buildings and related commercial development. The library is the major element in a composition of social and cultural facilities which includes a leisure centre, doctor's surgery, cafe and residential development. Necessarily, the facilities are grouped around a new square which opens off the high street in Epsom.

The square leads in turn to a concourse which links together the various civic facilities. Visible from the high street, the square and concourse signal the presence of the library to shoppers whilst also, according to the architects RMJM, 'organising and clarifying the scheme as a whole' (*Architecture Today*, 2002). Funded in part as a millennium project (using UK lottery grants and Capital Challenge Funding) the development was a partnership between Surrey County Council and a private developer (Trevor Osborne Property Group). The integration of public and private elements was necessary to ensure the scheme was economically and socially viable.

The 60 m long concourse is the main attraction to visitors. Being 8 m high, nearly fully glazed and south facing, the space has a grandeur befitting civic architecture. The concourse forms a promenade which leads to the three main public elements: the library, leisure centre (called a 'lifestyle centre') and doctors' surgery. It also provides access to retail outlets, bars, restaurants and a health club which are stitched into the development at various levels. The library is mainly at first floor level and has its own entrance foyer, lifts and stairs sandwiched between retail units. In effect, the shops provide the lure to bring young people into the library.

Set behind a glazed double height wall, the library is highly visible in spite of its elevated position. The glazed concourse wall provides natural ventilation and cooling via a 700 mm cavity, and sheds light onto the façade of the library beyond. With its own roof light above the entrance, the library provides an inviting well-lit space for readers. This small public library is on one level and has a soft

| Ebbisham Public Library, Epsom, Surrey | |
|---|---|
| **Architect** | **Special features** |
| RMJM | • First floor library with shops below and health centre above |
| | • Blend of lottery, local authority and private funding |
| | • Double height glazed entry promenade |

| Key design characteristics of libraries |
|---|
| Visible, recognizable and legible as a type |
| Adaptable to new information technology and physically extendable |
| Comfortable and disabled-friendly |
| Inviting, safe and secure for users |
| Protection and security of the collection |

---

**Key qualities for the design of public libraries**

| Access | • ensure safe, secure and legible routes |
| | • provide memorable spaces to aid navigation |
| | • use visual continuity to stitch library into cultural realm |
| Collections | • place major collection in major spaces |
| | • use collections to give mental map of building |
| | • integrate paper and IT provision |
| | • provide study rooms for special collections |
| Reader areas | • place reader desks in daylight |
| | • ensure soft seating magazine areas are near entrance |
| | • locate reader areas near cafes |
| Design quality | • ensure library looks like a cultural institution |
| | • make building inviting and stimulating irrespective of the collection |
| | • provide meeting spaces overlooking the city |
| Control desk and circulation | • ensure the information point is visible to all |
| | • provide circulation routes which celebrate movement |
| | • provide visual continuity by avoiding 'walls' |
| | • avoid fortress impression |

---

seating magazine area to one side of the entrance and computer terminals to the other with the book stacks and control point beyond. What is worthy of note in this example is the way a range of public facilities has been provided, integrated with private leisure and retail developments. The integration has been achieved primarily by the careful attention given to urban design in both plan and section.

## References

*American Libraries Association Journal* (2007). November.

ASLIB (1995). *Review of the Public Library Service in England and Wales*. Association for Information Management.

*Architecture Today* (2002). Issue 124, pp. 36–40.

*Architecture Today* (2005). Issue 160, June, pp. 89–90.

*Atlantic Monthly* (1992). August, pp. 84–87.

Blackman, D. (2003). More library revamps by the Idea Store team. *Building Design*, 25 April, p. 7.

Blundell Jones, P. (1994). Brought to book. *Architectural Review*, 42. February.

Boddy, T. (2006). Les Chambres de Bois. *Architectural Review*, June, pp. 73–74.

Brawne, M. (1997). *Library Builders*, Academy, p. 179.

*Building Design* (2006). 13 April, p. 4.

Evans, B. (2004). Ideas in Store. *The Architects Journal*, 12 August, p. 24.

Evans, B. (2005). Read all about it. *The Architects Journal*, 3 May, p. 24.

Glancey, J. (2000). *Guardian*, 4 March, p. 19.

Gregory, B. (2006). Between the lines. *Architectural Review*, 65–70. June.

Harper, P. (2006). Library design has arrived. *Update*, July/August, Vol. 5, p. 37.

Kaplan, S. *et al.* (1993). The museum as a restorative environment. *Environmental Behaviour*, 25, pp. 725–742.

Lamprecht, B. (2004). The nice and the good. *Architectural Review*: 52–54. August.

LeCuyer, A. (2006). Midwest modesty. *Architectural Review*: 56–62. June.

Library and Information Update (2006) Vol. 5, November, p. 4.

Melvin, J. (2000). Peckham Rise. *Architects Journal*, 30 March, p. 22.

Rattenbury, K. (2004). Toying with Uncle Sam. *Building Design* 6 August, p.11.

Ross Barney, C. (2007). Interview conducted with author, 17 December.

Slessor, C. (1995). Suburban bibliophile. *Architectural Review*, 53. March.

Spring, M. (2000). Temple of Learning. *Building*, December, pp. 37–43.

Sudjic, D. (2000). Keep your Eyes on the Prize. *Observer Review*, 20 October, p. 5.

Taylor, V. (1999). Postcard from the President. *Library Association Rec.*, 101, p. 632.

Webb, M. (2004). Cultural hub. *Architectural Review*, August, p. 46.

# 11

# The university library

Historically, universities have helped define and give form to the library as a distinctive building type. The demands of education, particularly in the seventeenth and eighteenth century, led to the construction of a new generation of efficiently planned, rationally organized libraries. It was during this time that the library matured into a recognizable building within the taxonomy of types. The library ceased to be a wing of a bigger building and became a structure with meanings all of its own. Higher education demanded of libraries the same rigour and intellectual discipline that was displayed in the laboratories and lecture theatres of Europe's expanding universities. Well before the public library had emerged on the scene (mostly from 1850 onwards), the university library had evolved with its own distinctive shape and form of spatial organization.

Central to this formal construct was the lack of distinction between reading and storage. Although the extent of books and journals required of university scholars was large, only a small portion was not on permanent display. Bookcases held the bulk of the material with only the rarest study collection held in secure storage.

By 1750, the academic library was less a visible trophy of scholarship and rather more a practical resource for all. To signify this change, the university library was built all on its own and often placed centrally on campus as a symbol of independent intellectual inquiry. The library at this time ceased to be what today would be called a faculty library and became instead a true university library. The library held all of the printed material required by undergraduates, arranged according to a standard system of classification. In fact, the introduction after 1780 of a standard classification system (increasingly the almost Darwinian Dewey Decimal System) helped give shape to the library building itself. In this sense, those who evolved this system had accidentally helped design the modern university library.

Today the university library holds a central position in the innovation of cataloguing and retrieval systems, and in the design of library buildings themselves. The challenge of computer-based learning and the infiltration of IT into all fields of education have revolutionized the university library. Just as higher education led advances in the design of libraries in the eighteenth century, the university has been at the forefront of technological innovation over the past decade. The modern university library has expanded to become a computing centre where both traditional and electronic data can be accessed almost simultaneously. Books and computer terminals stand side-by-side, with students flitting between paper and digital information. What was once a simple ordered world of books and journals has become a complex and plural place. Many new university libraries are known as learning resource centres and, where the old title of university library is retained, there are floors of computer terminals, media centres and sometimes cafes. If you want to see the shape of the municipal library of the future, then visit your nearest university library.

A comparison of plans of university libraries from the 1960s with those of today is revealing. Space has become more complex and multifunctional. Areas in the past that were corridors, reading areas or stack rooms have become multi-purpose, with the former distinctions of private and public, quiet and noisy, now blurred. The change has been necessary to accommodate new forms of data and new philosophies of learning triggered by the computing revolution. The university library is typically an extension of the classroom with seminars and joint student projects often undertaken within its walls. The ready access to electronic information in the modern university library makes it a teaching resource of unprecedented potential. A comparison of the plan of Thames Valley University library (1996), designed by Richard Rogers, with that of the University of East Anglia library (1964), designed by Denis Lasdun, shows the magnitude of changes brought about by this revolution. Whereas Lasdun's library is a collection of reading rooms and stack floors, the library designed by Rogers is fluid space containing dynamic interacting functions.

The university library is usually the most prominent building on the campus. Its visual dominance is justified by the crucial role played by books, journals and IT systems in learning and research. Since the library is a magnet for all members of the academic community, it requires a central position, prominent form and sheltered, well-lit approaches.

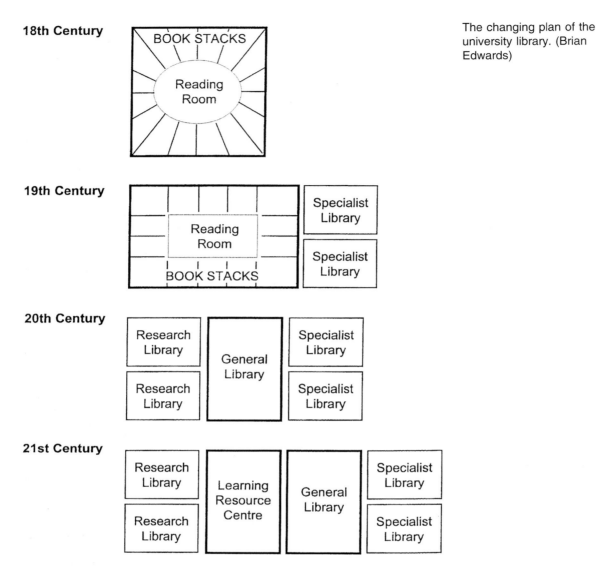

**18th Century**

BOOK STACKS

Reading Room

**19th Century**

Reading Room

BOOK STACKS

Specialist Library

Specialist Library

**20th Century**

Research Library

Research Library

General Library

Specialist Library

Specialist Library

**21st Century**

Research Library

Research Library

Learning Resource Centre

General Library

Specialist Library

Specialist Library

The changing plan of the university library. (Brian Edwards)

As library collections are rarely static and have a tendency to grow in an unexpected fashion, there also needs to be space for outward expansion. How growth is accommodated varies with circumstance but three strategies are often followed:

1. physical outward expansion, either laterally or vertically
2. the separation of study from book storage with the latter provided in another more distant building
3. the shift from traditional to electronic information systems.

These conditions are common of all libraries, but the university library experiences the pressure for change more acutely than elsewhere. This is particularly true in periods of rapid growth in higher education (as in the 1980s in the

USA and the 1990s in the UK) and during times of change in information technology (e.g. the mass availability of the printed book after 1650, the developmental of the scientific journal around 1840, and the revolution in computer-based information which has gathered pace since the 1980s). As a general rule, technology rather than management is the main motor of change in the design of library buildings.

University libraries tend to be long-lived buildings. Their collections may grow but the architecture fabric tends to remain, though frequently under stress of various kinds. Many university libraries contain book, journal and special collections of national importance. The library at Harvard holds 10 million volumes, Berkeley 7 million, Yale 6 million and Oxford and Cambridge each about 5 million. Inevitably with such a scale of provision, most university libraries of any size separate reading areas from storage. The argument is simple: reading rooms and study space can remain fairly constant whilst storage areas (usually some distance away) can grow to accommodate the expansion in the written word. As for digital information, this requires only storage for the computer network servers and system equipment, since the net is all-pervasive.

Computing has not only led to the death of distance but the extinction of storage in the traditional sense. The space required for CD-ROMs, discs, etc. can readily be accommodated within the library. The computer terminals themselves tend to be distributed throughout the building to facilitate access to the catalogue, and to be in dedicated areas given over exclusively to electronic browsing. The latter areas are often attached to large rooms of PCs where students can analyse the data collected and prepare their research reports or essays. Under such pressure, the university library resembles a hybrid of old library types and modern high-tech offices – a kind of trading area of new knowledge where, as the Vice Chancellor of Sunderland University put it in 1995, the library reflects the ethos of 'a university without walls, a gateway to global knowledge' (Wright, 1997, p. 25).

For many students, the large reading room of the traditional university library is where much study tends to take place. The eighteenth and nineteenth century academic library celebrated the reading room by setting it within a generous domed space. Typical is the work of the architects McKim, Mead and White, who placed grand circular reading rooms at the heart of their libraries for New York and Columbia Universities. These were the days when the book was dominant; today a similar gesture of spatial significance is often given to the computer suite. In fact, in some modern university libraries, known increasingly as 'learning resource centres', the computer screen is more in evidence than the book. In these libraries, walls are not lined with bookcases but rows of computers placed neatly on tables. Since the environmental needs of computer space are quite different from that of book-based reading, the approach to lighting design and ventilation varies according to the type of library. As computers release heat and require glare-free lighting, the shape of the technology-rich library reflects the environmental engineering of the space. The grand domed reading room of the past is quite unsuitable for computer-based library use just as the modern electronic library is ill-fitted for book and journal use. The media of the library determines not just the use of space but its basic architectural form.

## Centrality of the university library

The university library has always been at the geographical and intellectual centre of the campus. However, this role, which was formerly based upon the importance of the book and journal collections, has been reinforced by the revolution in IT provision, interactive learning and multimedia. Now the library is the primary focus of campus connectivity through both its provision of technology-enhanced educational provision and the use of wireless networking (Marmot, 2005, p. 50). This has enhanced the importance of the central university library at the expense of faculty libraries and in turn has encouraged the library to innovate in its provision of support for learning and research. At the same time, the university library has assumed the role of flagship for their institutions with the emphasis on innovative architectural design, high quality construction and fittings, generous use of space, accessibility and transparency (Wilson, 2008). The centrality exists on three levels: as an intellectual centre, as the focus for wire and wireless information connections, and as an architectural symbol. Disraeli's dictum that universities are places of 'light, liberty and learning' is nowhere more evident than in the design of the university library.

The sense that the college or university library is the major vehicle for campus connectivity in both paper-based learning support and IT provision has had two main effects. First, there is growing pressure to ensure that library facilities are available 24 hours a day and every day of the week. This in turn has encouraged the construction of social spaces and cafes in the library, which through WiFi have become informal learning zones often away from the gaze of library staff. Here students can network not only with peers but teachers and professors who may be using the cafes to take refreshment. Studies have suggested that these informal social spaces have become an important arena to support more structured teaching (Marmot, 2005, pp. 21–25). To maximize these benefits it is necessary to create congenial, stimulating and inspirational public areas in libraries (Wilson, 2008, p. 36).

The second main consequence is that more students are using the library than ever before and this is leading to pressure to expand provision to meet student demand. Since many are part-time or international students, there are often training spaces whereby students can be inducted into the technologies available. Coupled with this – the demands for group and project working whereby a range of sources (paper and digital) is employed and spoken word communication essential – there is growing pressure to provide study rooms for such activities. Formerly these were in the schools and departments elsewhere on campus, but by centralizing the information resources (often using the term Learning Resource Centre) the library has become the focus of much teaching. The growing importance of libraries has reinforced their role not just in the provision and interconnectivity of information services but critically in providing space where that information can be employed. After all, in the digital age information can be accessed almost anywhere so the library needs to provide attractive and inspirational areas which encourage knowledge exchange.

Partly as a consequence of these changes, the quality of the library becomes an important component of measures employed to assess the standing of different universities. For instance, the *Times Good University Guide* uses library provision and annual library spending to score the relative merits

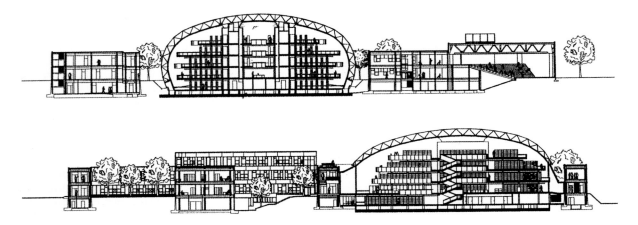

Sections through the central library at the Free University of Berlin designed by Foster and Partners. (Foster and Partners)

of the hundred or so UK universities. Similarly, the Higher Education Funding Council in its periodic audits makes an assessment of a university's library. Here the judgement is not just in the size and comprehensiveness of the collection but how well it is used in the pursuit of teaching, learning and research. To use a collection well invariably involves redesigning all or part of the building in order to accommodate the updating of library facilities for the needs of the twenty-first century. Hence, annual investment is a measure employed by those who audit library quality.

| Key qualities for the design of university libraries | |
|---|---|
| Access | • Ensure easy access for all |
| | • Provide high level of security around entrances |
| | • Provide clear way-finding through building |
| | • Ensure legibility of information points and collections |
| Collections | • Store collections of books in logical relationships to academic subjects taught |
| | • Place book and IT areas away from sunlight |
| | • Provide for expansion of material – paper, research and digital |
| | • Ensure integration of paper and digital media |
| Reader areas | • Place study spaces in natural light |
| | • Ensure sufficient study space to use a variety of media |
| | • Create quiet study spaces in corners |
| | • Form research study areas close to special collections |
| Control desk | • Ensure the circulating and information desk is readily visible at entrance and on each floor |
| | • Scatter staffrooms around library to ensure student contact |
| | • Use electronic controls for stock security, thereby liberating staff to be subject navigators |

As academic libraries assume greater importance, their architectural design has enjoyed a renaissance over the past few years. Many recent university libraries have been innovative and award-winning buildings, such as Lord Foster's central library at the Free University of Berlin. Nicknamed the 'brain' because of its organic shape and central cortex of information services (Wilson, 2008, p. 36), the new building has centralized library provision on this campus of 35,000 students. Another example of the library as landmark is Herzog and de Meuron's academic library at the Brandenburg Technical University in Cottbus in former East Germany. Built as a futurist castle encased in etched glass that reflects the sky by day and glows after dark, the library, which is both media centre and traditional book repository, signals the academic values of the twenty-first century (Wilson, 2008, p. 37). This building, which won the 'Library of the Year' award in 2006, acts as a gateway to knowledge and as a container of memories.

## Changing pattern of teaching and the library

Academic libraries, both university and school, are rapidly adapting to new forms of teaching and learning. The growing use of group projects means that students study as a team. This inevitably entails discussion and leads to the

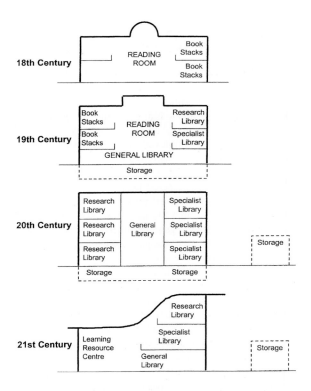

The changing section of the university library. (Brian Edwards)

provision of group study areas in libraries away from those areas for quiet study. Group work, especially around projects, involves interaction between members, access to IT and physical space which encourages team working. Large tables are needed surrounded by chairs and, ideally, the furniture layout should be flexible enough to allow for a variety of configurations. Rarely are projects undertaken without academic guidance, which leads to the erosion of boundaries between teaching and library space. Rarely too are projects tackled without the use of both traditional and electronic sources – hence the need to integrate book, journal and IT provision within the place of study.

Projects are a growing aspect of student-centred learning. It is argued that projects encourage intellectual cross-fertilization, are a deeper source of learning than traditional lectures, and mimic more closely the world of work. Project-based teaching has a profound impact upon the use of the library, especially when accompanied by a rise in student numbers. Where, at one time, libraries were quiet and relatively under-occupied buildings with individual readers surrounded by books in personal carrels, the reality today is one of bustle, social interaction and knowledge exchange. The library caters for these changes in a variety of ways – in the use and zoning of space, in the provision of silent and discussion areas, in the choice of furniture layout, and in the integration of IT and book facilities around the concept of PC study clusters. As students are now required to type most of their projects, there is great pressure upon word-processing facilities. This further breaks down the barrier between library and computer buildings, leading inevitably to the provision of learning resource centres where book, IT and especially multimedia packages can be integrated into a single space.

There are consequences too for library staff who will increasingly be involved in the support of learning. Old demarcations between academic staff and librarians become irrelevant as new forms of teaching and learning around IT packages take hold. This changes staff roles and the use or location of staff offices. To be most effective in supporting student-centred learning, library staff need to be accessible close to the material held. They become stall-holders in a market place of subject zones, each with their own clusters of PCs and learning packages. The book stacks, if they exist at all, simply define the territories within which student projects take place.

## The changing library: the learning resource centre

If universities have led the recent revolution in library design (to the benefit of public and national libraries alike), the impetus for change, in the UK at least, was the Follett Report published in 1993 (Joint Funding Council, 1993). The Follett Inquiry was set up by the bodies which fund higher education in the UK in response to perceived stress

189

upon academic library space, equipment and collections. The timing was critical – just as IT was biting into budgets and disrupting buildings – and the conclusions drawn by the committee of inquiry rightly put technology high on the agenda of reform. In his report, Sir Brian Follett made five recommendations, which had profound implications for the design of academic libraries:

- information storage and access should take greater account of new digital technology
- the emphasis upon the 'collection' should give way to facilitating 'access'
- IT should not be separated but integrated with traditional library sources
- research and teaching material should be more closely integrated and organized around the emerging reality of the electronic library
- extra funding should be available for universities to develop new IT libraries and modify existing academic libraries.

The Follett Report, which was accepted by the UK government with the allocation of additional resources, led to much innovation in library design in the 1990s. When one examines some of the new academic libraries created under the influence of the Follet Report (e.g. at Thames Valley University), it is evident that space within the library has become more fluid and, as a consequence, flexible. The integration of IT and traditional library material (books, journals) within the same general volume has led to what have been described as libraries without walls – places of information exchange across storage systems (Wright, 1997, p. 26).

The Follett Report anticipated the impact new technology was to have upon the library both as a building and in terms of its contribution to teaching and learning. In directing the bulk of its recommendations to IT, Follett effectively championed change within libraries, not just academic ones. The emergence of 'learning resource centres' is one manifestation, another is the rebalancing of 'library physical space with electronic service innovation, underpinned by changing technological infrastructure capabilities and new systems developments' (Brindley, 1995, p. 3). Although a few people have subsequently questioned the concept of a library as a physical building, what Follett effectively championed was a new type of space to serve new forms of library technology.

The new library has to accommodate flexibility but without excessive initial cost. Recent library design has moved away from characterless interiors towards more interesting expressive space. It is increasingly realized that short-term modification can be less costly than building in infinite flexibility at the outset. Certainly, the quality of the architectural interior suffers from an inexhaustible quest for adaptability. The open flexible library has also to balance the need for ventilation with acoustic separation, and

workspace privacy with trading floor activity. In addition, in an age of wireless networks, the dominance of cable-led determinism should not fashion building layouts.

All libraries face the same general problems, not just academic ones. Ultimately the library is a building which, like all others, is judged by quality of experience, not performance against abstract notions of flexibility or technological innovation. Space, light and ambience are enduring factors which can exist across changes in library technology. It is easy to be seduced by IT, but experience suggests that the promised flexibility sometimes fails to be delivered. If the academic library provides a vision for the future, recent learning resource centres offer many lessons in the difficult choices faced by library managers and their designers.

What is evident from learning resource centres is the fact that, though they are shrinking in size as they seek to accommodate less stock, they are becoming more expensive. The IT provision, wiring systems and environmental standards required of computer-based libraries results in them costing 20–25% more per square metre than traditional book-based libraries. So, although learning resource centres are slimmer and leaner than old-fashioned libraries, they are more expensive to build. However, once built they can often accommodate a variety of uses beyond library ones. This inbuilt adaptability offers institutions great advantage in an age of educational change.

### The changing nature of Learning Resource Centres

Since their introduction in the 1980s learning resource centres (LRC) have begun to take on new characteristics. Formerly, they were primarily computer-orientated libraries, essentially open-plan but with limited enclosed or semi-enclosed study areas. In such buildings books and journals were rarely employed since they were held in adjacent libraries, so students worked either digitally or used paper sources. Studies suggested that having two separate buildings discouraged integration of study material in spite of their physical proximity. This was partly because the library and LRC had their own staffing cultures, study methodologies, facilities, opening hours, policy on noise, etc. Over the past decade there have been attempts to combine the book and computer-orientated-cum-IT library within not just a single building, but within a single culture of information and study provision.

The LRC highlights a characteristic of the modern library. The physical collection of books requires a building whilst information services such as the Internet require only a laptop: one is space specific, the other exists in universal space. If new information technologies are busy dissolving the solidity of knowledge and making fluid its boundaries, the library still has to compete in architectural terms in order to retain its clientele. Although dedicated IT areas are needed in such buildings, scholars also require ready access to the book collection, theses and reference library. Digital and paper sources can be integrated at the study desk or nearby seminar room as long as media interaction is an objective at the outset of design. Also, since flexibility of space provision is needed and future trends in both technology and modes of pedagogy are hard to predict, there are certain principles to follow:

- use raised floors throughout, except in the book-stack areas
- provide proximity of all media, especially digital and paper-based sources
- provide a perception of other study areas and sources of information by ensuring visual connection
- use folding or sliding doors to create a spacious interior
- use lightweight walls on top of raised floors for flexibility
- zone the space for acoustic protection
- provide small teaching rooms in LRCs, some under the control of students for undertaking project work
- consider using mobile compact storage of rarely used book sources.

## Informal learning spaces in the academic library

Recent research has highlighted the need to provide casual corners where students can develop their own ideas within libraries. The idea of peer-to-peer and social learning spaces has assumed greater importance as higher education has moved from a teaching to a learning and research culture. The new environments of learning affect the campus as a whole but the university library is not immune to these wider changes in educational practice. Traditional teacher models of learning are giving way to study which is self-motivated, informed by a diversity of knowledge or theoretical sources, and underpinned by respect for research as the primary means of cultivating new knowledge. The role of the library is to provide a range of study environments to suit a diversity of learning styles and student preferences.

The four principles of effective learning are:

- learning by private study
- learning by reflection and testing
- learning by application
- learning through group work and conversation.

All four can be supported through the facilities provided in academic libraries if their role is seen as cultivating an ability to think critically rather than simply gain factual knowledge. Facts and knowledge are needed but it is the use made of that knowledge which characterizes an effective learner. Here architectural design has a role to play in creating the internal

Informal study space at the Sydney Jones Library, University of Liverpool. (Brian Edwards)

spaces which promote connectivity, intellectual exploration and deep (rather than shallow) thought. Hence, the trend is towards libraries without walls, spaces which can be used for informal working and networking, and architectural volumes which display the interdependence of knowledge rather than subject specificness.

The ubiquitous world of computing and all the associated benefits of e-learning allow facilities on and off campus to be exploited in both formal and more casual ways. From the students' hall of residence or home to the university or faculty library there are countless opportunities to cultivate informal opportunities for academic pursuit. The old distinction between lecture theatre, library, laboratory and seminar room, with their formal overtones of traditional modes of teaching, is being rapidly overtaken by what is called 'blended learning'. Here the emphasis is upon social learning spaces, often enhanced by IT (especially wireless networks), which are provided around the edges of formal teaching spaces such as lecture theatres and libraries. The ability of a college or university to adapt to changing student numbers, age profiles and abilities depends increasingly upon the development of new library environments geared to changing pedagogic styles (Wilson, 2008, p. 39).

New libraries, however, are not always essential or affordable in order to meet the learning environments required of the twenty-first century. It is often possible to adapt older university libraries to accommodate new pedagogic practices. The key here is intelligent refurbishment where the emphasis is upon maximizing natural light, acoustic separation and ventilation (qualities often overlooked in earlier academic libraries), creating spaces for social learning, providing informal as well as more structured IT areas, and (where the climate permits) forming external areas for the exchange of ideas and networking. Such adaptation often includes a large measure of physical extension and here (as at De Montfort University library refurbished and extended by Eva Jirinca in 2001) the design orientates students towards informal learning clusters placed on the bridges between the paper library and the electronic one. These are often bathed in natural light and naturally ventilated, thereby creating rooms (often under the students' control) which are stimulating to use and have a good social ambiance.

The challenge is not just to meet the changing world of university and college libraries, but to anticipate future trends in the designs we produce today. Certain principles are evident such as:

- growth in research-based learning
- emphasis upon problem-orientated study rather than theoretical pursuits
- using, assessing, applying and synthesizing information from a diversity of sources
- providing space which allows people to work together
- designing university libraries as meeting places both socially and academically.

Libraries are part of the university knowledge web that includes the production (through research), distribution

The Koener Library at the University of British Columbia signals the building's pedagogic importance. (Brian Edwards)

(through teaching), acquisition (through personal study) and application (through projects and theses) of knowledge. In this chain, the library as a pattern of architectural volumes and functions performs an ever-changing role in knowledge transfer (Arets, 2005). Hence, flexibility is important and so is the quality of the library as a building.

## Planning for growth

Mention has already been made of the main strategies for accommodating growth in the library. The stresses imposed by expansion in the library stock, or change in library technology, have impacts beyond physical enlargement. These stresses are felt within the library itself – the use and management of space, the integration of traditional and electronic information systems, in staff resources, furniture layout, access strategies, security, etc. Managing growth so that the library maintains coherence as a working entity is a subtle art.

The library should anticipate growth at the outset by placing flexibility and expansion strategies in the design brief. Libraries that are overly monumental do not readily accommodate change. However, libraries which place almost total flexibility high on the agenda often lack character as a building. 'Libraryness' is a quality all university libraries should contain. Incremental growth in study material is inevitable in the academic library. Books and journals continue to expand and at roughly predictable rates (3–5% increase in published stock per year). However, expansion is harder to predict in the area of electronic library resources. Although digital data is undergoing rapid growth, it demands less space than other information systems. Here it is not computing space which is the problem, but people space and the expectations placed upon the quality of that space (environmental standards, high-tech ambience).

Various strategies are available to harness growth for both library efficiency and architectural advantage. There are three common approaches:

1. To plan for growth by providing flexible, loose-fit space with obvious areas for expansion at the periphery. Here all areas are well serviced in terms of air-conditioning, cabling and access to lifts, hoists, ducts and stairs. Such libraries are systems based upon repeating modules of accommodation and the integration of space for books, journals, reading and electronic access. Libraries built to this approach are airy, open, transparent and often energy efficient.

2. To plan for growth by separating the library into 'served' and 'servant' zones. Here there is a distinction between the elements which support space and the space itself. The served spaces are the library and reading rooms, which are large and fairly fixed

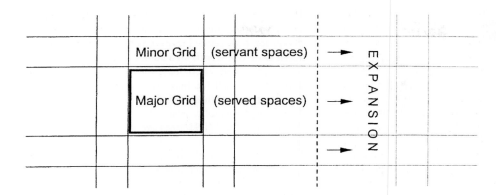

Plan of major and minor grids in a typical university library. (Brian Edwards)

elements. The servant spaces are the areas of circulation, ducting of services, staff offices and storage areas. These, essentially the supporting areas, are also the parts which are put under the greatest stress by library growth. The separation of the two types of space (in both plan and section) provides a dissimilar dimensional grid of accommodation through the building. The stress of growth or change in stock can be accommodated by such a measure since it allows for different types of space and servicing to occur on a rational basis.

3. To plan for growth by separating the main building elements from the lesser ones. Here structural columns, floors and roofs are distinguished from enclosing walls, partitions, lighting finishes and furniture. This allows the operation of the library to change without affecting the main structure or sheltering elements. This approach requires a different level of investment at the outset in the different components of the building. The basic structural frame and enclosing façade, since they last a long time, enjoy a higher cost threshold than those parts with a shorter life. Although this adds to cost in the short term, the building enjoys longer adaptive value. Related to this strategy is the increasing use of separating the library itself from library storage. The spatial

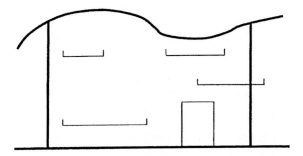

Section of a modern academic library. Activities and space can change without interfering with the main structural elements. (Brian Edwards)

segregation allows each to expand according to different functional agendas.

Unless it is well handled, flexibility can compromise architectural quality. Total flexibility is itself expensive because all areas will need to be air-conditioned, and the ducts and floor area required of highly serviced buildings take up valuable library space. Building plant should not exceed 10% of the volume of the library. It is better to have high-serviced and low-serviced zones than full air-conditioning. It is preferable too to employ natural means of ventilation rather than mechanical ones. This creates more attractive libraries (e.g. it overcomes the drowsiness suffered by some in such buildings) and can enhance the spectacle of the building as an object on the campus.

The expansion in electronic library systems adds a further complication to facilities and space management. Computing saves space but adds environmental complexity. However, since terminals release heat whilst in operation, the stack effect can be used to ventilate the library naturally as long as the interior profile encourages air movement. This explains the curvaceous cross-section of many modern learning resource centre libraries (e.g. at Sunderland and

**Trends in university libraries**

Growth in student numbers

Increase in student-centred learning

Longer opening hours

Growth in number of books and journals

Integration of library and computer services

Clearer focus on research

Increase in use of IT

Provision of teaching and seminar rooms in libraries

Increase in security

| Typical percentage of total stock of books and journals held on open shelves by library type | |
| --- | --- |
| **Type of library** | **Percentage** |
| National library | 10% |
| Large civic library | 60% |
| Small civic library | 80% |
| Mobile library | 100% |
| Research university | 50% |
| Typical university | 70% |
| Specialist university library | 20% |

the two principal working areas for undertaking academic study. Space is needed, usually in the form of tables and chairs, for both retrieving information and using it. Between these two worlds sit a number of supporting areas – photocopy rooms, short loan, interlibrary loan, security, staff offices, small teaching areas and sometimes a cafe. The distribution of these various elements is horizontal and vertical, and generally arranged on the principle that the most commonly visited areas are nearest to the point of entry.

In the smaller university, scholars have direct access to much of the stock, which is primarily held on open shelves. In larger universities, particularly those with a strong research presence, the percentage of the total stock on shelves is much lower. Here, specialist subject libraries are more common and much of the material within these is held in secure storage. A typical university of 25,000 students will house around 500,000 books and 10,000 journal volumes on open shelves. In addition, about the same number of books and four or five times the number of journals will be held in secure book stacks elsewhere (i.e. in the basement, a separate wing or separate building).

Thames Valley Universities). But since walls and columns impede air movement, the environmentally-friendly library tends to be open-plan and have a fluid section. Openness is an important characteristic of the flexible library but privacy, security and noise abatement can be problems with excessive spatial connectivity.

## Elements of the university library

The book and journal stacks on the one hand, and the computer areas on the other, represent the two main information sources for the student. They are also commonly

Books, journals, theses and electronic data all require their own type of accommodation for browsing, use and storage. Whereas books are commonly placed on open shelves (commonly at right angles to the perimeter wall) in stacks spaced about 1.2 m apart, current journals are normally placed face out on display shelving, whilst theses are placed in dedicated and secure quiet areas. Since the student typically moves between the type of study material,

| Typical library provision in two large universities in USA | |
| --- | --- |
| **University** | **Facilites** |
| UC Berkeley | Doe Library (undergraduate) |
| | Moffit Library (postgraduate) |
| | Bancroft Library (rare and specialist materials) |
| | 20 branch libraries in faculties |
| | Own website providing electronic database to Encyclopaedia Britannica, images from the Louvre, etc. |
| | Total collection 8 million books |
| Stanford University | Green Library (undergraduate and postgraduate) |
| | Hoover Library (research and specialist) |
| | 24 branch libraries in faculties |
| | Own website providing comprehensive electronic database |
| | Total collection 7 million books plus 100 million archive documents |

The library has a duty to give protective weight to the collection. Ruskin library designed by MacCormac Jamieson Prichard. (Peter Durant)

proximity is preferred to rigid spatial degradation. This is true too of computer-based information and retrieval. Whereas a dedicated IT suite is commonly a substantial feature of modern university libraries, much electronic media is integrated. Hence, books, journals, theses and computer terminals share the main spaces of the library – though each may also have its own dedicated area.

As a general rule, about 6–8% of a university's budget is allocated to the library. About a half of this is absorbed by salaries, the other half being spent on book and periodical

---

**Space standards commonly used in planning university libraries**

Library 8–10% of total academic floor area

One reader space for every three–four students based upon 2.5 m$^2$ per reader.

1 m$^2$ of shelf-based storage space for every 100 books

75% of total stock held on open shelves in teaching universities, 50–60% in research universities.

Library office space is 12% of total library space.

Circulation areas represent about 20% of total library space.

8–10 books per sq. ft in open-shelf reading room, 10–12 in open stack, 12–15 in closed stack, and 40–60 in compact storage

Computer-based material occupies 20–25% of total library area.

---

acquisitions, binding, copying and administration. Most universities spend about the same amount each year on book and journal acquisition, but the trend is towards expanding electronic systems. Computers, network, cabling and data sources (CD-ROMs) account for about 25% of total library expenditure each year, but in many newer universities the space and money spent in this area can exceed that given to traditional library resources. The modern IT-based university library suits business and professional courses, and has a particular appeal for students at universities with an ethos of computer-based learning. The balance of expenditure and space is both a library and a cultural issue.

The division of library and book storage into separate buildings is driven largely by cost concerns. As a general rule, the cost of library buildings is about three times that of library warehouses (currently in the UK about £1,200/m$^2$ as against £400/m$^2$ for book storage bindings). Purpose-built warehouses can also store up to three times the amount of books that can be housed per square metre in libraries. The efficiency on cost grounds of warehousing for book storage can be nine times that of the library (Urquhart, 1981). This explains the growing tendency in large university libraries to separate reading areas from storage – a separation which can be over several kilometres. With the cost differentiation in the region of a factor of 6–9, the extra burden of transport and administration can readily be absorbed. The main disadvantage is the time delay in bringing study material to the reader.

In planning university libraries, the general standard is to allow 1 sq. ft of floor area for every four volumes (1 m$^2$ for 40), resulting in a library containing a million books of about 250,000 sq. ft (25,000 m$^2$) in total area. Another useful rule of thumb is to allocate 1 m$^2$ per student – hence a university of 20,000 students will need a library of about 20,000 m$^2$ (or 200,000 sq. ft). However, the type of university influences the basic space calculations. It can be assumed that arts courses make greater demand upon library use and the books here tend to be larger. Science students on the other hand are more likely to use journals and IT systems. So whereas the space could be reduced to 0.8 m$^2$ per student, the overall cost may be much the same since journals and computing are more expensive to acquire than books. Since the tendency is for students and library resources to expand, it makes little sense to build to minimum standards initially. Growth is an unavoidable reality of university life but, whereas faculty growth can be accommodated by constructing new buildings, the library can only grow by building new wings.

Storage and circulation are important elements of the university library. Corridors, stairs, lifts, service ducts and toilets account for about 20% of the total floor area. In well-designed libraries, corridors and stairs are often part of the open-plan reading areas. Walls are often unavoidable and should not be built unless absolutely necessary – they impede flexibility and undermine transparency and security. Although fire regulations have an impact, the skilful architect will plan the library to reduce their damaging effect upon the building as an open interactive learning environment.

Readers' seats in the library should be provided at a rate of about 20% of the student population of the university. Hence, with a university of 20,000, there should be 4,000 tables and chairs. Where table working is replaced by screen scanning, the percentage can be as high as 40%. This results in 8,000 computer terminals distributed throughout the modern IT library. As an economy, however, most academic libraries have a general spread of IT facilities at a fairly low level and concentrate terminals in special IT suites or learning resource centres. However, whereas the shelf and storage needs of IT learning are low, the cost of tables, chairs and equipment makes the computer-based library more expensive to provide than the traditional academic library.

Although circumstances vary according to the type of university, about 75% of the total stock of books and periodicals is normally on open access with the remainder in storage. Clearly, when the total collection exceeds 1 million items, an increasing amount is held in storage. In research-based institutions, the balance of open-shelf access and secure storage is roughly equal and, in special libraries such as the Ruskin Library at Lancaster University, only a minority of the study collection is on open access. For calculating library space needs, the designer should assume 9 m of shelf storage per 1,000 volumes and 4 m where the material is held in compact storage.

These figures apply to typical large universities, but in college libraries the proportion of books to journals and study to research material varies. Normally a large college will contain 100,000 books and subscribe to 800 periodicals and newspapers. Since colleges often accept endowments of books from distinguished former students, they have the habit of growing erratically. Space tends to be a greater constraint in such libraries rather than the availability of funds or the generosity of benefactors.

---

**Accommodation needs in the university library**

Display on open shelves of books and periodicals

Storage of books and periodicals

Storage and use of audiovisual material

Tables for electronic media with supplementary storage

Catalogue search areas

Counter and control points

Copying facilities

Quick reference and short loan area

Library offices

Seminar and tutorial rooms

Private study space (especially for postgraduates)

Exhibition area

Media and video rooms

---

**Typical UK university library: Huddersfield University, UK**

| | |
|---|---|
| Number of students | 16,474 |
| Visits to library per year | 962,000 |
| Number of books in stock | 416,000 |
| Number of periodical titles | 1,938 |
| Number of reader's seats | 1,258 |
| Number of computer workstations | 1,447 |

---

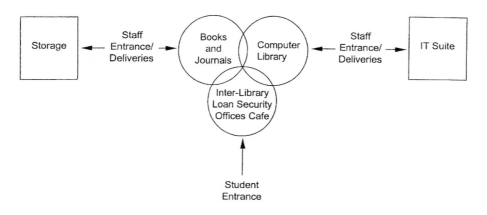

Conceptual diagram of a typical university library. (Brian Edwards)

As a rule of thumb, the higher the degree level of course provided at a university, the greater the demand made upon library space and the larger the collection. Whereas in a typical university the area of the library is usually about 8% of the total academic floor area, in a research-based university the library may approach 10–12% of total space provision. Universities with a large number of masters programmes, research students and active research staff require more library space, more books and journals, and more plentiful access to computers than other institutions. Guidelines in the UK allow for a variation of 30% depending upon the level and type of education. Normally the design team strives for a library which is heavily used, since it indicates a good utilization of resources and suggests a lively learning environment. Under-used libraries reflect poor design and management, and duplication between central, faculty and domestic facilities.

Academic libraries require space for quiet study and reflecting upon the material, and areas for intensive periods of writing. Hence, most libraries zone activities to create quiet individual study areas, space for group work, and areas where interaction can exist between library use and teaching. With the growth in both computer-based study and peer group learning, the importance of silent working areas should not be overlooked. Besides the culture change brought to university libraries by digital and electronic systems, the growth in student numbers, triggered by the concept that university education is for all, has also changed the nature of the university library. It is now an open access building serving both students and non-academic visitors; it is often available (at least in part) 24 hours a day and throughout the year. With these changes come new demands upon space, security and systems. Electronic tagging of all study material is now common-place (journals as well as books) and security cameras are installed in the most vulnerable areas. Also with the expansion of use comes a broadening of the facilities available. Copying, video conferencing and e-mail all change the nature and type of resources demanded, and with the concept of the library as a study centre comes pressure to provide cafes, bookshops, exhibition and video loan facilities.

## IT and library layout

Journal acquisition can be an expensive undertaking for a university. A typical university such as York University spends about £750,000/year on the purchase of journals. Newer universities, such as those formed in 1992 in the UK from former polytechnics, tend to subscribe to electronic versions of journals. With electronic journals, library authorities need to ensure that adequate networks and computers exist to access the electronic material both in the library and outside. So whilst the investment in journals is lower, the investment in PCs and networks is higher. But there are two further benefits of electronic journals.

First, there is an economy of space since extensive journal storage will not be required. Although the PCs take up a considerable volume of space, they are used extensively for other purposes and hence afford an overall efficiency gain. The balance between provision cost (CD-ROM as against traditional journal material) and space use varies according to the type of library, but the trend is towards electronically formatted journals. The other benefit concerns the access CD-ROMs give to study or research material for students who are studying part-time. For masters and doctoral students, it is fair to assume that they have their own networked PCs at home. Hence, accessing library information material from home makes part-time study more attractive. The ramifications for the design of libraries are quite obvious: to provide space and connections for PC use throughout the library on the assumption that information will be accessed electronically over the lifetime of the library (at least 50 years).

Evidence suggests that with computer-based access systems and electronically formatted information, the use of books and journals actually increases. The idea that traditional library material will become redundant is not borne out by evidence from a typical UK university (B. Kirtley, University of Lancaster, personal communication, 2000). What computing provides via electronic referencing and the Internet is ready access to catalogue material. This allows the student to make better use of books and journals, both in the immediate library and via interlibrary loan to obtain journals, theses and other study material held elsewhere.

The pattern in academic libraries is likely to be followed in public ones. Although universities and colleges invest more in their libraries than the public sector, they provide a useful model of design and investment for the whole library system. This is true not only of new library provision but of the refurbishment of older libraries to meet new IT demands. The upgrading of traditional academic libraries through internal rebuilding and the construction of new computer-based wings (as at the Jagger Library, University of Cape Town) sets a precedent for the whole library sector. Here the new IT wing acts as a bridge between the old library and the student union building – it is in a sense a social and electronic gateway to the library.

An interesting arrangement has been created by architects MacCormac Jamieson Prichard in their extension to the library at the University of Lancaster. Here, open-fronted computer rooms on every floor line a central three-storey street, glazed at roof level. The arrangement is not unlike a shopping mall with different retail units defining a wide airy route. Beyond the bank of computer suites sit the traditional book stacks, which act as a sound barrier between the quiet study area by the exterior windows and the relatively noisy central street. The street, or more

| Brotherton Library, University of Leeds, UK | | |
|---|---|---|
| **Architect** | **Special features** | **Date** |
| Lanchester and Lodge | Domed reading room | 1935 |
| | Special collection of early books | |
| | New provision for conservation and security | |
| | Bold new addition. | |

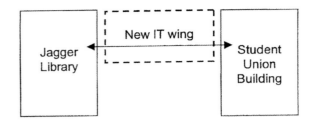

Conceptual diagram of the linking IT wing at University of Cape Town. (Brian Edwards)

correctly 'linear atrium', acts as a communication spine through the new library providing access to the reading room, which itself focuses upon the detached Ruskin Library beyond. This street with its library desk at one end is a place to shop for access to the knowledge held elsewhere in the library.

## Brotherton Library, University of Leeds, UK

The Brotherton Library at the University of Leeds is typical of university libraries created substantially by private donation. Although the university library dates from 1919, it was a modest affair until Lord Brotherton gifted his collection in 1935. The Brotherton Collection (as it is still known) was an extensive private library of medieval manuscripts and rare books, and came with sufficient funds to construct a new library building and an endowment to cover running costs. Brotherton sought a library where students and the general public could 'wander freely through the rooms of a great library' (Cox, 1981, p. 95). The emphasis was upon open access, large promenade space, generous stairs and lofty interiors.

The collection was particularly strong in material from the period 1600–1750, and today represents an archive of national importance. Around the Brotherton Collection grew other gifts and donations, making the library of value beyond the needs of that of teaching, research and scholarship within the university. Today, the original collection is housed in a self-contained suite within the Brotherton Library (which remains the central library for the university). The fragility of some of the books and manuscripts requires the material to be housed within special air-conditioned rooms. The growing monetary value of the collection (and consequent risk of theft) has also resulted in much of it being moved from open shelving to secure accommodation.

The Brotherton Library, a fine example of 1930s architecture, and its management regime has had to adjust to the changes brought about by mass education and the growing

value attached of the original collection. New wings have been constructed to accommodate the expanding library and former open reading areas have been partially enclosed to enhance the level of security. Library resources too have had to be spent on conservation measures of various kinds, adding to costs. The Brotherton donation and endowment makes the library at Leeds University exceptional, but the recurrent costs exceed the normal provision of 6% of total university expenditure spent on the library. Special collections make for libraries of exceptional interest to the academic community, but they also lead to special problems of funding, access and coherence of purpose between the provision of modern texts for students and the care of rare books (Cox, 1981, p. 100).

## Jagger Library, University of Cape Town, South Africa

The Jagger Library at the University of Cape Town is typical of a modern university – over 1 million books, 7,000 volumes of journals, extensive special collections and little space for expansion. Built in 1918 and expanded

Jagger Library, University of Cape Town, with congregation hall on the right. Both designed by Sir Herbert Baker. (Brian Edwards)

| Jagger Library, Cape Town University, South Africa | | |
| --- | --- | --- |
| **Architect** | **Special features** | **Date** |
| Sir Herbert Baker (extension by Louis Karol Architects) | Edwardian classical design | 1918, extended 2000 |
| | Extension acts as a bridge between old library and student union building. | |
| | IT facilities in new wing with emphasis upon interaction. | |

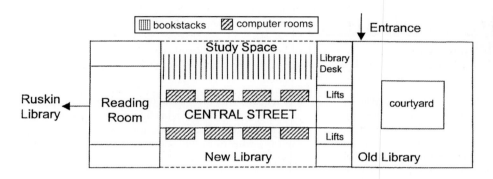

Conceptual diagram of the library arrangement at Lancaster University. (Brian Edwards)

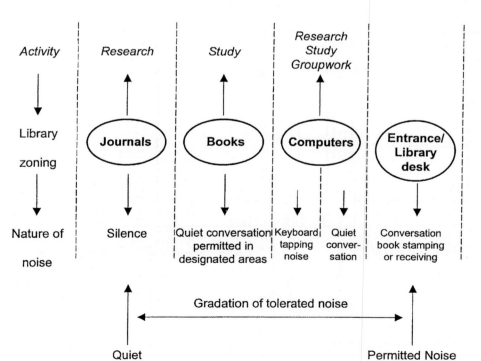

Noise zoning in a typical academic library. (Brian Edwards)

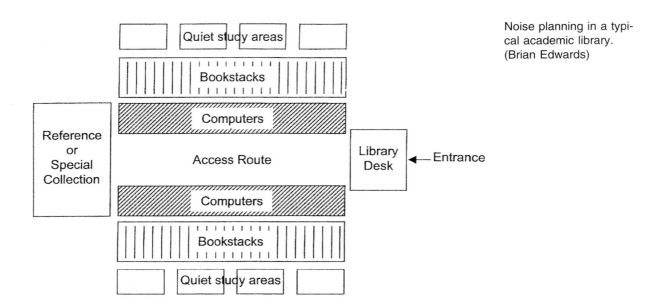

Noise planning in a typical academic library. (Brian Edwards)

periodically, it had by 1999 become quite inadequate especially in terms of student access to IT resources. Growth, which had over previous decades been accommodated partly through the development of faculty libraries, had reached the limits of what peripheral space was available.

The decision was eventually made to build a new wing to the Jagger Library, but in such a way that it formed a connection with the student union building nearby. This allowed the extension to act as a bridge between the social aspects of higher education and academic ones. The bridge itself is a wing of mainly student resource centre material (computer workstations, CD-ROM library), which allows the Jagger Library and the student union building to form a U-shaped block around Jameson Hall — the central

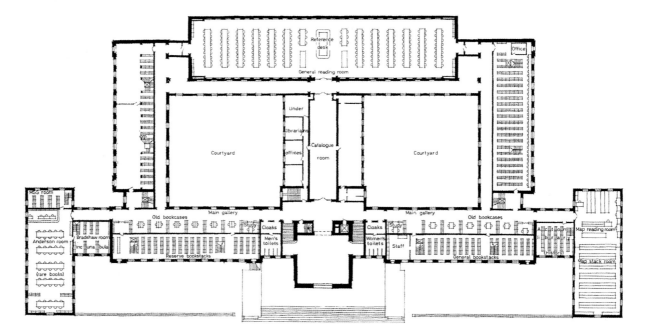

The university library of the 1930s is well represented by this example designed in 1934 by Giles Gilbert Scott for Cambridge University. (D Insall and Partners)

Electronic data is fairly economical of space use but expensive to acquire. Hence, the new wing is not large but intensively used by students. It is a high-tech gateway to learning with multiple connections to faculty, departmental and, for some academic staff, private electronic libraries. As the special collections and other research material are converted into electronic formats, the new wing also helps to break down the barriers between teaching and research by making the material more available in the classroom.

The new IT wing is known as the 'knowledge common' – a shared grazing area for students exploiting computer-based learning. Library management allows group work and talking to take place in small seminar rooms provided around the perimeter. So, whereas traditionally teaching takes place in the various departments of the university, new student-centred learning occurs mainly in the library. The advantages are twofold for the university: first it relieves space elsewhere and second it allows knowledge systems and skill acquisition (analytical, IT, presentation) to be integrated via the power of the computer. To allow the latter to occur successfully, the new IT wing contains its own area for training staff and students in the use of the new technology.

By concentrating the bulk of the library computer facilities in one dedicated area, laptop noise becomes concentrated and does not disrupt the remainder of the library. Also, as training and group learning takes place in the same space, the insistence upon silence becomes unnecessary. The new wing has become a high-tech gateway of learning driven by new IT-based knowledge systems, fresh approaches to skill development, and increasing reliance upon students teaching each other.

## Learning Resource Centre, Thames Valley University, Slough, UK

Designed by the Richard Rogers Partnership in 1995, the Learning Resource Centre at Thames Valley University was one of the first libraries to respond architecturally to the IT challenge. The client wanted a building which harnessed the latest technology in a design which would prove a model for other universities (Anon., 1996, p. 30).

Open learning study center with university registry behind at Saltire Centre, Glasgow. (Brian Edwards)

congregation building on campus. Conceptually, the new wing reflects the move toward a learning, rather than teaching environment at Cape Town University. The new wing provides direct access one way to the traditional stock of books and journals, and the other to refreshment and social facilities. There are extensive computer-networked positions integrated into the book-based library floors, but the new IT wing, with over 200 dedicated workstations, signals a change in emphasis in library use.

| Learning Resource Centre, Thames Valley University, Slough, UK | | |
| --- | --- | --- |
| **Architect** | **Special features** | **Cost** |
| Richard Rogers Partnerships | One of the first learning resource centres | £1,113/m² in 1996 |
| | Designed to reflect IT rather than book use. | |
| | Employs many sustainable features. | |
| | Creates a relaxed and stimulating learning environment. | |

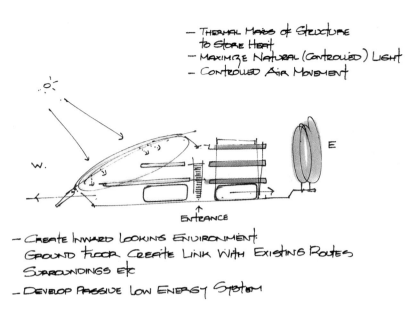

— THERMAL MASS OF STRUCTURE
to STORE HEAT
— MAXIMIZE NATURAL (CONTROLLED) LIGHT
— CONTROLLED AIR MOVEMENT

W.

E

ENTRANCE

— CREATE INWARD LOOKING ENVIRONMENT
GROUND FLOOR CREATE LINK WITH EXISTING ROUTES
SURROUNDINGS etc
— DEVELOP PASSIVE LOW ENERGY SYSTEM

BUILDING ORIENTATION / ENERGY

TVU–JUNE 94–RRP

Environmental sketch, Learning Resource Centre, Thames Valley University, by the Richard Rogers Partnership. (Richard Rogers Partnership)

In exploiting the potential of IT to enhance the learning environment for students, the university sought a model for a new generation of libraries which would have 'a relaxed and comfortable atmosphere' (Anon., 1995, p. 30).

Learning resource centres combine elements of the traditional library and computer suites. They allow students to study at their own pace, in their own time, and using a variety of learning styles (Anon., 1996, p. 30). As the electronic and information hub of modern universities,

The Internet has changed the face of the modern library. Thames Valley University Learning Resource Centre designed by the Richard Rogers Partnership. (Katsuhisa Kid/RRP)

learning resource centres require an image which signals the links to the 'wider global community'. This was the challenge put to the architects and which, to a large degree, they have met in the design. The design in particular is symbolic of the university ethos that 'learning and knowledge should be accessible and enjoyable' (Anon., 1996, p. 30).

The design breaks down into two elements. There is a rectangular book and journal storage area which represents 'knowledge', and an open reading, computer and entrance area which represents 'access'. The latter area is contained within a lofty curved glazed volume; the former is a traditional three-storey building which provides its buttressed support. The open volume houses videos, CD-ROMs, laptops and open learning areas, while the closed 'book-stack' area contains traditional book and journal material with carrels along the outer north-facing edge. The image produced is one of a factory of learning – a huge industrial shed of computers, books and people.

With so much computer use, the problem of creating an environment that is not stifled by air-conditioning led to many design decisions at a strategic and detailed level. The site arrangement places the open computer area to the east where morning sunshine encourages stack effect ventilation. Here the shape and smooth profile of the roof promotes air movement with the adjoining concrete constructed book-stack area providing sufficient thermal capacity to moderate temperature peaks. It is a good example of architectural elements and books resources combining to provide optimum conditions without resorting to air-conditioning.

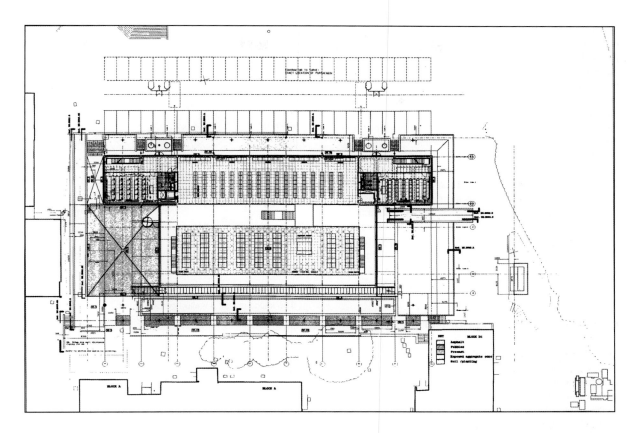

Plan, Learning Resource Centre, Thames Valley University, by the Richard Rogers Partnership. (Richard Rogers Partnership)

Night-time view, Learning Resource Centre, Thames Valley University, by the Richard Rogers Partnership. (Katsuhisa Kid/RRP)

The library is entered from the south where a cafe provides a welcoming counterpoint to the library control desk. The cafe projects into a small courtyard, defining movement patterns and signalling the entrance to the learning resource centre. Upon entering the building, visitors face a long vista with the open reading and computer area to one side and the book-stack floors to the other. A central staircase on the entrance axis leads visitors upwards to two further floors. Routes are clearly identified within a large open-plan building and, with totally glazed gables, students have no trouble orientating themselves by external features.

Transparency and the interconnection of function are themes of the building. The idea that computers and books can be combined in student-centred learning finds direct expression here both in the plan and, more noticeably, in the section of the building. The fluidity of volume is helped by the incorporation of a deck in the main reading room which avoids direct contact with the perimeter walls. Light and space flow around the deck encouraging a relaxed atmosphere where the mind can wander across the boundaries of subjects.

203

This is a library where both subject barriers and distinctions between modes of learning are deliberately eroded. Flexibility is provided by extensive use of raised floors with integral cable and ducting space. Air movement (necessary for maintaining a stimulating and comfortable working environment) relies upon mechanical fans, opening windows (on a computerized building management system) and on the profile of the building itself. It assumes that the life of the learning resource centre as represented by the students and their computer use play an active part in creating an environment of learning – both physical and intellectual. The heat generated, plus that of the sun, provides most of the energy needed for heating and ventilation. In this sense, the Learning Resource Centre at Thames Valley University is a useful model of the sustainable library of the future. Although the building services costs of this energy-efficient design were slightly higher than the norm, the building has substantially reduced running costs, giving a payback period of under 10 years (Anon., 1995, pp. 34, 38).

## Law Library, Cambridge University, UK

Constructed alongside James Stirling's History Faculty Building on the Sidgwick arts campus, the Law Library at Cambridge designed in 1994 by Foster and Partners, accommodates the largest law faculty library in the country. It serves over 1,000 students of law and nearly 100 faculty staff. The 9000 m$^2$ building houses the library, teaching rooms, five auditoria and staff offices. The library, which serves both undergraduate and postgraduate needs, has significant research collections and is conceived as one large interconnecting space. The compartmentalization into rooms, common in some faculty libraries where research

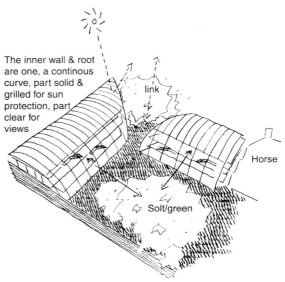

The inside is solt, a walled garden, quiet, contemplative, tranquil, an oasis.

Exterior concept sketch of Law Library, Cambridge University, by Lord Foster. (Foster and Partners)

occurs, is avoided in order to create one shared volume for intellectual exchange. It is an arrangement which provides an immediate feeling of spaciousness and offers the further advantage of embedding flexibility in the use of space.

An unusual form of structure is employed in order to construct a library of largely column-free interiors and spatial connectivity. The floors are built as a series of stepped levels interdependent of the roof and the perimeter wall. The latter consists of one huge curving glass façade,

Working tables provided at the perimeter of the Law Library, Cambridge University. Designed by Foster and Partners. (Dennis Gilbert/View)

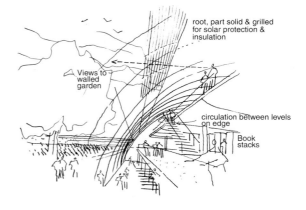

Interior concept sketch of Law Library, Cambridge University, by Lord Foster. (Foster and Partners)

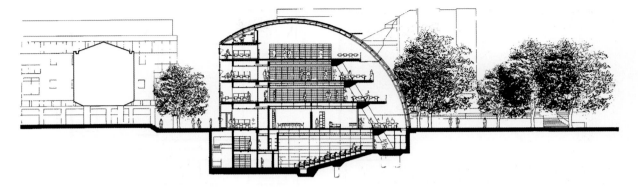

Section, Law Library, Cambridge University. (Foster and Partners)

| Law Library, Cambridge University, UK | | |
| --- | --- | --- |
| **Architect** | **Special features** | **Cost** |
| Sir Norman Foster and Partners | Energy-efficient library | £2,000/m$^2$ (approx.) |
| | Large faculty library combined with teaching space | |
| | Fluid cross-section and open plan | |
| | Partly underground to reduce visual impact and conserve energy | |
| | Employs unusual steel triangulated construction. | |

which encloses the library on its long northern elevation and sweeps over the roof to form the stainless steel cornice of the southern façade. The effect is to produce a triple height volume and a sense of flowing activity with islands of intensity at key points.

Each floor plate has a different dimension in order to accommodate the curving wall. The supporting columns are not vertical but angled. Thus, the columns define two types of space – an open working promenade alongside the glazed façade and an area of book stacks in the centre of the building. The promenade has tables and study space positioned so that the students are midway between the views out over adjoining lawns and the library resources positioned in the core. It is an arrangement which balances distant prospect with intensive close work and contrasts narrow aisle space between book stacks with the spaciousness of the promenade.

There are no problems of solar heat gain as the curved glazed façade faces north. Instead, the light is even with the sun shining onto the external view rather than penetrating into the building. The neutrality of daylight is ideal for both book and computer screen use. The tables are arranged at right angles to the promenade space, with task lighting provided from a strip just above eye level. Background lighting is relatively low (for energy efficiency), allowing pools of light to be employed as a means of orientating users through the building (e.g. reception desk, staircases and auditoria entrance).

Light and space relate activities to zones of the building. The curved section and triangular entrance make for an unusual library. Visitors arrive at a projecting prow and are taken along the glazed western façade. Opposite, and affording some protection from low-angled sunlight, is Stirling's history faculty building (now listed), whose alignment determined Foster's splayed entrance. Visitors enter a shaft of light which extends the perception upwards to the main library (on the first, second and third floors) and downwards to the auditorium and teaching rooms on the lower ground floor. Major routes are taken through the well-lit areas, with the main diagonally placed staircase always bathed in bright light (and often sunlight). As a result the circulation strategy and lighting design are in step, with the available routes being easily perceived, and hence the functional spaces reached effortlessly.

Except on the west gable where sunlight identifies the entrance, solar penetration is controlled by careful

205

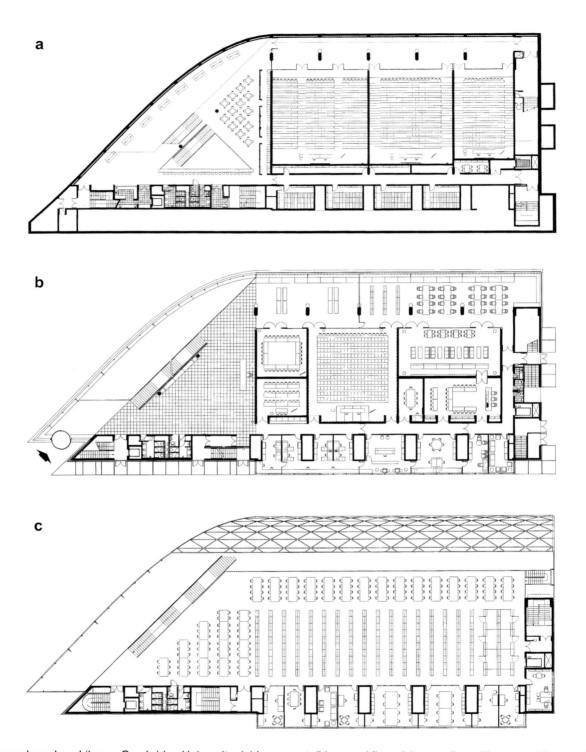

Floor plans, Law Library, Cambridge University: (a) basement; (b) ground floor; (c) upper floor. (Foster and Partners)

Exterior view, Law Library, Cambridge University.
(Dennis Gilbert/View)

planning. The staff offices and seminar rooms are positioned on the south side where the elevations can be designed to limit sunlight penetration. Here a combination of Portland stone cladding, louvres and solar glass ensures that light penetrates to the interior without glare or excessive heat gain.

The building is relatively energy efficient for a specialist faculty library. By positioning the main 250-seat auditorium, large teaching rooms and bookstore below ground, the library benefits from earth cooling – thereby reducing air-conditioning loads. Above ground the building is mainly naturally ventilated. The mixed-mode system reduces duct volume and provides the opportunity to extract heat from one system to benefit the other (by employing heat recovery technology). It is the search for energy efficiency which gives shape to the cross-section and makes for an interesting landmark amongst distinguished neighbours.

## Library, University of Abertay, Dundee, Scotland

A key aspect of the brief for the main academic library at the University of Abertay outside Dundee in Scotland was the need to respond to the growth in IT and the corresponding reduction in 'hard copy' (Fresson, 1998). The university has a static book collection and expects this to decline as the digital library expands. The three key elements of the new library are:

- IT learning resource centre
- specialist study collection
- training library for local businesses.

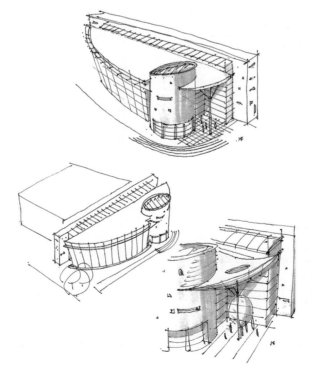

Concept sketches Library, University of Abertay, Dundee. (The Parr Partnership)

207

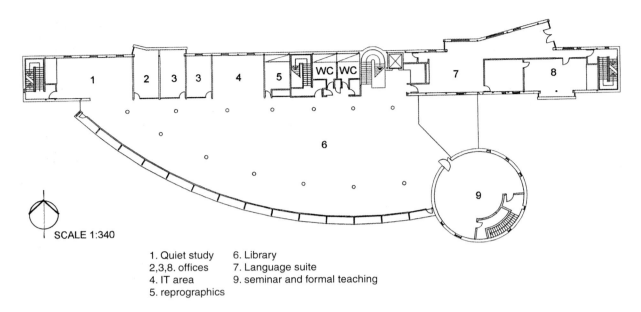

SCALE 1:340

1. Quiet study
2,3,8. offices
4. IT area
5. reprographics
6. Library
7. Language suite
9. seminar and formal teaching

Plan, Library at the University of Abertay, Dundee 1, Quiet study; 2,3,8, offices; 4, IT area; 5, reprographics; 6, Library; 7 Language suite; 9, seminar and formal teaching. (The Parr Partnership)

The challenge for the architects, the Parr Partnership, was to create a building which expressed the high-tech nature of the library whilst also providing a strong architectural statement at the centre of a new campus.

The library has three main zones: a highly glazed open-plan library reading room, IT and book-stack area; a circular teaching and seminar drum; and back-up office and service areas. The first of these zones has a curving line of study desks against the outside wall, the second is an inward-looking room for intense library-based group work and for conducting seminars, while the third forms a bank of cellular accommodation on the north side of the building. These different zones are expressed separately to provide legibility to users of the library and to allow each part to be designed according to specific functional and technical needs.

The main segment-shaped library is glazed continuously on the outside and has book stacks towards the rear to create introspective study areas. These are served by IT facilities which employ floor cable peninsulas running from ducts constructed in the rear wall. The subdivision of this area into study bays is achieved by a combination of book-stack alignment and structural columns, which establish working zones. The columns are on two patterns: one follows the linear line of the offices, the other the curved façade to the south. The presence of these contradictory grids creates an ambiguity which helps reinforce casual use of the large library reading room.

Between the bank of offices facing north and the curved southerly reading room is a corridor with a roof light on the top floor. The effect of the roof glazing is to form a slot of daylight to help articulate the zones of the library. The office 'wall' acts as a barrier between the car park to the north and the study areas to the south. It projects out on both east and west gables, forming an element that clearly services the whole. Within the 'wall' are positioned offices,

| Library, University of Abertay, Dundee, Scotland | | |
|---|---|---|
| **Architect** | **Special features** | **Cost** |
| The Parr Partnership | Flexible library to accommodate growth in IT and decline in book use | Not available |
| | Creates transparent reading room as gateway to new campus. | |
| | Clearly articulated library to express three main functional zones. | |
| | Has intelligent double-glazed 'energy' wall. | |

photocopying rooms, language suites, staircases and toilets. Constructed of concrete and faced in sandstone, the solidity of the 'wall' makes a deliberate contrast to the transparency of the main parts of the library.

Unusually the main library has a southerly aspect. Normally this would provide almost insurmountable problems, but in Scotland the problem of solar gain and glare can be overcome. The southern façade, built on a sweeping curve, is double-glazed with air drawn between the layers of glass, which are constructed 400 mm apart. Mature trees outside provide useful summertime shade, which is augmented by external-fixed bris-soleil and automatic internal blinds which adjust according to the intensity of the sun.

By placing working desks against the façade, the library always appears to be enlivened by student industry. Having a peopled elevation facing the centre of the campus creates a good impression for the university, whilst providing an opportunity for the students to exercise surveillance over the central campus. This is particularly evident at the library entrance where the glazed façade is pulled back to directly overlook the external courtyard alongside the library control point.

\A stone-faced drum penetrates the glazed reading room, providing a further measured contrast to the general air of transparency. Inside on three floors are the formal teaching and intensive IT training areas. These areas need more controlled daylight and environmental conditions than in the main reading room. Windows are deeply set into the stone wall, creating a keep-like quality which hints at Scotland's castle style. The drum has its own staircase so that it can operate independently of the library. Between the drum element and the office wall is an over-sailing canopy which protects the library entrance and signals its presence.

## Library, Cranfield University, UK

The library at Cranfield University designed in 1991 by Foster and Partners broke the mould of library design. It was one of the first academic libraries to establish an integrated provision of book and IT, and the first to incorporate library and lecture theatres in a single building. As Cranfield University is primarily a postgraduate institution built around industrial collaboration in the science, management and technology areas, the library was seen as reinforcing this character by the provision of a high-tech, user-friendly building. As much of the material housed in the library is of a research nature (particularly collections relating to aerospace technology), there was also a need to balance access with security. furthermore, postgraduate library users were often part-time masters or doctoral students and their demands were increasingly met by electronic rather than book or journal sources.

Open reading room sparsely furnished at Cranfield University Library. Designed by Foster and Partners. (James Morris/Foster and Partners)

The image of the library was seen at the outset as an important consideration. Its role was not only to provide effective library services, but to act as a building which would attract students to Cranfield University. Hence the streamlined shape with metallic curved roof forms, extensive glazing and use of expressed solar control – all creating a modern high-tech, environmentally conscious image. The latter was perceived as important because of the 'building's symbolic placement at the focal point of the Cranfield campus' (Blagden, 1997).

The library is square in plan and three storeys high with an over-sailing arched roof. It is a shape that offers both adaptability and extendibility. The internal columns order the accommodation into logical bays. In effect, the building

Library, Cranfield University, designed by Foster and Partners. (Foster and Partners)

| Library, University of Cranfield, UK | | |
|---|---|---|
| **Architect** | **Special features** | **Cost** |
| Sir Norman Foster and Partners | Postgraduate, technology-based library | £1,600/m$^2$ (approx.) |
| | Integrated library, teaching and lecture facilities | |
| | Integrated book, journal and IT access around perimeter study desks | |
| | Has high-level IT access and small collection. | |
| | Exploits daylight to reduce energy use. | |
| | Has a high-tech appearance to symbolize university's technological ethos. | |

is a simple well-lit case which can accommodate a variety of uses over time. The absence of walls and the presence inside of the triple height arched bays provides a sense of openness which encourages academic and social interaction. One criticism voiced by users, however, was noise leakage from the atrium to study areas, from the lecture theatres to the library itself, and from group working areas to those set aside for private study (Blagden, 1995, p. 45). These problems emanate from the modern concept of the academic library as a place of exchange rather than the traditional one as a place for private reading. At Cranfield, the decision to combine lecture rooms and library space into a single shell carried inevitable consequences for acoustic control.

The four parallel steel-framed bays provide the essential functional order for the library. Activities are arranged along the grain of the bays, whose vaulted ceilings provide orientation for users. Legibility, so important in complex libraries, is achieved by synchronizing the activity zones with the character of the architectural space. Book stacks and study carrels provide sub-bays which fit tidily into the structural order. Since daylight is introduced via the roof vaults as well as by perimeter glazing, the effect is to bring natural light into the interior in a fashion which reinforces the pattern of use.

Since most readers prefer to work at the building perimeter, where one can balance quiet study with exterior views, the challenge is to provide optimum conditions for both book and computer use. In an ideal world, IT facilities would be located in areas away from external glazing where screen glare can be controlled. However, readers and computers do not share the same performance objectives and the challenge at Cranfield was in creating good working conditions for a variety of study modes at the building edge. To achieve this, the glazing on the east and west elevations (where low-angled sun is a problem) is set well back behind the over-sailing vaulted roof. On the south elevation, the glazing is protected from the sun by aluminium louvres set between the steel columns. In addition, the glass is coated

for both sunlight protection and energy conservation. These measures not only provide good working conditions at the edge of the building, they also give good daylight penetration without unwanted glare or solar gain.

A continuous study desk now runs around the perimeter of the library with working bays set at the generous provision of 1.6 m – a width which provides for simultaneous use of book and personal computer (Blagden, 1995, p. 44). Data, network communications and power points are provided every 800 mm on the desktop. It is a level of provision which reflects Cranfield's ethos as a postgraduate technology-based university.

Small study areas also exist for group work with larger seminar spaces dispersed on the upper floors. Although the library is mainly on the first and second floor with the lecture theatres on the ground floor, the library storage is placed on the ground floor for ease of external access. The Aerospace Research Archive is also placed here where it can be air-conditioned in conjunction with the lecture rooms.

The three-storey configuration of the library is based upon the logic of dissertation, archive and lecture facilities on the ground floor, books on the first floor and periodicals on the second. It is an arrangement which makes the use of the library straightforward, but is not readily transferable since most academic libraries would normally seek to hold a far larger book collection and rely less on journals. Also, unlike some recent university libraries, electronic and traditional sources are fully integrated though at the cost of extensive perimeter ducting. Since Cranfield recognized the growing impact of IT systems on postgraduate training, the decision was made as early as 1991 to provide a fibre optic wiring infrastructure which would meet future needs as well as current ones (Blagden, 1995, p. 44). This IT resilience added to the initial cost but helped structure the building into its present form. It also allowed the library to be smaller than one would expect of a research facility, since most students and staff were expected to access material electronically. The comparatively small hard copy collection and large IT provision was a forerunner of a new generation of libraries (Blagden, 1995, p. 46) – ones which are smaller but more expensive to build and equip. If access is the key then cost yardsticks need to be modified to reflect quality rather than quantity of provision. The Cranfield Library opened up an important debate about how far academic libraries should rely upon electronic access as against developing a study collection of their own.

## Learning Resource Centre, Anglia Ruskin University, Essex, UK

Known as the Queen's Building, the Learning Resource Centre at Anglia Ruskin University in Chelmsford, Essex is a library that integrates new concepts of low-energy design and IT provision into a coherent whole. The building successfully explores energy-efficient environmental practices in the fields of heating, lighting and the choice of construction materials whilst incorporating these in a fashion which provides for optimum conditions for computer-centred library use. Flexibility and simplicity of operation are the keys to this successful design (it won the UK's Green Building of the Year award in 1996).

The library, designed by ECD Architects with engineers Ove Arup & Partners, creates a landmark building for a new campus. It signals both the presence of an IT library and also the location of a university on a site which was formerly used for industrial purposes. In this sense, the image of the library was important in signalling the type of university it served (Benny, 1995, p. 34). As a focal building with a high level of transparency, it was designed to give identity and unify a fragmented city landscape.

The Queen's Building is an early example of a library designed for retrieval from an IT resource rather than book or journal sources. It was not conceived as a quiet place filled with book stacks, but as a busy, bustling, high-tech library. This different character allowed for the integration of low-energy systems such as open-plan atriums exploring natural ventilation and daylight instead of air-conditioning. It also led to the provision of social space — restaurant and common

Learning Resource Centre, Anglia Ruskin University, designed by ECD Architects. (Anglia Ruskin University)

rooms — within the library. Thus, the openness of the building supported the concept of an interactive IT library and facilitated flexibility of future layout by employing the minimum of enclosing walls. The open nature of the building occurs both in plan and section, allowing space and activities to flow freely both horizontally and vertically.

The Queen's Building rises from three to four storeys in height and is topped by the glass lanterns of the two atriums. The ground floor is a social hub and the top floor houses research, TV studio and staff offices. The use of two atriums brings daylight into the centre of the library and allows ventilation to occur using the stack effect. Book stacks are positioned at right angles to the atriums with study spaces served by computers with video links arranged around the perimeter of the building. Each of the 700 study desks is wired for IT, which is threaded inwards from perimeter trunking (rather than raised floors).

The brief for the new library required 'an environmentally conscious, low-energy building' (Benny, 1995, p. 35). The client was keen to avoid a sealed, air-conditioned building on the grounds of inflexibility in the face of changing IT and educational needs, and because of

| Queen's Library, Anglia Ruskin University, UK | | |
|---|---|---|
| **Architect** | **Special features** | **Cost** |
| ECD Architects | Atrium-based low energy design | £680/m² in 1993 |
| | Maximize natural light and ventilation. | |
| | Intelligent triple-glazed façade with double-light shelves | |
| | Integrated environmental strategy with IT provision. | |

running and maintenance costs. Since the main element of energy use in libraries is in lighting, the decision was made to maximize the use of daylight and, at the same time, to exploit the secondary heat of the lighting sources. This led to a range of consequential decisions from narrow plan depth, central atriums, triple-glazing with twin light-shelves, lofty ceiling heights and high structural thermal capacity (Edwards, 1998, p. 107). With so many computers in use, the problem through the year is not one of heating but cooling – hence the use of through ventilation with opening windows operated by a computerized building management system and exposed concrete construction to absorb the heat and dispense it through night-time cooling.

The integration of library functions with environmental design is a feature of the Queen's Building. For example, the two atrium spaces provide social hubs for the library whilst aiding orientation through a typically large academic building. The use of internal light-shelves and high-level opening windows also has the effect of deterring the theft of books and computers. Task lighting is widely employed, allowing readers to adjust conditions to suit their needs. With a plan depth of 11 m up to the central atrium, spaces have a feeling of openness and tranquillity – an effect enhanced by the unusually high ceilings (3.2 m).

The environmental strategy seeks to provide comfortable conditions for readers and staff without complex controls. Typically of new universities, the library has to provide a good working environment when subject to a high density of use by people and a high level of computer use. The combination of people and computers stresses working conditions through noise, pollution, casual heat gain and humidity. Density of occupation by readers and IT rather than by books is a feature of modern academic libraries. What is noteworthy about the Queen's Building is the way natural systems of lighting and ventilation, and natural materials with low toxicity in construction, add up to a library which is attractive to use and efficient in operation, which provides flexibility without excessive cost (in fact at a price of £680/m$^2$ in 1993 the library is below cost norms (Edwards, 1998, p. 104) and quietly landmarks a new campus.

One consequence of these features was the occupation of part of the building by the vice-chancellor. The vice-chancellor's office and supporting administration took over part of the top floor just prior to occupation. The library was sufficiently flexible to accommodate this late change of use. Clearly in a world of rapid change, libraries need to be able to absorb the unexpected. A key to this occurring at the Queen's Building was the shallow plan depth, regular structural grid and optimum use of windows. Had the library had the normal 22–40 m floor depth, there would have been no opportunity to convert part of the building into a conventional office (Benny, 1995, p. 36).

## Aldham Robarts Learning Resource Centre, Liverpool John Moores University, UK

The Aldham Robarts Learning Resource Centre, designed in 1992 by Austin-Smith: Lord, was one of the first academic libraries in the UK to effectively combine traditional library and computer services into a single integrated building. It is a large building in excess of 6000 m$^2$ with 720 networked PC-based workspaces and a capacity of a quarter of a million volumes. The Aldham Roberts Learning Resource Centre, named after its Canadian publishing benefactor, is one of three integrated centres built to serve a university of 14,000 students. This one meets the needs of the Schools of Business, Built Environment, Design, Media Studies, Social Work and Law. The building is the result of the convergence of two services – library and computing – and does so with a design which deliberately erodes boundaries between types of provision.

The Aldham Robarts Centre anticipates the age of the fully electronic campus with its network connections to all staff and some student PCs. The building has a raised floor throughout for flexibility of power and data cables. It also has shelving which can be turned through 90 degrees or converted to study places (Revill, 1995, p. 56). The design, based upon a deep plan with a cruciform of roof-glazed corridors that radiate out from an entrance atrium, provides a rational grid of structural bays (7.2 m$^2$) capable of use by traditional library or IT services. The Learning Resource Centre is able to accommodate six networked services – CD-ROM, multimedia, interactive sound, MAC, PC and Dec Athena – with workstations typically connected to 3–5 of these services according to subject need (Revill, 1995, p. 56).

Since it is estimated that students at the university spend seven hours per week in library study and a similar number of hours on computing activities (Revill, 1995, p. 58), the decision to combine both in equal measure was a natural response. Not all universities would expect the same results – traditional universities depend more upon teaching. which creates orthodox library use. However, newer universities, such as those in the UK based within former polytechnics, rely more upon a student-centred learning environment with its more extensive computer use. With 14 hours a week devoted to library and computer activities (or about a third of overall student study time), the quality of the Learning Resource Centre is critical. As a result, the Aldham Robarts Centre is designed as a central feature on campus and has an inviting large glazed entrance foyer. This leads to an information desk whereby students are directed to study material and given advice on the computing facilities available.

Some group working areas have book stacks, providing partial noise baffles. Generally, the emphasis is upon quiet personal study space arranged mainly around the building perimeter. Book stacks, where they occur, are absorbed

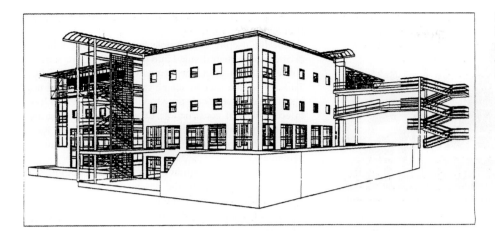

Design sketch, Aldham Robarts Learning Resource Centre, Liverpool John Moores University. (Austin-Smith: Lord)

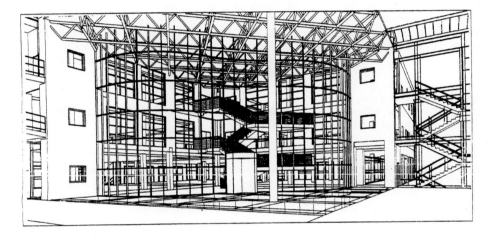

within the library's structural grid. Columns (spaced in both directions 7.2 m apart) define use either as book or journal shelving, as group study areas or as staff offices. The rationality of the configuration supports flexibility and leads to economies in servicing layout.

Two glazed corridors bisect the space at right angles. These terminate in staircases and, at the crossing, define the information or help desks placed on each of the building's three floors. The corridors each feed directly from the large entrance atrium and act rather like high streets leading to

| Aldham Robarts Learning Resource Centre, Liverpool John Moores University, UK | | |
| --- | --- | --- |
| **Architect** | **Special features** | **Cost** |
| Austin-Smith: Lord | Deep planned learning resource centre | £1,510/m$^2$ in 1994 |
| | Raised floors and artificial lighting throughout. | |
| | Fully integrated IT and book systems. | |
| | Has networked PCs able to access six IT services. | |
| | Designed as a symbolic learning gateway to twenty-first century. | |

Large simple volumes provide greater flexibility than irregular shapes, University of Hertfordshire Library. Here the shelving units and cantilevered floor soffits contain noise absorbent panels provided by Forster Ecospace. Architects: Architects Co. Partnership. (Forster Ecospace)

a variety of 'shops' along their route. In this sense, the students browse the facilities on offer in the different subject zones reflecting the client's objective of a 'symbolic gateway to the world of learning and the twenty-first century' (Revill, 1995, p. 55).

A constraint on the design was the presence on an adjoining site of a listed but derelict neoclassical church. Its generous proportions and height were, the city planning authority suggested, to be respected. By setting the new building partly underground, the cupolas of the church were able to rise above the general roofline. By adopting a building based upon cubes, and solid and void elements, the Aldham Robarts Centre also reflects the scale, rhythm and proportional harmonies of the church. Not only is the church able to stand in dignified prominence amongst newer and larger neighbours, but the general character of

the 'fine-grained conservation area' has been preserved (Sunderland, 1995, p. 60).

The philosophy of a simple box of learning which is divided and further divided into basic cubic forms mirrors, conceptually at least, the Windows programmes of PCs. This allows the user to search through the scales of provision relating physical space to virtual space. It also leads to economies of construction, of wiring and cabling, and the development of a consistent language of built forms and assemblies (from glazing and shelving to IT equipment).

The zoning of the building puts the noisier activities on the ground floor and in the basement; the progressively quieter ones occur as the building rises. High-level links connect the Learning Resource Centre to adjoining faculty buildings, with the possibility of a connection to the adjacent derelict church. Study spaces are arranged in groups of four around the building perimeter and determine the glazing grid, which itself informs the structural grid (two study bays per column bay). This symbolically at least allows the particular dimensions of private study to determine the geometry of the whole.

## Library, Delft Technical University, The Netherlands

The new library at Delft Technical University breaks with the modernist tradition of rational rectangular volumes. Designed by Mecanoo, this is a library of sloping roofs, angled walls, tilting façades and complex internal spaces. The logic derives from landscape metaphors – especially the Dutch fascination with ground planes, water and formal planting. In effect, this large new university library is an extension of the campus landscape rather than a building. To achieve this end, it is built partly sunk into the ground with the grass sward swept over the roof. The building reads as a series of slices of landscape capped by a cone which signals the presence of the reading room. This one

| Library, Delft Technical University, The Netherlands | | |
|---|---|---|
| **Architect** | **Special features** | **Cost** |
| Mecanoo | Large technical university library with national scientific collection | Not available |
| | Places collection below ground for security and ideal environmental conditions. | |
| | Building conceived as an element of landscape | |
| | Dramatic cone shaped reading room. | |

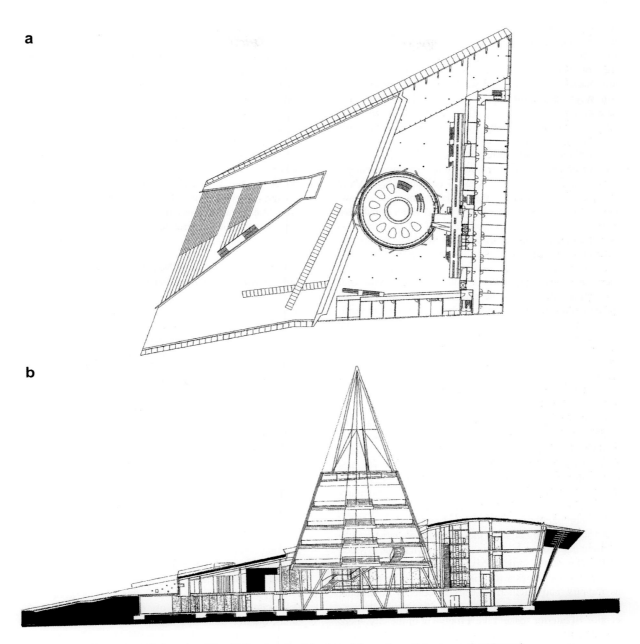

a

b

Library, Delft Technical University, The Netherlands: (a) plan; (b) section. (Mecanoo Architects)

gesture to nineteenth century library typology rescues the building from anonymity and signals the presence on campus of a building of significance, if not actually a library.

The tilting glass façade, curved roof and irregular trapezoidal plan give the library the appearance of a 'sleek, shimmering glass wave' (Van Cleef, 1999, p. 45). Constructed alongside a canal and in a country where rising sea levels due to global warming are an ever-present threat,

the wave is perhaps an ominous warning. It is not a dark wave, but a wave of light, which in the evenings seems to be pushing across the campus. Metaphors aside, this library demands attention as an exercise in new forms of library planning – and it is the nature of the collection which largely determines the architectural response.

This library houses the Dutch national archive for technical and natural sciences. The library's collection of over a million publications is housed in the basement where environmental conditions are best controlled. Here temperature and humidity can be maintained more readily than above ground, and there is greater security against theft or sabotage of the collection. Only 80,000 volumes are housed on accessible steel bookcases reached by walkways and gantries. The remainder of the library collection is accessed by staff who retrieve the material via glass lifts which travel to the basement and rise theatrically into the reading areas.

The library creates different types of working environments from private cellular study cubicles to airy, communal reading rooms (Van Cleef, 1999, p. 47). About a thousand study spaces are available, most in a grand double height reading space overlooking the tree-lined canal alongside the library's northern edge. It is an orientation which avoids solar heat gain whilst maximizing daylight penetration by the use of continuous façade glazing. As a general strategy, study areas and library offices face outwards over the campus with book stacks and open bookcases facing inwards towards the centre. Such an arrangement provides good working conditions (natural light and ventilation) at the building perimeter whilst affording optimum conditions for book and journal storage at the centre.

The core of the library is dramatically penetrated by a cone that rises from the basement to break through the roof and rise above it by two storeys, culminating in an open structure of steel members. This houses, on four floors, a circular reading room with a central void of cylindrical space providing a sense of physical and intellectual connection. Where the cone punctures the ceiling it is surrounded by a ring of roof lights and is itself roofed by a glazed ceiling. Light and geometrical volumes evoke an idealized image of cosmic harmony whose origins extend back to libraries of the early nineteenth century (e.g. University of Virginia Library, USA).

The non-parallel geometry of the library contrasted with the strict geometric order of the reading room cone creates exciting collisions which animate the internal space. Much of the apparent disorder derives from the wedge-shaped entrance which brings readers into a position off centre. The asymmetry and angularity seem at odds with rational planning: in plan the bookcases appear to impede the perception of interior space. Like a fragment of the city, there are elements of the Delft Library which are arranged with the discipline of the right angle, but other areas are fractured or collaged by the colliding geometries of the whole.

Many aspects of Mecanoo's design are the result of seeking to provide ideal conditions for study and book storage. The outward tilted glazed façades ensure the maximum of daylight penetration without solar heat gain. Air is pumped through the 140 mm thick double-glazing to ventilate at roof level, thereby avoiding drafts for readers at the building edge. The turf-clad over-sailing roof provides shelter and shade. The thick-planted roof (which extends as a continuation of the grass-planted campus) provides good

thermal and acoustic insulation. Evaporation of rainwater helps with summertime cooling, assisted by subterranean tubes linked to rainwater tanks (Van Cleef, 1999, pp. 47–48). These cool the building in the summer and assist with heating in the winter via a heat exchanger. The books and journals are stored in a sealed basement where air-conditioning provides optimum conditions for conservation.

The Delft University Library creates a distinctive building out of unusual conditions. By combining the demands of building functionality with site planning and sustainable practices, technical and aesthetic elements are fused. Though as much metaphor as rigorous design, this library transcends the limits of rationality to forge a modern democratic monument for a large technical university with a national science collection.

## The Catherine Cookson Reading Room, University of Sunderland, UK

This reading room, dedicated to silent learning, stands as an independent structure within the courtyard of an earlier university library. The original library, mainly of learning resource centre character, suffered from keyboard noise and the disturbance of group study. Students felt the need for a sanctuary for quiet reading away from the bustle of the main library.

The free-standing room is set into the horseshoe-shaped courtyard, allowing light and ventilation to reach the main library. The reading room has an irregular piano-shaped plan with a continuous glazed edge. To emphasize the sanctuary nature of the building, the windows are set down low to give views only when seated. From the windows, the readers look onto a planted courtyard and beyond to the outside walls of the university's electronic library. The roof-deck upon which the reading room is built serves as a terrace where students can read in the open air. Seats and planting form an intimate garden which complements the tranquil interior of the reading room.

The irregular shaped reading room is inspired by the Finnish architect Atvar Aalto (Edwards, 1997). Nature is deliberately evoked by the use of mushroom-shaped columns, the tree trunk-like outline of the reading room and the use of vertical timber battens inside and out (in beech on the interior, Oregon pine on exterior). Light enters the reading room via a perimeter skirt of glazing and through roof lights, evoking a sense that the forest canopy is opened to allow light to flood onto tables.

Although some books are stored in the reading room in free-standing bookshelves, this is essentially a place for quiet study. The design seeks to create a relaxed and contemplative environment, conducive to deep book-based study. Being a silent space (for both staff and students), there is an undeniable sense of reverence for the printed word. The building is a deliberate counterpoint to the

Catherine Cookson Reading Room, University of Sunderland, designed by Building Design Partnership. (M Hamilton-Knight)

| Catherine Cookson Reading Room, University of Sunderland, UK | | |
|---|---|---|
| **Architect** | **Special features** | **Cost** |
| Building Design Partnership | Reading room dedicated to silent study | £905/m$^2$ |
| | Placed in courtyard of an older electronic library. | |
| | Has external terrace for outside reading. | |
| | Inspired by architecture of Atvar Aalto. | |
| | Evokes spirit of forest clearing. | |

market hall ambience of the encircling IT library. It is a fitting reminder of the importance of traditional values in modern library design.

## The Saltire Centre, Glasgow Caledonia University

The Saltire Centre designed by BDP is one of a new generation of university libraries which effectively combine in one building a large book-based study collection, extensive IT-orientated study areas, cafes, bookshops, university registry and student union facilities. The emphasis is upon accommodating wireless technology and making it the primary focus of library usage. The aim is to use new technology to reach out to a generation of school leavers who would not normally enter higher education (Marmot, 2005, p. 78). The premise is that IT enhances the excitement of learning in contrast to the intimidating culture of book-based education.

The building is designed to be fashionable and fun, attractive and accessible at any hour, and a place for shared

Exterior view of Saltire Centre, Glasgow Caledonia University. (BDP/J Cooper)

ideas and knowledge (Marmot, 2005, p. 78). The Saltire Centre, opened in 2005, goes further than many of its LRC ancestors. There is greater emphasis given to the social role of informal learning through peer conversation, to self-orientated learning supported by sympathetic teachers based in the library, and in encouraging students to learn from each other by the provision of cafes and information points in the library. The building also acts as a beacon of new pedagogic practices on a typical inner city campus, in this case alongside Glasgow's bus station.

The entrance to the building is raised with the library front doors reached at the end of a ramp that climbs gently alongside a square which opens from the cafe on the ground floor. As a consequence, the library functions are separated somewhat from the registry and social ones, and this results in the library users having an attractive panorama over the double height cafe areas on arrival. From this elevated deck most of the library facilities can be viewed upwards through the generously proportioned atrium which rises through six storeys. The different levels — two social, two given over primarily to the book collection and

Study pod at Saltire Centre, Glasgow Caledonia University. (BDP/J Cooper)

| Saltire Centre, Glasgow Caledonia University | |
| --- | --- |
| **Architect** | **Special features** |
| BDP | • Integrates student facilities, registry, cafe and bookshop into library |
| | • Creates many informal learning spaces |
| | • Uses compact shelving to release space for inter-active learning |
| | • Large central atrium |

two to IT provision (although there is a large measure of integration on each floor) – are connected by a graceful staircase which encircles the round lift tower placed centrally in the building. At each floor level, bridges span across to informal study or meeting areas; many of these are placed on platforms overlooking the atrium. Between the atrium and the learning zones there is a large six-storey media wall designed to take a range of graphic representations from video projection to flying text using plasma screens. High-level routes also extend from the Saltire Centre to adjacent faculty buildings, making the campus permeable above ground.

First impressions are that this is a new kind of university library – a hybrid of older types but with the addition of significant new ones. The Saltire Centre has books and research journals but many of these are housed in compact storage stacks which are operated by the students using electronic motors. Books that are primary source material for projects or lecture courses are on open shelves, face rather than spine out. They are available on short-term loan but much of the relevant text is available as photocopies presented in study packs. This material is taken to the cafe where the students use a laptop to write an essay or meet with fellow students undertaking group work. Paper and digital media are hence readily mixed in an atmosphere which is relaxing and a far cry from many university libraries.

The building is transparent and colourful: glass is used widely to open up internal activities to external gaze. As such the building acts as a lighthouse of learning through the long Glasgow winter nights. With study spaces for over two thousand students in the building (about 20% of the university total) and many informal seating areas, the Saltire Centre is the hub of the campus – socially and academically. Mobile phone use is allowed in the bulk of the library, as is conversation; the cafe serves pastries and sandwiches as well as coffee, and there is much comfortable furniture to encourage lounging.

As architects, BDP has evolved a largely new solution to a new library type – one which is based upon 'conversational learning' and the integration of library, IT and student services (welfare, housing, visas) as well as the shop window for registry. The latter provides information on grants, examination timetables, how to apply for late submission and voluntary suspension, and many other things which students need to know but often have difficulty finding out. The library also provides access to external examiners' reports, thereby keeping students informed of issues facing their education.

The design approach incorporates three main elements. First, the external form of the building is eye-catching and colourful with large areas of glass making the building attractive and legible on arrival. Second, a great deal of effort has been devoted to the atrium in order to make the routes both vertically and horizontally inviting to use.

These are more generously proportioned than one would expect, and detailed with the glass and chrome aesthetic of retail malls. Although the south facing atrium acts as an environmental buffer to the main learning accommodation (*Synergy*, 2005), its main role is rather more celebratory. Third, there has been a great deal of thought given to flexibility and ensuring that at each floor level as much natural light (including sunlight) penetrates the library as possible.

A key to the success of the design is the use of an atrium rising through the building: it provides high levels of daylight and allows the library user to see all that is going on. It contributes significantly to energy efficiency and provides a model of environmental design for other libraries to follow. The large atrium also means that students working on the various galleries can spot their friends and set up the informal learning networks essential to the ethos of learning at Glasgow Caledonia University.

The building is graded from a noisy ground floor to a silent top floor, and from noisier group study areas closer to the atrium to private study desks in silent zones near the outer periphery. Undergraduate interactivity occurs nearer the ground with the research and masters study areas higher up. Book stacks, whether fixed or mobile, provide acoustic barriers around the atrium, but generally the emphasis is on the process of learning rather than the storage of study material. One of the main contributions the building makes is the way it expresses the educational philosophy of the university with an admirable lightness of touch.

## Magdeburg University Library, Germany

University libraries have a long tradition of pushing at the frontiers of campus architecture. Their longevity and symbolic role has encouraged the type of innovation rarely found in faculty teaching buildings. Here at Magdeburg University, west of Berlin, architects Auer and Weber have fashioned a building which, like folded paper, encourages the juxtaposition of thought rather than its isolation. The building is conceived as a 'continuous strip of concrete folded six times' with each fold forming a new level for separate faculty libraries. In effect this is an amalgam of

| Magdeburg University Library | |
|---|---|
| **Architect** | **Special features** |
| Auer & Weber | • Zig-zag plan aims to juxtapose knowledge |
| | • Central atrium acts as reading room |
| | • Exploits solar gain for heating and ventilation |

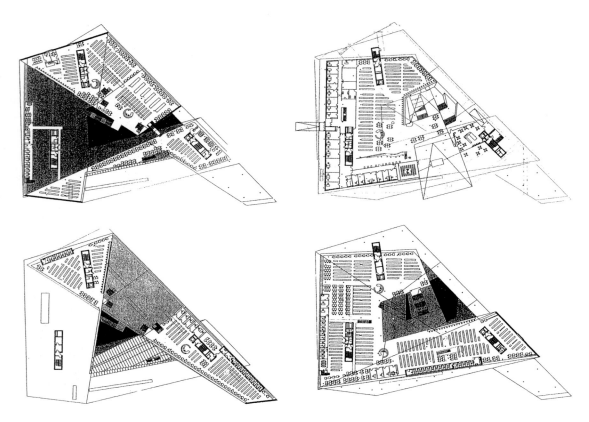

Plans, Magdeburg University Library. The ground floor is lower left, first floor upper left, second floor lower right and top floor upper right. (Auer and Weber/AR)

semi-independent libraries placed within a single, spatially interconnected building (Brensing, 2004).

The library zigzags in narrow sections, gradually rising to a height of four floors. A central atrium acts as a shared reading room overlooked by galleries and a cafe. Like much of the building the reading room is complex in both plan and section with angled wings of book stacks flying in different directions. The angles of stairs and lifts, which join the separate wings, open up views of the wider campus landscape. The effect is to see the 'library as a landscape' rather than as a conventional faculty building.

In total there are six acute-angled wings each containing its own subject library with supporting study and IT spaces. Generally the book stacks are in the centre with carrels and group study tables around the perimeter. The internal transparency allows the reader to gain views of the whole library and to gain a sense that although the collection is in separate wings, the world of knowledge is rather more comprehensive and interconnected.

The narrow plan depth and use of a glazed atrium allows the library to exploit the benefits of solar gain for both winter heating and stack effect summer ventilation. It also ensures that the building has high levels of daylight penetration – an important consideration when lighting can constitute the major area of energy use. The employment of prismatic technology in the atrium roof and on southern façades allows sunlight to be filtered out, allowing students to study in well-lit spaces without glare and reflections on computer screens (Brensing, 2004). In addition, the stepping of the building provides solar shade whilst also sheltering the library entrance and adjacent campus routes.

| Portsmouth University Library | |
|---|---|
| **Architect** | **Special Features** |
| Ahrends, Burton and Koralek (1986) | • Library extension helped clarify campus routes |
| Penoye and Prasad (2005) | • Library acts as knowledge gateway to campus |
| | • Central street through library acts as 'learning mail' |

## Portsmouth University Library

The latest extensions to Portsmouth University Library display the changing space needs of academic libraries. From its origins as a polytechnic library in the 1970s, through the extensions designed in 1986 by Ahrends, Burton and Koralek, to these recent additions by architects Penoyre and Prasad, it is possible to detect the way university libraries have had to adapt to changing academic priorities. The evolution of this university library follows a familiar pattern: a change from polytechnic to university status led to growing emphasis upon research; the aim of widening access to the university in the 1990s resulted in the addition of a cafe and extensive computer suites; and the early twenty-first century brought a fresh awareness of the role of libraries as image-makers on campus. Growth in student numbers from around 7,000 in the 1970s to 18,000 today also stressed the library and provided justification for the additions.

As with many university projects, the configuration of the new library provided the opportunity to address perceived shortcomings in the campus masterplan (Pearce, 2007). Here the extensions helped define the major routes between university facilities and form a gateway into the central campus. The library also established links to new seminar rooms and computer facilities which were also

Exterior at night, Portsmouth University Library. The entrance to the library is well lit and overlooked by other campus buildings, making it an attractive place to meet after lectures. (Tim Crocker/Penoyre and Prasad)

constructed to respond to changing academic practice at Portsmouth. Student-centred learning, part-time study and links to local professions and businesses meant that the new library had to be an open and inviting building. As such the emphasis is upon transparency and the creation of a central street to encourage informal learning and socializing by students across the different academic disciplines.

The original library maintains its position as the primary book repository. The extensions provide much needed reading room, group and small study spaces, plus individual research workstations. Although there are additional stack areas on upper floors, the extensions, built intriguingly at 45 degrees to the axis of the original building, has a knowledge use rather than knowledge storage function. The new street forms a connection between the original building and its extensions. Here readers access the whole library, gain information from the various desks in the foyer, and gain a perception of what is on offer at the various levels. What was originally a rather deep plan and uninviting library has become a light-filled space accommodating the needs of both book and IT provision. Externally, a new square has been created which organizes the gathering of students to the various new facilities and, with the cafe and bookshop around its edge, provides an element of animation to what could have been a mere exercise in space making.

Interior, Portsmouth University Library. (Tim Crocker/Penoyre and Prasad)

The new library now has a lofty reading room which is roof-lit and naturally ventilated. Unusually for academic libraries, advantage has been taken of the southern exposure to maximize the environmental benefits of its location. The orientation reduces the problem of low-angled east and west light on computer screens, and in the winter the solar gains are used to augment the heating load. Similarly the serrated profile of the extension provides semi-private study spaces around the edge which are light-filled but, due to their angle, suffer little from direct sunlight.

The extensions help make sense of the campus as a whole and allow the university library to meet changing academic priorities. The values expressed through the design also mirror the imperatives of the age — noticeably in the area of low-energy architecture. By retaining the original buildings, the university was able to upgrade its library and learning resource facilities without undue disruption to academic provision. Many other universities are facing similar demands to refurbish and extend their libraries. Portsmouth University provides a lesson in intelligent and sensitive upgrading of the main academic library to meet the learning aspirations of the twenty-first century.

## Library, Brandenburg Technical University

Located at Cottbus in Germany, this academic library designed by Herzog and de Meuron forms a link between town and gown. Catering for both communities, the library is a curvaceous glazed structure, patterned with a silk-screen imprint, which reflects the sky by day and glows like a beacon in this former industrial heartland at night (Webb, 2006). Like many recent buildings by Herzog and de Meuron, this library challenges the orthodoxy of university libraries. The architects argue that the organic free flowing shape was the result of a 'purposeful configuration of many different flows of movement...and their ability to reorganise and restructure urban space' (Webb, 2006). These different flows are those of the students accessing the library collection between lectures as well as those moving around the campus, for the library helps smooth external pedestrian movements between faculty buildings by removing sharp angles.

With all undulating plan-shaped buildings, the entrance is by no means obvious since the curved skin denies hierarchy. Here the problem has been overcome by providing two library entrances on opposite sides of the building. These link up to form a two-storey axial bisection of the amoeba-shaped plan, which in turn leads to a double height entrance hall. The hall provides essential information on the library services available and helps orientate readers through the building by the use of sculptural staircases and walls of bright colour. Above the entrance hall are six floors of book stacks interspersed with double and triple

| Brandenburg Technical University Library | |
|---|---|
| **Architect** | **Special features** |
| Herzog and de Meuron | • Large curved library with decorative surface tratment<br>• Organic form to help erode subject boundaries<br>• Library restructures campus<br>• Variety of types of study space |

height reading rooms. Unlike the usual practice of arranging reading carrels around the edge of central book stacks or providing one large reading room, here Herzog and de Meuron slice the stack areas to form lofty voids for quiet study. These, and the more deliberately located perimeter reading rooms, offer students a choice of type of study environment.

The irregular plan and sectional cuts through floor plates produce a spatially complex library. The aim was to break the volumetric monotony of typical academic libraries and provide instead a building which was a pleasure to use. In this way the university hopes that the library will appeal not only to its students but to the wider community of Cottbus.

## Seikei University Library, Tokyo

Seikei University Library in Tokyo, designed by the architect Shigeru Ban, follows the orthodox layout of a central atrium-cum-reading room surrounded by two wings of book stacks counterbalanced by glazed walls and open views on the cross-axis. Five storeys high, this academic library sits above a further three storeys of basement storage. Readers enter into the library via wide steps which are centrally placed and lead to a large 'chat zone', which in turn takes the students into the library's information floor. Here the students enter the first quiet zone, which

| Seiki University Library | |
|---|---|
| **Architect** | **Special features** |
| Shigeru Ban | • Central atrium acts as reading room<br>• 'Chat zone' at entrance with cafe<br>• galleries in atrium for group learning<br>• quiet study pods suspended in atrium |

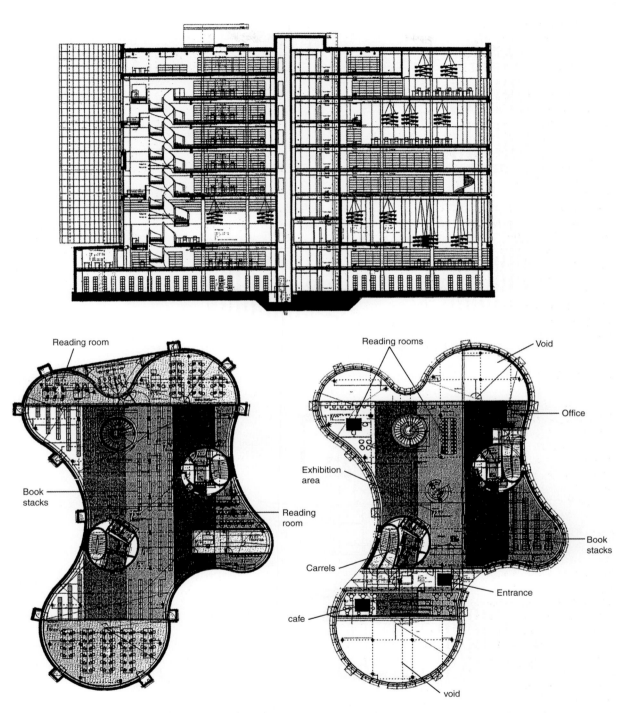

Plans and section, Brandenburg Technical University Library, Cottbus, Germany, designed by Herzog and de Meuron. (Herzog and de Meuron/AR)

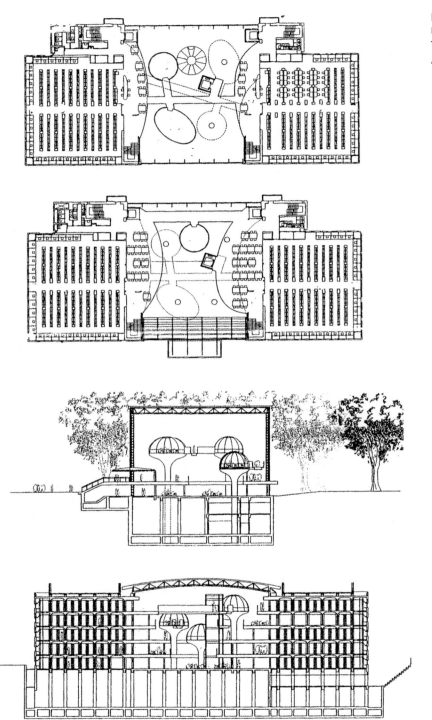

Plan and section, Seiki
University Library,
Tokyo. (Shigeru Ban/
AR)

permits talking but not mobile phone use and where guidance is provided to the collection. The entrance sequence takes the user up to an elevated first floor with the ground floor below reserved for study and social purposes not unlike that at the Saltire Centre in Glasgow.

The five-storey high central atrium doubles up as a reading room where students are encouraged to interact between paper and digital media. This handsome volume contains galleries which overhang the space at each floor level, thereby providing a great deal of academic animation. The galleries are designed for group learning use and contrast with the private study pods which stand like elevated mushrooms within the atrium. Here silence is required (unlike the policy in much of the library) in an attempt to encourage more reflective learning. The pods form distinctive landmarks within the building and are joined by elevated bridges which add to the architectural drama.

The two book-stack wings have closely spaced fixed shelving with a central spine for book and journal access. Each stack area has its own information point where the subject librarians guide students to the material. Around the edge of the stack area there is a ring of individual study carrels which provide views across the campus as well as back into the library. The proximity to the book collection means that the carrels are much in demand and their position at the perimeter gives life to the building.

The layout provides an economical and flexible arrangement for an academic library. The large storage basement absorbs books, archives and research journals which are less in demand and gives the library a buffer zone for future growth. Here the material is stored in compact shelving where environmental conditions are more favourable than in the main library.

Externally the library faces a square which provides pedestrian links to other faculty buildings. The square helps establish the centrality of the main library at Seikei, thereby signalling its importance to academic life. The square and atrium are axially aligned adding further significance to the reading room whilst also adding to the legibility of the library.

## References

Anon. (1995). Learning Curve. *Architects Journal*, 10 October, pp. 30, 34, 38.

Arets, W. (2005) *Living Library*. Prestel, pp. 381–382.

Benny, J. (1995). Designing for change. In *Building Libraries for the Information Age* (S. Taylor, ed.). Proceedings of a symposium held in York, 11–12 April 1994. Institute of Advanced Architectural Studies (IAAS).

Blagden, J. (1995). Cranfield's library of the future. In *Building Libraries for the Information Age* (S. Taylor, ed.). Proceedings

of a symposium held in York, 11–12 April 1994. Institute of Advanced Architectural Studies (IAAS).

Brawne, M. (1997). Cranfield Library. In *Library Builders*. Academy Editions, p. 67.

Brensing, C. (2004). Unfolding knowledge. *Architectural Review*, February, pp. 62–66.

Brindley, L. J. (1995). Introduction. In *Building Libraries for the Information Age* (S. Taylor, ed.). Proceedings of a symposium held in York, 11–12 April 1994. Institute of Advanced Architectural Studies (IAAS).

Cox, D. (1981). Rare books and special collections. Case study of the Brotherton Library, University of Leeds. In *University Librarianship* (J. F. Stirling, ed.). Library Association.

Croft, C. (2005). Literary connections. *Architecture Today*, Vol. 163, pp. 56–64.

Edwards, B. (1997). Homage to Aalto. *Architects Journal*, 27 March, pp. 25–35.

Edwards, B. (2003). *Green Buildings Pay*. E & F N Spon. See also: Learning Resource Centre, Anglia Polytechnic University, *Building*, 20 January 1995, pp. 39–46.

Fresson, M. (1998). Switched on. *Prospect*, August, p. 40.

Joint Funding Council (1993). *Joint Funding Council's Libraries Review Group: Report*. Joint Funding Council. (Known as the Follett Report after its chairman, Sir Brian Follett.)

Marmot, Alexi Associates (2005). *Spaces for Learning*. Scottish Funding Council, Edinburgh.

Pearce, M. (2007). Penoyre and Prasad in Portsmouth. *Architecture Today*, April, pp. 28–41.

Revill, D. (1995). Liverpool John Moores University: The Aldham Robarts Learning Resource Centre. In *Building Libraries for the Information Age* (S. Taylor, ed.). Proceedings of a symposium held in York, 11–12 April 1994. Institute of Advanced Architectural Studies (IAAS).

Sunderland, A. (1995). Designing a better shoe box: the architects' view. In *Building Libraries for the Information Age* (S. Taylor, ed.). Proceedings of a symposium held in York, 11–12 April 1994. Institute of Advanced Architectural Studies (IAAS). See also: *Building Design*, 18 February 1994, and *The New Builder*, 18 February 1994.

Sykes, P. (2007). Letter from Phil Sykes, University Librarian to Shepheard Epstein Hunter dated 20 August 2007 and made available to author.

*Synergy* (2005). February, p. 8.

Urquhart, J. A. (1981). Acquisitions and relegation: a case study of the University Library, Newcastle-upon-Tyne. In *University Librarianship* (J. F. Stirling, ed.). Library Association, p. 41.

Van Cleef, C. (1999). Book bunker. *Architectural Review*, March, pp. 45, 47–48.

Webb, M. (2006). Cottbus Kaleidoscope. *Architectural Review*, April, 2006 pp. 65–67.

Wilson, A. (2008). Re-thinking Berlin's academic libraries. *Update*, January/February.

Wright, A. (1997). *Architects Journal*, 27 March, pp. 25 and 26 (the quote is from the vice-chancellor, Anne Wright, of Sunderland University).

# 12

# The specialist library

---

This type of library is normally dedicated to a person, subject or place. Typical of the genre is the Reagan Library, based upon US presidential papers, memoirs and personal artefacts. Typical also is the Ruskin Library where a collection of material by this famous Victorian artist, author and critic is housed as a self-contained annex to a university library. Like the Reagan Library, special collections normally contain a wide range of material – books, journals, newspaper cuttings, letters, drawings, photographs and videos. They also frequently include personal furniture and household goods (coffee cups, telephones, television sets, etc.), which help to create a well-rounded view of the individual involved. Specialist libraries dedicated to individuals are necessarily personal and sometimes idiosyncratic in nature. The challenge here is to design a library that captures the mood of the collection and which embraces the values of the person involved.

Specialist libraries may be topic based. Here it is the subject material which is being housed and made available to scholars. Examples include poetry libraries, sports libraries, photographic libraries and video libraries. The design of these buildings has to consider the special accommodation and conservation needs of the material. As with personal libraries, the collection contains more than paper-based material. Frequently there are artefacts which make up the collection, producing the blurring between library and museum use. With specialist libraries, security, conservation and access are part of a web of interconnected library tasks. In most specialist libraries, visits are made by appointment and the emphasis is more upon research than loan. Unlike in public or academic libraries where the bulk of material is held on open shelves, only a small percentage is visible in specialist libraries. Most is held in secure storage and much will be subject to periodic preservation, often involving sophisticated conservation measures.

The third common type of specialist library is that built up by professional institutes. Here the material may go back to the founding of the body, making some of the books, journals and committee papers nearly 200 years old. The professional library was originally a private library for members, but increasingly the material is made available to the general public. Typical is the British Architectural Library at the Royal Institute of British Architects (RIBA). When the RIBA secured funding from the Heritage Fund Lottery in 1998, its considerable library became a quasi-public facility. Today the extensive collection of books, drawings, photographs and letters is available via appointment, though none of the material is available for loan. Professional institute libraries are by no means small – the RIBA Library contains nearly a million items, that at the British Medical Association (BMA) over two

The Scottish Poetry Library in Edinburgh, by Malcolm Fraser Architects, is a place to reflect upon the written word. (Malcolm Fraser Architects)

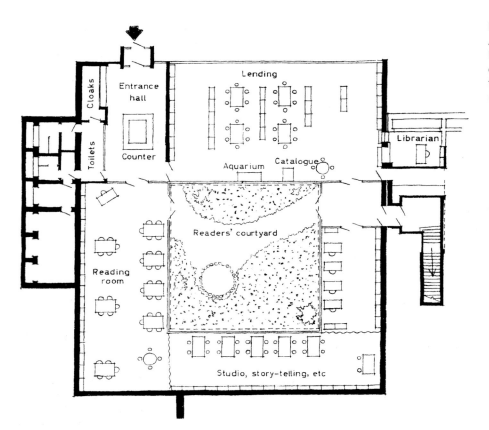

Plan, Children's Library, American Memorial Library, Berlin. Note the courtyard surrounded by tables for contemplation. (D Insall and Partners)

million, and that at the Institution of Civil Engineers (ICE) over a million.

With all special libraries, conservation and security are paramount. Access is often made available only in controlled circumstances and readers are normally required to wear gloves, to use pencils only, and may be accompanied for the whole period of use. Closed circuit television (CCTV) is also commonly employed, especially in the most security sensitive areas. Library staff are also well versed in conservation techniques and, with the most rare material, may have modern copies available rather than risk damage to the original.

Storage is often more complex in specialist libraries than in other types of library: drawings and prints require storage in secure, fireproof plan chests; photographs are normally stored in acid-free boxes; letters are frequently placed individually in plastic holders; and old committee papers, journals and newspaper cuttings all have their own special storage and conservation needs. For the architect there are implications for the level and method of ventilation, the degree of natural light permitted, the potential exposure to fire, and the means necessary for speedy evacuation of material in the event of a hazard. With fires, the greater damage normally occurs as a result of water saturation and here both architect and librarian need to

co-operate on the best security strategy in the event of fire, flood and sprinkler system operation.

Specialist libraries come in two forms – they are either self-contained or they exist as annexes to larger libraries. Typical of the latter is the Afro-Caribbean Collection at Peckham Public Library, London and of the former, the Scottish Poetry Library in Edinburgh. In both cases, there is a clear identity for the collection and, also in each, the design of the library reflects the character of the collection. In the Peckham Library, the collection is an ark which floats loftily within a double height public reading room. In the Edinburgh example, the building plan follows a figure of eight pattern, returning to the starting point via recurring themes in the fashion of a poem.

Specialist libraries are often under the control of a trust rather than a public body. Such trusts, normally charitable in nature and instigated to provide a legal basis for the development of the collection, grow from local enthusiasm or the gift, perhaps at death, of exceptional library material. Trusts do not always have the expertise to undertake building development and the task of the appointed architect is often to advise on possible sources of grant aid, to choose an appropriate site or location for the collection, and to offer advice not only on building design but also on the best measures to be adopted for storage, security and

Surrey History Centre
Library, Woking,
designed by W S Atkins.
(W S Atkins)

conservation. Specialist libraries often require specialist advice from professional advisors; their complexity can exceed that of other libraries though frequently the collection is smaller in scale.

Another specialist library is the Surrey History Centre in Woking designed by W S Atkins. It provides an archive and local study collection – parts of which date back to the twelfth century – in a new building constructed in 1998 with financial support from the Heritage Lottery Fund. The building cost over £6.4 million and attracts 4,500 visitors a year to a history archive noted for its emphasis upon working and social conditions. The library is divided into three parts – public reading rooms, archival storage and conservation areas. The special nature of the collection led to the early involvement of the Library Furnishing Company (LFC) in the design process. Here the expertise of

Special collections often require special shelving systems. This example shows the library at the Shakespeare Institute, Stratford-upon-Avon, developed with the Library Furnishing Company. (LFC)

LFC aided the multidisciplinary team of W S Atkins with the result that the sophisticated storage and security systems do not conflict with the architectural ambitions elsewhere. The History Centre uses northern light, thereby avoiding shadows and damaging sunlight and, in the search-room and archive area, glass-fronted shelving is employed for security and ultraviolet light screening purposes.

Two further specialist libraries should be mentioned: the Shackleton Library in Cambridge and the Fawcett Library in London. The first consists of an extension to the Scott Polar Research Institute Library and contains photographs, lanternslides, maps, diaries and letters representing the work of the explorer Sir Ernest Shackleton. The design by John Miller and Partners evokes a feeling of ice by employing extensive areas of glass and white walls. The second library of note is the National Library of Women (formerly the Fawcett Library), where an extensive study collection, exhibition space, cafe and shop exist thanks to funding from English Partnerships, the Heritage Lottery Fund and the Higher Education Funding Council. As with other specialist libraries, the facilities are wide-ranging and many sources of finance have been tapped to bring the libraries to fruition.

## Presidential libraries

Presidential libraries are a group of specialist libraries which share the honour of recording in print the lives of former US presidents. They are endowed and mainly funded by deceased presidents often in association with American universities and hence are found predominantly on academic campuses. Presidential libraries are principally archive collections and consist of a diverse range of material from books to congressional papers, personal files, photographs, films, letters and artefacts. Though housed in the main on university campuses, they tend to be managed by the National Archives and Records Administration. Since presidential libraries carry a great deal of genuine or perceived prestige, they tend to be architecturally distinctive buildings. Typical examples are the George Bush Senior Library at Texas A and M University, the Ronald Reagan Library in California, the Jimmy Carter Library in Atlanta, the Richard Nixon Library in Maryland and the William J Clinton Library at Little Rock, Arkansas (Sudjic, 2006).

In many ways presidential libraries share some of the characteristics of museums. Reagan's Library, for instance, also contains his personal telephone, the typewriter used to send messages to aids, and even his car. However, in spite of the glamorizing of presidents these libraries contain a great deal of valuable archival material and attract a number of serious academic scholars. As such they need to perform as libraries with attention given to the storage, conservation and safe use of the study material.

One characteristic of this type of library is the copious use of architectural symbolism. For example, the George Bush Library is circular in shape recalling Jefferson's rotunda library at the University of Virginia. Similarly, Lyndon Johnson's Library has an oval office where his most valuable papers are stored. Although presidential libraries display the changing tastes of the American political class they are particular to the person honoured and are one of the defining legacies of the political culture of the USA. Whereas UK prime ministers leave little more than collections of letters and manuscript memoirs to already established libraries, ex presidents mark their place in history in the architecture of libraries. Umberto Eco is rather scathing of the type: he refers to the Lyndon Johnson Library as a 'fortress of solitude' where genuine texts are mixed with fake reconstructions, making the library rather more a wax museum than a genuine archive (Eco, 1987). The fashion is spreading to adjacent countries with the opening in 2008 of the Fox Centre – the presidential library of Mexico's President Vincent Fox at Guanajuata. This example, designed with its study carrels to serve the needs of academic researchers, is modelled on the Clinton Library.

## The Ruskin Library at Lancaster University, UK

The library was designed to accommodate the Ruskin collection of papers and artefacts, geological specimens, pictures (unmounted as well as framed), sketches and early slides. It makes, therefore, an interesting specialist library and one which is both library and museum. It is not possible to ignore the elliptical building, with its incised two-storey window, used as a metaphor for Ruskin's life and ideas. The external cladding of white concrete blocks with marble aggregate and green polished bands blends with the surrounding buildings of the campus. One significant feature are the entrance doors constructed of bronze-clad aluminium. These are a solid reminder of the arts and crafts period in which Ruskin was writing and echo the traditional craftsmanship found throughout the building.

The entrance floor is made of glass and slate. The materials used throughout the building are natural and reflect Ruskin's interest in construction. Internal finishes on the rendered walls are either natural ochre limewash or finished with black pigment sealed with linseed. Roof timbers are grit-blasted to expose the grain. The device of inserting an ark-like construction in the centre of the building is extraordinary in library architecture – it rises to the full height of the building. The ark is held within an oak frame, its side walls rendered in red Venetian plaster. It is viewed from the foyer through a glass-etched panel containing a copy of one of Ruskin's own daguerreotypes.

There are two staircases, one on each side of the building, each accessing the upper gallery floors. The

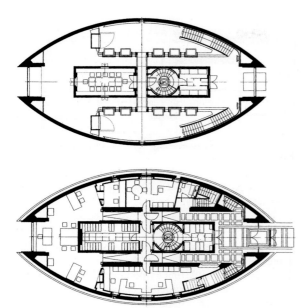

Plan, Ruskin Library, Lancaster University, designed by MacCormac Jamieson Prichard. (MacCormac Jamieson Prichard)

meeting room lies between them and above the storage areas. It opens onto the glass walkway, which is also etched with the names of benefactors to this project. Observers can look down onto the reading room from the western end of each gallery and from there the view extends towards Morecambe Bay.

Storage areas, office space, a reception area, workroom, meeting room and a gallery have been accommodated within this deceptively small building. The equipment to view the non-print material and the library catalogue all has specific power and data requirements. Plans to disseminate information about the collection are ambitious and exploit the potential of the IT age.

The staffing includes a curator who is a nineteenth century art historian and a librarian. This fits the mixture of conservation/preservation activities associated with a specialist library collection, as well as the information storage and retrieval for scholarly purposes necessary to fulfil the aim of the project. There is dependence upon the facilities and staff of the University Library, housed in an adjacent building. Staff offices have curved footprints and are found on the outer perimeter of the ground floor; workshop space is provided adjacent to the loading bay which is covered and located at basement level.

Once within the Ruskin Library, each artefact is subject to some movement as it undergoes conservation, cataloguing, scholarly investigation or display in addition to storage. This internal mobility is achieved by the use of a book lift, in conjunction with specially designed trolleys and by the internal spiral staircase with half landings. The large storage requirements of this wide-ranging collection bring about specific solutions. This is a common feature of specialist library collections, which by their nature are dynamic organic growing entities. The library contains small reading rooms and staff work areas for specific projects. One example is the room used to create the database of press and media cuttings about Ruskin. The main book archive is kept on Rackline rolling stacks on three floors. This and the two picture stores are not accessible by the users. Readers are expected to adhere to the regulations common to many specialist collections and archives. These include the use of cotton gloves for handling original manuscripts, the use of pencil only in the main reading room and archive area, and closed access to the artefacts with staff facilitation of objects.

The internal decoration and furnishing have been designed to achieve a high degree of harmony with the subject. This attention to detailed planning ensures that the Ruskin Library is entirely suited to its purpose as a scholarly resource. The study area is a reading room of about 70 m$^2$. It will seat up to eight readers. A specialist examination table for drawings or large folios has been provided. The catalogue is available through a computer terminal located on the desk of the reading room supervisor. All furniture is sympathetic with the collection, having been specially commissioned and executed. It also includes some original pieces from Ruskin's own collection. Bookcases have been built in the reading rooms and specially designed display cabinets for prints and artefacts are found in the gallery areas.

The building has a passive airflow system with ventilation through the floor. This solution allows the housing of collections needing differing environmental controls. The only direct air-conditioning is within the gallery and

| Ruskin Library, University of Lancaster, UK | | |
|---|---|---|
| **Architect** | **Special features** | **Cost** |
| MacCormac Jamieson Prichard | Library and museum combined | |
| | Embodies Ruskin's ideas in design of building. | |
| | Linked to university library. | |

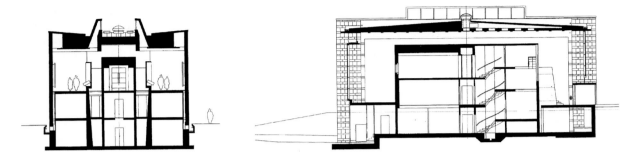

Sections, Ruskin Library, Lancaster University, designed by MacCormac Jamieson Prichard. (MacCormac Jamieson Prichard)

reading room areas. One disadvantage of the floor ventilation system is the transmission of the noise from the book trolleys vibrating on the wire mesh floor of the bookstore areas to other parts of the library.

## The Scottish Poetry Library, Edinburgh, Scotland

The Scottish Poetry Library in the heart of Edinburgh's Old Town is a small specialist lending library devoted to poetry. The collection of about 36,000 volumes is divided between two-thirds reference and one-third lending. Though modern in spirit, the building is rich in historic reference – both to its surroundings and to the traditions of Scottish poetry. As a library, it is conceived on a figure of eight plan with stairs and lift providing the crossover points between a larger double height reading room and smaller specialized library spaces (Bevan, 1999). This configuration allows the interior

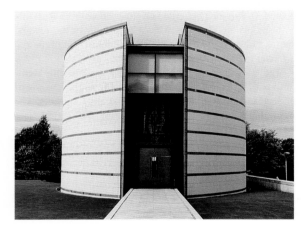

Ruskin Library, Lancaster University, from the ramp linking the building to the main campus library. (Peter Durant)

space to flow yet be always connected – perhaps evoking the nature of poetry itself.

The Scottish Poetry Library designed by the Edinburgh practice Malcolm Fraser Architects was shortlisted in 2000 for the Stirling Prize, Britain's premier architecture award. For such a small building, it captures the spirit of 'libraryness' in the handling of external entrance and related façade, and in the interior procession. The approach to the building is via Crighton's Close, a linear courtyard placed at right angles to historic Canongate. Necessarily the new building is placed parallel to the Close but is set back slightly from the building line to form a room at the library entrance. Within this space sits a small external amphitheatre whose projection into the courtyard signals the presence of a public not private building. Details around the threshold further reinforce the message of a library – there are inscriptions such as 'By leaves we live' from Patrick Geddes, with carved oak leaves in the stone paving adjoining the door. Inside further quotations are set into walls and glass panels or hang as tapestries. One such quotation, 'This house, this poem, this fresh hypothesis' from Iain Crighton Smith, is etched in a glass screen running practically the length of the building.

The interpenetration of interior and exterior space allows the activities of the library to influence the outside world. One can stand in the Close and watch the process of reading, lending, searching and reflection take place without interrupting the world inside. Being transparent at the edge and well lit inside, the feeling is almost one of a sophisticated city street cafe. Although the interior is tranquil, at times poetic in the play of space, light and materials, the ambience is never precious or exclusive. Instead there is an inviting air which, via the books on display, draws the visitor inside.

The building is two storeys in height and four structural bays in length. This is a framed library where the elements of construction – steel frame, glazed panels, oak screens, blue-glazed brick walls – are all articulated and separately expressed. Again one seeks a metaphor in poetry where the

232

Scottish Poetry Library, Edinburgh, from Crighton's Close. (Malcolm Fraser Architects)

| Scottish Poetry Library, Edinburgh, Scotland | | |
|---|---|---|
| **Architect** | **Special features** | **Cost** |
| Malcolm Fraser Architects | Lottery-funded national poetry library | £1160/m² |
| | Specialized library for deposit, reference and lending | |
| | Design inspired by poetry and historic context | |
| | Employs modern constructivist aesthetic language. | |

| Katharine Stephen Rare Books Library, Cambridge, UK | | |
|---|---|---|
| **Architect** | **Special features** | **Cost** |
| Van Heyningen and Haward | Protective library for rare books | £1,895/m² |
| | Heavyweight building construction to moderate temperature and humidity variation | |
| | Use of open metal shelving to encourage air movement around delicate leather-bound books | |
| | Strict dust, humidity and temperature control | |
| | Strict fire security. | |

233

| Science Library, University of California, Irvine, USA | | |
| --- | --- | --- |
| **Architect** | **Special features** | **Cost** |
| James Stirling, Michael Wilford and Partners | Rotunda to act as subject integration | Not available |
| | Wings to facilitate links to research and teaching facilities | |
| | Study carrels around centre and perimeter | |
| | Landmark building around central park | |
| | Study collection and teaching spaces in wings. | |

| Common types of specialist library | |
| --- | --- |
| **Type** | **Notes** |
| Government bodies | Including legislative or special sections (Civil Service) |
| Major industrial headquarters | Central and branch |
| Commercial and industrial firms | Large manufacturers, small legal firms or GP surgery libraries |
| Learned institutions and research associations | Providing a service to members as well as a source of specialist knowledge and an obligation to support research and scholarship. |
| Adapted from Thompson (1989). | |

lines of construction, down to the smallest part, inform the whole. The resulting staccato modernity reminds the visitor that there are still fresh shoots of creativity in a literary tradition.

The design is inevitably fashioned by the nature of the collection it houses and the physical context in which it is built. This is a library where the container and the contained seek a dialogue. It is also a library which seeks sustenance from the historic fragments surrounding the site. Immediately to the east stands the Old City Wall of Edinburgh, to the north historic tenements lining the Royal Mile, and to the south there are long views between nine-teenth century warehouses to Salisbury Crags. It is a landscape as rich in history as any in Northern Europe and it is this landscape which has not only inspired the poets whose work is housed here but the design of the library itself.

Light is a recurring theme of the design. The visitor is guided through the building via natural light. Fraser sees the library as a glade in woodland with light filtering through clearings in the forest canopy (Bevan, 1999). Domes of roof light punctuate the route through the library, bringing daylight into the centre of the building. The ceiling is tilted so that clerestory light defines the library perimeter, giving a sense that the forest has an edge as well as clearings. The

metaphor is carried further in the use of oak construction, dark green tapestries and a pale green paint finish to plaster surfaces. Underfoot there are woven wool carpets of leaves and grasses reminding the reader that nature and landscape have been the dominant sources of Scottish poetry.

The main lending library is positioned on the ground floor with carrels around the edge. The upper mezzanine floor houses open reading areas, a children's library and a members' room. Readers are encouraged by the presence of an open central staircase to carry their books upstairs to the reading area where carpets, easy chairs and low tables are located. The practice is akin to that of monks in the monastery who, having retrieved their books from dark secure rooms, took them into sunny cloisters and gardens to read. The upper floor reading area of the Scottish Poetry Library is generously glazed facing west (and hence filled with afternoon sunlight) and looks directly onto Crighton's Close at its widest point. The arrangement gives expression to the process of selecting and reading a book of poems, and gives life to the outside courtyard where a high-level balcony overlooks the space.

The building confirms that even small libraries are important cultural magnets. In awarding the Scottish National Library a Civic Trust Award in 2000, the citation said:

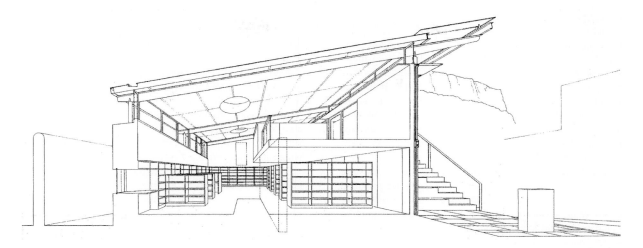

Section, Scottish Poetry Library, Edinburgh, designed by Malcolm Fraser Architects. (Malcolm Fraser Architects)

*like a short poem, this building delights and inspires, and demonstrates that small buildings can have a positive impact far greater than their modest scale suggests (SPL, 2000).*

## Katharine Stephen Rare Books Library, Newnhan College, Cambridge, UK

The Katharine Stephen Library was established in 1995 as a special library to house the rare books held by Newnham College. The building, designed by Van Heyningen and Haward, creates ideal conditions for the storage, conservation and use of rare and fragile books. Previously stored on open shelves or in cardboard boxes, the new building creates a safe environment for the collection by paying particular attention to fire security and the environmental conditions of humidity and temperature. As with many such libraries, the value of the collection exceeds the value of the building (Anon., 1997) though the building is by no means cheap by library standards (nearly £2,000/m$^2$ in 1995).

The library is a long roof-lit rectangle of double height with an access balcony constructed around the perimeter of

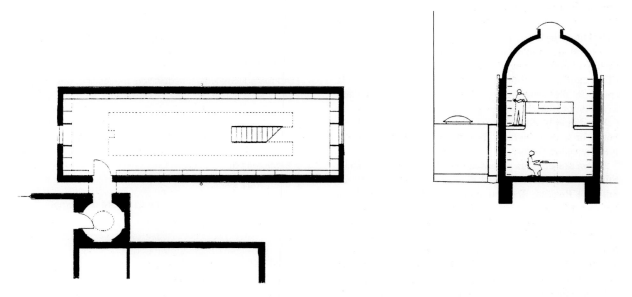

Plan and section, Katharine Stephen Rare Books Library, Newnham College, Cambridge University. (Van Heyningen and Haward)

the central space. A straight staircase on the axis of a long spinal roof light provides access to the gallery and terminates in a small space marked by a square window. The rare books, many of irregular size, are housed on metal shelves set slightly forward of the walls to allow air to flow freely around the leather bindings. Open metal shelves set within a traditionally brick-built library provide the means to monitor the condition of the books whilst creating a relatively stable library environment. For security reasons, some of the most valuable material is kept in open-locked metal bookcases.

The Katharine Stephen Library is more a secure store than a study library. Although reading desks are provided in the centre of the building, this is primarily a repository rather than a working library. Scholars are required to make an appointment in advance and can only handle the scarce books under controlled conditions. For security reasons, there is only one entrance into the building and this is via an octagonal vestibule with a security camera. The vestibule skilfully handles the change in axis from the adjoining college and, like the library, is marked by a roof light – in this case circular.

Architecturally, the new building borrows construction details and stylistic motifs from adjacent buildings. From these it derives the language of colour-banded brickwork, vaulted ceilings and an underlying classical symmetry. Within this repertoire, a modern interpretation of college library architecture is provided for a rare and valuable collection of books and manuscripts.

## Science Library, University of California, Irvine, California, USA

This library in Irvine provides a specialist science collection for students at a high-tech university. It is one of six faculty libraries arranged around a circular park at the heart of the campus. The library itself consists of a large rotunda space in the centre, surrounded by study carrels, and a series of subject wings placed either tangentially or perpendicularly. Students are encouraged to retrieve their books or science journals from the wings and bring them into the centre for use.

There are obvious precedents for this design by James Stirling of Michael Wilford & Associates. One is James Smirke's Reading Room at the British Museum, another is the circular library by James Gibbs in Oxford, the third and geographically more appropriate is Thomas Jefferson's Library at the University of Virginia. What these libraries have in common, and which the Science Library at Irvine also exploits, is the sense that a library is a kind of collective consciousness. The knowledge banks are held in wings with the reader bringing the material together physically in the centre and psychologically in his or her mind. The plan gives architectural structure to this

notion, affording the building the dysfunction of being also a campus landmark by virtue of the way its spatial clarity is expressed three-dimensionally. This is a plastic, dynamic design, which seeks to integrate the sciences around the notion of rational space. In the process, it expresses the unification of the sciences, especially the role of the reading room in providing a shared interdisciplinary study area for students engaged in their own subject specialisms. The wings contain specific subject material, but the central rotunda is the 'mind' where it is integrated.

The Science Library is linked to a bioscience research laboratory which acts as a bridge between itself and the medical school. The use of radiating wings allows the linkage to be achieved smoothly. Students and researchers pass through a sequence of well-engineered spaces, edged by study material and linked by a pattern of corridors and larger sunlit-filled spaces. It is a passage through ideas as well as through space, with the student journey culminated by the terminus of the central rotunda. This rotunda or drum extends through four floors and is split to expose views outwards over the campus. The axis produced aids orientation whilst giving definition to the different subject collections (chemistry, biology, physics, bioscience, etc.). As each subject library leads also to teaching or research areas, the wings act as gateways to subject classifications.

The plan of the Science Library has as a central premise the idea that all the sciences are unified by certain principles. The rotunda is the point of meeting and exchange; it is

---

**Main activities in specialist libraries**

User-based activities (registration, records management, security check)

Staff areas (workroom, public areas, rest areas and personal facility areas)

Audiovisual materials, acquisition, processing, recording, lending

On-line services, organization and provision

Book acquisition, cataloguing, processing and lending

Journal acquisition, cataloguing, processing and management

Interlibrary loans

Searches by database, on-line CD-ROM or Internet

Catalogue production

Conservation

Photocopying

Enquiry and research function

Communications

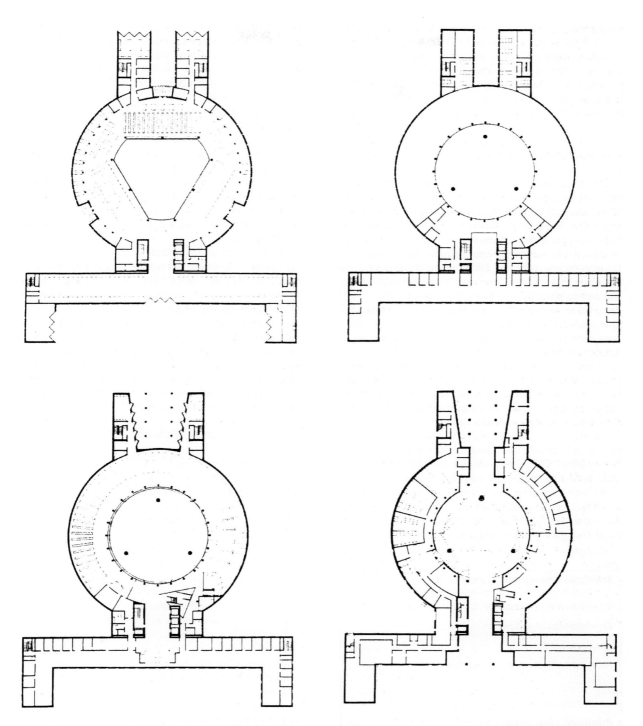

Plans, Science Library, University of California, Irvine, designed by Michael Wilford and Partners. (Michael Wilford and Partners)

where subject interface is encouraged by contact with space, light and external views. The sense of inside and outside is deliberately blurred to allow the mind to wander and to explore complex knowledge from a variety of angles. In this the building aids rather than impedes the imagination. As a 24-hour library, it also acts as a beacon of learning and investigation all through the day.

## Archive Library, Jersey

The archive library designed for the Jersey Heritage Trust by MacCormac Jamieson Prichard in collaboration with BDK Architects is typical of small independent community-based libraries. The aim was to preserve the island of Jersey's heritage of manuscripts and early photographs in a building which is attractive to use but also offers the latest facilities in conservation. The building consists of three main elements – a reading room, a suite of specialist study and conservation spaces, and a repository for the collection. These elements are arranged in a composition of right-angled wings anchored around the large four-storey repository. In the latter are the 7 km of shelving needed to house the archive.

Jersey is an island where war has been a recurring theme of its history. As a result much of the collection is devoted to military history, particularly the French invasion of 1781 and the German occupation of the island during the Second World War. Perhaps symbolic of this was the decision to locate the library beneath the cliffs of a quarry whose rugged and fractured rock faces counter the smooth lines of the building. The library has an inviting entrance and landscaped forecourt where curved seats are arranged casually to encourage passers-by to relax before exploring the building. The entrance itself is surprisingly large and doubles as an exhibition area. It leads via a staircase to a first floor gallery and archive information point. Here the

researcher can begin to access the material along a corridor that leads to the right to the reading room and to the left to a suite of offices which provide an increasing level of security. Only staff can access the repository held at right angles in the nearly windowless white tower.

The double-storey entrance provides an inviting first point of contact with the building. The reading room is the other space designed to evoke reflection on the material at hand. It is cantilevered out to afford solar protection to the rooms below and has a large south facing window and clerestory lighting which is filtered through daylight shelves. The diffused sunlight of the reading room strikes the green panelling of the walls providing a reminder of the landscape outdoors. This is an archive library where cultural memory and landscape play an important part in island life.

The theme of landscape finds its way into the selection of materials both inside and outside the building as it does at the Ruskin Library designed by the same architects. The horizontal timber cladding set on a stone base allows for a play of colours and textures which relate directly to the island context. Added to this, the use of natural materials and exploitation of solar gains, cross-ventilation and thermal mass allows the building to absorb peaks in temperature and humidity without resorting to air-conditioning (Prichard, 2007). As such the Jersey Archive Library (shortlisted for the Stirling Prize in 2001) provides a model for other specialist library buildings.

## Women's Library, Whitechapel, London

This specialist library and archive remodelled from an existing building by architects Wright and Wright includes a museum, conference centre and extensive study spaces for London Guildhall University. It provides for conventional scholarship and cultural research in the area of women's studies whilst also acting as a catalyst for the wider regeneration of this part of East London. The collection, which extends back to the sixteenth century, is of international importance and centres on the social and political history of women. The library has an important conservation and archival role whilst also acting as a library for the use of students and the general public.

The Women's Library occupies part of a former Victorian public baths (built in 1846) which is now engulfed by extensions that step from three to six storeys in height. Surrounded by public housing and other university buildings, the library faces the street with its own leafy courtyard to the rear. The entrance to the library is taken through the former baths on Old Castle Street via a new opening cut into the mellow brick walls. Inside there is a long double height entrance hall with an information desk and cafe on the first floor. From here space flows through to the lofty brick-lined exhibition area and seminar room beyond. Sandwiched between the entrance hall and exhibition area

---

**Specialist professional libraries**

Governmental departments

Governmental organizations

Voluntary agencies

Professional trade and learned societies

Legal organizations

Commercial organizations

Pharmaceutical companies

Management and information consultants

Adapted from Library and Information Statistics Unit, Loughborough University.

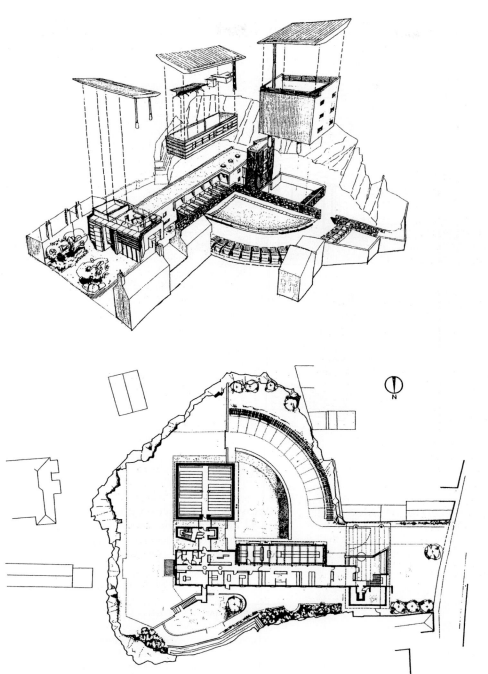

Plan and exploded
perspective, Jersey
Archive Library.
(MacCormac
Jamieson Prichard/
AR)

a staircase leads up through the building to the various study collections on the upper floors. The archive is located in the basement for security and conservation of the valuable and fragile artefacts, and on the third floor for less precious parts of the collection. In both areas the environment is carefully controlled to prevent damage from fluctuating temperature and humidity.

There is a Louis Kahn-like quality to many of the library spaces (Slessor, 2002). The use of large areas of exposed red brickwork, segmental arched ceilings and a discipline of served and servant spaces suggest a debt to Kahn's

Perspective sketch,
Women's Library,
Whitechapel, London.
(Wright and Wright/AR)

library at Phillips Exeter Academy in New Hampshire. The plan and section are both highly articulated and help with communicating the rationale behind the collection and the routes through the building. The Women's Library is a densely occupied and compact building where architecture and light (often from above) are used to guide the reader to the different facilities available. The use of natural light and passive ventilation reduces the energy

| Archive Library, Jersey | |
| --- | --- |
| **Architect** | **Special features** |
| MacCormac Jamieson Prichard with BDK Architects | • Large manuscript collection<br>• Extensive conservation facilities<br>• Building responds to quarry site<br>• Shortlisted for Stirling Prize, 2001 |

| Women's Library, London | |
| --- | --- |
| **Architect** | **Special features** |
| Wright and Wright | • Includes museum and conference centre<br>• Linked to London Guildhall University<br>• Catalyst for wider social and economic regeneration<br>• Conversion of Victorian baths |

footprint of the building whilst adding considerably to the pleasure of using the collection.

## References

Anon. (1997). *Library Builders*. Academy Editions, p. 89.

Bevan, R. (1999). Slim volume. *Building Design,* 4 June, p. 14.

Eco, U. (1987). *Travels in Hyper-reality*. Picador, pp. 6–7.

Prichard, D. (2007). Personal communication with author, 26 June 2007.

Scottish Poetry Library (SPL) (2000). *Newsletter*, July, p. 12.

Slessor, C. (2002). Making History. *Architectural Review*, January, pp. 50–57.

Sudjic, D. (2006). *The Edifice Complex*. Penguin Books, pp. 224–254.

Thompson, G. (1989). *The Planning and Design of Library Buildings*. Butterworth Architecture.

# Part 5
# Speculations

# 13

# The future of the library

## Why libraries matter

It has been suggested that with electronic media the library as a special place will disappear (Davey, 1998). As society adopts digital technologies, the storage of paper (and within it books) will become redundant with the exception of special collections. This is an argument which fails to acknowledge the role of the library as symbolic domain — a place for the public to meet, a refuge away from the commercialization of cities. Even with the growth of computers, the book continues to enjoy great popularity. With books you need storage and reading space, and this is fundamentally what a library provides. Yet beyond function, the library serves to signal the value of the written word, of learning (as against knowledge) and the importance in this compact to the reader. The reader requires space as much as the books, and it is the dialogue between the reading room and the storage of the written or electronic material which makes a good library. Such space is both interior and exterior, and functional and spiritual. It is the way libraries are redefining civic architecture that makes the building type so interesting today.

More books are printed today than at any time in history. More reading, learning and research are undertaken today than in any previous age. Even with our current computing sophistication, few books are held in their entirety in electronic formats. Books may become obsolete more quickly than updateable electronic formats, but they still retain value as a source of wisdom, intellectual stimulation or theoretical discourse. A book can contain knowledge, but information becomes out-of-date more rapidly than theory. The pattern emerges, therefore, whereby both book and IT systems are needed: the modern library has to accommodate both on an equal footing.

The library provides space for the reader, the book and the means of accessing electronic data. All three require attention and in certain civic or academic libraries, the reader can be both a casual browser and a serious scholar. A classification begins to emerge between type of library (national, deposit, civic, academic, private), between type of information (book, journal, graphic, special collection, photographic) and type of reader (casual, researcher, student, child). All require their own ideal conditions, yet a successful library is one which unites rather than divides its users, and one which integrates its systems and material. Security poses a threat to openness, noise (especially computer noise) limits the degree of shared accommodation, and the needs of the researcher are quite distinct from those of the everyday library user.

A good library is one which is alive with activity. Successful libraries are living dynamic buildings which provide interaction between books and readers, and between the public life and private imagination. They are market places in which people shop for knowledge or entertainment — searching both traditional and electronic material for their needs. Living libraries are open and inclusive, the democracy of space signalling freedom of public access. Being a living and dynamic system, libraries need to be able to change and to grow.

Change is needed to reflect the evolving technologies of information storage and retrieval. Modern IT and earlier systems of microfilm or microfiche all challenge the use and politics of space. Even traditional printed material, which has been readily available for three centuries, continues to grow in volume, although the sizes of books are falling. Added to this, the library is increasingly expected to house back copies of newspapers, to have a deposit of old photographs and plans and, in some libraries, to hold special collections of local or regional interest. Some libraries (such as national deposit libraries) necessarily have ever-expanding storage needs, whilst others (such as academic libraries) may find themselves in receipt of a major research archive. Libraries, like cities, need to be able to grow outwardly and renew themselves inwardly. Since libraries are particularly long-lived buildings, the initial size may only be 40% of the final dimensions.

New media impose fresh storage or display needs upon an existing library. The demands of electronic media are quite different in terms of environment compared to traditional paper systems. New technologies alter the use of space, the expectations of readers and the engineering of the library. Growth in the size of the collection can be accommodated by splitting storage of rarely used material from the popular collection — often using separate buildings. But electronic data is ubiquitous: it cannot be shelved elsewhere. For the modern library there is no alternative to

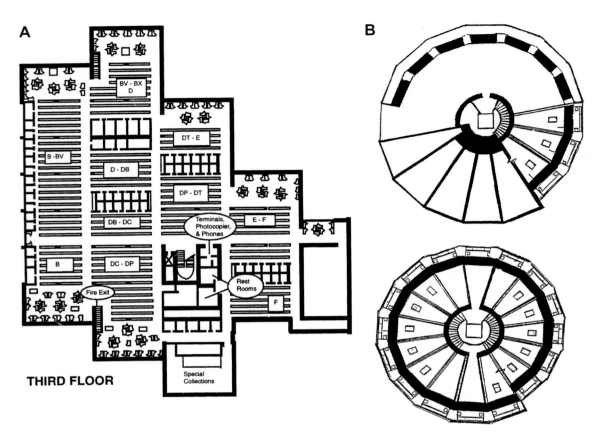

A clear arrangement of book storage in the centre and reading space at the periphery characterizes a well-designed library: (a) Green Library, Stanford University; (b) Library, Jubilee Campus, University of Nottingham. (Brian Edwards)

comprehensive recabling, giving book space over to computers, and putting electronic screens on every reader table. The flickering computer screen – though it can jar the serenity of the well-mannered library – is an essential tool for reader, researcher, casual delver and staff member alike.

## The library as a building type: the importance of words and forms

To most people, the word 'library' evokes a mental picture of a particular type of building. The picture is both an external image and an internal one. The form of the library upon which personal and public perception is based draws upon four interconnecting mental constructs. There is the geometry of space, the grasp of mass and surface, and the effects of light, colour and other optical phenomena and, most importantly, the presence of people (paraphrased from Markus, 1993, p. 11). These together, plus the overriding presence of books, allow function (or what librarians call 'operational requirements') to generate distinctive plans and arrangement. It is the four acting together which carry connotations of 'meaning'. Such meaning is expressed in the architecture of the building, the meeting of function and the celebration of the civic realm.

To a typical library user, the building has a recognizable plan and image which are rich in cultural meaning. Those who design libraries have a responsibility to convey 'libraryness' through the manipulation of form, space and light. A library fails in its social discourse if, no matter how functionally efficient, it does not evoke library character. To be successful, the library should be according to Frankl (cited in Markus, 1993) a 'complete, closed, self-sufficient unit' as opposed to an 'incomplete fragment'. Only mature building types (museums, railway stations) have this wholeness of form and harmony of meaning/function relationship. Out of this compact comes the idea that forms are both containers for function and metaphors for meaning. The library is, therefore, a type of building whose image is already well established in the collective mind of

A library which gives equal weight to book and IT information systems. Free University Library Berlin. (Nigel Young Foster and Partners)

society. The mental picture of 'libraryness' is in this sense a sign — a particular type of shape and volume which signals a particular function. Society reads the built sign and receives the meaning codes.

The difficulty for architects today is how to communicate the presence of the library when IT has eroded the principal element upon which the library as a building type is based — namely the book. By changing the nature of the library and the specific functional demands of its elements, computing has undermined the fundamentals upon which the social codes are based. Form, space and light — the key elements which allow the mental picture of a library to be constructed — have vastly different qualities depending upon the type of material in the library. An electronic

library has neutral space, the book-based library informed space. Eco has developed an argument which relates language in a linguistic sense to architecture (Markus, 1993, pp. 37–38). He proposes a direct link between words and the consequences in architectural design for construction or use. This allows the architect to differentiate between types of libraries, giving each their own identity. For example, a traditional library will raise different expectations of built form from a learning resource centre. Each in their way is a library but the function/meaning metaphors will vary and, as a consequence, so will their exterior shape and interior volumes.

IT has not only revolutionized commerce, education and our access to information, it has changed the very nature of

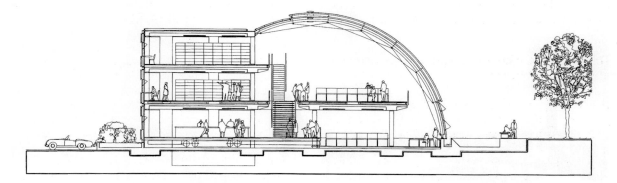

Traditional library material (on the left) and modern computer-based systems (on the right) are combined effectively in the Learning Resource Centre at Thames Valley University. Designed by the Richard Rogers Partnership. (Richard Rogers Partnership)

building types. The library, like the bank, faces the prospect of redundancy as a traditional urban element – a form destined to landmark history but with an ambiguous relationship with the future. What the next generation of libraries will look like is likely to be different from inherited expectations. The mental picture of a library held by society at large does not suit the e-library. The challenge is to evolve a new, shared mental construct for the electronic library which allows the building type to both serve function and signal meaning in a cultural sense.

The form/function/meaning equation is society's way of defining a building type. The 'library' as a functional label had until recently a predictable formal consequence – one which architects could draw upon to communicate the presence of a library. Such constructs are threatened not only by the IT revolution but the trend in western society towards the erosion of single building types. For example, the airport terminal is also a shopping mall and, in the typical urban shopping mall, you may find an airline ticket office, certainly a travel agency selling airport services, and perhaps a branch library. Singular functions have given way to multiple functions. Labels like *library*, *school* or *office* are convenient classifications since they give validity to typologies, but in an age of multiple functions the clarity of form can appear as a hollow gesture. Society is moving towards multiple typologies, hybrids of old building types. The library is not immune to the trend – in fact in many recent library buildings (e.g. Saltire Centre, Glasgow) the architect has sought to redefine the typology. If the library is to survive as a cherished social institution, designers have a duty not to create mongrels of building types or

The library at the Saltire Centre, Glasgow Caledonia University pushes at the frontiers of the academic library. (Brian Edwards)

The interior of new public library in Copenhagen designed by Henning Larsen Architects captures the spirit of new design approaches. (Henning Larsen Architects)

thoughtless repetition of old solutions but to advance the library typology to meet the challenge of the IT age.

There is a further important point for library design which Eco (1987) makes of all buildings. It concerns the importance of ordinary language in communicating the social meaning of institutions and as a consequence the structures which serve them. Eco argues that terms like 'library' are not only a language of words but also of built forms. If society ceases to use the word 'library', it will lose sight of function, form, construction and meaning in libraries themselves. Other terms are increasingly employed for libraries – learning centres, resource centres, computer suites. Without the everyday use of the term 'library', architects will not be able to give authenticity to new libraries, even electronic ones. Markus (1993, p. 38) makes a similar point: he argues that the anchor of language protects society against the disintegration of social fabric and the buildings evolved to serve it. 'Library' is, therefore, a term we must protect in spite of the fundamental change to the media upon which it is increasingly based.

The word 'library' is applied to a wide variety of library types – national, university, civic, branch and specialist. The spread of written media from archival to digital spans a similar spectrum of architectural responses as described earlier. However, what has begun to emerge is the use of libraries beyond their mere functional purpose. For example, many universities see their libraries projecting a high-tech and progressive image to their students and the outside world. The centrality of the library both physically and academically has encouraged universities from Berlin to Glasgow to shop window their institutions via the design of the library. A similar trend has occurred in public libraries where the need to signal regeneration – social, cultural and economic – has encouraged the construction of some imageable new libraries from Tower Hamlets in London to Seattle and Alexandria. Where modernism once produced quasi-identical libraries we now have greater specificness and regional authenticity. The latter has been partly the result of more attention being paid to climatic design spurred by the pursuit of sustainable development. In summary, three forces have come together – ecology, cultural identity and image branding – to produce a fresh and interesting generation of library buildings.

## Lessons from the library at Alexandria

The library at Alexandria in Egypt is generally considered the world's first library in a modern sense. It occupied a wing of the Museum of Alexandria and was surrounded by gardens and observatories. The library was for inner contemplation, the gardens for outward contemplation. The museum stored the artefacts of a civilization, the library its written records. Both played a part in storing the knowledge of the age and making it available to scholars. What is significant about the library is that when Ptolomy Philadelphius set it up in 260 BC he gave it an annual grant from the royal treasury and put it under the control of a priest nominated by the pharaoh. The library was perceived as

The library as a street corner university – the metaphor of shop and display counter. UMIST Library, designed by Building Design Partnership. (BDP)

a collection under state control: it was not trusted to scholars to maintain the collection or the building (Davey, 1994).

In many ways it is the organization and management of the library at Alexandria which makes it the precursor of modern practice, especially that of national libraries. No civilization is complete without a state-run library; no country is truly democratic without its written records being made available to all. It is not scholars or researchers who should manage such libraries, but administrators appointed directly by government. It is this connection between the library as a state-funded service and the library as a collection which allows the public library to reflect certain democratic principles in its plan and organization.

The universality of literacy in the twentieth century made knowledge available to all via the public library. In this compact between the book and the borrower – extended by the recent invention of the Internet – the design of libraries has profound implications for how society sees its relationship to knowledge. The library at Alexandria was one of the high points of Hellenistic civilization – not just for its collection, but the way the state made the books available to scholars throughout the classical world and provided gardens and observatories to refresh the mind between periods of intense private study.

## The library as shop

One current trend in library design is to break down the barriers between libraries, education and shopping. The motive for this comes from the popularity of shopping as a leisure pursuit and the success of large bookshops (such as Waterstones in the UK) with their relaxed environment. Big modern bookshops allow the customer to browse, to listen to music and to enjoy coffee and cakes whilst they shop. Since many public libraries are seen as 'dowdy and somewhat intimidating institutions' (Slavid, 1999), there is pressure to learn from the retail industry.

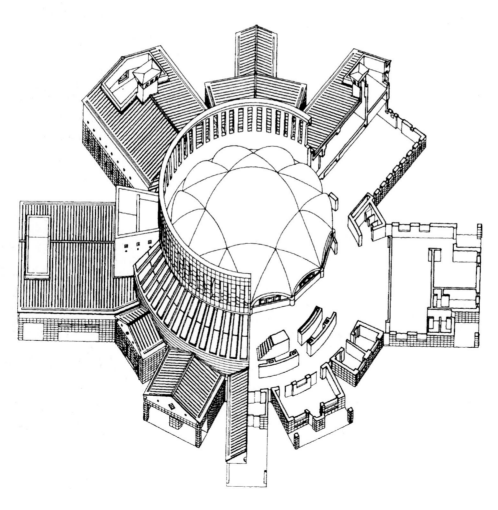

A particular geometry of space allows us to recognize the library as a building type. Mito West City Library, Japan, designed by Chiaki Arai Architects. (Chiaki Arai Architects)

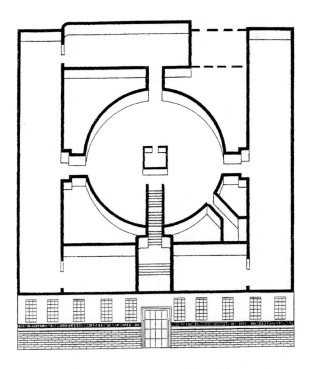

The blending of modern and traditional forms at Stockholm Public Library. Designed by Gunnar Asplund. (Stockholm Public Library)

The modernist library designed by Denys Lasdun at the University of East Anglia expresses 'libraryness' through measured monumentality. (Brian Edwards)

One such example is a plan by the London Borough of Tower Hamlets to create a string of 'idea stores' where newly constructed libraries will be near supermarkets (Sainsbury's, Safeway, Tesco, etc.) and offer access to library services and training programmes (Slavid, 1999). The designs are deliberately eye-catching with highly glazed façades, bright colours on the inside and dramatic roof shapes. The design for the Whitechapel site in East London, for example, features a large electronic message board on the front elevation, which communicates news of library, educational and social activities to passers-by.

Like supermarkets, these new 'ideas stores' libraries will have a brand identity, setting them apart from traditional libraries and other public or commercial buildings. Chris Smith, the then UK government minister responsible for culture, referred to this new generation of libraries as having the 'potential to bring great benefits to the people of Tower Hamlets' (Slavid, 1999). Such a remark signals the change in emphasis required of twenty-first century public libraries – they need to be people-orientated and to address social issues in a broad sense, bringing library, education and leisure together in a single building. Smith further expressed the view that these new libraries were in the 'street corner universities' of the future.

## Authenticity in design

The modernist library departed from past typological traditions. The rational language of planning represented by deep shoebox structures combined with increasingly abstract technological detailing produced a generation of libraries that banished historical references. Architectural theory impacted little on these functional entities. Five hundred years of library building was cast aside by new typological, spatial and technological imperatives. Many building types of the twentieth century suffered from a similar loss of cultural continuity (Brawne, 1997). Recent library designs, especially those in the UK by architects such as MacCormac Jamieson Prichard and Michael Hopkins and Partners, have sought to rediscover an inheritance and make it relevant to the future. With such designs, the approach taken is one of using an abstract language of space and order rather than the stylistic of historic styles motifs. Some of these new libraries take the idea that architecture is a form of collective memory and

251

that books are the individual elements of cultural capital. Here authenticity in library design is, like in literature and art, part of the fundamental landscape of cultural continuity (Brawne, 1997).

If this is the role of the library of the twenty-first century, then what plan should the building adopt in terms of the relationship between readers and books? Where in this configuration does IT fit? Is the library a building within an IT learning centre – a kind of casket of bound volumes of print surrounded by promenade space sprinkled with reader tables and computer screens? Should the library be more akin to the shopping mall where the reader can enter 'shops' for specific study needs, but generally negotiates the cafe zone in-between? Where should the reader sit once books have been retrieved? Traditionally, the readers had their own cavernous 'reading room', but the current trend is towards placing reader carrels at the building perimeter.

The choices are by no means simple; much depends upon the type of library and the needs of different categories of reader. If the library is a form of cultural memory with a social significance as great as that of other public institutions such as art galleries and museums, then the relationship between the object (book) and the user (reader) is infused with meaning. Old typological

classifications were disrupted by the functionalist agenda of the twentieth century, yet building types as robust as the library have a habit of surviving fashion. Although time leads inevitably to typological adjustment, it rarely leads to the extinction of a whole class of building.

Libraries exist because people value the collections they hold, their role as meeting places and their proximity to other cultural facilities. In the UK, over 350 million visits a year are made to public libraries and over half the population holds a library card (Glancey, 2000). A trip to the library is usually planned and has an objective and normally a physical outcome (a borrowed book). The outcome may be intellectual nourishment for its own sake, information about local facilities, a search for a job or details of college courses. The material, whether paper based or electronic, represents the means of making connection in an increasingly fragmented world. The library is concerned with overcoming physical, social and economic disconnectedness. In an age of digital, all-pervasive knowledge where place, time and depth have a tendency to erode, the library as a building gives symbolic presence to that contained within.

Design is not a question of abstract efficiency but of expressing cultural value. The building has a duty to give

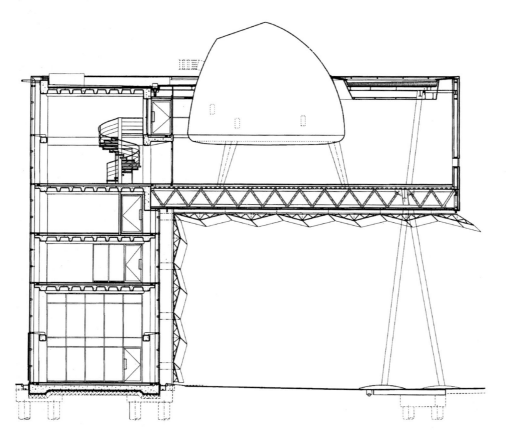

Peckham Public Library responds to new cultural agendas by developing a fresh architectural language for the library. It seeks to make reading fashionable again. (Alsop and Störmer)

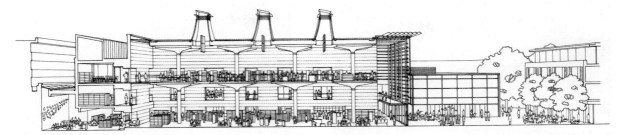

Brighton Public Library brings environmentalism to the fore, developing another direction for library architecture. Designed by Bennetts Associates. (Bennetts Associates)

protective weight to the collection, to provide interior spaces which are social and intellectual commons, and to express outwardly the publicness of the institution. In these endeavours, 'design' is not neutral but expressive of symbolic ambition. The human memory contained by the collection is a form of living heritage which the building must make available. The library, almost uniquely, bridges past and future; it feeds the imagination as directly as an art gallery. The cognitive space of the library, the electronic space of the data, the cultural space of the books, and the physical space of the building, together make a library. No single part should be evolved independently: the integration and adaption of the elements over time creates richness. It is important that the architecture of the building shares not only a common language but a common intent with the collection, the catalogue, the reader and the information systems.

## Design challenge for the future

After a long period of stagnation as a building type, the library has begun to change. Those architects familiar with the design of libraries are currently enjoying the prospect of participating in the development and transformation of the library typology (Long, 1995, p. 70). As discussed earlier, two forces are reshaping the library – the revolution in computing and IT, and the pursuit of more sustainable approaches to design. The first is epitomized by the change in nomenclature from 'library' to 'learning resource centre', the second by the rejection of deep planned, air-conditioned libraries.

Typologies do not change without considerable external pressure. Designers and library clients form a conservative body that historically has held on to the tried and tested. The domed reading room library survived as a general pattern from around 1850 to 1950; the deep plan, square grid, air-conditioned library from 1950 to about 1990. Only in the past decade has the grip of the deep shoebox library weakened. In many ways the currents of IT and sustainability have been complementary in refiguring the library. Old

assumptions about flexibility and economy have proved false. The deep plan, square box library provided little opportunity for energy efficiency, it was a disorientating type of building to use, the heavy loads of deep compact shelving made the building structure expensive to build and hard to adapt, and the concrete construction gave little scope for threading new IT cables through the building. In short, it proved inflexible and dull at the same time.

The deep plan library led inevitably to a great deal of artificial light and forced ventilation – frequently to the use of full air-conditioning in all areas. Flexibility even dictated structural loads throughout the building so that floors could support compact shelving in any location. The expansion in published material from about 1960 led clients to insist upon the accommodation of high impact loads as a means of housing the growth in books and journals. Over-specification of both structural elements and environmental systems led to dull and expensive libraries. The lack of variety of space and light intensity led to complaints from users (Long, 1995, p. 70) and, ironically, when IT offered the chance to house or access information spacelessly, these libraries proved incapable of ready adaption to new cable layouts. It was a case of the search for flexibility without thought or discrimination.

More recent library designs have almost reversed the principles upon which earlier generations of buildings were based. The question of orientation and legibility on the one hand, and access to natural light, view and ventilation on the other, has allowed library typology to go through a profound change. Most recent libraries are shallow (as against deep) in plan, have a variety of type of space inside, have daylight throughout (and often sunlight in selected areas too), have clearly identified routes with their own architectural language, have distant views as well as close desk ones and, as a consequence, more organic configuration. Functionally, the computing and book material is integrated so that the reader can move readily between both types of information. The furniture and book stacks provide zoning, allowing areas to be identified into subject zones without either walls

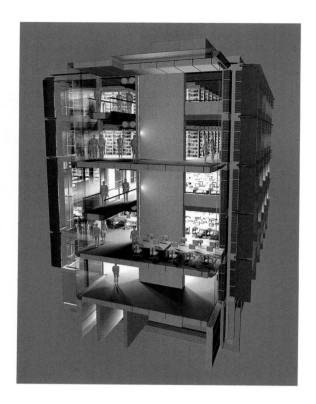

*Existing scheme section perspective of University of East Anglia*: CAD modelling of the extensions to the library at the University of East Anglia. (Shepheard Epstein Hunter)

*Previous scheme for the external environs of University of East Anglia*: CAD modelling of the extensions to the library at the University of East Anglia. (Shepheard Epstein Hunter)

or featureless open planning. Many recent libraries have streets and squares (rather than corridors and rooms) to create the feel of a public building rather than a warehouse of books. Reading spaces, some with carrels, occupy the perimeter with book stacks acting as thermal stores near the building centre. The planning of library use and environmental servicing is more closely related than in preceding buildings.

Flexibility in a library is not a question of the use of space as such but the variety offered in three key relationships:

- between traditional (i.e. book, journal) and electronic information systems
- between reader space and book-stack space
- between staff offices and reader space.

Abstract flexibility has given way to selected intelligent flexibility. Only in the most expensive libraries (such as national or major academic ones) is high-level flexibility justified on cost and operational grounds. Elsewhere the trend is towards long-life quality with the avoidance of

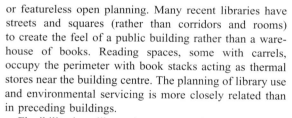

*Future phase in context, University of East Anglia*: CAD modelling of the extensions to the library at the University of East Anglia. (Shepheard Epstein Hunter)

cheap systems (such as suspended ceilings) and expensive and difficult to control engineering (such as air-conditioning) (Anon., 1989).

Nowadays the typical public or academic library exploits daylight and sunlight, both as an energy source and as a means of providing legibility through the building.

The library as a language of recognizable forms translated in: (a) the Faculty of Medicine Libray, University of Paris (1770); (b) Phoenix Public Library (1995). (Brian Edwards and Andrew North)

Readers placed around the edge of the building enjoy views out to relieve the close work of study, and have the benefit of daylight or controlled sunlight. Light-shelves are employed to deflect daylight deep into the building and to provide solar shading at the edge. Where solar gain is a problem (such as on south facing walls), book stacks can give useful protection if used in conjunction with a reduced glazing area. Cabling for task lighting and computers is

The civic status of the public library has grown following CABE's pronouncements. Here Brighton Public Library, designed by Bennettes Associates, shares a square with shops and cafes. (Bennets Associates)

taken around the perimeter of the building, with IT service peninsulas directed inward to connect nearby desks or tables.

It is commonplace today to integrate the IT and book-based collection within the same subject space. Large libraries may also have a dedicated area for computing where readers can use PCs to access the Internet and undertake word processing. It is important that different strategies are developed for different types of library area in terms of heating, lighting, ventilation, electrical cabling, IT cabling and mechanical distribution systems. It is not economical to create the highest standard and level of provision in every area. Design judgement is needed to ensure the appropriate level of facilities for each type of space. There needs to be an 'intelligible order for the building, and positive differences of visual environment within a simple structural shell' (Long, 1995, p. 71). The search for visual variety driven by technological, ecological and functional need is a defining feature of contemporary library design.

Visual variety matters as much in the sequencing of rooms as in the library rooms themselves. The routes through a library provide an essential part of the human experience: legibility through different types of volume (entrance, corridor, stair, reading area) depends upon the manipulation of key architectural elements. Height, proportion, light, colour and axial termination are important physical characteristics; sound, activity and perceptions of hierarchy are crucial psychological ones. Many recent libraries exploit the interface between people, books and computers to generate a legible dialogue of activity volumes within the library.

The intelligible sequence of spaces expressed in an architectural order of light and volume is, however, sometimes undermined by the excessive noise emanating from computer suites. Here the tapping of keys and conversation between users can, especially in an open-plan library, lead to acoustic disturbance. As a consequence there is a trend in modern libraries, particularly academic ones, towards noise zoning whereby conversation is permitted in IT areas but not elsewhere. But with the increase in group study in schools and universities, and the growing use of atrium-based public libraries on low-energy grounds, the problem of noise transfer from computer to reading areas is likely to grow. This has led some to suggest the physical segregation of multimedia and IT areas from traditional material – for example, placing the computer suite on a separate floor or wing. Although this may assist noise management, it does run counter to the concept of the contemporary library as a market place integrating different types of information and reader within a common environment. It also discriminates against those users for whom the computer workstation is an alternative to pen and paper. Walls also obstruct the natural flow of air, which is the very basis of low-energy library design. At the University of Sunderland, the vice-chancellor Anne Wright declared that she wanted 'a library without walls – inside or out' (Wright, 1997). The modern library is a building where ideas and the

The "Black Diamond" is formed by two black cubes which slightly tilt over the street. The atrium's exterior wall is made of glass, through which you get a stunning view of the harbour and luxury buildings on the opposite side. (Brian Edwards)

fresh breezes of technological innovation are allowed to flow unimpeded by traditional construction.

## IT and space

IT has not only changed the way we use libraries, it has also led to more fluid space use (less walls) and easier communication between librarians, support staff and information managers. To some extent, users also become their own subject librarians as they search through electronic catalogues and download information. A book about libraries is essentially a study of function, space and structure, yet each is made redundant to a greater or lesser degree by the IT revolution. As libraries stabilize after the first shock waves of universal e-information (1980–2000), one can begin to take stock. The library is still a 'repository of knowledge, a focus for reflection and a centre for exchange' (Worthington, 1995, p. ii). The medium of knowledge has changed: reflection may be via the screen rather than the book, and exchange is more likely to be electronic than paper based, but the library still exists as a distinctive type of contained architectural space.

As digital technology becomes more universal, it could paradoxically be argued that space should become more specific. Identity is not destroyed by IT rather the need for image and identity is reinforced. In a placeless world of electronic data, the real world of place takes on greater meaning. This paradox allows new library buildings to take on a character which transcends the immediate needs of technology. Certainly, within the lifespan of a typical library (100–150 years), many technologies come and go. Buildings are intergenerational assets that should rise above the transient pressures of emerging technologies. Whilst they need to accommodate new ways of storing and accessing information, libraries are more than giant containers for the technology they house. Meaning is an essential ingredient beyond that of function, and the character of space is fundamentally more important than the technology it houses.

New typological adjustment for the library. Adsetts Centre, Sheffield Hallam University, Designed by Faulkner Brown Architects. (Sheffield Hallam University)

## A new typology for the library and learning resource centre

Library designers today face a particular dilemma. The value of precedent upon which typological classification depends is made increasingly irrelevant by new functional demands. It is not only the revolution in IT services which erodes typological clarity, but the blending of library, education and leisure interests into a new kind of single building. A typological construct into building types depends upon grouping based on certain 'inherent characteristics which makes them similar' (Bandini, 1993, p. 388). This conceptualizing into specific categories is concerned with aspects of human thought (i.e. design) and aspects of human need (i.e. function). Both have seen unprecedented change in terms of libraries over the past decade.

Like most recognizable public buildings, libraries are rich in historic precedent and typological reference. Such buildings do not exist in a vacuum but in a context. It is a context which can be employed or rejected but cannot be ignored. No architect can ignore the cultural significance of the library – it has fashioned at least two centuries of architectural thought. But as the cultural and technical parameters that gave credibility to a recognizable typological classification are eroded, the designer today faces a challenge of evolving a new order for the library. The old formal expression, whether it was the domed reading room of the nineteenth century or the deep planned shoebox library of more recent times, has become irrelevant. The task for today is to evolve a fresh generation of libraries which represent 'libraryness' in the mind of society yet signal the presence of learning resource centres effectively.

Architects need to manipulate the concept of cultural parameter in order to create a new typological order for the electronic, ideas-rich, knowledge-based library.

Most buildings are designed as an exercise in 'seriality' (Bandini, 1993, p. 388). They develop from a recognizable order, with each new building introducing 'newness' into the lineage. The concept of seriality depends upon the presence of a formal typology. This sharing of inherent characteristics allows the grouping into types to occur and offers the chance to break free of constraint. Until the computer revolution of the 1980s and growing global concerns about environmental stress (about half of all man's ecological impact is building related), the library was a reproducible form. Its basic footprint – the relationship between plan, section and elevation – and its internal sequences of space and control were all predictable and exploitable as a language. Countless libraries from the 1950s to 1990 followed the same recipes. Whilst it was not an ideal type which evolved, it did represent the power of precedent to fashion thought.

Today's architects face two particular difficulties – the first is to evolve a new typology for the modern library, the second is to create a new ideal building construct (called a 'library' or 'learning resource centre') which signals meaning by making reference to social codes of understanding. The first is primarily about function, programme and performance; the second is to ensure that architectural invention coexists with the 'tradition and authority of precedents' (Bandini, 1993, p. 389). Whereas the thought processes which underpin modernity provide the means to tackle the first, those of post-modernity are better equipped for the second. And here we have the key

The Michael Howard Reading Room at the Liddle Hart Centre for Military Archives, King's College London. Designed by Shepheard Epstein Hunter, the reading room successfully integrates historic and contemporary information systems. (Shepheard Epstein Hunter)

| Changing characteristics of library design 1850–2000 | |
| --- | --- |
| 1850–1950 | Large, often circular, reading room |
| | Separate subject rooms |
| | Seating normally in centre |
| | Non-electronic security |
| | High ceilings |
| | Large, tall windows |
| | Steel and timber construction with load-bearing walls |
| | Card index or ledger type catalogue |
| 1950–1990 | Deep plan |
| | Uniform, low suspended ceilings |
| | Horizontal bands of windows |
| | Concrete construction with columns |
| | Square reading room |
| | Open plan |
| | Electronic security |
| | Seating at perimeter |
| | Air-conditioning |
| | Microfiche catalogue |
| 1990–onwards | Shallow plan |
| | Relatively high ceilings |
| | Perimeter windows and central atriums |
| | Open fluid plan |
| | Natural light and ventilation in most areas |
| | Mechanical ventilation in 'hot spots' (photocopying, etc.) |
| | Perimeter cabling for IT |
| | Task lighting |
| | Book stacks used as thermal store |
| | Streets or areas of computers as anti-rooms to main library |
| | Computer catalogue |

Natural light enters deeply into the library known as the Saltire Centre at Glasgow Caledonia University, designed by BDP. The fluid spaces in the library encourage interdisciplinary study. (Brian Edwards)

to resolving the central dilemma of typology for the electronic, non-book-based library. Designers need to assign to type an ideal role for IT in society. The type will then fashion the various library buildings created in its wake. The conventions of precedent and tradition will in time generate a new typological order for lesser designers to adopt.

The first signs of the evolution of a new ideal order for the library are to be found in the fusion of library and computer buildings on university campuses. Typical of these are the Thames Valley University Library, designed by the Richard Rogers Partnership, the libraries at Cranfield and Cambridge Universities designed by Foster and Partners, the Adsetts Centre at Sheffield Hallam University designed by Faulkner Brown, and the library at Sunderland University designed by BDP. What they have in common is a search for new, more fluid arrangements in plan and section. The buildings flow as activities change in space and time: the currents of movement (both human and electronic) fashion the whole. The mental construct upon which these buildings are based represents a new model which is not rooted in history but the geometrical demands

Eye-catching shape of the library at Temasek Polytechnic, Singapore. Designed by Michael Wilford and Partners. (Michael Wilford and Partners)

Distinctive entrance canopy at the Surrey History Centre Library, Woking. (W S Atkins)

New construction technologies used at the Law Library, Cambridge University. Designed by Foster and Partners. (Dennis Gilbert/View)

of new technology, new ways of accessing information and fresh environmental concerns. The conventions of tradition are not entirely ignored but, as at Peckham Public Library designed by Alsop and Störmer, given fresh meaning by transformation. The social codes are altered in the process creating new cultural understandings of what a library looks like. Meaning, function and form – the basic elements of typological understanding – are skilfully manipulated.

A key to facilitating this transformation lies in the use of transparency. Being primarily an internal and introverted space, the library requires a high level of permeability for its activities to be perceived as accessible. Such permeability is both physical and perceptual – visitors need to feel they can readily reach the interior spaces. Walls, where they are needed, should be fully glazed to allow the interior world to impact upon the exterior realm. It should be possible to 'see' and 'read' the interior volumes using a language of understood codes. Such reading is a dialogue between solid and transparent elements, in the use of shape and colour and interpenetration of function. It is no coincidence that the new libraries listed earlier are highly glazed – the merest containers of glass to house highly visible internal activities.

Author's sketch of the main reading room at Alexandria Public Library designed by Snohetta Architects. The room seeks to symbolize modern knowledge systems and learning on the site of the world's first library built nearly 2,000 years ago. (Brian Edwards)

## Libraries in a state of flux

Since the first edition of this book libraries of all types have displayed even more characteristics of a building type in rapid evolution. New information technologies coupled with a growing interest in the role of architecture to enrich the civic realm have liberated libraries from older design stereotypes. A number of other factors has been at work as well, such as the concept of life-long learning, the community benefits of literacy training in an age of peoples migration, the awareness amongst national governments of the cultural inheritance embodied in library collections, the massive expansion in higher and further education, and, finally, the merging of cultural institutions around media centres. These have stressed the library as a service but for the architect, the expansion in functions and facilities associated with the twenty-first century library has had the effect of expanding the design potential of the building type.

Public libraries, like art galleries a decade earlier, have awoken from half a century of functional slumbers. They have assumed their role as one of the great civic institutions, providing access to knowledge (and hence power), to democracy via their classless world of free books and journals, and to public space and heroic urban shelters for rich and poor alike. Libraries are the first port of call for many people who are new to neighbourhoods, countries or continents, and here these people are as likely to start their visit with a sip of coffee in convivial surroundings as engage immediately with the book catalogue. The old dialogue in built form between the reading room, reference library and lending library has been replaced by grand public spaces, made possible by replacing many books with digital volumes. With the book repository relegated to basement floors or placed in compact shelving units, the library has assumed a new role as public learning and meeting place. Coupled with this, the former emphasis on silence has been overtaken by the tapping of keyboards and the excited chatter of knowledge seekers and Google searchers. This has been beneficial to many communities and to local businesses which increasingly use public and university libraries to meet their knowledge needs (Boddy, 2006).

Libraries now trade on comfort, 24-hour access, retail type facilities, colour and glamour. The fortress world of many modernist libraries has been replaced by mediateques inhabited by people who take a pride in their city and want to invest in the public realm. This expansion in aspiration has been matched by a fundamental reassessment of the design of the public library by librarians and their architects. New functions have led to the generation of new forms or hybridized old ones. The early twenty-first century has been an exciting time for libraries, particularly public ones.

With the expansion in services provided by libraries, their entrance floors have gone through the most fundamental change. No longer is security the primary objective; instead libraries have an open doors policy like shopping malls. All are welcome through these new democratic portals of knowledge exchange. With this change has come a greater attention to the external civic space and the external image of the building. A new generation of library squares, gardens and sculpture courts has been provided at the entrance, many containing benches and play areas for children. This stitching into the civic realm has allowed public libraries to contribute towards wider urban regeneration.

Public libraries are the most enduring buildings of many cities and academic libraries, often the most durable buildings of university campuses. Their survival reflects their importance and their ability to adapt to changing priorities. However, recent changes have exceeded the capacity of many libraries to accommodate the storage of new forms of knowledge and to make it available in attractive surroundings. Hence, many new libraries have been built linked to museums or retail areas in the hope of engaging in cross-cultural dialogue. The new generation of libraries is refreshingly innovative both in design and in terms of the diversity of their information provision. In this they are built statements confirming our commitment to democratic ideals and social progress.

In some ways libraries have become engaged in the theoretical debates surrounding architecture in the twenty-first century (Davey, 2005). As the case studies in the book demonstrate, libraries have been at the forefront of new forms of social engagement through design. From Seattle to Kyoto, libraries have pushed at design frontiers just as art galleries did a decade or two earlier. The need to make statements has often superseded the imperative of functionalism with its emphasis upon programmatic fit and high-tech solutions. New libraries have engaged in more art-orientated design approaches with the emphasis upon colour, fluid spaces and cultural resonance. Functional efficiency, though laudable in itself, is a poor guide in an age of rapid social, environmental and technological change. Too close a fit is a sure recipe for speedy obsolescence. Many architects are aware of this and seek instead to connect with symbolic meaning.

After all, as Umberto Eco reminds us, a distinction exists between the abstractions of information and the cultural resonance of the media which carries it (Eco, 1989). This distinction adds meaning and value to the knowledge. However, the meaning behind the concept of the library lies in a number of different cultural and social ideals. In an age when information has few walls, when knowledge is transmitted and shared at an unprecedented pace, the justification for the library as a building resides in notions of democracy and collective space. The creation and design of a library is ultimately a political act.

## References

Anon. (1989). *Architects Journal*, 17 May.

Bandini, M (1993). Typological theories in architectural design. In *Companion to Contemprorary Architectural Thought* (B. Farmer and Louw, eds). Routledge

Boddy, T. (2006). Libraries have reassumed their role as places of learning and civic spirit. *Architectural Review,* June, p. 44.

Brawne, M. (1997). *Library Builders*. Academy Editions, p. 27. (Paraphrased from a contribution by R. MacCormac writing about the Ruskin Library.)

Davey, P. (1994). The ghost in the library. *Architectural Review*, February, p. 4.

Davey, P. (1998). Book cases. *Architectural Review*, June, p. 5.

Davey, P. (2005). Bling, blobs, burgeoning problems of figure. *Architectural Review,* March, pp. 72–85.

Eco, U. (1987). *Travels in Hyperreality*. Pan in association with Secker & Warburg. (Translated from the Italian *Semiologio quotidiano* by W Weaver. Originally published as *Faith in Fakes* by Secker & Warburg in 1986.) (See particularly Chapter 2.)

Eco, U. (1989). *The Open work*. Harvard University Press, pp. 52–53.

Glancey, J. (2000). Shelf Life. *Guardian*, 4 March, p. 19.

Long, M.J. (1995). The University of Brighton Library: the development of a building type. In *Building Libraries for the Information Age* (S. Taylor, ed.). Proceedings of a symposium held in York, 11–12 April 1994. Institute of Advanced Architectural Studies (IAAS).

Markus, T.A. (1993). *Buildings and Power: Freedom and Control in the Origin of Modern Building Types*. Routledge. Markus, in turn, cites Frankl, 1914, Giedion, 1944 and Kanfmann, 1955.

Slavid, R. (1999). Libraries go retail-style to pull in East End punters. *Architects Journal*, 29 April, p. 12.

Worthington, J. (1995). Preface: planning the virtual library. In *Building Libraries for the Information Age* (S. Taylor, ed.). Proceedings of a symposium held in York, 11–12 April 1994. Institute of Advanced Architectural Studies (IAAS).

Wright, A. (1997). *Architects Journal*, 17 May, p. 26.

# Bibliography

*Academic Libraries as High Tech Gateways – a Guide to Design and Space Considerations* (2001). American Libraries Association, Chicago.

*Accessible Building Design.* New York: Eastern Paralysed Veterans Association. www.epva.org/

Alexi Marmot Associates (2005). *Spaces for learning.* Scottish Funding Council, Edinburgh.

American Association of College and Research Libraries (ACRL). See www.acrl.org/

Ardis, S. (ed.) (1994). *Library Without Walls: Plug In and Go.* Special Libraries Association, Washington, D C.

Arets, W. (2005). *Living Library.* Prestel.

*Better Public Libraries* (2003). Cabe and Resource, London.

Bosser, J. and de Laubier, G. (2003). *The Most Beautiful Libraries in the World.* Thanes and Hudson, London.

Brawne, M. (1997). *Library Builders.* Academy Editions, London.

Brophy, P. (2000). *The Academic Library.* Library Association, London.

Brown, C. (2002). *Interior Design for Libraries: Drawing on Function and Appeal.* American Libraries Association, Chicago.

Building Regulations (2000). *Part M: 'Access to and Use of Buildings'.* HMSO, London.

CABE and Resource (2003) *Building better libraries.* See www.cabe.org.uk/assetlibrary/2151

CILIP papers (Chartered Institute of Library and Information Professionals). See www.cilip.org.uk/professional

Connecticut State Library (2002). *Library Space Planning Guide.* See www.cslib.org.libbuild.htm

Conway, J. (2000). *America's Library: the Story of the Library of Congress 1800–2000.* Yale University Press, New Haven, Conn.

(2003). *Creating Excellent Buildings: a guide to clients.* Cabe, London

Department for Culture, Media and Sport (2003). *Framework for the Future: Libraries, learning and information in the next decade.* HMSO, London.

*Designing Libraries database.* See www.designinglibraries.org.uk

*Designing spaces for effective learning.* See www.jisc.ac.uk

*Disability Discrimination Act* (1995). HMSO, London.

*Disability Discrimination Act* (2005). HMSO, London.

Eco, U. (1987). *Travels in Hyperrealty.* Picador, London.

Eco, U. (1995). *The Search for the Perfect language.* Blackwell, Oxford, UK and Cambridge, USA

Eynon, A. (2005). *Guidelines for Colleges: recommendations for learning resource centre.* Facet Publishing, London.

Harrison, D. (1995). *Library buildings in the UK 1990–1994.* Library Services Limited, London.

Hoffer, C. and Eco, U. (2006). *Libraries.* Thames and Hudson, London.

Leighton, P. and Weber, D. (eds) (1999). *Planning Academic and Research Library Buildings.* American Library Association, Chicago.

*Library building projects database.* See www.sconul.ac.uk/lib/build

Mayo, D. and Nelson, S. (1999). Wired for the Future: Developing your Library Technology Plan. American Library Association, Chicago.

McCabe, G. (2000). *Planning for a new generation of public library buildings.* Greenwood Press, London.

Metcalf, K. D. (1996). *Planning Academic and Research Library Facilities.* American Libraries Association, Chicago.

Neuman, D. (2003). *Building Type Basics for College and University Facilities.* John Wiley and Sons, London.

Sannwald, W. (1997). Checklist of Library Building Design Consideration. American Libraries Association, Chicago.

Stonehouse, R. and Stromberg, G. (2004). *The architecture of the British Library at St Pancras.* Spon Press, London.

St John Wilson, C. (1998). *The design and Construction of the British Library.* British Library Press, London.

Sykes, J. (1998). *Choosing Library Furniture.* SCONUL.

The Commission for Architecture and the Built Environment (2005). *The Better Public Building Initiative.* HMSO, London.

Webb, M. (ed.) (1999). *Building Libraries for the 21st century: the shape of Information.* McFarland and Company, London.

Worpole, K. (2004). 21st century Libraries: changing forms, changing futures. *Building Futures*

# Index